The International Theological Library.

PLANNED AND FOR YEARS EDITED BY

THE LATE PROFESSOR CHARLES A. BRIGGS, D.D., D.LITT.,

AND

THE LATE PRINCIPAL STEWART D. F. SALMOND, D.D.

THE DOCTRINE OF THE PERSON OF JESUS CHRIST

BY PROFESSOR H. R. MACKINTOSH, D.D.

THE DOCTRINE

OF THE

PERSON OF JESUS CHRIST

By Professor H. R. MACKINTOSH, D.D.

INTERNATIONAL THEOLOGICAL LIBRARY

THE DOCTRINE

OF THE

PERSON OF JESUS CHRIST

BY

H. R. MACKINTOSH, D.Phil., D.D.

PROFESSOR OF THEOLOGY, NEW COLLEGE
EDINBURGH

EDINBURGH

T. & T. CLARK, 38 GEORGE STREET

Printed in England by
Billing and Sons Limited,
Guildford, London and Worcester

FOR

T. & T. CLARK LTD., EDINBURGH

ISBN 0 567 27218 4

Latest impression . . 1978

TO THE MEMORY OF

Marcus Dods

I INSCRIBE THIS BOOK

PREFACE.

It may not be unnecessary to inform the reader that the present book is designed chiefly as a student's manual, which, with a fair measure of completeness, should cover the whole field of Christology. This so far excuses two of its more prominent features: the large space given to historical narration, and a certain frequency of allusion to modern literature. My purpose was not simply to formulate the results reached by a single mind—results, as I give fair warning, in no sense original or extraordinary—but also to furnish what might be considered a competent guide to the best recent discussion, in this country and Germany. If these pages should have helped any student to take his bearings in the world of Christological thought, or suggested fruitful lines of new inquiry, their object will have been fully achieved.

Nothing in the book, it is probable, may seem so indefensible as the more or less speculative tone of the concluding chapters. Some, I fear, will judge that, all protestations notwithstanding, I have added one more to the vain attempts to explain in detail how God became, for our redemption, incarnate in the person of Jesus Christ. I am conscious that a problem of method is indicated here on which opinions are widely divergent, and are likely to remain so. To abstain from all efforts to reach a constructive synthesis of the data which faith apprehends would, as is known, have been in harmony with well-marked and ably championed tendencies of our time. I can only plead that, while it certainly "has not pleased God to save His people by argument," it nevertheless does not seem possible to vindicate the absoluteness of Christ as an intelligent conviction except by passing definitely into the domain of reasoned theory. It is not that Dogmatic starts where faith ends. It is rather that Dogmatic is called to fix in lucid conceptual forms the whole rich truth of which faith is sure. The revelation and self-sacrifice of God in Christ—which forms the very heart of the New Testament message—cannot really be presented to the mind without raising problems of an essentially speculative character. Hence there will always be metaphysic in theology, but it is the implicit metaphysic of faith, moving ever within the sphere of conscience.

My sincere thanks are due to my friend and colleague, the Rev. Professor H. A. A. Kennedy, D.D., who has helped me to revise the proofs, and has guided me at many points by valuable counsel and suggestion. I am also indebted to the Editor of the *Expositor* for permission to use some portions of an article lately contributed to its pages.

H. R. MACKINTOSH.

NEW COLLEGE, EDINBURGH,
October 1912.

IN the Second Edition I have made a few corrections, which do not affect the substance of argument or exposition.

H. R. M.

February 1913.

CONTENTS.

BOOK I.

CHRISTOLOGY IN THE NEW TESTAMENT.

INTRODUCTION.

CHAPTER I.

CHAPTER II.

CHAPTER III.

CHAPTER IV.

CHAPTER V.

CHAPTER VI.

BOOK II.

HISTORY OF CHRISTOLOGICAL DOCTRINE.

CHAPTER I.

CHAPTER II.

CHAPTER III.

CHAPTER IV.

CHAPTER V.

CHAPTER VI.

CHAPTER VII.

CHAPTER VIII.

BOOK III.

THE RECONSTRUCTIVE STATEMENT OF THE DOCTRINE.

PART I.

PRELIMINARY QUESTIONS.

CHAPTER I.

CHAPTER II.

CHAPTER III.

PART II.

THE IMMEDIATE UTTERANCES OF FAITH.

PART III.

THE TRANSCENDENT IMPLICATES OF FAITH.

CHAPTER X.

CHAPTER XI.

CHAPTER XII.

ABBREVIATIONS.

DCG. . . Hastings' *Dictionary of Christ and the Gospels* (1906–1908).

DG.. . . *Dogmengeschichte.*

EGT. . . *Expositor's Greek Testament* (ed. Sir W. R. Nicoll, 1897–1910).

HDB. . . Hastings' *Dictionary of the Bible* (1898–1904).

RE.. . . *Real-Encyclopädie für protest. Theologie u. Kirche*[3] (ed. Hauck, 1896–1909).

ZTK. . . *Zeitschrift für Theologie und Kirche.*

THE PERSON OF JESUS CHRIST.

BOOK I.

CHRISTOLOGY IN THE NEW TESTAMENT.

INTRODUCTION.

It may be well to state clearly that in the sketch of New Testament Christology which follows, I have advisedly made no attempt to expound the numerous minor phases of opinion. On the contrary, my range has been confined somewhat severely to the main types of apostolic doctrine. These, we may compute, are six in number: the Synoptic, the primitive (which here includes 1 Peter), the Pauline, the types represented by the Epistle to the Hebrews and the Apocalypse, and the Johannine. It is not assumed that all six types are totally independent of each other, but only that in a broad way they are capable of being distinguished. By the Synoptic type, in the enumeration just given, is denoted the mind of Jesus Himself as it may be gathered from the Synoptic Gospels; with this explanation, the order of types may be taken also as approximately

Literature on the New Testament Christology as a whole—The text-books on New Testament Theology by Baur, Feine, Holtzmann, Schlatter, Stevens, Weinel, and B. Weiss; Beyschlag, *Die Christologie des Neuen Testaments*, 1866; Denney, *Jesus and the Gospel*, 1908; Granbery, *Outline of New Testament Christology*, 1909; Shailer Mathews, *The Messianic Hope in the New Testament*, 1905; J. Weiss, *Christus, die Anfänge des Dogmas*, 1909 (Eng. tr. 1911); Clemen, *Religionsgeschichtliche Erklärung des Neuen Testaments*, 1909.

chronological. Nothing has been said about Christology in Deutero-Paulinism or in the less prominent Catholic Epistles (James, Jude, 2 Peter). These are of course matters which demand to be carefully investigated in their own time and place, but the aims of the present treatise, I felt, would be best attained by keeping to the main stream of Christological statement and reflection.

That there is a main stream, that the authors of the New Testament are eventually one in their view of Christ, with a unity which is powerful enough to absorb and subdue their differences of interpretation, is not indeed to be lightheartedly assumed. But it is rendered extremely probable by the simple experimental fact that the Church has always found it possible to nourish her faith in the Redeemer from every part of the apostolic writings. Further, this natural presumption is vindicated by a closer scrutiny of the facts. Two certainties are shared in common by all New Testament writers: First, that the life and consciousness of Jesus was in form completely human; second, that this historic life, apprehended as instinct with the powers of redemption, is one with the life of God Himself. In Christ they find God personally present for our salvation from sin and death. Yet in spite or rather because of this basal agreement it is the more impressive to contemplate the sovereign freedom with which they surveyed Christ, telling what they saw in books which have been quite justly described as literature, not dogma. Each looked at Jesus with his own eyes; each spoke out of his own mind; and to force their words about Him into a mechanical and external harmony is simply to misconceive the genius of Christian faith.

We may venture to determine the motives operating within the New Testament mind and leading its spokesmen to "christologise" in modes which transcend the theocratic ideas of Judaism. In the main, they appear to have been four in number.[1]

(1) Reading the Old Testament with Christian eyes,

[1] Cf. Harnack, *Dogmengeschichte*⁴, i. 92.

they felt that its revelation terminated in Jesus. His person, His deeds, His fate and subsequent victory were recognised as constituting a real and even a precise fulfilment of prophecy. From the days of the fathers God had foretold His advent and prepared His way. God had foreseen and pre-ordained Him, and in Him the Church, and had committed to Him the task of establishing the Divine Kingdom. How great then must this Man be, and how inevitable that minds like St. Paul should seek to express His greatness under the highest forms provided by first-century thought.

(2) The characteristic Christian faith in Jesus' exaltation to a place of supramundane and universal power impelled to reflection those who held it. Their sense of His Lordship concerned the present and it concerned the future. It signified the joyous assurance that the Holy Spirit given by Him was powerfully energising in believers and begetting in them a transcendent life; it signified also that He would come at last in glory, that in the final scene of all He would be revealed as central and omnipotent. This consciousness of the Spirit and this hope of the Parousia form the vital heart of the primitive Christology. But if Jesus is now so great, can He have reached this place by becoming? Must not the antecedents of His career be such as harmonise with His present dignity?

(3) Thought was stimulated by the success of missionary enterprise. Apostolic men went out beyond the Jewish circle, and found everywhere that the Gospel made its own impression. With ever-increasing vividness it became clear that Jesus was for the whole world. His significance was as universal as the hunger for God and righteousness. He must therefore be defined in absolute and universal terms.

(4) Finally, the witness of Jesus to Himself could not but quicken thought regarding His consciousness of a unique Sonship and the presuppositions on which it rested. The time came when searching questions were put by hearers

of the Gospel respecting Jesus' *right* to faith, and Jewish monotheists could not decline the challenge. Just as little could they omit to attach fundamental importance to the Lord's own words concerning His relationship to God.

These four kinds of impulse represent with tolerable completeness the religious forces by which the Christological activity of the first generation was controlled and inspired. And in a real sense, though in different measures, each of the four still retains its old value. "The New Testament writers," it has been said, "did not think of Christology and of the Atonement without sufficient motives, and as long as their sense of debt to Christ survives, the motive for thinking on the same subjects, and surely in the main on the same lines, will survive also."[1]

[1] Denney, *Jesus and the Gospel*, 101

CHAPTER I.

CHRIST IN THE SYNOPTIC GOSPELS.

OUR point of view in this study of Jesus' personality, as depicted in the Synoptic Gospels,[1] is determined chiefly by two facts, each important in its own way. To begin with, we are interested more in convictions than in the

LITERATURE—Scott, *The Kingdom and the Messiah*, 1911; Holtzmann, *Das messianische Bewusstsein Jesu*, 1907; Porter, *The Messages of the Apocalyptical Writers*, 1905; Bruce, *The Kingdom of God*[2], 1890; Sanday, *The Life of Christ in Recent Research*, 1907; Dalman, *Die Worte Jesu*, 1898 (Eng. tr. 1902); Schweitzer, *Von Reimarus zu Wrede*, 1908 (Eng. tr. 1910); Steinbeck, *Das göttliche Selbstbewusstsein Jesu nach dem Zeugnis der Synoptiker*, 1908; Monnier, *La mission historique de Jésus*, 1908; Titius, *Reich Gottes*, 1895; Moffatt, *Theology of the Gospels*, 1912.

[1] Jesus is presented from much the same point of view in Mark, Matthew, and Luke, the broad impression being identical (cf. our familiar phrase, "the Jesus of the Synoptics"), though in each case a variation of light and shade is observable. Thus the standpoint of Mark is indicated by 1^1: "The gospel of Jesus Christ, the Son of God." He has a specific Christology; Jesus was Son of God (*i.e.* one with God in nature) even while on earth, and is so addressed at the Baptism, the first recorded incident of His life. Mark draws Him as He appeared to contemporaries, living out the truth of Divine Sonship. There is no story of birth or infancy. While the general conception has close affinities with Paulinism and the Fourth Gospel (cf. J. Weiss, *Das aelteste Evangelium*, 42 ff.), the human limitations of this Divine personality are not forgotten—witness the report of His inability to do mighty works in Nazareth (6^5). In Matthew, on the other hand, Jesus appears as the fulfilment of Old Testament hopes and Messianic predictions; He is the Son of David and of Abraham. But though the true Christ of prophecy, with a special mission to Jews, He has been rejected by His own nation and has in consequence established a Kingdom of all peoples. The name Immanuel (God-with-us) belongs to Him. Matthew strongly inclines to omit statements of Mark which might seem incongruous with a proper reverence for Jesus' person (see Allen's *Commentary*, xxxi ff.), and gives prominence to our Lord's place as future Judge. Luke, while not obtruding a Christology (he resembles Q in this), seizes every opportunity to accentuate the universality of Jesus' mission.

mental processes by which they were attained. We wish to know what the writers of the first three Gospels believed concerning Jesus; it is for us a less urgent question how far we can ascertain the exact order in which the varied elements of this belief arose, or the influences under which it was formulated in words. That the Evangelists should have regarded Jesus as Messiah is obviously a fact of much greater significance than anything now discoverable as to the successive stages of their faith. Once we have made out their convictions, we are justified in pleading that the content of an idea must not be confused with its history, inasmuch as "things are what they are, not what they came from." Whatever the story of its genesis, these writers had gained a wonderful impression of Jesus; this impression they enshrined in books which now are in our hands; and from these books we may catch that impression on our own minds without a too disturbing pre-occupation with matters of chronology or the affiliation of conceptions.

But indeed—and this is the second decisive fact—the character of the Gospels is of a kind which makes chronological exactitude quite impossible. We cannot date any of the three with certainty, nor can we arrange their contents in a temporal order which commands anything like unanimous assent. To a considerable extent the investigation of the life of Jesus, in recent times, has been stultified by a radical error in method; the error of supposing that the Gospels are biographies in the

He is the Son of God, seeking *all* men; hence His genealogy is traced not merely to Abraham, but to Adam. The evangelist's chief interest centres in His supernatural healing ministry. Both Matthew and Luke narrate the Virgin-birth, thus apparently referring Jesus' special Sonship to His birth from the Spirit.

Q is an entity so hypothetical and nebulous that any attempt to draw out its Christology must be in a high degree precarious. Harnack makes an interesting contribution to the subject in his *Sayings of Jesus*, 233 ff., based, of course, on his special construction of Q. He finds that the compiler of Q regarded Jesus as the Messiah, consecrated as Son of God at the Baptism; also that he never calls our Lord ὁ κύριος, but simply Jesus, or "the Christ."

modern sense. It is true that biography involves much more than a precise system of dates based on careful inquiry into the relation of different episodes to each other, yet it is totally inconceivable apart from some such chronological framework. We have only to glance at the Synoptics to perceive that they have not been composed on this plan. Their purpose is simply to convey the impression of a great Personality, but they make no attempt to cover the entire life. The available sources of information are not subjected to an exact scrutiny, in the manner of a modern scientific historian; nor are the person, experience, and beliefs of the central Figure exhibited as conditioned by the circumstances of His *milieu.* Details, whether of the career of Jesus, or of the modes in which the whole image of His person stamped itself on the minds of His disciples, are treated broadly, with the essential selective freedom of the preacher. They depict Jesus, in short, as any onlooker of goodwill might have watched Him in Palestine. Two things stand out boldly in their narrative—the portrait of Jesus as He lived in His familiar habit among men, His personality laden with Divine grace to the sinful; and on the other hand, the believing response to this personality more and more evoked in human souls. But in neither case can we fix the exact progress of events. The course alike of Jesus' self-revelation and of the disciples' adhesion to Him is only discernible in part. And yet it scarcely matters. The character and work of Jesus, in its unique redemptive significance, and the reflection of it gradually formed in the apostolic mind, may be more than sufficiently realised and interpreted by means of the evangelical memoirs we possess.

This being so, we may justly put aside here most of the difficulties in the Gospel record which modern criticism has unearthed. The difficulties, or many of them, are there undeniably; but their importance may easily be overestimated. It makes comparatively little difference in our view of Jesus, for example, whether the cleansing of the Temple belongs to the commencement of His career or to its close. No one can be quite sure whether His public ministry lasted three years or one; in either case our belief regarding the greatness of His person is the same. Similarly, we must not exaggerate the importance of the question how far the picture of Jesus furnished by the Synoptics has been substantially affected by later Christian experience. The possibility of this cannot be denied. But it is only upon the hypothesis that the Christian view of Jesus is mistaken that the incidence of this modifying force would form a legitimate subject of complaint. If in some transcendent way He was Son of God, those who believed in Him must have required a certain period of time to realise fully the magnitude of His person. When their eyes were opened, in consequence of the resurrection, what they beheld was no free and independent creation of religious fancy; it was the deeper, eventual truth of facts now appreciated for the first time. Faith, in other words, did not incapacitate the evangelists as narrators; it showed them, rather, how infinitely the life of Jesus deserved narration. The impulse to select, to fling upon words or incidents a light answering to the later situation of the Church, is natural and intelligible; what is not so is an impulse to deform or to fabricate. "Fidelity to the historical tradition," a sympathetic writer has said, "was undoubtedly the chief aim of the Synoptic writers. Their work may here and there bear traces of theological colouring, but their first interest was in the facts. Their part was not to interpret, but simply to record."[1]

We assume, then, the substantial correctness of the Synoptic portrait. It appeals to the mind of the true seeker with self-evidencing and harmonious power. The writers have nothing of pose, of doctrinal inflexibility, of mis-timed literary artifice. Their subject has been *given* to them; it would be against nature for them to take liberties with its essential meaning. Besides, the

[1] Professor E. F. Scott, *The Fourth Gospel*, 2.

uniform quality of the whole guarantees its truth; its pure originality constitutes a certificate of origin. As the fragrance dwells in each rose-leaf, so all the uniqueness of Jesus is present in each word. *In jeder Aeusserung steckt der ganze Mensch.*

To repeat, our task is interpretative rather than historical in the narrower sense. It is to take a cross-section of the Synoptic view of Jesus, with the object of differentiating the elements which blend in it, so registering the composite impression held and fixed in tradition. Now in the deepest sense, the Synoptic view of Jesus is simple, with the simplicity of nature. He is greater, indeed, than any record of His life; yet it also has caught from Him the consistent tone of simple majesty. On the other hand, within this great unity we encounter differences, contrasts, individually distinguishable aspects, each of which contributes a vital element to the whole. His person is exhibited in a variety of relations to God and man. Very specially what He claimed to be was expressed, by Him or on His behalf, in a few profoundly significant titles. In these titles are gathered up the ideas which believers, by the time our Gospels were composed, had come to cherish regarding Jesus, but which, as they held, sprang originally from His own self-consciousness. To understand what such names or titles mean is perhaps to solve the hardest and most elusive problem in Synoptic Christology. But first we must scrutinise the human portrait the evangelists have drawn.

In contemplating Jesus the man, as mirrored in the Synoptics, we must safeguard ourselves against the tendency to signalise in His character those features exclusively which attract the modern mind. A not

[1] Harnack has a scathing passage on "the extreme and mutually exclusive" views of Jesus' individuality to be found in modern literature (*Sayings of Jesus*, p. xiii). On the humiliating controversy as to the "mythical" Christ and the "historical" Jesus, see Muirhead's articles in the *Review of Theology and Philosophy*, vol. vi. 577 ff., 633 ff.

unnatural revolt has taken place from the mediaeval image, which sank deep into the common heart, and which had represented Him chiefly as a mild and lowly Sufferer, quiet, patient, averse to conflict, whose life and death breathed only gentleness and calm. To-day, the pendulum bids fair to reach the opposite extreme. In many a modern sketch, Jesus is given a fiery and imperious temperament, with a capacity for indignant or scornful passion which now and then escapes from His control. For the idol of our time is strength, and the supreme religious personality must be all compact of power and energy. The Gospels confirm neither of these opposed delineations. Indeed, the fashion in which different minds draw from the same record widely differing conceptions of the central Character is surely a suggestion that in His person there met, wondrously, the most diverse attributes and dispositions elsewhere manifested only in disparate and one-sided forms.

The evangelists nowhere seek to prove Jesus' manhood: it is for them a tacit and self-evident assumption. He is revealed to us within the lines and dimensions of human experience; and the general trustworthiness of the narrative may be reckoned from the fact that His higher being, though accepted by the writers, is never obtruded incongruously or at random. Church history is rich in evidence that Christians forget the manhood of their Lord with amazing ease; but they have done so only because they read the Gospels with veiled face.

Jesus' bodily and mental life plainly obey the rules of natural human development. Luke sums up the scanty recollections of His childhood in the statement that "Jesus continued to advance in wisdom and stature, and in favour with God and man" (2^{52}); and the words enunciate a principle that covers the entire life. It is impossible to conceive a point at which the evangelists would have held that He had nothing more to learn of His Father's will. In the physical sphere He is authentically man. When the Temptation was past, He hungered; on the cross He thirsted and longed to drink; He slept from weariness in the boat upon the lake. His career closed in pain and death and burial. And His soul-life is equally normal. There were hours when He rejoiced in spirit; the unbelief of His own countrymen moved His astonishment; He marvelled at the centurion's faith; glimpses of His heart break out in His compassion for the unshepherded multitude or for the widow of Nain, in the brief anger with which He drove the money-changers from the Temple, in the desire for the companionship of the Twelve, in His tears over Jerusalem. Every wholesome emotion touched Him, finding fit outlet in word or act. Most significant of all, His piety is human. The Baptism and Temptation were scenes of prayer; He was found by disciples praying in secret; it was with prayer on His lips that He healed the man deaf and dumb, that He fed the multitude, that in the garden He wrestled through the agony and at the end gave up His spirit. No shadow of estrangement fell on His communion; yet the unquenched longing with which He resorted to the Father betokens a deep, consuming sense of need.

Three characteristics of Jesus' personal religion are placed by the Synoptic Gospels in strong relief. First, His *faith*, His conscious trust in God. Here lay the source of the felt power in which He accomplished every duty. It rested, doubtless, on the consciousness that the Father and He were bound by unseen ties, yet as it filled and controlled thought and act we feel it to be something which we are being called to imitate, because ideally and distinctively the faith of man. So He was enabled to cast His burden on the Lord, all the more completely as the Cross drew near. Nowhere does Jesus' trust in God appear more wonderful than in presence of the catastrophe which, in outward semblance, was to sweep down His person and His cause to common ruin. If He triumphed in prospect of a death for sin, it was through a confident reliance on the Father. And from this flowed His *peace*. The untroubled calm of soul we mark in Him was manifested less during His passion, when He was faced by His foes, than in the more testing hours just before, when He parted from His friends. But frequently in the course of His public ministry there is visible a profound contrast between tumult and uproar round about Him and the interior calm of a heart at rest in God. This inward rest He strove to impart to others (Mt 11^{28}; cf. Jn 16^{27}). Finally, He was actuated by an infinite *love*, which may be said to have formed the very substance of His nature. It was primarily love to God, in whom were the well-springs of His life, but it overflowed in a comprehensive love to man.

Jesus felt keenly the pressure of temptation. The impulse of self-preservation could not become conscious without inducing the distress of moral conflict. We find Him wrestling with the desire to evade pain, to enjoy things wholesome and lovely, to command success and acquire influence. Had He not shrunk from death, He would have belonged to another race than ours. And in the struggle thus forced on Him, He knew the power of sin so far as it may be known apart from self-identification with its evil; so far, yet no further. Christendom speaks of "the Temptation," as if that which followed His baptism were an isolated fact. But the pressure lasted to the end; and few things in the Gospels are more subduing than the words in which Jesus gratefully acknowledges the fidelity of those who had remained with Him throughout His trials (Lk $22^{28f.}$).

The Jesus of the Synoptics shares in the common secular beliefs of His own time. His human faculties operate in media coloured and impregnated by the great movements of the past. He appears on the page of history as a Jew of the first century, with the Jewish mind and temperament. To interpret His message we need not travel out beyond the Hebrew frontier; nothing is here from the wisdom of Buddha or Plato, nothing even from the fusion of Hellenism and Hebraism in the crucible of

Alexandria. He was nurtured in Galilee, where He must have encountered some impressions of the larger world; but little in His teaching recalls Greco-Roman civilisation. Nevertheless, the universality of His spirit has affinities with the nobler mind of Greece. In the main His soul drew its nourishment from prophet and psalmist; yet there was that in Him, He knew, which would make Him comprehended and efficacious in the world outside Palestine. "The character of Jesus," it has been said, "does not reveal Jewish traits merely, but such also as are Hellenic in the larger sense, so that in Him these definite types of manhood wonderfully complement and balance each other. The fulness of the times had come."[1]

It has gradually become clear that to make Jesus responsible for such things as the details of an ethico-political system, valid for all time, or to invest His words with legal authority in matters of Biblical criticism and history, is wholly misleading and irrelevant. The realm of scientific knowledge is one in which He became like unto His brethren. Incontestably He exhibits at different times a wholly abnormal penetration, a perception of men's thoughts which far outstrips the insight even of prophets. But we cannot speak of His omniscience except as we desert the sources. "Of that day or that hour," He said plainly, "knoweth no one, not even the angels in heaven, nor yet the Son, but the Father" (Mk 13[32])—a declaration of ignorance which, it is suggestive to note, is not insisted on after the resurrection (Ac 1[7]). Along with this goes the fact that He makes inquiries and manifests surprise; but that in doing so He was acting a part is credible only to the incurably docetic mind.

It also appears from the Synoptic narrative that the mighty works of Jesus were not done out of (as it were) independent personal resources, but through power received from God. The Father had bestowed on Him the Messianic Lordship over all things embraced within

[1] von Soden, *Die wichtigsten Fragen im Leben Jesu*, 110.

His life-work; this delegated authority He exercised in faith and acknowledged with thanksgiving. He ascribes the glory of His miracles to the Father. At the same time, the verdict passed on Nazareth to the effect that, owing to the unbelief He encountered there, Jesus could work no miracle (Mk 6^5), has often been misconstrued. The meaning is not that the people's mistrust deprived Him of Messianic power; it is rather that the ethical conditions of reception being absent, a moral impossibility existed that He should put His power in active operation.

Christology of an *à priori* tendency has too often been permitted to encroach upon the interpretation of the first three Gospels, with results equally disconcerting and incoherent. Attempts, for example, to vindicate for Jesus a "double consciousness" or a "double will"—the one human and beset with limitations, the other infinite and Divine—merely impose on the evangelic data a dogmatic schematism of much later origin, thus gravely impeding the work of objective inquiry. Not only do they break the marvellous unity of impression created by His person; they are the outcome of a tendency, mistaken though devout, to reflect on these earthly years the radiant glory of the exalted Christ. But this is to ignore the well-marked New Testament distinction in the manifested being of Jesus before the resurrection and after. To the apostolic mind, the life of the Ascended One was no mere prolongation of the earthly career. It was an existence charged with a higher power, because invested with new and universal attributes. To ignore the human conditions of the historic life, therefore, is to miss the contrast of earthly humiliation and ascended majesty. It is also to miss the vast redeeming sacrifice of God; for these circumstances of self-abnegating limitation form the last and highest expression of the love wherewith the Father bowed down to bless us in the Son.

A constitutive element in the faith of Israel had long been the hope of the Messiah, conceived not as a second

God, but as the Saviour-representative of Jehovah. This Messianic faith is a projection into history of faith in the living God. It is natural, accordingly, that the first article of the new Christian creed should have been the Messiahship of Jesus, the crucified and risen Nazarene. In the Synoptics the name "Christ," the Greek equivalent of Messiah, is always an official, never a personal, name.

The problem of the Messiahship, however, entered on a quite new phase when certain recent scholars, and particularly Wrede, taking up the suggestions of Lagarde and Volkmar, put forward the contention that the Messianic claim was never made by Jesus, but was read back into the history in the sub-apostolic age. The hypothesis cannot be regarded as a happy one. We can point to a series of incidents which make it virtually certain that Jesus felt Himself to be Messiah, and declared His consciousness of the fact to others.[1] Proof positive is furnished by the narrative of the Temptation, which is meaningless except as related to a preceding Messianic experience; by His message to the Baptist in prison (Mt $11^{2ff.}$); by the epoch-making words of Peter at Cæsarea Philippi (Mk 8^{29}); by Jesus' solemn entry into Jerusalem; by His open confession before the high priest; by the mocking cries flung at Him during the crucifixion; finally, by the inscription placed above His head. Even the view defended by certain recent writers, to the effect that Jesus claimed Messianic dignity only for the future, as *Messias designatus*, but refrained from asserting it as an actually present fact, fails to satisfy the recorded data. It brings out the cardinal truth, however, that for Jesus' own mind the future coming of the Messiah in glory constituted His most characteristic and decisive

[1] This is quite compatible with the view that, prior to the resurrection, it was only in hours of specially heightened feeling that His disciples recognised His Messiahship, that they used the name with only a partial consciousness of its implications, and that as He hung on the Cross their faith was eclipsed (cf. Lk 24^{21}). Von Soden has a fine passage on the experimental basis of the disciples' faith in Jesus as Messiah in *Theologische Abhandlungen Weizsäcker gewidmet*, 167 f.

Messianic work. Death would invest Him with the full exercise of His official power.

A more important question yet remains: Jesus believed Himself to be Messiah; where lay the meaning of this title for His mind? We are so far able to determine its meaning for His contemporaries. In Jewish religion (cf. Ps 2) "the Christ" denotes the anointed Head and Lord of the Divine Kingdom, ruling over a redeemed people in bliss and majesty. The Messiah was conceived now as a superhuman figure, now as a man chosen and endowed for His unique task. Bousset remarks that the Messianic hopes of the Jews in our Lord's day must have oscillated between the poles of pure earthliness and pure transcendence. No universally acknowledged type of faith prevailed. Even John the Baptist, with his robe of camel's hair and his thundering prophecies of judgment, could be taken for the Messiah. But in general the function of the Coming One was believed to be the inauguration of the new Kingdom, a catastrophic judgment being the essential prelude to His work.

Jesus' attitude to this ancient hope may be defined by saying that while retaining the traditional outline of the idea, He infused into it a fresh and spiritual content. It still pointed to the King of the Divine Kingdom; it still involved the redemption of the subjects by One anointed for the task; but the significance both of "kingdom" and of "redemption" underwent a radical transformation. His reading of the name was new even when compared with the prophetic thought of the Old Testament. Every political suggestion fell away, every hope of national predominance; the office was conceived for the first time in spiritual and ethical—even if eschatological—terms. At this decisive point, therefore, Jesus broke with tradition. His purpose declared itself at the Temptation, when He turned once for all from the received Messianic ideal to identify Himself with a conception till then unheard of. Thenceforward to be Messiah signified for His mind not the work of a religious Teacher, or of a new Lawgiver, but the vocation of One who must bring complete salvation for sinful men, opening the Kingdom of God to all believers. His life and death are the only worthy comment on His thought. "Jesus was greater than any name, and we must interpret the names He uses through the Person and His experiences and powers, and not the Person through a formal definition of the names." [1]

The consciousness that He was the Messiah must have come to Jesus not later than His baptism. No other point of time has any claim to rank as the commencement of the fully recognised vocation. We cannot tell through what inward experiences this certainty took possession of Him; and it is vain to guess. The vision vouchsafed to Him at the Jordan was such that He Himself must be regarded as the source of the main elements of the narrative. In that hour He knew Himself summoned by the Father to fulfil the Messianic work, and was filled with the power and knowledge requisite for His task by the reception of the Holy Spirit.

It is at first disconcerting to find that Jesus' self-avowal as Messiah was characterised by singular reserve. Nor is this explicable by the inadequacy and unspirituality of the traditional conception; for, as we have seen, it was still open to Jesus to make of the title what He chose. It has been suggested that Jesus was silent concerning His Messiahship simply because it was for long a problem to His own mind; we ought to think of it as dawning on Him gradually, through a process of doubt and struggle. But this seems to be incompatible with the decisive importance of His baptism, which called Him to a task He must have regarded as Messianic. The true explanation appears to lie in the familiar consideration that Jesus' novel conception of the Kingdom, as the reign of the loving and holy Father, entailed also a novel conception of His own function. His partial concealment is therefore due to the

[1] Denney, *Jesus and the Gospel*, 208. On the ethical side, we get our clearest look at what our Lord meant by Messiahship in His message to the Baptist in prison (Mt 11$^{2ff.}$).

all but insurmountable difficulty of proclaiming Himself as the Messiah without stirring into flame passions of a kind which would have rendered the people deaf to His unique message. Thus it is significant that in Nazareth (Lk 4^{24}) He is represented as assuming the rôle simply of a prophet.

The confession of Peter at Cæsarea Philippi was in all probability the first occasion on which the Messiahship of Jesus was made the subject of conversation by the Master and the disciples. It does not follow that Jesus' real dignity then for the first time suggested itself to the Twelve. There are facts (cf. Jn 1) which indicate that the possibility of His being the Messiah may have occurred to His followers from the very outset. What is new in Peter's confession is its personal assurance and devotion; and it is this, not its being a flash of religious genius, which evoked the unusual emotion vibrating in Jesus' answer. Here then, in Holtzmann's phrase,[1] lies the true *peripeteia* of the drama, on which the entire action turns. Jesus now explicitly accepts the Messianic name; nay more, in the fact that it has been attributed to Him He finds clear evidence that the Twelve were beginning to attain true convictions on the subject of His person. Yet there remained the possibility of further misconception; and Jesus therefore at once proceeded to check the formation of too secular hopes by uttering a definite prediction of His death (Mk 8^{31}). But it was only by His entry into the city and during the trial before Caiaphas that He announced His Messiahship to the world at large.

In Jesus' hands the idea of Messiahship came to be associated with unprecedented claims. "By His heathen judge He was condemned," Dalman writes, "as a usurper of the throne; by the Jewish tribunal, as One who pretended to such a place as had never been conceded even to the Messiah."[2] In short, for Jesus to use the title was *ipso facto* to supersede it. While therefore it is true that the Messianic claim was indispensable as a mode of express-

[1] *Das messianische Bewusstsein Jesu*, 86.
[2] *Die Worte Jesu*, i. 257.

ing our Lord's vocation within the lines of Jewish religious history, the title in itself is the product of a special development, and was bound to give place to forms more adequate and universal.[1] This is this truth which has been put falsely, or at least confusedly, by saying that Jesus always felt Messiahship a burden, and would have dispensed with it if He could. The hand which Jesus laid upon traditional Messianism was that of a creative master. At each point He was free of the conceptions of the past.

It was especially through His anticipation of the Cross that Jesus rose above the limits of the older thought. How early this anticipation visited His mind we have not the information to decide; but the view expressed by Holtzmann,[2] that any one who regards the story of the baptism as containing really credible recollections of a definite point at which Jesus' Messianic consciousness was born, and who holds also that His conception of "Messiah" is related to Dn 7, may reasonably believe that our Lord had the prospect of death before Him from the first, is a noteworthy concession to the inherent probabilities of the case. However this may be, at all events it is certain that Jesus was the first to make current coin of the idea of a suffering Messiah. In pre-Christian Judaism, Is 53 had never been interpreted in a Messianic sense. In that sublime picture of vicarious pain, however, there lay truths which found a perfect echo and fulfilment in Jesus' soul.[3] Thus it was, we may surmise, that for Him the ancient conception of Israel's national Messiah was so glorified as to pass into that of the Redeemer of the world.

We now turn to what has justly been described as the most confused and intricate problem in New Testament

[1] But as Peter used it, it expresses in its own way the same idea of uniqueness and absoluteness as we find elsewhere in the names *υἱός* and *κύριος*.

[2] *Op. cit.* 88.

[3] Cf. Professor H. A. A. Kennedy's articles in the *Expository Times* for 1908. Is 53 also contains the idea of the Servant's resurrection and His subsequent career of effectual activity.

Theology. This is the meaning given by Jesus to the name "Son of man." From the point of view both of ideas and of history we are still engaged with the preceding topic, since the adoption of the title "Son of man" may itself stand for a quite definite interpretation of Messiahship. It broadens and universalises a conception which had shown itself capable of very narrow limitations.

"Son of man" is only used by Jesus in the Synoptics, virtually always as a self-designation. It is at least obvious that the evangelists understand it so. The name occurs as early as Mk 2^{10}. Many scholars believe that Jesus employed it only after Peter's great confession; but it is possible that He had used it long before. Not till His trial, however, did the significance of the claim dawn upon the wider public. Its total absence from New Testament writings other than the Gospels (except Ac 7^{56}) is easily explained by its practical inconvenience, since it is "as curious a phrase in Greek as in English,"[1] and would be familiar only to Jews. But the later disappearance of the name at once puts out of court the suggestion that in the Synoptics it is due to interpolation.

In Matthew, Mark, and Luke the title is found on Jesus' lips about seventy times, representing forty occasions more or less. The notion that it properly means "somebody" may be put aside. In such verses as "The Son of man is come eating and drinking" (Mt 11^{19}), and "Betrayest thou the Son of man with a kiss?" (Lk 22^{48}), it is manifestly applied by Jesus to Himself. That our Lord should speak of Himself in the third person is not necessarily unnatural, for St. Paul does the same thing (2 Co 12^{2}); besides, the title was tolerably familiar as a title. We have no guarantee, of course, that all these three-score texts give a perfectly accurate report of Jesus' words; and allowance must be made for the possibility that "Son of man" has in some cases been inserted by the evangelist. But the necessary deductions under this head are so few as to leave the main result unaffected. It is

[1] Burkitt, *Earliest Sources for the Life of Jesus*, 64.

noticeable, further, that the passages containing the name fall naturally into two groups according as they refer (*a*) to Jesus' earthly work, especially as it culminates in suffering and death, or (*b*) to the final glory of His Parousia. Speaking broadly, "Son of man" occurs more frequently towards the close of the Gospel story, while the proportion of passages tinged with eschatology mounts rapidly at the end. These facts are themselves a valuable indication that some intimate relationship existed in Jesus' own mind between the name "Son of man" and His impending death.

The first source of the name is irrecoverably lost in far-past ages,[1] but we are justified in believing that its nearer, proximate source is Dn 7[13]. This, it may be noted, is one of the few points on which scholars have reached virtual agreement. We are carried back, then, to the Danielic vision in which, after the bestial forms symbolising the four heathen empires, there emerges a symbolical human Figure on whom the universal Kingdom is conferred. "Behold, there came with the clouds of heaven one like unto a son of man . . . and there was given him dominion, and glory, and a kingdom, that all the peoples, nations, and tongues should serve him." Whether "one like unto a son of man" denotes the ideal Israel or an individual is uncertain, though the former view is more convincing. But in the Similitudes of Enoch, as Professor Burkitt puts it, "the figure of Daniel, the Son of Man who was with the Ancient of Days, is personified and individualised. From of old this Son of Man, this celestial human being, has been hidden with the Most High, but one day He will be revealed."[2] Jesus was probably familiar with this circle of ideas, and nearly everywhere His use of the name is only intelligible if it denotes an individual person. It has indeed been argued that the distinction which exists in Greek between "man"

[1] For the "religionsgeschichtlich" view, see Weinel, *Biblische Theologie des NT* (1911), 30; Bousset, *Hauptprobleme der Gnosis*, 149 ff.

[2] *Op. cit.* 65.

simply and "Son of man" could not have been expressed by one speaking, as Jesus did, in Aramaic; and that accordingly the phrase for Him must have really meant nothing more than "man in general." In the first place, however, the linguistic facts are doubtful. Dalman, with whom Dr. Driver agrees, has stated what seem excellent reasons for denying that "man" could be expressed in Aramaic in no way except this; "Son of man," it is possible, may be a literal rendering of an independent Aramaic phrase. Apart from this, however, even if we concede that the Aramaic term was equivalent to "man" simply, still "the Man," used by Jesus as a title for Himself or His office must have been employed *in sensu eminenti*; must have meant the special, or well-known, or unique "Man."[1] Nor can Dr. Sanday's suggestion be overlooked that, since Jesus may have spoken Greek, *ὁ υἱὸς τοῦ ἀνθρώπου* may have been one of His own phrases.

But what does the term mean? To begin with, it is almost certainly unbiblical to explain it as equivalent to "man in idea" or "the ideal man." Baur, slightly modifying this, takes it as equivalent to one *qui nihil humani sibi alienum putat*; Wellhausen thinks it equal to "man normal in relation to God," although, since Jesus was neither a Greek philosopher nor a modern humanist, this signification, in his judgment, proves sufficiently that the phrase was never used by Jesus. He is at least right in the contention that ideal humanity is a Greek or modern, not a Jewish, conception; and while it is undoubtedly embodied in the character of the Son of man as realised in Jesus, it forms no part of the connotation of the term. On the other hand, there is no foundation for the older dogmatic theory that our Lord's intention, in using the title, was to assert distinctly His real manhood; for of His real manhood the audience could not be in doubt. The truth, so far as I can judge, appears to be something like this: Jesus took the name, in a spirit of complete freedom, from the familiar Danielic verse, possibly being influenced

[1] Cf. Bousset, *Die Religion des Judenthums* (1 Aufl.), 252.

in some degree also by the Similitudes of Enoch. He began by using it to denote His own special or representative humanity, as appointed to future glory and transcendent sway; but with this, especially in the later months, He combined a note of sharp contrast, defining and enriching the primary signification by the added thought of suffering.[1] In any case, contrast is of the very essence of the truth. Triumphant glory, over-against which is set utter self-abasement and humiliation—this, on the whole, is the meaning fixed for us by a careful scrutiny of the Synoptic usage.

It is not too much to say, indeed, that Jesus, in His selection of the name, had an educative purpose. It was a spiritual mystery, a problem not less than a disclosure. Tradition had defined the title only imperfectly; it awaited final interpretation: and this Jesus gave by stamping on it the impress of Himself. As the marble takes shape under the sculptor's chisel, masses of rejected matter fall away; so Jesus drew forth from the potentialities of the conception that which harmonised with His own higher thought. In His hands the name provoked reflection. While in no sense an obvious appellation of the Messiah—otherwise the question of Mt 16^{13}: "Who do men say that the Son of man is?" would be inept—it yet proved suggestive of Messiahship to those who cared to search deeper. Into the title furnished by tradition He poured a significance of His own which transcended the past; for in affirming, *e.g.* that the Son of man had power on earth to forgive sins (Mk 2^{10}), He rose above inherited and conventional ideas. The name was designed to indicate not so much the nature as the vocation of its Bearer; it signalised the transcendent place and function still awaiting Him. Of the available modes of self-description it was the least political, and as on other occasions He appears to deprecate the title "Son of David' as too provocative, or at least as irrelevant to the true conception of Messiahship, so Jesus chose the apocalyptic

[1] We must never lose sight of Is 53; cf. Feine, *Theologie d. NT*, 68.

name of Son of man, especially near the end, as one which laid the required emphasis on the future greatness thus far concealed under obscurity and destined to be still more darkly eclipsed in death. And the solution of this apparent antinomy He found in the decisive significance of His cross. So far from rendering His future glory impossible, it was to be the gate of entrance to His consummation.

In the Synoptics, accordingly, our Lord's usage of the title "Son of man" constitutes a paradox. Just as the idea of the Kingdom points to a transcendent order of things which, though future, is none the less actually present;[1] so the correlative name of Son of man embraces likewise the "hereafter" and the "here." Its point of departure is the thought of coming glory, but that eventual triumph is mediated through suffering and death. It unites anticipation with reality. Yet this seeming contradiction is vital to the inward spiritual coherence of the idea. It is through indignity and pain and death that He who must reign passes to His Kingdom. As it has been put: "The 'Son of man,' in the mature mind of Jesus, is the Person who unites a career of utmost service and suffering with a sure prospect of transcendent glory. And herein we touch at once the depth and height of His originality."[2] The work of Jesus, in a large measure, came to consist in training the disciples to understand this novel thought of Messiahship, to perceive and appreciate inwardly the mystery of the fact that "not in spite of His death, but in and through His death, He was to assert Himself as Son of man."[3] When therefore they at length seized His drift, what their minds fixed upon as forming the vital content of the title He had chosen was the Divine destiny which lay veiled in the future, and

[1] Kaftan has put it excellently: "Only a paradoxical formula will cover the ascertained historical facts. It must run thus—*The future salvation is become present, yet has not ceased to be future*" (*Jesus und Paulus*, 24).

[2] Muirhead, *Eschatology of Jesus*, 203.

[3] Scott, *The Kingdom and the Messiah*, 243.

the experience of self-sacrifice through which it must needs be attained. The Son of man must suffer many things ere He comes with the clouds of heaven.

The last of the special titles predicated of Jesus in the Synoptics is "Son," or, in its fuller form, "Son of God." We cannot, of course, ascribe precisely the same meaning to every instance of its use. In the lips of the possessed (Mk 3^{11}), of unbelieving Jews (Mt 27^{40}), of the centurion at the cross (Mk 15^{39}), and, by implication, of Caiaphas (Mt 26^{63}), it obviously carries something less than its full significance. From the words of the centurion, "Truly this man was a son of God," we may judge that he found in our Lord a man of such sublime courage and righteousness as indicated a greatness more than human. How near this poetic or symbolic usage may have approached to theological conviction, it is less easy to determine. But in the majority of cases belonging to this class, our wisest course is to regard "Son of God" as a synonym of Messiah. Even when at the baptism a Divine voice hailed Jesus as "My beloved Son," what stands out most clearly is His consecration to the Messianic task.

In the Old Testament, we may note, the title "Son of God" is given a varied application—to angels, to the chosen people, to the theocratic king who reigns over and represents them, to the Messianic Deliverer of the future. The promise to David concerning Solomon is most typical: "I will establish the throne of his kingdom for ever; I will be his father, and he shall be My son" (2 S 7^{13-14}). In this passage and others like it, the name guarantees to its bearer the special protection and love of God, a relationship which in Ps 2 is actually represented under the symbol of paternity. The outer side of the relation was represented by the certain possession of Divine glory and power; the inner consisted in the peculiar enjoyment of His love as its chosen object.

It was primarily on this inner aspect that the mind of Jesus dwelt. Nowhere in the Synoptic records does

He adopt for Himself the fully-phrased name "Son of God," perhaps as finding in it a too familiar designation of the Messiah, or one too certain to evoke political expectations. Everything goes to prove that His supreme conception of His own person was expressed simply in the name "Son." Not merely does it occur in two exceptionally striking words, of indubitable authenticity (Mt 11^{27}, Mk 13^{32}, cf. 8^{37}); certain other pieces of indirect evidence bear directly on the same point. Such are, for instance, a veiled allusion to His special Sonship in the parables of the Vineyard and the Marriage Feast; His question to Peter about the taxing of kings' sons; and His conversation with the scribes as to the relation between David's Son and David's Lord. We may perhaps catch the tone of unique filial self-consciousness in His custom of naming God the "Lord of heaven and earth," but never His Lord. However this may be, no one can miss the significance of the name "My Father" so frequently applied by Him to God (Mt 7^{21} 10^{32} 12^{50} etc.); a deliberate and selected phrase which sets His personal relation to the Father in a distinct place by itself. No parallels from pagan thought are of the least use in illustrating this; the Hellenic conception of the Divine Fatherhood, for example, starts not from ethical but from cosmic presuppositions. Nor is any real equivalent to be found in the religion of the Old Testament. If ethnic ideas leant with more or less decision to a naturalistic pantheism, Judaism had long stood in peril of the petrifying rigidities of deism. Jesus' incommunicable consciousness of filial oneness with the Eternal is a new thing in the world.

In his second chapter, Luke represents the consciousness of this unique Sonship as already present at twelve years (2^{40-52}). There can be little doubt that from this indication and others we are justified in concluding that Jesus knew Himself Son before His call to the Messiahship. The sense that His life flowed from God directly, having in Him all its well-springs, laid upon Him more commanding obligations than those of earthly affection. In the narrative as it stands there is no suggestion that the episode formed the birth-hour of Jesus' special consciousness of God and Himself; one is rather led to think of processes only now becoming visible upon the surface. The grace by which He lived brooded over His development. As He stands in the Temple, not answering questions merely but asking them, the curtain's edge is for a moment lifted from a hidden life which we must conceive of as sustained and informed perpetually by the clear knowledge that the Father and He belonged wholly to each other. To Him the word came unceasingly: "Son, Thou art ever with me, and all that I have is Thine."

But the study of our Lord's filial consciousness must always centre in the great words of Mt 11[27]: "All things are delivered unto Me of My Father; and no one knoweth the Son, save the Father; neither doth any know the Father, save the Son, and he to whomsoever the Son willeth to reveal Him."[1] These words, the most important for Christology in the New Testament, were apparently spoken on the return of the disciples from their first preaching mission. They are instinct with a high and solemn joy. As commentators have remarked, the whole passage has a Johannine quality which is unique, or all but unique, in the first three Gospels. The words come home to us not so much as the sudden flash of a transient emotion as rather the overflow of an habitual mood of feeling. To question their authenticity is a desperate expedient, and it is difficult to take seriously the insipid suggestion that they are more than half a quotation from the Son of Sirach. What it is of supreme moment for us to note is "the unqualified correlation of the Father and the Son" these words proclaim. We are brought face to face with a relationship of absolute intimacy and perfect mutual correspondence,

[1] On Harnack's argument in favour of the "Western" text, so far as it changes the present (ἐπιγινώσκει) into the aorist (ἔγνω), see Denney, *Jesus and the Gospel*, 272 ff.; Kühl, *Das Selbstbewusstsein Jesu*, 21 ff.

which is intransferable by its nature. Not merely is the Father's being, to its inmost secret, open to the soul of Jesus, without that sense of mystery and inscrutable remoteness of which the greatest prophets had been conscious; not merely is the Son's knowledge of the Father complete, final, and inaccessible to every other save those to whom the Son is mediator: along with this goes the fact that Jesus' inmost being is known to the Father, and to nóne else. "Between Jesus and God, one may say, all is common."[1] This is not to repudiate Old Testament revelation as worthless; it is to declare that nothing which can be called revelation of the Father is worthy to compare with the knowledge given in and through the Son. The revealing medium has an absolute and exclusive harmony with that which is revealed. All others become children of God by way of debt to Jesus; in His case alone Sonship is the constitutive factor of His being. The life of the Father and the Son is one life, and either can be known only in the other. In these inexhaustible words, accordingly, there is presented something far greater than a new conception; the conception is expressive of a new fact beyond which religion cannot go, for "the sentence as a whole tells us plainly that Jesus is both to God and to man what no other can be."[2] It was a final intimation of truth which the apostles kept ever after in their heart. Never again could they attempt to realise the Divine Fatherhood but there rose before them the person of the Son, as life and death had revealed Him; in like manner, to possess the Son was literally to possess the Father also. Looking both at Jesus' own mind and at Christian experience, there is no reason why we should not use the word metaphysical to denote this special Sonship, not as though metaphysical stood in contrast with ethical, but to mark the circumstance that this Sonship is part of the ultimate realities of being.

[1] Goguel, *L'apôtre Paul et Jésus-Christ*, 199.
[2] Denney, *op. cit.* 272.

Harnack has unduly minimised this aspect of the truth in his too categorical statement that "the name of Son means nothing but the knowledge of God."[1] Jesus' relation to God, he urges, consists merely in the fact that He knows God thus and thus, that He has come to recognise the sacred Being who rules heaven and earth as Father, as *His* Father. Yet we may not thus reduce what is evidently presented as a mutual unity of life to a phenomenon of religious knowledge; and if Jesus could declare (Mk 13^{32}) that He stands closer to God than even the angels, whose nature is heavenly, it is scarcely credible that in Mt 11^{27} He is not claiming a place in an order of things far transcending all mundane relationships.[2] Knowledge of God, moreover, in Harnack's sense, is something which begins to be; if Sonship, then, is constituted by this knowledge, it also must begin to be; but can it be reasonably held that Jesus would have confessed His filial relationship with God to be a fact of temporal origin? I cannot think so. Every attempt to conceive of Him as *becoming* the Son of God makes shipwreck on the unconditioned character of His self-consciousness. It is quite in accord with this that the Jesus of the Synoptics nowhere *affirms* His pre-existence. He simply refers the origin and secret of His personality to the perfect love of God, His mind moving always within the limits of the human fact. For deeper truth, if deeper truth can be expressed in speech, we must turn to the Fourth Gospel.

On a careful estimate, our results up to and including this point are these: Neither in the self-disclosure of Jesus nor in the faith of disciples have we encountered anything which could even plausibly be described as a theory of incarnation, or of two natures hypostatically united in a single person. The Christology of Jesus and His followers yields rather the picture of One who by a career of faith, service, and mighty works—a career culminating in death—is cognizable as the perfect revela-

[1] *What is Christianity?* 128.

[2] Cf. Titius, *Jesu Lehre vom Reich Gottes*, 118.

tion of the Father and the destined Sovereign of the world. The terms of description are so far immanent, while yet it is clear that His consciousness of unique Sonship lifts Him beyond the plane of normal human life. By His chosen name of Son He proclaims what He *is* to God and for God; of the fact that He occupies this place no doctrinal interpretation is offered, nor is the fact analysed in its eternal implications, before and after. These implications, we ought to note, are neither denied nor asserted; and it is quite conceivable, even from the present standpoint, that they may yet emerge as welcome or even necessary elements of deeper Christian thought. There are, to say the least, points of attachment for what apostles may yet divine as to the pre-existent glory of "the Son" or "Word" and His place within the Godhead. Nevertheless, it remains true that the self-consciousness of Jesus was, in the main, historically conditioned. When He spoke of Himself as Son *par excellence*, the name indicated a perfect and redemptive filial life which took shape and form in unclouded fellowship and ethical solidarity with the Father.

For the mind of Jesus this unshared Sonship is the supreme reality. All other facts concerning Him receive from it their whole value and meaning. In particular, it shed a revealing light on His personal vocation. It was not that He awoke to find Himself Messiah, rising afterwards on this stepping-stone to the consciousness of Sonship. Exactly the reverse is the truth; He was Son of man, Messianic Head and Sovereign of the Kingdom, in virtue of the still more fundamental conviction that He was Son of God.[1] This, and this only, interprets to us such things as His magisterial criticism of the Law; and makes it all but impossible to believe that His view of the Kingdom did not quite consciously embrace the whole world. The ground of

[1] "With the most careful and reverent application of psychological methods, it is obvious that our's Lord's consciousness of Sonship must have preceded in time His consciousness of Messiahship, must indeed have formed a stepping-stone to the latter. In spite of all that has been deduced from the apocalyptic and dogmatic Messianic conceptions of the times, we must assert that the consciousness of Divine Sonship and of Messiahship

His vocation, then, lies in the uniqueness of His nature. Because He is God's Son, He does and can do God's work. Yet in the last resort these two are inseparable. As human life mounts in the scale of greatness, vocation and personality become more and more coincident; in the case of Jesus the coincidence was absolute.

Apart from these select titles or modes of self-description, we must glance at the evidence contained in the Synoptic Gospels of a peculiar and indeed unexampled authority to which Jesus habitually laid claim. He assumed a place within the relations of God to man, as of man to God, which none but He could occupy. Thus it is not too much to say that He Himself, as King, came by degrees to displace the Kingdom as the main subject of His teaching. Meek and lowly of heart, He yet displayed an incomparable majesty of bearing, which gave sanction to each new commandment by a simple 'Verily, I say unto you." This elevation of tone and mien was recognised on every hand. The possessed, the crowd at Nazareth, the Pharisees of the capital, His own disciples—all were conscious of it. But more; the utter loyalty He demanded was instinctively accorded. If the claims of Jesus to personal obedience are felt to be amazing, not less wonderful is the free and joyous acquiescence with which men responded to His call.

The secret of this overwhelming impression lay not in His miracles, obviously; for according to Mark His first disciples had been gained ere the first miracle was wrought. It lay rather in Himself. Somehow He was able to impart the certainty that in Him men were face to face with God. In His voice sounded a tone—we can still hear it—of boundless and unconditioned power.

could not have existed together from the beginning; for the consciousness of Messiahship never meant anything else for our Lord than a consciousness of *what He was about to become*. In His soul the consciousness of what He was must have come first, and only when this had attained to the height of consciousness of Sonship could the tremendous leap be taken to the consciousness of Messiahship" (Harnack, *Sayings of Jesus*, 245–246).

Amongst the founders of religion He is unique in the fact that His claims were not so much argued as presupposed. Without explaining His title or reasoning about His place as Divine Redeemer, He announced that in His person the saving power of God was present; present to make all things new. Never does He refer, like the Baptist, to one who should come after Him and complete His task. He was Lord, not only of all things for the Kingdom's sake, but of the very Kingdom as such. He had the keys; with Him it rested to declare for men the conditions of entrance. How completely He refused to be one in a series we gather most clearly from His attitude to the ancient Law. August and sacred as were its precepts, He put them royally aside, setting in their place the perfect principles of the transcendent Kingdom over which He should come to reign.

In recent years it has been emphatically denied that Jesus claimed to forgive sin, yet on grounds which must be pronounced insufficient. To the guilty who sought Him out, His presence formed the medium of pardon. Few episodes are more obviously authentic than the healing of the paralytic (Mk 2), where the narrative simply falls to pieces if we strike out Jesus' self-presentation as Forgiver. His rejoinder to the angry protest of the scribes would be pointless, but for the implied assertion that His gift of pardon was as real and as immediately verifiable as His gift of bodily strength. From the incidents of the woman with the issue of blood and the dying malefactor, it appears that our Lord frequently made use of this power. The significance of this can hardly be overestimated. By coming forward as incarnate pardon He proclaimed His ability to lead the sinful, there and then, into the Father's presence. His person, as they saw it, was a sure guarantee of God's mercy. But when we think it out, clearly forgiveness is a Divine miracle, something which in its infinite marvel is inexplicable by the resources of nature or humanity; it presupposes the very grace and might of the Eternal. By the claim to impart peace of conscience, therefore, Jesus laid His hand, with quiet assurance, on a unique prerogative. And by its exercise He opened the Kingdom of heaven to believers.

Jesus, then, was habitually conscious that in His person Divine power had entered the world for the accomplishment of all that can be called salvation. He was the Chosen One, by whose presence evil was already overcome in principle; the predicted Deliverer who should save many by His death; the Victor who should conquer the last enemy by rising from the grave and in due time appear in glory as Judge of all mankind. His claim to be Judge in the great future has occasionally been denied, but in one who knew Himself to be the inaugurator of the perfect Messianic age it is in fact neither novel nor incredible. One who remits sins on earth in the consciousness that God's holy love is present in His person, may well discharge that solemn function at the End. Bousset has argued that the steps are even yet discernible by which the later Church mounted to this ascription of Judgeship; but it may be pointed out that even in the most primitive form of the tradition—"Whosoever confesseth Me before men, him will I also confess before My Father who is in heaven" (Mt 10[32])—Jesus definitely takes a place as Intercessor or Advocate in the heavenly world which is certainly not less superhuman in significance than the claim to be final Judge of men. The uniqueness of Jesus for His own consciousness could not be more startlingly demonstrated than by this fact, that He who forbade His followers to judge each other should have foretold that He Himself will judge the world.

Thus with ever-increasing power it was borne in upon the disciples that no comparison or parallel could be instituted between Jesus and the great figures of the past. No prophet had invited men to confess his name; no prophet had declared that the relation of men to himself would fix their destiny in the future Kingdom; no prophet had dared to say: "All things have been delivered unto Me of My Father." For these great souls it had been enough to announce, "Thus saith the Lord." Jesus, however, as it has been put, "knows no more sacred task than to point men to His own Person."[1] He is the object of saving faith; this we may conclude with whole-hearted assurance, albeit the phrase "believe in Me" occurs seldom or never in the Synoptics.[2] No serious mind will miss the significance which was bound to be assigned to such professions by all who gave them credit. The disciples could not but have their own thoughts regarding One who made such claims and wielded such power over the spirits of men. And it is a crucial circumstance that Jesus, who must have perceived the trend of their reflections, welcomed with joy the absolute religious trust and incipient worship of the Twelve.

In the foregoing pages we have studied the main features in the Synoptic representation of Jesus Christ. Our materials have been derived partly from the manifest self-consciousness of our Lord, partly from the impression He produced on other minds. As regards the witness of Jesus to Himself, it is at all events such as to demonstrate the futility of saying, with Bousset, that He simply ranks Himself by the side of struggling humanity, or with Wellhausen, that He nowhere assigns a central place to His own person. So far from this, He may be better described as having identified the Gospel with Himself.[3] Moreover, the impression made by Him on others was of such a kind that far-reaching questions in regard to His ultimate identity could not be evaded; and when once these questions as to what lay behind His redeeming influence, and explained it, had been asked, it was inevitable that the attempt should be made to furnish an intelligible and coherent answer. This answer, as it took shape in the apostolic mind, is present in solution in the Epistles and the Fourth Gospel. It was no false metaphysical scent which drew St. Paul and his successors into the difficult

[1] Herrmann, *Communion with God*, 93.

[2] Cf. Feine, *Die Theologie d. NT*, 26–34.

[3] Cf. Mk 8^{38}, "Me and My words."

paths of Christological reflection; it was a resolute endeavour to set forth convictions which had been borne into their hearts with an irresistible force of evidence—the conviction, above all, that in the life of Jesus God had been personally present in their midst. The question whether they were well or ill advised in their affirmation of His Divine being is one which necessarily is insoluble by the methods of historical science. Then as now, only those could attain to evangelical faith in the Godhead of Jesus who knew that in Him they had met with the Father. Nothing but irrefragable religious experience will explain the amazing fact that, without a tremor of hesitation, the apostles took the responsibility of asking men to believe in Christ as Son of God from all eternity.

NOTE ON THE SINLESSNESS OF JESUS.

The testimony to Jesus' sinlessness which may be gathered out of the Epistles rests on no *à priori* dogma, but is a transcript of convincing facts of which we have a clear view in the Synoptics. Historical argument will not of course carry us all the way, yet it does prove that Jesus thought of Himself as sinless. It also permits us to believe that in affirming His sinlessness the apostles cannot have been at war with their recollections of His life, "suppressing defects in His character which they had observed, or acknowledgments of shortcoming made by Himself."[1]

The Synoptics certainly record no explicit claim to moral purity on Jesus' part; nothing so direct as the question, "Which of you convicteth Me of sin?" (Jn 8^{46}). But neither do they anywhere eulogise Him or attempt to prove His innocence; they offer simply a plain tale of His words and works. Various minor traits of bearing and conduct, however, reveal undeniably His own conviction. When we recollect that His mission opened with a call to repentance, that He condemned "the righteous" unsparingly, that He urged personal confession on His followers yet was Himself a stranger to the language of contrition, we can explain this only by the supposition that He reckoned Himself inwardly pure. This absence from the mature mind of Jesus of any consciousness that sin had tainted Him is

[1] Forrest, *Authority of Christ*, 26.

the really decisive fact. He stood without fear or shame in the light of God. There is no trace of healed scars, no memories of defeat. He was no penitent, like St. Paul or Augustine, nor does He confess sin when He is dying. Men may of course be sinful unawares, but not such men as Jesus. The intense moral pain that vibrates in His rebuke of Peter (Mt 16[28]) implies an exquisite sensitiveness to the presence of evil. Not only so; as Goguel has remarked, a personality of this depth and ethical intensity, had He felt conscious of sin in even the slightest degree, would have been overwhelmed by feelings of poignant and consuming grief.[1] Further, in view of the obligation resting on Him to dispel erroneous impressions, His persistent silence, notwithstanding the presence within Him of a bad conscience, would have been the last hypocrisy. Finally, on every page of the Gospels, we encounter such imperial demands for obedience, as well as gracious promises of help and pardon, as it would have been an enormity for a sinful man to utter.

Traces of moral imperfection have nevertheless been discovered at various points in His career. His denunciation of the Pharisees has been characterised as harsh and unfeeling; His behaviour to His mother and brethren has been censured for a grave lack of affection; and to some His cleansing of the Temple has appeared as a blameworthy excess of zeal. Still more graceless accusations have been based on other narrated acts. Most readers will feel that His conduct on each of the occasions specified is a quite intelligible manifestation of fidelity to His Messianic task. It was a task which provoked resistance, necessitating counter-resistance in its turn; and it would have been a vice in Jesus, not a virtue, to shrink from the painful duty. Enough that such a one as He was conscious, even in these and similar instances, of complete adequacy to His own ideal.

Against the view that Jesus had no interior experience of sin, it is illegitimate to urge His self-subjection to baptism. For in His case also acceptance of the rite signified the definite resolve to associate Himself with the Messianic community in expectation of the Kingdom and in the corresponding passion for righteousness; but while for the people the advent of the Kingdom demanded penitence and the abandonment of known sin, from Jesus it asked self-consecration to the Messianic activity by which the Kingdom was to be brought in. Jesus' baptism, in

[1] *Op. cit.* 202.

short, formed a crucial stage in His deepening self-identification with sinful men—"a great act of loving communion with our misery," as it has been described, in which He numbered Himself with the transgressors and took all their burdens as His own. More difficulty will be felt in interpreting His reply to the young ruler, whose salutation, "Good Master," He waved back with the uncompromising rejoinder, "None is good save one, even God" (Mk 10^{18}). The words cannot be a veiled confession of moral delinquency, which certainly would not have taken this ambiguous and all but casual form. What Jesus disclaims, rather, is *God's* perfect goodness. None but God is good with a goodness unchanging and eternal; He only cannot be tempted of evil, but rests for ever in unconditioned and immutable perfection. Jesus, on the contrary, learnt obedience by the things which He suffered, being tempted in all points like as we are (He 5^{8} 4^{15}). In the sense of transcendent superiority to moral conflict and the strenuous obligation to prove His virtue ever afresh in face of new temptation and difficulty, He laid no claim to the "absolute" goodness of His Father. Which reminds us emphatically that the holiness of Jesus, as displayed in the record of His life, is no automatic effect of a metaphysical substance, but in its perfected form the fruit of continuous moral volition pervaded and sustained by the Spirit. It is at once the Father's gift and progressively realised in an ethical experience. This follows from the moral conditions of incarnation.

It may also be held, with much reason, that Jesus' words to the young ruler must be interpreted exclusively in the light of the incident itself. In that case, they are simply meant, like so many of Jesus' utterances, to throw the man back upon his own mind. And accordingly they cannot be relevantly cited in a discussion of our Lord's sinlessness.

For some recent thinkers the concept of sinlessness is disqualified by its unduly negative character, and they accordingly propose to replace it by the idea of Jesus' perfect fidelity to His vocation. Sinlessness, if predicated of a child, might mean no more than incapacity for conscious transgression. Now not only does the concept of fidelity to vocation bring out a characteristic of fundamental importance in Jesus' personality, but several New Testament passages usually quoted under the head of sinlessness might be still more fitly placed under the other category (*e.g.* 1 P 2^{21}, Ph 2$^{7.8}$, 1 Jn 3^{5}). Nevertheless, the specific thought of sinlessness is one which we cannot afford to lose. We need a predicate which bears directly, not merely on Jesus' fulfilment of His task, but on the inner life which made this fulfilment possible—the private hidden stream of thought, feeling, and volition which flowed out of a stainless development dating from very birth. "In a so-called civil vocation," writes Haering, "it is possible to be faithful apart from perfect inward purity; in the case of Jesus fidelity was possible only through an unperturbed communion with the Father in the hidden deeps of the heart."[1]

Such moral perfection is to us inexplicable; yet, as Mr. Bradley has said, "not to know how a thing can be is no disproof that the thing must be and is." Ethical psychology, based on the experience of sinners, must ever find sinlessness a mystery. We are sure of the fact; sure also that the fact was mediated in ethical and spiritual modes. Jesus alone was sinless, because He felt as we do not the powerlessness and insufficiency of the human will to sustain itself in goodness; also because He felt as we do not man's sheer dependence on the Holy Father whose response to simple and complete faith passes understanding.

[1] *Der christliche Glaube*, 398.

CHAPTER II.

PRIMITIVE CHRISTIAN BELIEF.

THE initial stage of primitive Christian thought is reflected most typically in the early speeches of the Book of Acts. Especially in their Christology, it is agreed, these Petrine sermons are of the highest value, containing as they do precisely the kind of teaching that might be expected from men for whom the resurrection of Jesus had created a new world of feeling and anticipation. We can see the apostolic mind begin to adjust itself slowly to a great and novel situation, though naturally a considerable time was to elapse before an effort could be made to formulate the doctrinal conclusions implied in their practical religious attitude.

St. Peter's message may be briefly summarised in the statement that Jesus—a person well known to his Jewish hearers—is the Messiah; that His Messianic dignity has been proved by resurrection from the dead; and that He will return presently to bring in the last consummation. In simple outlines he pictures the Prophet whom their leaders put to death. "Jesus of Nazareth," we read, "a man approved of God to you by mighty works and wonders and signs, which God did by Him in the midst of you" (2^{22}), by the side of which we may place a later verse: "God anointed Jesus of Nazareth with the Holy Spirit and with power: who went about

LITERATURE—Weizsäcker, *Das apostolische Zeitalter*[3], 1902 (Eng. tr. 1894–5); McGiffert, *History of Christianity in the Apostolic Age*, 1897; Gunkel, *Die Wirkungen des heiligen Geistes*[3], 1908; Spitta, *Christi Predigt an die Geister*, 1890; Monnier, *La première épître de l'apôtre Pierre*, 1900; Wernle, *Die Anfänge unserer Religion*[2], 1904 (Eng. tr. 1903–4).

doing good, and healing all that were oppressed of the devil; for God was with Him" (10^{38}). But this Man whom they had slain is now vindicated marvellously; the hopes set upon Him have become certainties. As we read in a verse the importance of which for the primitive Christology we cannot overestimate: "God hath made Him both Lord and Christ, this Jesus whom ye crucified" (2^{36}). These words reveal the secret of the new faith. For the first time it has broken on human minds that Jesus is Lord. It is by resurrection that He has taken His place openly as the Christ. We need not interpret the words as meaning that He was not Messiah previously, a position which makes a chaos of the Synoptic narrative; but certainly we may affirm that not till after death and resurrection was He the fully manifested Christ, in a perfect manner all that which the Christ was to be. This is in harmony with the general conviction expressed throughout the New Testament (cf. Ro 1^{4}) that resurrection opens a new transcendent stadium in the career of Jesus. He was the Christ even during His lifetime on earth, and was acknowledged in that character by faith; yet His true status could be then disclosed only in a restricted and conditioned measure. "The fact that He was raised from the dead did not make Jesus the Christ; but it showed Him to be such."[1]

Thus the gospel preached by St. Peter may be condensed in the one truth that Jesus, crucified and risen, is the promised Christ of God. He is attested by miracles wrought by Himself or done later in His name, but supremely by the amazing miracle of the resurrection. This appeal to Jesus' miracles, it is worth noting, is the

[1] Mathews, *Messianic Hope*, 130. The name of J. Weiss is prominently associated with the opinion that for the primitive faith the earthly Jesus was not yet Messiah, but even he is unable to carry through so drastic an interpretation. Thus we find him conceding that the disciples who preached after Pentecost "must have known or believed that Jesus in some form or other regarded Himself as the fulfiller of the prophecy (Dt 18^{18}), the final messenger of God to Israel, in some sense or other the Messiah" (*Christ: the Beginnings of Dogma*, 23).

only direct and concrete allusion to the events of His earthly life. Even His work as Teacher is barely mentioned (10^{36}). The speaker's mind is drawn irresistibly to other topics. Less than we might have expected is said as to the bearing of Jesus' death on the forgiveness of sins; though His death is described freely as foreseen and pre-ordained of God; and, what is very significant, it is distinctly alleged to have been necessary, presumably as a part of His redeeming work (2^{23}). But what absorbs the preacher is Jesus' deliverance from the grave and entry into glory. "This Jesus did God raise up," he declares, "whereof we all are witnesses" (2^{32}). He is speaking not merely in view of the resurrection appearances, but in the power of that ineffaceable impression left by Jesus in the long intercourse of their discipleship. The Easter faith is the living resultant of the vision of the Risen One acting on and harmonising with the pure and sublime image of Jesus which had been stamped upon their memory. The hall-mark of New Testament religion, faith in an exalted Lord, is thus shown firm and clear at the very outset. Men who had been daily in Jesus' company knew that they were still in relations to Him. He was still the same Person they had known and loved; death and resurrection had not impaired His individuality. "We ate and drank with Him after He rose from the dead" (10^{41}). Even if a saying of this kind may reveal traces of unconscious materialisation, at all events it proves how different the intercourse of the risen Christ with His followers is felt to be from a merely subjective and transitory vision. As it has been put: "There is no such thing in the New Testament as an appearance of the Risen Saviour in which He merely appears. He is always represented as entering into relations to those who see Him in other ways than by a flash upon the inner or the outer eye: He establishes other communications between Himself and His own than that which can be characterised in this way."[1] To be related thus to the exalted Lord is the differential feature

[1] Denney, *Death of Christ*, 67.

of Christianity. His presence inspired believers, and so trustfully did they lean on it that death was nothing more terrible than falling asleep (7^{60}).

Various epithets have been appended to this first sketch of Christological doctrine. By some writers it has been roundly described as humanitarian; but every sympathetic reader must feel that in the conceptions of "Christ" and "Lord" there lay from the beginning a wealth of content and of implication far transcending the limits of mere manhood. Others, in view of a passage like Ac 2^{32-36}, prefer to speak of it as Adoptionist; and in this questionable *terminus technicus*, better reserved for the view which dates Jesus' special Sonship from the baptism at the Jordan, there is at all events this much truth, that Jesus *is* represented as entering on full Messianic dignity at the resurrection, and as having first manifested His new sovereign power by the outpouring of the Spirit. But a better adjective than either is "rudimentary." The total absence of the idea of pre-existence, for example, is significant for the theological *naïveté* of the belief.

At the same time, there are positive features which prove that Jesus was already viewed as having His place somehow within the sphere of Godhead. To be raised to God's right hand is to participate in the Divine power and glory. The gift of the Spirit is bestowed by Him, and this Spirit is the Spirit of God. We ought not to forget that this claim to possess the Spirit was largely an appeal to something which even the onlooker could recognise and verify. The acceptance of Jesus as Christ manifestly led to a new experience. Spirit-filled men rose up to proclaim a gospel of salvation from sin, death, and all diabolic powers, and it was impossible to deny that their inspiration was really due to their connection with Jesus. In other ways also His person had the religious value of God. Prayer is offered to Him as well as in His name,[1] and God

[1] 7^{59}; possibly 1^{24} also, for just before St. Peter speaks of Him as Lord. Cf. 2 Co 12^{8}, Rev 5^{13}, Jn $14^{13\,\text{f.}}$, and on the whole subject Zahn, *Skizzen aus dem Leben der alten Kirche*, 1894, 271 ff.

is said to have appointed Him judge of quick and dead. He is Himself the theme of gospel preaching, the object of faith, the source of penitence and forgiveness. Over and over again, His name, *i.e.* His person as revealed and known, is proclaimed as sole medium of redemption (2^{38} 3^{16} 4^{12} 19^{43}). Most significant of all is His possession of the title "Lord," a familiar Old Testament designation of Jehovah. In the same way, verses from prophecy or psalm which at first referred to God are applied directly to Jesus, and the conception of Him as occupying the throne of Israel is merged in the vaster thought that He is King of the world. As Feine has pointed out,[1] these lofty predicates are only intelligible if we suppose that the disciples in retrospect were conscious that even Jesus' earthly life revealed traces of His higher being. Even then He had been anointed with the Holy Spirit, and had been "holy and just"; even then He was known by the sublime name of the "Son of Man" (7^{56}). The primitive Christology can be best interpreted as the fruit of adoring memory quickened by the experience of a risen and glorified Redeemer.

We are now in a position to consider the suggestion that in the earliest faith two forms of faith in Christ went side by side, in peaceful rivalry: that to which He was but a prophet and forerunner, and that to which He already appeared as authentically Divine in majesty and redeeming power. If this means that these forms of Christological belief were held respectively by two different groups of Christians, it must be said at once that so far as the New Testament is concerned the hypothesis is without foundation. Both estimates were held by *all* Christians. Jesus was indeed "a prophet mighty in word and deed" (Lk 24^{19}),[2] but also from the very outset He was the Messiah-King who had been vindicated by His rising from the dead and reception of universal authority. From which

[1] *Theologie d. NT*, 203.

[2] The term παῖς (3^{13}, 4^{27}) is "Servant" rather than "Son," and all but certainly contains an allusion to Is 53.

we may draw two inferences: first, that the difference of view between St. Paul and the primitive apostolic society was not one of principle, but of degree, since the risen Jesus was *never* regarded as an ordinary man. And secondly, that it is needless to have recourse to a supposed "Messianic dogmatic" for the august epithets from the first attributed to Christ. They are sufficiently accounted for by the appearances of the risen Lord.

This primitive conception of Christ is pervaded by an intense eschatological feeling. While it is an exaggeration to speak of Jesus' earthly life as being for St. Peter no more than "a preliminary career," yet there is certainly a startling preoccupation, or rather absorption, of mind in the hope of the Parousia, which may break on the world any moment. The impending return of the Messiah is the keynote of the whole. "Repent ye, therefore, and turn again . . . that He may send the Christ who hath been appointed for you, even Jesus" ($3^{19.\ 20}$). The period of waiting will be short. Men still think in the forms of national Messianism.

Into these forms, however, rudimentary though they be, a new and infinite content has been poured. We find, indeed, scarcely an effort to create a system of conceptions adequate to the revolutionising experience through which the witnesses of the glorified Lord had passed. Doctrine could not begin till men had first lived themselves into the new thought of Christ. But already their attitude is that of faith and worship. Jesus' nature is seen to be universal and absolute in the sense that everything which can be called salvation is mediated by His power. Exaltation has set free His influence from all limits, whether of place or time; He is now available everywhere and always. It could only be a question of time until a theological master-mind should rise to set forth the unsuspected significance of these elemental facts of faith and life.

Turning now to the First Epistle of Peter, we find a writer who is interested, it may be fairly said, rather in the salvation accomplished by Christ than in theoretical problems relating to His person. The Epistle, like the speeches in Acts, rests on and revolves round the contrast of the passion of Jesus with His present sovereignty, "the sufferings of Christ and the glories that should follow" (1^{11}). In both the evidence of Old Testament prophecy is appealed to, and more than once the same quotations occur. Both emphasise the Divine fore-ordination of the Cross; both refer to the sinless perfection of the self-sacrificing Victim. We may gather the writer's favourite thought of Christ from the fact that "Jesus" is never used by itself, while "Christ" has become a proper name. Weiss is probably correct in explaining this as "due to the fact that the person of Jesus is contemplated by the Christian always and exclusively in His specific quality as Mediator of salvation."[1] It is a point in Christology where a slight change of accent has taken place as contrasted with the Petrine speeches.

Is there a further advance in 1^{11}? When it is said that the Spirit of Christ in the prophets "testified beforehand to the sufferings of Christ," and in a related verse (1^{20}) that Christ "was foreknown indeed before the foundation of the world, but was manifested at the end of the times for your sake," may we conclude that the writer believed in the pre-existence of Christ? The arguments on either side will be found in the commentaries; here it can only be said that the language of 1^{11} by itself apparently means no more than that the Divine Spirit, now so much identified with Christ as properly to be called *His* Spirit, moved also in the prophets of old time. The principle of life and power that filled the manifested Christ was operative even prior to His coming. But on this view the passage after all marks a stage towards the full assertion of pre-existence, though it does not assert it quite directly. The Spirit in which the inmost being of Jesus was constituted had pointed on to the sufferings that befell Him. On the other hand, 1^{20} is distinctly more significant. While the word

[1] *Biblical Theology of the New Testament*, i. 226.

"foreknown" (προεγνωσμένου) in no way involves the pre-existence of Christ, since it is used even of Christians in 1^2, yet the unusual combination of "foreknown" with "manifested" may justly be considered as placing the matter beyond doubt. Only that can be manifested which was in being before manifestation. Thus, even though the point is not insisted on, the person of Christ is already lifted clear of the contingencies of time, viewed as the embodiment of a Divine Spirit, and given a place within the redeeming world-plan of God. More and more the historical is being fused with the eternal.

The Christ so characterised, then, was revealed in the last times. We have a vague hint as to the constitution of His person in the difficult phrase (3^{18}), "being put to death in the flesh, but quickened in the spirit"; where the two datives (σαρκί and πνεύματι) are exactly parallel. The flesh is the sphere or element in which death took place; similarly, the spirit is the sphere of resurrection, the element of life that made it possible. In virtue of one aspect of His being, Christ died; in virtue of the other and higher, He was raised again.[1] The verse at first sight comes very near to the orthodox doctrine of the Two Natures; what it really does, however, is to contemplate the personality of Christ from two different points of view, as capable of death on the one hand, and on the other of resurrection. Spirit means here the Divine vital principle, in a higher potency than it attains in man, and thus characterised by an essential and indestructible energy. The evidence that Christ's spirit was laden with vast abnormal powers is that "He went and preached unto the spirits in prison" (3^{19} 4^6). Whatever this means, it proclaims that wherever men are, Christ can save. Even in the region of the dead He must have manifested His power.[2] Formerly, in Ac 2^{24}, the ground of Jesus' resurrection had been found merely in Old Testament prediction, but now the step is taken of attributing it to

[1] In a sense Ro $1^{3.4}$ may be compared.

[2] Cf. Denney, *Jesus and the Gospel*, 48.

the energies inherent in His nature and due to the unction of the Messianic Spirit.

We are entitled to say, I think, in view of these data, that First Peter exhibits a form of Christology slightly more developed than that of the first chapters of Acts. Yet its tone is thoroughly primitive; there is nothing in the way of precise analysis or speculation. If the epistle was written by St. Peter, as it may well have been, we must recollect that a man of his type would probably care little for reasoned theories regarding the loved person of His Lord. He lived amid the memories of the past and the ardent hopes of a near and glorious future.

Nevertheless, there can be no reasonable doubt that he shared the specifically Christian estimate of Jesus. The Spirit of God, as we have seen, is definitely spoken of as "the Spirit of Christ"—in itself an amazing fact. "Son of God" is nowhere used, but we meet with the significant and full-toned phrase, "the God and Father of our Lord Jesus Christ" (1^3), with an undeniable implication of Christ's special Sonship. The declaration that angels and authorities are subject to Him (3^{22}) does more than assert His risen glory; it affirms that He is personally participant in the sovereignty of God, whom angels serve as messengers. The somewhat unusual phrase, "Sanctify in your hearts Christ as Lord" (3^{13}), echoes Is 8^{13}, where "Lord" has reference to Jehovah. And in 4^{11} we read: "Through Jesus Christ, whose is the glory and the dominion for ever and ever." The balance of the verse is in favour of an interpretation which ascribes the doxology to Christ, but in the last chapter (5^{11}) virtually the same form is used in reference to "the God of all grace."

Details of this kind can never be quite conclusive, but at all events they mark with some clearness the direction of the stream. The primitive apostolic Christology lays due stress on the subordination of Jesus Christ to God the Father, while yet already He begins to fill the sphere of the Divine. He is believed in with adoring trust, as monotheists can believe in none but God. If this is the attitude taken by men of unspeculative minds, the fact is only the more full of suggestion. It implies that the normally Christian intelligence cannot refrain from predicating of Jesus Christ the religious value of God. Not metaphysics in the wrong place, but faith conscious of its own significance and therefore reaching out to a clear expression of its proper content, has been responsible for the high Christology to be found even in the first origins of our religion.[1]

[1] The materials for an exhaustive treatment of the primitive Christology would of course have to be drawn also from St. Paul (*e.g.* 1 Co 15[3 ff.]) and the synoptic Gospels. But I have not entered on this field, my object being merely to sketch the main distinguishable *types* of Christology present in the New Testament.

CHAPTER III.

THE CHRISTOLOGY OF ST. PAUL.

In the following statement of St. Paul's view of Christ it has not been thought necessary to make a sharp distinction between the four great Epistles—to the Galatians, Romans, and Corinthians—and the later group, known as the Epistles of the Imprisonment. For one thing, excellent critical opinion may be quoted for the statement that all the Imprisonment Epistles are genuine, so that post-Pauline developments, say in Ephesians, need not so far be allowed for. Moreover, if we have already in Ro 9^5—and perhaps even in 2 Th 1^{12}—[1] an explicit assertion of Christ's deity, it is plain that quite early the apostle had expressed an estimate of our Lord's being beyond which it was impossible to go, and we may discount the hypothesis that in his later years he gave himself up to unbridled and fantastic speculation, of a sort wholly alien to his previous thought. This means that chronological charts of St. Paul's advance in Christian knowledge, which have pleased no one but their authors, may be laid aside. It is a better plan to attempt a comprehensive view of his thought in its plastic and vivid unity. Enough if we mark here and there a difference of accent in earlier and later formulations.

Literature—Schmidt, *Die paulinische Christologie*, 1870; Somerville, *St. Paul's Conception of Christ*, 1897; Moffatt, *Paul and Paulinism*, 1910; Olschewski, *Die Wurzeln der paulinischen Christologie*, 1909; Goguel, *L'apôtre Paul et Jésus Christ*, 1904; Weinel, *Paulus der Mensch und sein Werk*, 1904 (Eng. tr. 1906); Wrede, *Paulus*[2], 1907 (Eng. tr. 1907); Kaftan, *Jesus und Paulus*, 1906; Feine, *Jesus Christus und Paulus*, 1902; Brückner, *Die Enstehung der paulinischen Christologie*, 1903; Kölbing, *Die geistige Wirkung der Person Jesu auf Paulus*, 1906.

[1] von Dobschütz, *Kommentar* (1910), *in loc.*

Is a genetic account of St. Paul's view of Christ possible? Can we tell what set his mind a-working on the subject, or what quickening influences shaped his beliefs? Holsten, preceded by Baur, long maintained that we must take the apostle strictly as a theologian, whose letters are brief statements of dogmatic. He wrote primarily as a logician, only in the second place as a missionary. Like his other doctrines, Christology took form in his mind as the outcome of a reasoning process, of pure logic applied to the fate of Jesus. Confronted by the Messiah's death on the cross, an event, as he felt, laden with the Divine redemptive purpose, St. Paul, yielding to a strictly intellectual compulsion, gave up the theological system of Judaism and replaced it by one in which Christ appeared as a synthesis of historical tradition and Hellenistic doctrines of a pre-existent "Heavenly Man." It is a theory deeply marked by the influence of Hegelian dialectic. On such terms St. Paul's gospel, as Kaftan puts it, is simply the *gnosis* of the Messiah's death; not the fruit of a great religious experience, but the cold, rational production of a patient theorist.

More recently the place of Holsten's purely immanental theory has been taken by that of a large and active school of writers, united by keen devotion to the methods of scientific history of religion. Their interest for the most part has lain in tracing the descent of ideas. And the gist of their conclusions, so far as we are now concerned with them, has been expressed with admirable clearness in Weinel's somewhat audacious words: "The Christological dogma already existed in all essential particulars before Jesus was born. Jewish Messianic speculations had already imagined a picture for the completion of which nothing was wanting but the Nicene dogma that the Father and the Son were of the same substance. . . . Even the statement that the world was created by the Son of God was as current an opinion among the Jews as everything else that Paul tells us of Christ's life from the beginning of the world until His second advent in judgment."[1] The value of this may be gathered from the single fact that in Jewish Messianism the ideas of a redeeming death and triumphant resurrection are nowhere to be found. Apart from this damaging circumstance, however, it is of interest to note that, according to Brückner, Wrede, and other scholars, the elements even of the Judaistic "Christology" had mostly been taken over from Oriental myths. In various lands and faiths the yearning dreams of salvation had created, in wavering outline, the imaginative figure of a "Saviour"; and the different features of the sketch came to deposit themselves, like crystals in a supersaturated solution, on the head of the Messiah hoped for by Jews. St. Paul, who fell heir to this creation of apocalyptic fancy, merely added the name of Jesus, and at once his Christology was complete. Instantly he felt that Jesus must have been and have done all things portrayed in the Messianic dogmatic. The Christ of the Pauline Epistles, therefore, has no relation at all to the historic Jesus. We need scarcely hesitate to regard St. Paul, indeed, as the real founder of our religion.

It is obviously an intellectualistic theory, as much so as that of Holsten. Waiving the fact, conceded frankly by Gunkel,[2] that of this pre-Christian apocalyptic "Christ" we are in complete ignorance, the entire hypothesis rests on the *à priori* assumption that there can have been nothing genuinely new and creative in the apostle's view of Christ. His ideas on the subject must all have come to him from outside sources: as for attributing the vital core and heart of his Christology to a vast, revolutionising experience, it is not be dreamed of. No doubt the Damascus vision counts for something; but what happened to him then, apparently, was not that he knew himself redeemed, but that he formed a reasoned opinion. He merely learned to give the name "Jesus" to the Divine heavenly being in whom he believed already. There is nothing to be said about this except that it is preposterous. If anything is sure about St. Paul, it is that his theology

[1] *St. Paul*, 313. [2] *Zum religionsgesch. Verständnis d. NT*, 94.

is, as Wernle puts it, "the theology of a converted man." Every idea is a *Christian* idea. At Damascus there occurred a real event which changed his life from the centre to the circumference, and once for all caused him to forget the things that were behind. It is vain to interpret his Christology, therefore, by the hypothetical contents of his mind in earlier years; as vain as to "explain" Shakespeare's historical plays by the materials he may have found in North's *Plutarch* or Holinshed's *Chronicles.* To suppose that the Pharisee became the Christian apostle merely in consequence of an intellectual readjustment, or that he could have induced the primitive society to tolerate, let alone adopt, a view of Christ thus generated, appears to me a theory out of all intelligible relation to human life. This is not to deny that certain inherited conceptions may have influenced the periphery of the Pauline doctrine, or determined the wording of some few phrases of description. But it is lost labour to start from these things. St. Paul's Christology is based on the experience of the glorified Lord vouchsafed to him in the hour of his conversion, illustrated and confirmed by the Spirit-sustained life of fellowship with Christ which was then begun. When he speaks of Christ, he is not combining ideas, but transcribing inwardly reported fact. For him the basis of true religion was not made by man, but given by God; and the knowledge of Jesus the Christ, through which he had peace with God and was become a new creature, he owed to a transforming spiritual experience.[1]

The living and dynamic centre, then, of the Christology of St. Paul is his experience of the glorified Lord, by whom he had been "apprehended." In this respect he is

[1] The drift of opinion away from Wrede and Brückner's view of St. Paul's indifference to the historic Jesus has been illustrated in a startling manner by the suggestion of J. Weiss, based on 2 Co 5[16], that the apostle came in contact with Jesus at Jerusalem prior to the crucifixion (*Paulus und Jesus*, 1909). Much more attractive is Moffatt's explanation of the passage, according to which "the *knowledge of Christ after the flesh* is probably the Messianic belief of Pharisaic theology such as Paul had

in agreement with the primitive society. Both he and they looked upward, not backward. The staple of his thought comes not from inherited ideas as to the Messiah, but from a wonderful inward sense of possession by the sovereign grace of Christ. As we shall see, it is impossible to fuse too intimately his doctrine of Christ and of the Spirit. Yet, on the other hand, this exalted One is identical with Jesus who died for sin. The apostle cannot think of Christ and not think also of the cross He bore; "I determined," he writes to the Corinthians, "to know nothing among you but Jesus Christ, and Him crucified" (1 Co 2^2). We must conclude that his mind started from the Risen One who encountered him in glory at Damascus, moved thence to the cross, which the Lord had endured, and came finally to rest on the person of the Crucified. His present experience of Christ is decisive as to what he must think of the death undergone by the Messiah; on the other hand, the fact that such a reconciling death was possible is an index of the inherent dignity of Him who suffered. The full truth, accordingly, is not to be expressed either by saying that St. Paul's view of Christ's person is derived from his doctrine of atonement, or, conversely, that his Christology fixed his doctrine of the atonement. In reality person and work define each other. The exalted Lord, known from the first as such, would not *be* Lord unless He had died "for our offences" (Ro $4^{24f.}$); on the other hand, what Christ inherently is to God accounts, in the apostle's view, for the supreme religious value of His acceptance of the Cross.

St. Paul, like all the writers of the New Testament, is convinced that the exalted Jesus is "the Christ" or Messiah—"Christ" for him still keeps a flavour of its

shared in his pre-Christian days" (*Paul and Paulinism*, 18). If this be so, we may be said to have from the apostle's own lips a protest in advance against the modern radical derivation of his Christology. He is telling us, as in Gal 1^{15-17}, that "from the very outset, a better knowledge of Christ's nature had shone upon him." The whole question of the genesis of his Christological ideas is very ably discussed by Olschewski, *Die Wurzeln der paul. Christologie*, 1909, whom I have followed in some points.

official sense—but also he transcends *ab initio* the current Messianic idea, perceiving the cardinal significance of Jesus, not for Jews merely, but for mankind. He nowhere employs the title "Son of Man." The Kingdom of God he virtually merges in the person of Christ. The phrase "Kingdom of God" itself, which seldom occurs, was so completely Jewish in origin and associations that he must have found it unhelpful in his missionary work. At the same time, its eschatological reference is still retained in what the apostle means by "salvation" and "eternal life"; for he never ceased to look yearningly towards a consummation in which death, sin, sickness, demons, and every godless principality and power should be overcome and annihilated. Jesus the Christ was already clothed with universal power, and would ere long appear once more to bring all things to completion. Those who had accepted Him as Messianic King would at His appearance be made perfect members of the Messianic Kingdom, and thus be, in the full sense of the word, saved.

In tracing now his conception of Christ we shall endeavour to follow as far as possible the movement of his own mind, beginning with the thought of the exalted Lord, and passing back thereafter to the historical, and what may be called the eternal, antecedents of Christ's present glory.

It was due to his amazing experience of conversion that St. Paul's faith came to be fixed steadily, and from the very outset, on the risen and glorified Redeemer. He habitually conceives of Christ as clothed in the δόξα or Divine radiance in which he first beheld Him at Damascus. That moment was for him a piercing glimpse of a new world; his sight of the glory of God in the face of Jesus Christ he can compare with nothing but that first creative hour when God said: "Let there be light!" (2 Co 4^{6}). Here is the basis of his faith. From day to day he is preoccupied with the risen Lord, the Son whom it had pleased God to reveal in him (Gal 1^{16}). The attitude is one, of course, really common to all New Testament writers, but St. Paul's unique experience lent to it a peculiar intensity and passion. All redeeming influences are streaming out from Christ's risen power to fill the life of the believer. He is not to be separated, whether in thought or prayer, from God Himself. It is with this one purpose that He has been exalted, that in the Spirit He should bring home to men the universal reconciliation with God once for all accomplished on the cross. He is Head of the Church, which is His body; yet not of the Church alone, for His omnipotence, like His knowledge and His love, is complete and all-embracing. God has set Him far above all rule and authority and power and dominion, not only in this world, but also in that which is to come (Eph 1^{21}). The hour of doom struck for the power of darkness when He rose from the grave. Even yet He has not attained the full victory, which will culminate only in His final advent, when the last enemy shall be vanquished and God will fulfil His purpose to sum up all things in Christ, both things in heaven and things in earth. Nevertheless, this glorious, royal Lord is not far away from His people, too high for human need or for that sympathy and care on which they are dependent while yet in the body. On the contrary, He is within and beside them always, to guide, comfort, warn, inspire, so that the apostle could literally speak of himself as being in Christ, of his life as being his own no longer, but the life of Christ living in him (Gal 2^{20}), and could pray for his converts that Christ might dwell in their hearts by faith. Thus in Ro $8^{31ff.}$ the strain of confidence and praise sweeps up from point to point with gathering intensity; from the death of Christ to what is greater still, His rising from the dead, from His rising to His session at the right hand of God, and finally, as to a height at which imagination fails, to His work of intercession. This is the Christ before whose face St. Paul lives from day to day, and to whose advent he strains forward with keen desire.

No part of the apostle's teaching has a more vital bearing on his thought of the Exalted One than his mystic conception of the believer's union with Christ.[1] Round this idea his religious feeling crystallised. The phrase "in Christ" or "in the Lord" occurs nearly 240 times in the Epistles we have accepted as genuine, and it is used with reference to every side of experience. "I am persuaded in Christ," he writes (Ro 14^{14}); "if there be any consolations in Christ" (Ph 2^1); "the dead in Christ" (1 Th 4^{16}). It is as though Christ were the air or element in which the Christian moved and had his being, thinking with His mind and willing with His will. The believer has absolutely become the organ or instrument of the Lord, and is drawn, spirit, soul, and body, into His dominating and recreating life. It is a relation of spirit to spirit, yet not a relation individualistically realised; for—and this point is particularly accentuated in Ephesians—the Church is the body of Christ, in which old divisions of Jew and Gentile are done away. This final turn of thought, however, he has prepared for by the earlier conception of Christ as the Head of the body, of which individual Christians are the members; "we, who are many," he writes to the Church in Rome, "are one body in Christ." (12^5). The bond uniting Christ and Christians is such that the same predications can be made of both. In His death we also die, only to rise in His resurrection to newness of life. His power is made perfect in our weakness; and it is no contradiction of this, but its true expression, that the apostle bears about in his body the dying of the Lord Jesus (2 Co 4^{10}), for only in proportion as the private forces of the believer decay can his natural capacities be absorbed and utilised by the higher power of Christ. The fact that St. Paul conceived this union or communion as mediated by the Spirit may possibly explain how he feels at liberty to change from the phrase "in Christ" and speak of Christ dwelling in us; for the

[1] It has been expounded with a fine sympathy by J. Weiss, *Die Nachfolge Christi*, 83–98.

interpenetration between the Spirit-life of believers and the Spirit of Christ is perfectly reciprocal. Plainly this faith-mysticism lets in a flood of light on the Pauline Christology. A single verse like 2 Co 5[17], "If any man be in Christ, he is a new creation," reveals in a flash the last ground of his religious conviction about the Lord. He with whom men can be thus in a relation of mutual vital possession has obviously a nature which is more than human; that entrance of His life into us, met and appropriated by our absorption in Him—whereby we are able to denude ourselves of an unrighteous past and live anew to holiness—involves on His side something of the universality and transcendence of God Himself. It has been argued that this synthesis of personality and spiritual immanence in the Christ of St. Paul is in reality unthinkable, inasmuch as the two sides of the combined idea are irreconcilably opposed, and to take the combination seriously can only lead to the depersonalising of Christ in a quasi-pantheism. But we may reasonably urge that this is to beg the question of His divinity, in a negative sense. The figure of the head and the members (Col 1[18]) seems peculiarly fitted to represent the relation of Christ to His people in both lights—as characterised equally by transcendence and by mystic vital union.[1]

There is nothing more luminous or creatively original in St. Paul's thought than his living correlation of Christ and the Spirit as they are manifested in experience. It is not merely that the phenomena of the Spirit are for him a decisive proof of Christ's Messianic position; still further, the presence of the Spirit as a fact of power in the believing life is a self-communication of the Lord Jesus, who as Spirit dominates the new order of being into which Christian men have been translated. Spirit means supernatural power, yet not for St. Paul power revealed most typically in ecstatic rapture, but the ethical force from which spring such normal Christian graces as love, joy, peace, long-suffering, and kindness (Gal 5[22]),

[1] Cf. Olschewski, *op. cit.* 153–54.

which he sees to be more wonderful by far than speaking with tongues.[1] In Dr. Moffatt's words, "his first experience of the Lord was a vision of Jesus as the risen and exalted Christ. The reality of Christ's nature was Spirit, on his view; Jesus was installed or constituted Son of God with full powers by the resurrection, which revealed and realised his true nature as life-giving Spirit. His life in the flesh had limited him. It was a phase of being which could not do justice to him. But when that temporary impoverishment of nature was over, the heavenly reality shone out in its fulness. The Spirit radiated on men, it was poured into their hearts, as the Spirit of one who had died and risen for the sake of men. We must extinguish, however, the misconception that Paul regarded the Spirit as acting on the lines of a natural force in the evolution of the religious life. To him it meant the gracious power of God which evoked faith in Jesus as the crucified and risen Christ, and then mediated to the receptive, obedient life all that the Lord was and did for his own people."[2] Life "in the Spirit," his characteristic term for personal religion, can have its source only in the exalted or spiritual Christ, so that, when he describes men as being "in Christ" or "in the Spirit," he is thinking not of two rival or parallel realities, but of one revolutionary experience seen from two points of view; for life flows to men from Christ and the Spirit indifferently. The ground of this epoch-making combination is clearly to be sought in his conversion. He had met the Exalted One face to face; and that spiritual event, in which the Spirit was energising, had had the Lord Jesus for concrete and substantial content. This once for all fixed his conception of the Spirit, lending it precision of outline, and protecting it against the wandering and unethical fancies of paganism. The Spirit of God, long promised for the latter days, was now known to be the

[1] His perception of this difference of value marks a forward step in the history of religion.

[2] *Paul and Paulinism*, 37–38.

very Spirit of Jesus. It is a salient example of how God reveals new truth through the medium of life. Not only so; but we are thus once for all secured against the temptation to explain the Pauline Christology either as the product of mere theological reflection or as a mosaic of fragments borrowed from the traditions of Jewish apocalyptic. In point of fact, it is the offspring of creative religious intuition, working upon the felt realities of experience. "This inner fusion with the conception of the Spirit," as Olschewski puts it, "constitutes the specific and distinctive essence of Paul's Christology, and just on this account we must hold that its roots lie in the fundamental experience of Damascus."[1]

At the same time, the relation of Christ and the Spirit is not that of identity, but of vital unity. The opposite view has been taken strongly. "He could not distinguish the Son from the Holy Ghost," Weinel says;[2] a statement the force of which is naturally lessened by its retractation on the next page. The wording of 2 Co 3[17] may seem to decide the question; "the Lord," the apostle avers plainly, "is the Spirit." Yet the following clause faintly reaffirms the distinction in the words, "Where the Spirit *of* the Lord is, there is liberty." No one can imagine that "Christ" and "the Spirit of Christ" mean the same thing precisely. Not to speak of the fact that St. Paul does not regard Jesus as the incarnate Spirit of God, but affiliates his ideas on this subject to other lines of ancient thought, various minor data are significant. The person who died upon the cross, and rose again, and will come at last to judgment, is nowhere named "Spirit." Christ, moreover, *gives* the Spirit in its fulness. And in the triple blessing of 2 Co 13[14], the Spirit is co-ordinated with Christ and God as a separately discernible element in the one redeeming agency. It is important to recollect that the theological ideas of Christianity came first, and

[1] *Op. cit.* 161.
[2] *St. Paul*, 326; cf. Schmiedel, *Hand-Kommentar*, ii. 192.

that only afterwards were they fitted with more or less exact verbal distinctions, so that usage might for a considerable time show a certain fluidity or free play of expression. By the form of identification St. Paul indicates just the familiar experiential fact that Christ, by whom God saves men, and the Holy Spirit, in whom He conveys to them Divine life, are so indissociably one in significance and operation and media that from the point of view of practical faith they are seen as true equivalents of each other. Yet within the unity there is distinction. As it has been put, "Christ in you, or the Spirit of Christ in you; these are not different realities; but the one is the method of the other."[1]

We have already encountered the principle that on St. Paul's view the Lordship of Christ first came to full reality at His exaltation to the right hand of God. There is a sense in which His glory is superior even to His pre-existent life. He is now possessed of the Name above every name. It is represented as somehow a reward of His voluntary sacrifice: "He humbled Himself . . . wherefore God also highly exalted Him" (Ph 2^9). The classic passage for this side of the Pauline teaching is Ro 1^4, which declares that He was constituted or declared Son of God with power, in virtue of the Spirit of holiness, by rising from the dead. The Divine energy which effected the resurrection set Christ free from the confining limits of life in the flesh, and gave untrammelled and complete expression to His proper Sonship. With this we may compare Ro 14^9, a verse which points to the authority of Christ as now covering all men, in this life and the next. Similarly, it is always the *risen* Lord who bestows the Spirit. In these statements it appears to be implied, first, that Christ has ascended to be Lord of all things, taking this place subsequently to and as a result of the resurrection; and in the second place, that originally His personal nature was such as to qualify Him for this transcendent place. Presently He will come to judge

[1] Moberly, *Atonement and Personality*, 194.

the world in God's name. But in strictness no sharp line of distinction is drawn between God and Christ as regards this judicial act or function. The two names occur jointly, or as alternatives.[1] God, or Christ, or God through Christ, will judge men and work the last great change on believers. But we must not play off the future against the present, as if even for St. Paul the believer "never is, but always to be, blest." He shares to the full the ardent primitive hope of Jesus' return, as inaugurating the final consummation; none the less on his view salvation is already real through the present activity of the Lord who became incarnate, died, and rose again. The crucifixion had been the ruin of the hostile cosmic powers; having disarmed and exposed them, Christ triumphed over them in the cross (Col 2^{15}). The Kingdom of God, which is righteousness, and peace, and joy in the Holy Spirit (Ro 14^{17}), is actual even now. Christ died once, but the redemptorial virtue of His death is in Him for ever.

The relation of the exalted Christ to men as Life-giver leads the apostle, in one place, to designate Him by the title of "the last Adam" (1 Co 15^{45}). Adam was head, representative, and type of the race derived from him; through transgression this race became carnal and subject to death: so in like manner, Christ as risen is Head of a new redeemed race made one with God by His death and raised above the power of the flesh by contact with the Spirit. Adam was earthly, Jesus heavenly; Adam a transgressor, Jesus obedient; Adam only a living soul, Jesus a quickening spirit, "a Being above nature, who had life and was capable of giving it."[2] The new spiritual principle that came with Him is made incorporate with all who trust Him, thus vivifying their whole being in its relation to God, self, and all things else. The Spirit of holiness being the inmost reality of Christ, He becomes the organic head of a new spiritual creation; and as grace and life are more potent than sin and death, His reign

[1] Cf. Sanday and Headlam, *Romans*, 389.
[2] Fairbairn, *Christ in Modern Theology*, 311.

will far exceed in scope and triumph the doom entailed by ancient transgression.[1]

So deeply absorbed is St. Paul in the risen Lord that it has not infrequently been held that he was indifferent to the historic Jesus, his gospel only beginning when Jesus' career on earth had ended. This, however, is gravely misleading. To his mind the distinction of earth and heaven, so wide for modern thought, was relatively small. While he had no personal knowledge of Jesus like that enjoyed by the Twelve, it may be taken as an assured fact that he was acquainted with the evangelical tradition, and indeed knew about Jesus what the ordinary Christian knew. In Arabia, after his conversion, he need not have lived wholly apart from Christians. Besides, he had spent a fortnight with St. Peter in Jerusalem, and it will be admitted that much may be told in a fortnight if Jesus is the subject-matter, and the learner an apostle. There is nothing inconsistent with this in the striking language of Gal 1^{11}: "The gospel preached by me is not according to man; for neither did I receive it from man, nor was I taught it, except by revelation from Jesus Christ"; which is but a forcible declaration that the Messiahship of Jesus was once for all disclosed to him by no human intermediary, but by a vision of the Lord Himself. Jülicher, with a pleasing vigour, has observed that "an apostle of Jesus Christ who had no desire to know about the Messiah's earthly life, and for dogmatic reasons passed by with scorn, as mere carnal weakness, everything revealed by God's Son in the form of a servant, is not the Paul of history, but a monstrosity of modern logic."[2] As Drescher shows, it is possible to draw a fairly complete sketch of Jesus, and especially of His character and disposition, from the

[1] From all this we may gather what St. Paul would have said regarding the modern attempt to put him alongside of Jesus as part founder of Christianity. "Paul is not the second after Jesus," Deissmann remarks finely, "but the first in Christ."

[2] *Jesus und Paulus*, 55.

Pauline materials.[1] At the same time, the interest which guides his pen is not purely or even mainly historical. There is no reference to Jesus' miracles, His faith, His prayerfulness, His habits as a man amongst men. Certain words of Jesus are cited as authoritative, chiefly on minor points. His birth, His sinlessness, His institution of the Supper, His death on the cross and rising on the third day—these things are reported with a few lesser details. The reason for this comparative reticence must lie in the apostle's mind being engrossed chiefly with the great decisive fact of redemption as an experience. But it is clear that unless certain facts concerning Jesus were known to him, through historical tradition, the confession "Jesus is Lord" would have meant nothing. Hence it is an axiom for St. Paul that Jesus lived and was true man. He was made of a woman, born of the seed of David according to the flesh. He is the last Adam, founding a new humanity. There might appear to be a docetic undertone in the statement (Ro 8[3]) that God sent His Son "in the likeness of sinful flesh"; but the meaning is simply that while Christ's flesh is as real as ours, and as human, it was not like ours sinful. The flesh of man, with this one exception, was the pattern of His flesh, but in Him alone it may be seen in a perfected relation to the Spirit. But Jesus' sinlessness—St. Paul knew of it, as of His unique self-consciousness, from the impression made on the disciples and conveyed by them to the new convert—was not the mere absence of moral fault. The fulfilment of the law is love, and the figure of the Nazarene who bore the cross for sinners must have shone upon him with the radiance of ineffable and self-abnegating grace. A complete moral identity links the present Lordship to the past humiliation.

Yet the life lived by Jesus on earth, as St. Paul discerned, was a form of being wholly inadequate to His

[1] *Das Leben Jesu bei Paulus.* For some admirable pages on the harmony of detail in St. Paul's picture of Jesus and that of the primitive society, cf. Feine, *Theologie d. NT*, 200 ff.

true nature. It confined Him within limits; it prevented the full manifestation of all that which He really was. For His origin lay in a higher world, that of eternal being, from which by a voluntary act He came amongst men, taking the form of a servant. To the original disciples the astounding paradox had been, that the Jesus whose companions they had been, and who had died in shame, was now raised to the right hand of God; to St. Paul the paradox was rather that the Exalted One, proved by resurrection to be the Son of God and of heavenly nature, should have taken flesh and died at Calvary. They saw the resurrection against the lowly ministry with its still more lowly end; he viewed the earthly life in bold relief against the glory of ascension and pre-existence. The mere fact that Christ should have accepted human life, to surrender it in death for our sake, thrills him with a wondering gratitude.

The unique personal constitution of Jesus, during His earthly lifetime, consisted of a body of flesh and blood, and, in addition, of that which the apostle denominates "Spirit." The two elements are mentioned side by side in Ro 1[3.4]; on which Dr. Denney has observed that "the expression *κατὰ πνεῦμα ἁγιωσύνης* characterises Christ ethically, as *κατὰ σάρκα* does physically. Not that it makes the sonship in question 'ethical' as opposed to 'metaphysical': no such distinctions were in the apostle's thought. But the sonship, which was declared by the resurrection, answered to the spirit of holiness which was the inmost and deepest reality in the Person and life of Jesus."[1] It was a "Spirit" which sealed Him with a specific character; not merely energising as Divine power in His life, but supplying the efficient ground of His victory over death. To it St. Paul's mind recurred, most probably, when his mind dwelt on the theme of Christ's pre-historic life; "Spirit" was the element or medium, so to speak, of that life, in virtue of which there was continuity between the different phases of His career.

[1] *EGT*. ii. *in loc.*

In eternity, on earth, and now in the present and unending glory, His unity with God was a unity in or through "Spirit."

In the first paragraph of Romans, as in the great verses we have just examined, Jesus Christ is designated the "Son of God," a title never used by St. Paul save with a certain grave solemnity.[1] It is no longer a Messianic name of honour merely; it has been assigned the loftier function of expressing the original and inherent unity of life by which Christ is conjoined with God. According to the usage of the Old Testament, he was specifically God's Son on whom God's love was set, but in St. Paul this is a mode of thought transcended, even if not cancelled. If we take verses like Ro 8^{32}: "He that spared not His own Son," or Col 1^{13}: "the Son of His love," we can only agree with Weiss that "it would be a mistake to interpret these passages as though 'sonship' were merely another way of expressing love; because God so loved this being, therefore he was the Son of God. The reverse is true: Because he is the Son, therefore God loves him."[2] Son of God by eternal nature—it is in this character that He comes into the world. Already in that unbeginning life He had been the image of the invisible God (Col 1^{15}). We are not entitled to make the apostle responsible for an explicit doctrine of "eternal generation"; but unquestionably he does mean that the relation of Christ to God is increate and essential. It has been inferred from Ro 1^4, where the Sonship of Christ is put in connection with His rising from the dead, that the Pauline Christ is Son only after the resurrection. But the words really mean that only then was His Sonship fully and actually manifested; He is *known* as Son from that point onwards, but by inference the mind passes beyond and behind that fact to the Sonship which is superior to time.

[1] "With scarcely an exception it is only used in such portions of the letters as are marked by an especial elevation of style" (Weinel, *St. Paul*, 324). Examples are Ro 8^{32}, 1 Co 1^9, Gal 2^{20}.

[2] J. Weiss, *Christ: the Beginnings of Dogma*, 66.

It is observable that St. Paul touches on our Lord's pre-existence, always or nearly always, in a quite incidental manner. This does not prove that the idea was no part of his "gospel"—a point on which so far we have no evidence—but it proves, at all events, that pre-existence was an idea so familiar to Christians as to require no explanation or apology. Nowhere is his tone that of the sponsor for a doctrinal novelty.

As to particular texts, undue weight must not be placed on Gal 4[4], "God sent forth His Son," although the phrase is significant enough (cf. Ro 8[3]). Somewhat more explicit is 1 Co 10[4], where it is asserted that the Rock which followed the Israelites in the desert, and of which they drank, was Christ; He is conceived, that is, as having played a real part in Old Testament history. And there is general agreement that 2 Co 8[9] bears not upon the "poverty" of Jesus' lifetime on earth, but on His sacrifice in being born; for the "poverty" and "riches" in question must obviously be correlative, and since He neither was Himself rich in the literal sense, nor made others so, it is impossible to take literally the poverty here ascribed to Him. The verse is one which in import transcends the phenomena of time and space, announcing not merely that Christ's earthly life was inferior in glory to His prior condition, but—a yet more sublime thought—that He entered upon the lower state by His own volition. Finally there is Ph 2[5-7], a passage "marked by epic fulness and dignity," the amplest and most deliberate of all St. Paul's declarations on the theme. Lightfoot has thus paraphrased vv.[6] and [7]: "Though existing before the worlds in the Eternal Godhead, yet He did not cling with avidity to the prerogatives of His Divine majesty, did not ambitiously display His equality with God; but divested Himself of the glories of heaven, and took upon Him the nature of a servant, assuming the likeness of men."[1] Christ, that is, came into our world from a previous state of Divine existence; in that estate He

[1] *Philippians*, 110.

possessed self-conscious independent life, with a will that ruled itself; a will that might have been exerted in other modes, but actually was exerted in this mode of self-abnegation. It is asserted—and on the assertion hinges the thrilling moral appeal of the passage—that before He came as man Christ's life was Divine in quality; not merely *like* God, but participant in His essential attributes (μορφή). The crucial fact is that the apostle, even though refraining from speculation as to the relationship to God of the Eternal Son, does not scruple to describe Him as subsisting in, and then giving up, "a being so in the form of God that to be equal with Him is a thing of nature." He took a life of manhood through the abdication of infinite glory. And the *motif* of the passage—metaphysical only so far as it is ethical—lies in the subduing thought that when it was open to Christ so to employ the powers of His inherently Divine dignity as to insist on being worshipped as God, He chose to reach this supreme position, of Lordship acknowledged universally, by the path of lowliness, obedience, and death. Thus His descent reveals the vastness of His love, and justifies His later exaltation.

This exaltation is undoubtedly conceived as in a real sense the reward of the great sacrifice that went before; on the other hand, to talk of "deification" is out of all keeping with the apostle's mind. To a Jew the notion that a man might become God would have been flat blasphemy. Ascension only served to bring out in full actuality what was originally implicit; it but unfolded the essential glory and dignity of Christ's person. Pre-existence and Lordship, therefore, are in strictness relative to each other.[1]

It is of course possible to discount the impression made by such declarations. The first believers, it may be said, vied with one another in finding or inventing names

[1] Cf. H. A. A. Kennedy, *EGT*. iii. *in loc.* Too much importance should not be ascribed to Deissmann's interesting suggestions as to the influence on St. Paul of language associated with the worship of the Emperor.

by which to enhance Jesus' glory. But whether they spoke of His birth of a virgin or His eternal Sonship, it was only a hyperbolical attempt to utter His spiritual greatness. The idea of His pre-existence, Jülicher has surmised, may have been helped into currency by the widespread contemporary belief in the transmigration of souls. "If I have been man already, innumerable times, why should Jesus not have lived in heaven for centuries as the Son of God?"[1] In other quarters it has been maintained that for St. Paul's mind, as for the mind of his fellow-Christians, the thought of Christ's pre-existence was no more than a subordinate and ancillary symbol. It is obvious that whatever names St. Paul might use would have had their own previous history, but we must not beg the question whether he could or could not fill them with a new significance. Further, it is vain to urge that the conception of pre-existence is either peculiar to St. Paul or of merely peripheral importance for his view of Christ. It is present conspicuously in Hebrews and in the Johannine writings; there is some reason to believe, indeed, that it derives ultimately from Jesus. In the presence of these facts, it is gratuitous to plead that the writers of the New Testament attached to it only minor religious value, and would have waived it readily to satisfy an objector.

The origin of St. Paul's thought of pre-existence has been sought especially in the alleged Jewish-Hellenic idea of a pre-existent "heavenly Man," the archetype and pattern of created manhood. Following the Alexandrian theory, as various scholars have maintained since Baur, he taught that Christ pre-existed in heaven as a human personality, inclusive of a body. The evidence for this startling hypothesis is of the slenderest. In Ro 5 the parallel between Adam and Christ is more an illustration than anything else; it is St. Paul's way of saying that Christianity is the absolute religion. And in 1 Co 15$^{44-49}$—the *locus classicus*—all likelihood of

[1] *Paulus und Jesus*, 32.

Alexandrian influence, except possibly by way of implied polemic, is negatived by two main considerations: that the "heavenly Man" whom Philo names "the First Man" is emphatically named "the Second Man" by St. Paul, and that the passage is throughout concerned not in the least with the pre-existent but with the exalted Christ. It was only in virtue of resurrection that He became the archetype and head of a new race. It would be arbitrary to deny that the apostle's mind may have owed something to such floating conceptions of transcendence as the Philonic, but it is still more unfounded to describe it as in any intelligible sense the germ or organic core of his Christology, since in point of fact it is mentioned merely in one chapter of one epistle. A minor but equally decisive circumstance is its incompatibility, in its Alexandrian form at all events, with other Pauline statements as to the pre-existent One. A being who was from eternity in the form of God could not also be said to have eternally worn a human body. The notion, however, that St. Paul's view of Christ started from the idea of the "heavenly Man" will always fascinate those who are resolved to interpret his "gospel" in exclusively humanitarian terms.

The pre-existent Christ is further conceived as having mediated by personal Divine agency in the creation of the world (1 Co 8^{6}, Col $1^{15ff.}$). If there be a reference to Gnosticism in the latter passage, as is probably the case, it is by way of recoil, not of imitation. I quote again Lightfoot's paraphrase: "He is the perfect image, the visible representation of the unseen God. He is the Firstborn, the absolute Heir of the Father, begotten before the ages; the Lord of the Universe by virtue of primogeniture, and by virtue also of creative agency. For in Him and through Him the whole world was created, things in heaven and things in earth, things visible to the outward eye, and things cognizable by the outward perception. His supremacy is absolute and universal. All powers in heaven and earth are subject to Him. This subjection extends even to the most exalted and most potent of angelic beings, whether they be called Thrones or Dominations or Princedoms or Powers, or whatever title of dignity men may confer upon them. Yes, He is first and He is last. Through Him, as the mediatorial word, the universe has been created; and unto Him, as the final goal, it is tending. In Him is no before or after. He is pre-existent and self-existent before all the worlds. And in Him as the binding and sustaining power, universal nature coheres and consists."[1] In this picture of Christ, stimulated it may be in part by the Philonic conception of the Logos, the apostle moves onward from historical to cosmic modes of interpretation. We may single out the three main statements: first, Christ is the organ of creation, absolute in function and eternal in existence; secondly, in Him all things are held together, cohering in that unity and solidarity which make a cosmos; thirdly, as all things took rise in Him, so they move on to Him as final goal. The aorist tense is used to affirm that Christ created all things, for the writer is thinking of the pre-existent One; but the fact that he lapses into perfects and presents is a suggestive hint that he contemplates this pre-existence through the medium, so to speak, of the exalted Life. Or to put it otherwise, Christ is conceived as creator of the world *qua* the Person in whom the universe was in due time to find its organic centre in virtue of His work of reconciliation; He was the initial cause of all things, as being destined to be their final end. His function as Creator is proleptically conditioned by His achievement as Saviour. The apostle's mind, here as everywhere, starts from the risen Lord, and, as Professor Peake observes, "the work of the Son in His pre-existent state is referred to, that the true position of the exalted Christ may be understood."[2] It is interesting to compare an earlier form of the same idea. This is in 1 Co 8^6: "To us there is one God, the Father, of whom are all things, and we unto Him; and one Lord, Jesus Christ, through whom are all things, and we through

[1] *Colossians*, 144. [2] *EGT*. iii. *in loc.*

Him." Christ is the agent in creation, yet He is here designated not as Son, but by the title usually applied to the risen Saviour. As in Colossians, the ideas of creation and redemption are united—redemption being the present fact from which thought begins, and in the light of which alone creation can be interpreted. The Son before all time is visible through Christ's historic work in grace. On the other hand, what is last in knowledge may be first in reality. In the Colossian passage, therefore, we can discern also this inferential counter-movement of thought; redemption is a fruit of, and has its basis in, Christ's place and work in nature. The same oscillation of mind between the poles of eternity and time may be seen in the Prologue to the Fourth Gospel and in the opening paragraph of Hebrews.

In view of this exalted estimate of Christ, it is at first disconcerting to read plain statements in the same author which affirm His distinct subordination to God the Father. A candid exegesis will acknowledge, I think, that now and then the matter is too clear for dispute: Christ is given a place inferior to God, and His work as Mediator and Reconciler is eventually traced to the Father as originative cause. As examples we may take "God sent forth His Son" (Gal 4^{4}), "He that spared not His own Son" (Ro 8^{32}), "God hath highly exalted Him" (Ph 2^{9}), "It pleased the Father that in Him should all fulness dwell" (Col 1^{19}); and it should be noted that these phrases are selected indifferently from the earlier and later writings. The gift of Christ to men, His sacrifice in death, the saving content of His life, and the bestowal on Him of the glory of exaltation are in turn asserted to be due to God. The whole career of Christ, in short, with its vast issues, is regarded as having redounded supremely to the glory of God the Father (Ph 2^{11}). To this we scarcely need to add the explicit statement of 1 Co 11^{3}: "The head of the woman is the man, and the head of Christ is God," with which the great climax of 3^{23} may be compared: "All things are yours . . . and ye are Christ's, and Christ is God's." Even more striking, perhaps, is a third verse in the same epistle, where St. Paul anticipates the final surrender of the kingdom by the Son: "Then shall the Son also Himself be subjected to Him that did subject all things unto Him, that God may be all in all" (15^{28}). As Loofs has shown, it is a verse the mystery of which laid a spell on many of the Greek and Latin Fathers.[1] It appears to contemplate a point of time when Christ, having put all enemies under His feet, will abdicate and submit even Himself to the Most High. There is no parallel to this anywhere in the New Testament.[2] It may possibly be a relic of Jewish belief as to the destiny of the Messiah; and at a later stage, as in Col 1^{16}, the apostle seems to have put it on one side.[3] But at all events it is proof of the subordinationist aspect of his view of Christ.

Whatever inference we build on these expressions, they are at least no evidence that St. Paul was an early Arian. To say that "Christ is not God, but the Son of God," or that "The Son was called into life and endowed with power by God for the creation and redemption of mankind," is to signalise but one side of the Pauline Christology, and not the most remarkable. We are justified in saying that his view was not simply incoherent. But it is certain that he held the deity of Christ. If he nowhere puts it with dogmatic precision, at least the doxology in Ro 9^{5} is significant; also his habitual use of "Lord" as the proper title of the exalted Christ, and his frequent bracketing of Christ with God as the fount of all grace and peace. The mere fact that he could write Col 2^{9}: "In Him dwelleth all the fulness of the Godhead bodily," is really decisive; for the words mean

[1] Cf. article "Christologie," *RE.* iv.

[2] Weizsäcker long ago suggested Jn 16^{23}—"in that day ye shall ask Me nothing"—but a precise exegesis scarcely bears him out (see *Jahrb. f. deutsche Theologie*, 1857, 183–84).

[3] Cf. Titius, *Die neutest. Lehre von der Seligkeit*, 2 Abtheil. 35.

that in Christ there is to be found, as a unity or in organic relation, the entire sum of qualities and attributes by which the being of God is constituted. The subordination of Christ, therefore, was on his view compatible with His having a place within the sphere of Godhead. It was a subjection by which the unity of God was exhibited, not destroyed.

In the solution of this antinomy, St. Paul affords less aid than we might expect. In common with the primitive apostolic society, he looks to Christ equally with God for all things in the present or the future, representing now the one, now the other, as Judge, Saviour, and Lord without any sense of facing a painful problem, much less a contradiction. Questions on which a later age fastened had not arisen in his mind. One simple mode of relieving the strain has indeed been recommended. It is to identify the Pauline dualism in Christology with the twofold interpretation of Christ which has been felt to pervade the New Testament as a whole. The first or historical view moves always within the human fact of Jesus' life on earth, finding in His unique manhood the perfect vehicle of Divine grace. The other or transcendent view fixes upon the higher nature manifest in all Christ's life and work, and from this recurs to His pre-incarnate life in God and as God. Are not subordinationist phrases more easily intelligible (it is said) if we relate them simply to the former, or historical, interpretation? This would virtually be the theory of Calvin, who comments on 1 Co 3^{23}: *Hæc subjectio ad Christi humanitatem refertur.* Jesus Christ, as a historic person, who was entrusted with a vocation in and for mankind, and submitted Himself to God in the discharge of it—how else than in subordinationist terms *could* St. Paul speak of His relation to the Father? I do not wish to deny the force of this, which would indeed be quite convincing but for certain statements that unquestionably plant the subordination predicated of Christ within the eternal and transcendent sphere. The pre-incarnate One and the Risen Lord equally are pictured as subject to the rule of God the Father (Gal 4[4], Col 1[19]). The Son is personally one with God, yet also subordinate in the sense indissociably bound up with the very thought of sonship. And St. Paul, so far as can be seen, would not have consented to reduce either of these two forms of truth to the other—Christ and God are of one Divine nature, yet within this unity there obtain relations of higher and lower.

It will be seen that St. Paul's view of Christ represents a noteworthy advance on the primitive apostolic conception as indicated by the Petrine speeches in Acts. He was the first to speak of Christ as agent in creation, and to draw together closely the Spirit and Christ's inmost being. He led the way also in teaching a mysticism which has its pivot or point of departure in the Christian's union with Christ. In this sense his Christology is independent and unique. This originality has been turned into a grave charge against the credibility of his conclusions by those who argue that we cannot really expect a true estimate of the person and work of Christ from one who had not been an immediate disciple. Whether he did or did not spin Christology freely out of his own mind, at least we are unable to control the statements for which he makes himself responsible.

It is a striking fact, however, that his estimate of Christ never became, so far as we know, the subject of controversy in the primitive Church.[1] Men who dissented violently from his interpretation of the Law found no difficulty in his conception of the Saviour. His was one true way, they felt, of stating the impression made on him and them alike by the crucified and exalted Lord. He nowhere betrays a feeling that the idiosyncrasies of his thought are leading him on to dangerous ground where he must move with a tender regard for others. He can count on sympathy and comprehension. The categories he

[1] Not that controversy would discredit his interpretation; but in point of fact there was none.

employed were such as to gain the confidence and approval of Christian men.

Nevertheless, it may be argued that the aptness of the Pauline Christology to the first century is precisely the reason why it is impossible for us. Owing to the providential advance of human thought we have irrecoverably lost his point of view. The fact that primitive believers welcomed his estimate of Jesus is, moreover, no evidence of its real truth. Naturally all views of Christ that enhanced His glory or gave worthy expression to His redeeming influence were pleasing to their minds; but they would certainly have greeted a different set of thought-forms with equal fervour, provided they rose to the same level of imaginative and ideal power.

This is true no doubt in the sense that some important elements in the Christology of St. Paul are even yet of partially dubious interpretation; it is a vain question whether we accept them, for we cannot tell what they mean. Who will claim to know for certain the whole import for the apostle's mind of such phrases as "the form of God" and "the form of a servant" (Ph $2^{5ff.}$), as they are predicated successively of the pre-existent and the incarnate Christ? Nor can we deny that several pre-Christian influences—Jewish theology, Philo, Stoicism—may have left their mark on his language. Yet it is an unseeing criticism which finds in these anything more than the outward setting of the picture.[1] If the gospel

[1] Cf. a valuable page in Reischle, *Theologie und Religionsgeschichte*, 40. Harnack's recent statement is also worth quoting: "It is utterly improbable that St. Paul arrived at the central conception of a Son of God, who died and rose again, through the myths of Western Asia; the premises of his reasoning and the historical premises which lay in the death on the cross and the belief in the resurrection of Jesus must of themselves have led him up to it. But it is quite possible that the idea underlying those myths had won some influence over him, without his being aware of it, not only upon the cosmological development of the idea, but also upon the determination and power with which the apostle advanced it" (*Fifth International Congress of Free Christianity*, 1910, p. 104).

Similarly, how much had been done by the progress of Hellenistic religious thought to prepare the term σωτήρ for Christian usage we may learn from the

was for the men of that age, it must be conveyed in the vernacular of their minds, by those to whom contemporary ideas formed a natural and vital atmosphere. On the other hand, it is in no way fatal to the validity of an idea—that of pre-existence, for example—that it should have had a previous history in Jewish thought. The revelation of God in Christ, if interpreted at all, must of course be interpreted by ideas already present in the world; ideas, we may believe, not altogether unmoulded by a higher wisdom for the service they were to render. If in addition we contemplate the Pauline Christology as a whole, we perceive that in every age it has gained the free recognition and assent of the Christian mind. The thought, for example, that Christ by essential nature is such that He gathers men into union with Himself, opening the gates of His spiritual being to receive us as only God can; that in eternal love He bowed down to earth to bear man's sin; that the destinies of His Church and of the world are in His hands for ever—can we dismiss these things as the outworn formulas of a remote past, in which there remains no substance or value any more? On the contrary, they rise spontaneously in the intelligence of those who to-day are impressed by Jesus as they were who first believed in Him. But more, the Christology of St. Paul is possessed of that sublime and inexhaustible quality which is native to enduring truth. His loftiest descriptions of the Lord Jesus, far from having faded into obsolescence, still evoke our reflection, as they elude it, by their very greatness.

researches of men like Paul Wendland (cf. his article in the *Zeitschrift für neutest. Wissenschaft*, 1904, 335 ff.). Christians, we can see, employed that term to express the glorious fact that in Jesus they had found everything which can be called salvation—from sin, from death, from judgment, from the tyranny of demons. In the case of New Testament writers, however, it is scarcely questionable that the old form has been filled with a new spirit. Indeed, it may be argued that they "consciously and deliberately opposed the Σωτήρ who had appeared to them, and His influence, to the earthly σωτῆρες and their false titles of honour." This certainly holds true of the Apocalypse (see Moffatt's Commentary in the *Expositor's Greek Testament*, v. 307–17). Cf. Harnack, *Reden und Aufsätze*, i. 299 ff.

They are still beyond us as of old; we can but throw out our minds at an infinite reality; and to the last the believing consciousness will vainly strive to know the depth and height beheld by the apostle in Christ Jesus as he wrote: "In Him were all things created, in the heavens and the earth, things visible and things invisible . . . for in Him dwelleth all the fulness of the Godhead bodily."

CHAPTER IV.

THE CHRISTOLOGY OF THE EPISTLE TO THE HEBREWS.

IN point of time, the Epistle to the Hebrews is the first systematic sketch of Christian theology. A very complete picture of Christ is drawn, line after line being added to fill out the majestic introductory representation (1^{1-4}). His person is contemplated throughout as the source or presupposition of the work accomplished by Him as the High Priest of men. Jesus, we read, is "the Mediator of a new covenant" (12^{24}, cf. 9^{15} and 8^{6}); this is His essential function; and the pre-eminence of the new covenant over the old, as well as its lasting glory, is due to the incomparable dignity of the one eternal Priest. Christ is like Aaron in certain ways: His commission is from God, not self-assumed, and for all His unique superiority He keeps touch with the needs and frailties of the people, one with them in suffering and temptation. But still more He is unlike Aaron: He abides a priest continually (7^{23}); being holy, guileless, undefiled, and separate from sinners, He needs not to offer sacrifice for His own sin, as in the old order (7^{25}). Formerly men were made priests without an oath, whereas in constituting Jesus the Son a priest for ever "the Lord sware, and will not repent"

LITERATURE — Riehm, *Der Lehrbegriff des Hebräerbriefs*[2], 1867; Ménégoz, *La théologie de l'epître aux Hebreux*, 1894; Davidson, *Hebrews*, 1882; Bruce, *The Epistle to the Hebrews*, 1899; Milligan, *The Theology of the Epistle to the Hebrews*, 1899; Bousset, *Die Religion des Judenthums*[2], 1906; Fairbairn, *Christ in Modern Theology*, 1893; Drummond, *Philo Judæus*, 1888.

(7^{21}). With His life and death a new dispensation has opened:

> "In Him the shadows of the Law
> Are all fulfilled, and now withdraw."

His sole earlier type is Melchisedec, that ancient and mystic figure in whom king and priest are one, "the direct creation of God, without any of the accidents of time," independent alike of descent and posterity. Already we can see that Christology is the doctrinal centre of the Epistle.

The writer makes no profession of having been an eye-witness, yet his picture of Jesus is singularly vivid and arresting. He must, one feels, have had access to good original tradition. Nowhere in the New Testament is the humanity of Christ set forth so movingly; for "not even all the Gospels show us Jesus in the weakness of His flesh side by side with the purity of His spirit, as He is exhibited here."[1] We see Him proclaiming salvation (2^{3}), agonising in prayer (5^{7}), embracing the Cross with joy and faith (12^{2}), suffering the last penalty without the city gate (13^{12}). The name "Jesus" occurs by itself at least ten times. Sprung from the tribe of Judah, He passed through the normal development of human life, learning obedience, even though a Son, by the things which He suffered (5^{8}). Into His course there entered sinless frailty and dread temptation; no aspect of His life or character escaped the assault of evil. And thereby He was schooled in sympathy. Yet no corrupt strain existed in His nature to which temptation could appeal. His sinlessness is definitely affirmed, more particularly as a supreme qualification for His work as Saviour and Intercessor. A frank emphasis, without parallel in the New Testament, is laid on His human virtues. These constitute the ethical life of the Son of God. There are allusions to His fidelity (3^{2}), His trust in God (2^{13}), His piety (5^{7}), His patience under reproach (12^{3}). The strong crying and tears with which He is said to have prayed "to Him

[1] Bruce, *Epistle to the Hebrews*, 443.

that was able to save Him from death" are as unlike as possible to the ontological impassivity that has been ascribed to the Christ of Hebrews. When He is said to have been "made perfect" (5^{9}), it is not meant that He overcame fault or defect, but that He realised to the full what He had it in Him to be. He became perfect through experience, as the bud is perfected in the flower. Potencies of absolute goodness were evoked by a moral discipline which made Him the High Priest of mankind. Such unity with the will of God, however, finally expressed in death, is not something which He gradually acquired; in principle it is something which He brought with Him when He came (10^{5-7}).

Along with this realistic portrait of Jesus goes a Christology at least as lofty as that of Paul. Hebrews, like the rest of the New Testament, begins from the exalted Lord; "We have such a high priest," the writer sums up at one point, "who sat down on the right hand of the Majesty in the heavens" (8^{1}). It is the distinctive work of Christ to be Priest within the veil, "a minister of the sanctuary, and of the true tabernacle" (8^{2}). From the stress put upon exaltation we gather that Messianic ideas still come naturally to the writer's mind, but they are receding from the foreground, and other than Messianic terms are about to replace them for purposes of interpretation. Assuming, then, the present glory of Jesus, the writer's argument as to His personal dignity is regressive. He goes back to the original nature which renders possible the present majesty. From the first Christ was capable of what He now is.

In the exordium of the first chapter, accordingly, Christ is set forth as "Son," a name which defines His nature as in essential relation to the Father. In the character of Son, He is "the effulgence of God's glory and the very impress of His substance" (1^{3}). If "effulgence" or reflected brightness hints at essential unity between light at the centre and light diffused, "impress" or image or facsimile points to a distinctness in which one side of the duality is a perfect, yet dependent, reproduction of the other.[1] The language is no doubt that of the schools; but the writer is master of his terms, not their slave, and can mould them to the spirit of his exposition. "Son" is itself a metaphor, and there appears to be no good reason why an apostolic writer should not elucidate its meaning by other metaphorical expressions current in his own day. The Divine place of the Son is signalised by the fact that in 1^3 He is said to uphold all things by the word of His power, and in 1^8 is actually addressed as "God." Possibly in view of Jewish beliefs as to the mediation of angels, the writer is at special pains to emphasise their inferiority to the Son. They are bidden to adore Him; no angel has ever been named Son, as He is, or placed on God's right hand. He is also above Moses and the prophets.

In spite of this transcendence, Jesus on earth was made a little lower than the angels (2^9). It was a temporary but real humiliation, for the life to which He stooped in His redemptive purpose formed but an imperfect medium of His higher being. He assumed flesh, not only that He might be apprehensible, but in order to suffer by tasting death for every man; and there is more than one pathetic reference to the ignominy of the Cross. Nowhere is the writer's religious feeling more penetrating than when he insists (2^{14-16}) that at His coming into the world the Son did not stop half-way, but chose a veritable share in our lot. "Since then the children are partakers in flesh and blood, He also Himself in like manner took part of the same . . . for verily not of angels doth He take hold, but He taketh hold of the seed of Abraham." We are led to think of a descent on His part, even if nothing is said, here or elsewhere, regarding the effect on His previous form of existence produced by this sublime act. Thus He *became* High Priest (5^5), and His complete and perfect priesthood is the outcome of His having been made like men in all things, in suffering, in self-oblation

[1] Cf. Fairbairn, *Christ in Modern Theology*, 324.

(7^{27})—all leading up to and culminating in that death and victory by which He overcame the devil and accomplished an eternal salvation (9^{12}). God set the seal upon His work by crowning Him with glory and honour (2^{9}).

It has been held that in Hebrews the term "Son" takes on a certain speculative colour, and that the obviously ethical significance of the name as used by other New Testament writers tends to give place to a sense more explicitly metaphysical. Some justice there may be in this; yet the distinction of ethical and metaphysical is not one which we can press, at least to the extent of construing the two ideas as disparate alternatives. It is begging the question to say that because "Son," as applied to Jesus, denotes primarily a relation of special intimacy and fellowship, the psychological coefficients of which we can in some degree conceive, it cannot also mean a relation which is essential and transcendent. If, as all will concede, the name "Father" is not incapable of a sense equally ethical and metaphysical, may the same not be true of "Son"? There is a theological positivism which would deny even to apostolic men an interest in Christ such that it longs to know Him in His own nature.

It is a less simple question whether in Hebrews the name "Son" is given to the pre-existent One or exclusively to the historic Jesus. Our decision will rest on materials supplied by the first chapter. The writer's mind clearly starts from the Sonship revealed by exaltation following upon the career of earth; this is steadily before his mind at every point. But are there indications that he thought also of the pre-incarnate life as a life of Sonship? "The name," says Professor A. B. Davidson, "is not directly given to Him in His pre-existing state, but the inference that it was applicable is inevitable. It was the same Son in whom God spake to us, through whom He made the worlds (1^{2}); and there is no hint that the name Son became the possession of a Being already existing on His entering into the flesh."[1] And

[1] *Hebrews*, 74.

from a somewhat different point of view, Professor Bruce pleads that the writer's interest in magnifying the sacrifice of Christ required the Sonship to be of older date than the life on earth.[1] We may note for ourselves, in addition, that origination from God and precise likeness to God—both constituents of Sonship—are in 1³ plainly said to have characterised the pre-historic One. In favour of this view, though it has great names against it, is the fact, noted by Riehm, that the Subject of the three stadia of action—creation before all time, atonement on earth, and the heavenly ministry—is set forth as personally identical throughout. The same difficulty meets the expositor in what are virtual parallels, Col 1¹⁵ and Jn 1¹³.

However this may be, it is safe to say that Hebrews can be quoted for the pre-existence of Christ, and that this pre-existence is specifically conceived as personal. As Weiss puts it,[2] all theories to the effect that what is meant is no more than an impersonal principle go to wreck on 1¹⁻⁴. Christ's eternal being is repeatedly made a foil to the sorrow, tears, shame, and death endured by Him in the flesh; His earthly life is an episode, though not an episode merely, in a history without beginning and without end. It was the reproach of Christ which Moses bore; it was by Christ Himself, as Lord, that of old the foundations of the world were laid. Very few words in all are spent on His pre-temporal life, yet it fills a larger place than in any other New Testament Epistle. But the writer has no speculative key to incarnation as an experience. He says not one word as to the method of it, and although he points out how the Son came into our very midst by taking flesh and blood, there is no passage to be compared with Ph 2⁵⁻¹¹. What is underlined is the fact that He came into humanity, not out of it; His coming was a supernatural event. At the same time, docetism is excluded firmly. Christ's very purpose in taking flesh was that He might suffer. Not only so, but His experience has contributed to His present character. As the fruit

[1] *Op. cit.* 441. [2] *New Testament Theology*, ii. 189, note.

of His passion He is now a merciful and faithful High Priest in whom the frail and sinful are sure of sympathy purchased at a great price. Just because the once suffering Jesus is also the Exalted Head of the Christian society, the idea of imitation is raised to the supreme level of religious faith. He is the Forerunner who has passed through the heavens as our Priest; He is the beginner and finisher of faith, whose course of brave endurance we must consider, when tempted to faint or grow weary. He can help us in our suffering, inasmuch as He has Himself been a sufferer, but now lives in glory and universal power.

The writer's exposition of Christ's redemptive work is in keeping with the centrality of his thought of Sonship. It is as Son that Christ discharges priestly functions, sacrificing Himself in death, and, after death and resurrection, entering through His own blood as priest within the veil. In the character of Son, also, He offered Himself to God "through eternal Spirit" (9^{14}, cf. 7^{16}). This striking phrase almost amounts to a definition of His nature; it denotes that the Spirit which dwelt in Him and made Him what He was, proved to be inextinguishable by death, and thus enabled Him to carry on for ever a priestly work in the higher sanctuary. The importance of this heavenly function for the writer's mind is cardinal. But it too is based on Sonship. It is as Son that Christ intercedes (4^{14} 7^{25} 9^{24}); as Son He bears the once-made sacrifice before God on our behalf as He enters the holy place; as Son He sits down on the right hand of God (1^{4}), heir of all things, and destined to appear a second time to them that wait for Him (9^{28}). Thus the eternity and perfection of the new covenant are once for all guaranteed by the fact that Christ is Son of God.

Nevertheless, the antinomy we have found in St. Paul returns also in the Christology of Hebrews. On the one hand, the Godhead of Christ is explicitly asserted. The Son acts as Creator, and the relations of created things to God are mediated by Him. No proof is given of this, which is in itself significant. But on the other hand, the Godhead so enunciated is compatible with real subordination. Everywhere the Son is viewed as dependent on the Father—for appointment as heir of all things (1^2), for calling as High Priest (5^5), for resurrection (13^{20}), for exaltation (1^{13}). In 1^6 He is described without qualification as "the first-born." Not Christ, but God, is the final Judge of men. The Son's place is not on, but on the right hand of, the throne of God. The two views are there; and they must simply be acknowledged. It is idle to refer one of them to Christ's deity, the other to His manhood. As Baur has remarked,[1] if the words "This day have I begotten Thee" (1^5) seem to define Christ as posited by God's will, and therefore in a sense temporal and accidental, the metaphors of 1^3 as plainly teach that the relationship is one of essential nature. This may of course be criticised unfavourably as an unmediated conjunction of metaphysic and history in which justice is done neither to the logical character of speculation nor to the demands of exact historical inquiry. As a matter of fact, the duality is simply indissociable from the Christian view of Jesus. Faith is conscious of the personal presence of God in Him; it is therefore inevitable that He should be regarded alike in a Divine or eternal aspect—implying somehow a real pre-existence—and in an aspect for which He fulfils His mission under the conditions of time. It may turn out that the antinomy is insoluble by thought; but the writers of the New Testament at least obey a true instinct in affirming both estimates even if the grounds of their organic unity cannot be made apparent.

No man thinks or writes in a vacuum, and there can be no question that Hebrews reveals the influence of Alexandria, that crucible of all creeds. Some of the writer's phrases have a history behind them. There is a significant resemblance between his description of the Son and epithets applied by Philo and the Book of Wisdom to the Logos or Wisdom personified.[2] Philo

[1] *Neutest. Theol.* 237. [2] Cf. Holtzmann, *NT Theologie*, ii. 294 f.

had spoken of the Logos as the mediator between God and man, as the first-born creature, as the oldest Son of God, as the organ or instrument of creation and providence. But while we recognise the Alexandrian vocabulary, it is quite mistaken to infer from this that the underlying system of ideas is in each case the same. Philo in comparison with Hebrews is "as water unto wine." In Philo the Logos floats vaguely in a medium which is neither personal nor impersonal, as the unity of subordinate *logoi* that pervade the world; the soul which has been caught up in ecstasy and initiated in mystery may dispense altogether with the Logos; God is impassably severed from the world by a gulf the Logos only can bridge; and at no point is the Logos identified with the Messiah. But in Hebrews the Messianic Son—nowhere designated as Logos—descends into history as a Redeemer, and through a career of temptation, death, and victory becomes the great High Priest of men, by whom alone we come to God. It is clear that a wholly new religious interest is predominant. The author of Hebrews has carried over to Jesus predicates and epithets drawn from the cultured phraseology of his time which appear to him pre-eminently suited to declare His greatness. With a sovereign freedom he argues that what philosophy has aspired to is given in Christ. We must not make him responsible for more than this verbal debt. It is indeed difficult to conceive how an apostolic writer is to satisfy a certain type of criticism. Let him create a new world of ideas, and he is in danger of being pronounced unintelligible; let him use the categories of his day, even though baptized in the name of Christ, and he is scouted as a plagiarist who has nothing of his own to say. The Christ of Hebrews does replace the Philonic Logos, in which philosophy had, as it were, been dreaming of a Saviour; but to state the one in terms of the other is impossible.

The Christologies of St. Paul and of Hebrews are similar in many important features. Both teach that Christ did not begin to be at His earthly incarnation, but was Mediator of creation from the first; and in each case the argument moves in a regressive direction, from His exalted glory to His pristine estate. Both teach that He has reached a glory far above men and angels by way of the cross; it was at the resurrection that for the first time—in some sense as reward—He attained to a manifested greatness which was His always by right. Both teach His true Godhead yet real subordination. At the same time, vital differences prove that as constructions they are wholly independent. The idea of High Priest has no place in St. Paul, and much is said in Hebrews about our Lord's heavenly ministry to which in St. Paul there answers only the thought of intercession. Hebrews also brings out in a new way—here more or less anticipating the Fourth Gospel—the glory of Jesus' life on earth, with its riches of acquired sympathy. If in St. Paul imitation of the earthly Jesus is swallowed up in the thought of union with Christ (cf., however, 1 Co $10^{31ff.}$), in Hebrews the Leader of all the faithful is our pattern in temptation, who endured before us the gainsaying of the wicked, and suffered, as we also must suffer, without the gate. In the later book the mystical side of Paulinism is absent, even from 3^{14} and 6^{4}, and though the writer looks forward to the Parousia, there is no suggestion, as in 1 Co 15^{45-47}, of a future when Christ will abdicate, and His Messianic reign merge in the absolute dispensation of the Father.

CHAPTER V.

THE CHRISTOLOGY OF THE APOCALYPSE.

THE view of Christ which inspires the Apocalypse of John —the Domitianic date seems proved—offers a peculiarly interesting study in contrasts. On the one hand, whatever be its sources, the book is now rightly regarded as the product of an intensely Jewish form of Christianity. To the writer Jesus is the true Messiah. He is the Lion of the tribe of Judah (5^5), the bright, morning Star, the Root and Offspring of David (22^{16}), whose destiny it is to rule the nations with a rod of iron (5^{27} etc.)—all manifestly Old Testament predicates. On the other hand, so exalted is another vein in his conception, that Bousset speaks of it as apparently the most advanced Christology in the New Testament. Nor ought we too hastily to assume that this is due to Pauline influence. It may represent a late independent branch of primitive faith.

Here we are concerned less with the origins of the writer's symbolism, than with the immense significance he has forced it to carry. "His vision of Jesus," Dr. Moffatt has said, "came to him through an atmosphere of truculent and fantastic Messianism, which was scarcely lucid at all points, and which tended to refract if not to blur the newer light." The inconsistencies and inequalities of his usage "are mainly due to the fact that the writer's

LITERATURE—Bousset, *Die Offenbarung Johannis*[6], 1906; Moffatt, "Revelation," in the *Expositor's Greek Testament*, 1910; Porter, *Messages of the Apocalyptical Writers*, 1905; Briggs, *Messiah of the Apostles*; Peake, in *Mansfield College Essays*, 1909; Schmiedel, *Johannine Writings*, 1908; Titius, *Die neutestamentliche Lehre von der Seligkeit*, Abtheil. IV. 1900.

Christian consciousness repeatedly tends to break through forms too narrow for its fulness. Probably the materials at the author's disposal would have been better arranged had this been anything less than the presentation of a living Redeemer in heaven as the Messiah of God's people upon earth. The mere fact that the Messiah had lived, involved a readjustment of Messianic categories; the further fact that he had suffered and risen meant that many had to be reshaped."[1] It is the heavenly life and activity of Christ that occupy the foreground, although the days of His flesh are not wholly forgotten. The name "Jesus" occurs five times, twice in the now familiar phrase, "Lord Jesus." Primitive thought is revealed in the Judaistic appellations of the Messiah, as also in the Danielic reminiscence, "one like unto a son of man" (14^{14}). Eschatological forms are frequent. The Kingdom will be established by the advent of Jesus, not by the development of society. The past is His; but above all He is herald of the future, ushering in the day of final triumph when those who have kept His testimony shall be made priests of God and His Christ, and reign with Him a thousand years. His vestments in 1^{13} are priestly. But the seer's favourite title for Jesus is "the Lamb." It occurs twenty-nine times as a significant and touching index of His redeeming work and of the awed yet tender adoration evoked by it, for the blood of the slain Lamb which purges sin, guarantees to all the faithful a like victory through suffering and death.

Yet all memories of the past are virtually absorbed in the vision of Jesus' heavenly glory. He who was dead now lives to bless and rule. And it is not going too far to say that the song uttered in His praise passes upward from point to point, till, in all essential ways, He is frankly identified with Godhead and fills a Divine place. His power is far superior to the angels. Omnipotence, omniscience, and eternity are ascribed to Him. He is the "Living One" whose conquest of the tomb gave Him

[1] *Expositor's Greek Testament*, v. 297.

the keys of death and Hades (1^{18}); like Jehovah (Ps 7^{9}) He searches the reins and the hearts with eyes like a flame of fire; the seven spirits of God are His; He has power to unlock the secrets of human destiny (ch. 5); and, in the Christophany with which the book opens, such is the godlike and overwhelming radiance of His person that the seer falls at His feet as dead. He is source and end of all existing things, assuming thrice with solemnity the specifically Divine name, "the First and the Last," and the impression of absolute eternal power is deepened by the additional circumstance that the words, "I am Alpha and Omega, the beginning and end," spoken by God Himself in 21^{6}, are elsewhere uttered by Jesus (22^{13}) in an emphasised form. This makes it virtually certain that He is ranked with God, not with finitude, in such phrases as "the beginning (or principle) of the creation of God" (3^{14}), and that He is conceived as filling this place eternally, not merely after His exaltation.

Within this Divine sphere, His relation to God is that of Sonship. In the letter to the Church of Thyatira He designates Himself "Son of God," and His words make reference more than once to "My Father" (2^{27} 3^{5}). Once only He is described as "the Word of God" (19^{13}), a token that we are somewhere within the range of Johannine and Alexandrine ideas. Even if the phrase is not an interpolation, however, the nature of the context scarcely invites an immediate or unconditional identification with the Logos as conceived in the Prologue to the Fourth Gospel.

Throughout the book the praise of this Divine personality is echoed passionately. In 19^{10} the seer is bidden worship God only, but the Apocalypse as a whole heaps proof on proof that already the adoration of Jesus is a distinctive feature of Christian religion, this earthly praxis being no more than a reflex of the homage paid on high. "Unto Him that loveth us, and washed us from our sins by His blood . . . to Him be the glory and the dominion for ever and ever" ($1^{5.6}$). This is closely parallel to the doxology in $7^{11ff.}$, which is addressed to God. Along with this may be combined two salient passages, 5^{13} and 7^{10}, in which God and Christ are held forth as the objects of a single intense movement of adoration: "Unto Him that sitteth upon the throne, and unto the Lamb, be the blessing," is the worship offered in 5^{13} by the totality of animated creation; "Salvation unto our God which sitteth on the throne, and unto the Lamb," is in 7^{10} the song of the great multitude of the redeemed, which no man could number. In both instances God the Creator and Jesus the Redeemer are exhibited in the same indissociable unity, the same oneness with difference. And with this representation the mystical expressions harmonise which occur in the beautiful picture of the heavenly Jerusalem ($21^{22.\ 23}$), regarding which it is said, in fulfilment of the Old Testament ideal, that "the Lord God Almighty, and the Lamb, are the temple thereof," and again that "the glory of God did lighten it, and the lamp thereof is the Lamb." This last verse is obviously parallel to and a reminiscence of Is 60^{19}: "The Lord shall be unto thee an everlasting light, and thy God thy glory"; where a recent commentator points out the noteworthiness of the fact that in the closing phrase "the Lamb" occupies the place of "thy God" in the prophecy.[1] We have only to read the seven epistles to the Churches consecutively to realise with a vividness scarcely felt in any other part of the New Testament how central, incomparable, and all-determining is the place of Jesus in the life and faith of first-century believers, and how impossible any comparison is between His function as the medium and as it were the very atmosphere of redemption and that of any other, whether prophet, saint, or martyr. Christ does not live, as we do, by the grace of God, but we live by the grace of God and Christ. A monotheist Jew, of the first Christian generation, finds himself not only free, but actually bound, to identify Christ in His attributes with God, and can use with adoring freedom such

[1] Professor C. A. Scott, *Commentary* (Century Bible), 294.

unparalleled phrases as "the throne of God and of the Lamb."[1]

As in the rest of the New Testament, the transcendence of Jesus—His place within the Divine sphere—is still combined with a view of His person as subordinate to God. However misleading it may be to say, as Wernle does, that in the Apocalypse Jesus is only the highest in the great company of mediators; however obvious the author's conviction that in ascribing praise to Jesus he cannot go too far or far enough, since words must still fall short; yet this Person, alone, unapproachable and supreme, is yet uniformly presented as dependent on God the Father. In the opening verse, whatever rendering we choose, it is made clear that the revelation which forms the subject was *given* to Jesus Christ by God. And in 3^{21} Christ's risen glory is depicted as in some real sense the outcome and reward of His earthly fidelity, for He promises to all who overcome a share in His own acquired royal power and judicial dignity. Lofty as His position is, He still reveals Himself as the exemplar of His people. To object, as some writers do, that it is only because Jesus is not God that He can be conceived as the pattern of humanity, and that the naming separately of Jesus and God virtually disproves the author's belief in His Divine significance, is to assume the very matter in dispute. The same may be said of the contention that, since the gift of exaltation is *conferred* on Christ, we cannot be meant to take seriously various other expressions in which His original divinity appears to be asserted. Weiss has pointedly replied to this, that so far from one position neutralising the other, it really furnishes its sufficient ground. None but He who was Divine by nature could sit upon the Divine throne.[2]

[1] It is not as if the author had decided this question of Christ-worship unreflectively. The issue filled his whole mind. His book is a trumpet-call to Christians to worship Jesus and refuse to worship the Roman Emperor (cf. Moffatt, *op. cit.* 307–17).

[2] *NT Theology*, ii. 277.

Here, then, as elsewhere in the apostolic writings, the Christian view of Jesus stands firmly on a foundation of experience. It is the impression made by the historic Redeemer on hearts surrendered to Him, joined to the consciousness of the new life in the Spirit which He conveys to them from His place on high. To this Jesus belong "the glory and the dominion for ever and ever" (1^6). No one knew better than the author that the Apocalypse was a book for the people, not for the theologian,[1] and that the literary and mythological details of his symbolism have no unity but that of the religious passion which employed them. "The writer's Christology," it has been said, "may mingle naively archaic elements like the lion of the tribe of Judah, or the iron sceptre which dashes nations in pieces, with speculative ideas like the first principle of creation or the eternal Divine word—it matters not. What his work reveals is that Jesus is practically greater than any or all these ways of representing Him; neither the imagination of the Jew nor the philosophical faculty of the Greek can embody Him; in the faith and life of the seer He has an importance to which neither is adequate; the only true name for Him is one which is above every name."[2]

[1] Wernle may be right in his suggestion (*Anfänge*, 230) that the book is of lay origin.

[2] Denney, *Jesus and the Gospel*, 79.

CHAPTER VI.

THE JOHANNINE CHRISTOLOGY.

THE writer of the Fourth Gospel—on the evidence it is still possible to regard him as John the Apostle[1]—has explained very clearly the purpose of his work. In words which may have formed the conclusion of the Gospel as originally composed, he declares plainly: "These are written that ye might believe that Jesus is the Christ, the Son of God, and that believing ye might have life through His name" (20^{31}). He felt himself to be in line with primitive Christian belief. The point at which he passed beyond primitive ideas was not in replacing the Messiah by the Logos, but in perceiving how much is eventually implied in Messiahship. Jesus' Messianic function he construes uniformly in terms of Divine Sonship. Or, to put it otherwise, he formulates Messiahship in categories more universal and absolute, working back to those ultimate presuppositions which were best fitted to impress the wider contemporary intelligence.

But the specifically Messianic interest is never out of sight. Thus in chapter 1, Andrew reports to his brother

LITERATURE—Scott, *The Fourth Gospel, its Purpose and Theology*, 1906; Drummond, *The Character and Authorship of the Fourth Gospel*, 1903; Sanday, *Criticism of the Fourth Gospel*, 1905; Lütgert, *Die johanneische Christologie*, 1899; Barth, *Das Johannesevangelium und die synoptischen Evangelien*, 1905; B. Weiss, *Der johanneische Lehrbegriff*, 1862; Holtzmann, *Hand-Kommentar*[3], Bd. iv., 1910; Titius, *Die neutestamentliche Lehre von der Seligkeit*, Abtheil. iii., 1900; Schmiedel, *Johannine Writings*, 1908; Heitmüller on the Fourth Gospel in *Die Schriften des Neuen Testaments*[2] (ed. J. Weiss), 1907; Kirn, article "Logos," in *RE.* xi.

[1] This is not meant to negate the possibility that a later editor or editors may have arranged the apostolic material, or that certain passages in the Gospel as we have it are in the wrong order.

Simon that he has found the Christ, and Nathanael hails Jesus in that character on the ground of His preternatural knowledge. The woman of Samaria also is convinced, while a similar process of reasoning goes on in the minds of the Jerusalem populace, as revealed in their question: "When the Christ shall come, will He do more signs than those which this man hath done?" (7^{31}). The works of Jesus, moreover, are characteristically Messianic. He comes to raise the dead, to bestow the Spirit in fulfilment of the ancient promise, to receive the Lordship of all things (3^{35} 16^{15}). It lies with Him also to execute judgment; though, as has been pointed out, "the judgment is taken out of the future, and carried back into the actual life of Christ,"[1] an earlier conception of judgment thus being supplemented by the notion of a present and continued process. His miracles are placed in the same light, but it is significant of St. John's profounder and more spiritual interpretation that outward miracles are regarded (5^{20}) as but the signs of greater works still, wrought by Jesus in His function of awakening, animating, judging, and illumining the souls of men. He is represented, in short, as exerting a delegated but competent authority such as only the Messiah could assume. But the Jewish horizon has vanished. Whatever Jesus may be as Christ, He is definitely for the whole world.

The writer intentionally selects the *person* of Jesus Christ as the subject-matter of his Gospel. Our Lord's consciousness of His relation to God, His transcendent nature, His willingness to communicate eternal life, and the issues of the attitude which men take to His person—these form the real centre of the picture. "The point of view," says Mathews, "is certainly not that of the Synoptic Gospels, but it is precisely that of a devoted disciple, who, looking back upon the career of his Master through the course of years, would be quick to see how constantly Jesus was in reality presenting Himself as the subject of definition."[2]

[1] Scott, *Fourth Gospel*, 214.
[2] *Messianic Hope*, 246

The relation of Father to Son had already been signalised in a great Synoptic passage (Mt 11[27]) in terms which involve the uniqueness of Jesus' nature, so that in part the change of emphasis is prepared for. At the same time, the representation of Christ diverges from that of the older Gospels, in so far as the Fourth Gospel represents His discourse as revolving almost exclusively round His own person and the revelation it contains. He is alike the subject and object of His message. Thus the Gospel opens with a carefully constructed Prologue, the purpose of which is to affirm the eternal Godhead of the personal Word who became flesh in Jesus Christ; and (if chapter 21 is by a later hand) it virtually closes on the same note, in the adoring cry of Thomas, "My Lord and my God" (20[28]). In great measure, however, the distinction between the two readings is that of fact and theory. The first three Gospels had pictured Christ in His familiar habit among men, as any onlooker might observe Him; the fourth undertakes to penetrate behind this to its deeper ground. If they moved always within the fact of Jesus' human life, St. John offers an articulated view of the relationship of Christ to God, when followed up into its final implications.[1] Jesus is the Christ, in the last and highest sense of that term, because He is primarily the Eternal Word or Son, come forth in history as the perfect manifestation of the Father. The varied elements of the story—the miracles of Jesus, His sayings, His experiences—are so arranged as to focus the light directly on this Divine truth. Each incident, each discourse, reveals a new aspect of Jesus as the Christ who is also the Incarnate Son, and can be the first only because He is the second. Constant reference to this central aim lends the Gospel its singular uniformity of tone and language.

[1] Both readings are inspired by *religious* conviction. St. John's interest in the Godhead of Jesus Christ was, as Mr. Purchas has noted, "not philosophical; it was intensely practical. To him Christianity meant the love of God reaching forth and stooping down to men wandering in darkness" (*Johannine Problems*, 101).

As regards the authenticity of the Johannine discourses, a working compromise is being slowly effected between reasonable men on both sides. A few scholars would still claim for the evangelist a quite literal exactitude. At the other extreme, a large body of writers contend that the teaching of Jesus in the Fourth Gospel is really an expansion in philosophic terms of an estimate of Jesus which has virtually no point of contact with the person known to us from the Synoptics. On this view, the apostolic authorship is out of the question. Gradually, however, there is growing up a mediating party, who are more or less prepared to waive the question of authorship, but in any case are convinced that the Johannine witness of Jesus to Himself is at bottom historically trustworthy, while yet His actual words have passed through the colouring medium of the writer's personal reflection. His type of exposition, so unlike that of the Synoptics, is due to his having thoroughly worked over into his own style his recollections of what Jesus said and did. But it is incredible that a Christian apostle should have taken liberties with the self-consciousness of Jesus. We may say with Haupt that the teaching of Jesus has an authentic commentary bound up with it, or, in Burton's admirable phrase, that the Gospel is "a series of historical sermons";[1] but in either case there is a vital accuracy. The pregnant pictorial words of the Synoptics are gone, the original matter has largely been melted and recast in memory, yet we feel no final discrepancy between the Master's thought as we know it elsewhere and the evangelist's report and exposition. Truth learnt by St. John and the Church around him, ere the close of the apostolic age, was felt to have lain from the very outset in Jesus' words, and in the light of this perception the words themselves assumed a new aspect. Thus we may explain the comparative absence of development alike in Jesus' self-revelation and the apprehension of it by the disciples. Objects really separate in time merged in each other unawares; to the

[1] *Short Introduction to the Gospels*, 128.

evangelist looking back, as Dr. Sanday suggests, the evolutionary process was foreshortened.[1]

It is an axiom, therefore, that the apostle's view of Christ had passed through a rich and fruitful process of transformation.[2] We can imagine spiritual forces which may well have produced the change. Such were his fellowship with the exalted Lord; the common faith of the living and suffering Church; the challenge of the wistful religious longings which pervaded the Graeco-Roman world; not least, perhaps, the teaching of St. Paul, with which he must have been familiar. Unless experience is something of which God can make no use, these influences must have operated on St. John's recollections of the historic Jesus and have tended to evoke an ever profounder apprehension of His supreme religious significance. The Fourth Gospel is then fundamentally the work of an apostle, who, in the evening of life, and as a protest against the idealising tendency which sought to turn Christianity into a group of abstract conceptions, made known to the Church the intuition he had gained of the eternal value of the historic Lord—His unique relation to God as uncreated Son, His relation to men as essential Life and Truth. Throughout he strives to convey the total impression of this Christ. The secret of his Gospel lies in its unique combination of history with clear-sighted faith. It belongs to a class of writings which may be described as not merely historical but prophetic, and has the qualities rather of a portrait than a photograph. As it has been expressed finely: "The greatness of the Fourth Gospel consists in this, that it takes us back to the living Person of Jesus as the ultimate force in Christianity. There was a danger in the period immediately following the apostolic age that the religion of Christ would soon cease to bear any vital relation to its founder—John perceived that a religion thus severed from Christ Himself would be emptied of its real content and power. It was the life

[1] *Criticism of the Fourth Gospel*, 157.

[2] He is himself conscious of this; 14^{26} 15^{26} $16^{13f.}$.

which had been the Light of men."[1] The final import of the historic Personality had yet to be set forth; and St. John, essaying this task, has seized the inmost truth of Jesus' self-consciousness with a surer grasp even than the Synoptics. Thus the difference of interpretation is after all only a matter of degree. There is a close affinity, for instance, between the Christology of the Fourth Gospel and that of the Second.[2]

As a whole the Johannine picture of Christ makes on the reader's mind an impression of harmonious and sublime transcendence. *Incessu patet deus*; this is indeed the mien of God manifest in the flesh. At the same time it is a rather unfortunate mistake to regard the delineation of Christ as out of touch with the common experience of men. To say that the Logos-Jesus is incapable of human weakness, and that the writer has obliterated all traces of a moral struggle in His life, is totally misleading in view of the cry for deliverance from the passion in 12^{27}; and in chapter 5, where Jesus is represented as Judge, it is noticeable that His fulfilment of the office is made wholly dependent on His obedience to the Father. "I can of Myself do nothing; as I hear, I judge" (5^{30}). The real fact is that manifestations of the humanity of Jesus are recorded with greater vividness in the Fourth Gospel than in any of the first three.[3] He is shown to us wearied at Jacob's well, weeping beside the grave of Lazarus, grateful for the companionship of the Twelve, anticipating the cross with alternate shrinking and desire, athirst on Calvary, and bearing, even after the resurrection, the marks of the spear and the nails. He is bound to His fellows by ties of blood. He is guest with His family at

[1] Scott, *op. cit.* 291.

[2] Cf. J. Weiss, *Das älteste Evangelium*, 42–47.

[3] Cf. Weizsäcker, *Jahrbücher für deutsche Theologie*, 1857, 175; Drummond, *Character and Authorship of the Fourth Gospel*, 422 f. Professor F. C. Burkitt has said that "in no early Christian document is the real humanity of Jesus so emphasised as in the Fourth Gospel" (*Gospel History and its Transmission*, 233).

a wedding-party, receives advice as to His conduct, cares for His mother with His latest breath. He offers prayer. He is subject, moreover, to the limits of earthly experience; for although more than once very remarkable knowledge is attributed to Him, yet definite details, such as His inquiry regarding the place of Lazarus' tomb, make it impossible to say that He is depicted as omniscient.

His oneness of nature with us is specially exhibited in His uniform dependence on God. He prays to God as His Father, and gives thanks that His prayer is always heard (11^{41}). The will of God is throughout the source and background of His mission to the world. Consecrated and sent by the Father (10^{36}), He speaks only those things which He has seen and heard of Him, or, as it is expressed in one place, "as the Father hath taught Me" (8^{28}). He is in fact a commissioned deputy to whom both words and works have been "given." His higher knowledge is described as being His by communication, and He confesses that He can do nothing of Himself but that which He sees the Father do (5^{19}). Knowledge and power equally are mediated through the Spirit. Not only so; His relation to God is somehow conditioned by His moral attitude. "He that sent Me is with Me; He hath not left Me alone; for I do always the things that are pleasing to Him" (8^{29}); and again: "therefore doth the Father love Me, because I lay down My life" (10^{17}). But this human dependence, on the other hand, is no mere commonplace fact which might have simply been taken for granted: it is of the essence of this unique life; it flows ultimately from His special and unshared Sonship, and is the form of that special Sonship under the conditions of human experience. That He should do Divine works on earth results from His singular relation to the Father. The power necessary for His vocation is given from day to day, but it is only because He is Son that He can receive it.

While therefore the mutual love and knowledge of Father and Son are insisted on, the relationship is not such as to involve a simple equality. The Son is dependent at each point on the Father, but it would be gravely unfaithful to St. John's interpretation to speak of the Father as being dependent on the Son. There remains a true subordination, a human subjection and (as it were) inferiority, on Jesus' side. What has frequently been missed, however, is that this subordination is depicted as expressing itself in modes which are purely ethical. It is mediated, that is, by authentic human motives, desires, prayers, acts of submission and compliance, and nothing could be more inaccurate than to regard it as necessitated by the inherent properties of a metaphysical Divine "substance" or as illustrating the rigid, self-acting categories of an *à priori* ontology. To assert that "the moral attributes, trust, pity, forgiveness, infinite sympathy, are replaced by certain metaphysical attributes, which are supposed to belong more essentially to the Divine nature," is not to interpret what the evangelist has written, but to impose on him an erroneous modern theory. It is a reading of the facts wholly out of keeping with the character of One who, when exhorting the disciples to keep His commandments, could promise that thereby they would abide in His love, "even as I have kept My Father's commandments, and abide in His love" (15^{10}), and who, in another place, is presented as *entreating* the Father to glorify Him with the glory which had been His before the world was (17^{5}). Metaphysical attributes, in any sense in which they are represented as opposed to ethical attributes, are irrelevant to such a situation. All the predicates affirmed of Jesus by Himself are of a fundamentally religious type; they are meant to state personal relations humanly, so that human souls may lay hold upon the only true God in His Son, Jesus Christ (17^{3}). The Christ of the Fourth Gospel, then, is truly man, one with us in all points, except sin. The secret of His uniqueness lies in an unparalleled relation to the Father. Men can be children of God only by the new birth; Jesus is the Son of God by eternal nature. This combination of personal uniqueness with human dependence is put very strikingly in 5^{26}, where each side is brought out alternately: "As the Father hath life in Himself, even so gave He to the Son also to have life in Himself." The power to impart life is a derived power; on the other hand, as imparting it, Jesus is for men that which none can be save God—the source of life eternal. In like manner, He does nothing but what He sees the Father do, yet He does the same works as the Father.

Like the Synoptic writers, the Fourth evangelist represents Jesus as seeking by human fellowship to train the disciples into a spiritual conception of His purpose. By degrees, under His influence, they became aware that the gift He desired to impart was Divine and universal, namely, the possession of perfect life in union with Himself. A crucial stage in their progress is dated from St. Peter's words: "We have believed and know that Thou art the Holy One of God" (6^{69}); and it is a significant minor detail, testifying to the substantially historical character of the narrative, that there is no intrusion at this point of the ideas of the Logos or the eternal Sonship.[1] The disciples are coming to recognise the Messiah, but, as they rise to a religious point of view, the name is assuming a new content.

The distinctive name of Jesus in the Fourth Gospel, however, is "the Son of God," or, more briefly and simply, as in the Synoptics, "the Son." At least thirty times He employs the phrase "My Father," on nine occasions when speaking to God directly; seventeen times, by the lowest estimate, He designates Himself "Son" or "Son of God." In the Johannine writings, and throughout the New Testament as a whole, the primary reference of this name is clearly enough to the historic Person, known and remembered within the domain of human fact. So far then it denotes

[1] Those who regard the Fourth Gospel as a philosophical romance or a thesis in theology may still do well to read the essay appended by Renan to his *Vie de Jésus* (ed. 13).

our Lord as one who held towards God a unique relationship of intimacy and love, manifested in entire obedience to His will. This aspect of the matter we have had occasion to study closely, and at present we need not dwell on it.

But as one who loved ultimate conceptions, St. John felt the inadequacy of this, and he pressed on to elucidate its absolute eternal ground. He does so in the first place by expounding the witness of Christ to the identity of nature subsisting between Himself and the Father. That nothing less august than such a unity is meant may be gathered from the charge made by the Jews against His claim to special Sonship, namely, that He made Himself equal with God (5^{18} 10^{33}). In 5^{19-29} this identity or parallelism is drawn out in considerable detail, only a faint allusion being made to the subordination of the Son; the Father and Jesus are one in quickening power, in authority to judge, in worthiness to be adored. It is a remarkable passage, the distinctive note of which is audible in the words, "that all may honour the Son, even as they honour the Father." This unique relation of Son to Father is elsewhere described by the term "only-begotten" (3^{16}), joined to and explained by the phrase, "who is in the bosom of the Father" (1^{18}). Shades of meaning but faintly discernible in the Christology of St. Paul are thus deepened and intensified. Sonship is defined in its highest terms. The Son is of the same nature as the Father, Divine powers and qualities devolving on Him in virtue of His inherent birthright. Yet His possession of these powers is seen so steadily from the ideal or timeless point of view that it nowhere cancels the element of weakness and restriction inseparable from the personal presence of the Son in human life.

At various points the writer opens up, beyond this unity of Father and Son, a vista of its eternal character. He transcends the first three Gospels by insisting on the fact that the Sonship of Christ is increate and unbeginning, the presupposition of all time and history.

In the beginning (1^1, cf. Gn 1^1) He had been the Word with the Father. Ere coming from heaven He had lived a life somehow characterised by spiritual relationships (17^5); it was not some impersonal moment or tendency in God which had taken flesh and dwelt among men, but the Son, eternal object of the Father's love (17^{34}), and possessed thereby of a perfect knowledge of the Father which was capable of reproducing itself in His earthly consciousness. As one whose place is in the Father's bosom (1^{18}), He presents God *in propria persona.* He knows God thus because He has always known Him so. "I speak the things which I have seen with My Father"; "no man hath ascended into heaven, but He that descended out of heaven." Numerous other salient passages dwell on this prior life of Sonship. To the Jews' question where He will go that they cannot come, He answers, "I am from above" (8^{38}). In the mysterious declaration, "Before Abraham was, I am" (8^{58}), the tense is apparently chosen to denote, as far as human speech permits, the timeless and unbecoming eternity of His inmost being. And in the upper room, He speaks to the Father of "the glory which I had with Thee before the world was" (17^5), and prays that it may be restored to Him. Yet the main object of these statements is not to make certain speculative predications, in a so-called metaphysical interest, but to exhibit Jesus as *the final revelation of the Father.* This is the pivotal and organising idea in St. John's theology. We can see the conviction in his mind that none can reveal perfectly save He who *is* that which He reveals. In His essential love, accordingly, the Father has poured forth His being in Jesus, that a perishing world may have life through Him. "Believest thou not," Jesus asks, "that I am in the Father and the Father in Me? The words that I say unto you I speak not from Myself: but the Father abiding in Me doeth His works" (14^{10}).

It has been urged that Jesus' claim to a pre-existent knowledge of God must reduce His earthly experience to mere semblance. Could He learn what previously He had known? On the other hand, are we prepared to conceive the life of God and of man as so totally disparate in ethical and spiritual character that what pertains by origin to the one may not reproduce or mediate itself organically in and through the other? Are divinity and humanity to be thus defined by mutual exclusion? If not, there may be nothing self-contradictory in the view that Jesus' knowledge of God was experimental in kind — mediated, that is, by the unmeasured gift to Him of the Spirit, as acting on and interpreting to His mind the normal development of His own life—while yet its deepest fount lay in His eternal being as the Son. To take the parallel case of love, it is a frequent suggestion in the Fourth Gospel that Jesus, though loved eternally as Son, keeps Himself in the love of God by doing His will. "This is an assertion of the ultimate truth, that the union of Jesus with God depends on moral conditions; not that through His conduct He had in the first instance to gain His Father's love—it was there from the beginning—but that He can *retain* it only on the one condition, that He makes the will of God His own."[1] In some such way we may conceive His earthly realisation of the perfect knowledge of God. Apart from a theory more or less on these lines, the evangelist must have held that either no continuity or no difference obtained between the pre-existence of the Son and His earthly life. Humanitarianism or docetism would have been forced upon him.

The conclusions at which we arrive regarding the historic accuracy of the Johannine discourses is of course to be applied also to Jesus' recorded words about His pretemporal being. It would seem that these words were uttered in exalted hours of feeling, when our Lord's self-consciousness expanded to a length and depth and height that passes understanding. As we listen, we hear only the plunge of the lead into unfathomable waters. It is

[1] J. Weiss, *Christ: the Beginnings of Dogma*, 156.

possible, and we have to allow for the possibility in our interpretation, that lapse of time may have altered light and shade in the apostle's memory. One feels it scarcely credible that Jesus should have spoken on the subject so often or so clearly as to be at once intelligible to the great bulk of His auditors; for otherwise the silence of the first three Gospels is enigmatic. On the other hand, while He may have displayed a marked reticence on this theme, as on that of His Messiahship, we have reason to believe that He spoke regarding the antecedents of His life on earth with such significance that the brooding evangelist later became conscious of the claim to pre-existence implied in His words; a pre-existence not of an ideal type, but real and personal.

The last stage of Jesus' reported interpretation of Sonship is represented by His prediction of the glory to be resumed by Him after death, and of His abiding spiritual presence with the disciples (ch. 13 ff.). Resurrection would mark His entrance on a larger, unseen life, free from the limits of time or space, and this involved a change in the dignity of Jesus' person at least in the sense that it conferred on Him an omnipresence and universality of influence He had lacked on earth. We have seen that Sonship, in initial content, was a relation with God of unequalled love and intimacy. This is what we already find in the Synoptics: though even there, as Titius has remarked, the absolute tone with which the name Son is used in Mt $11^{25ff.}$ naturally suggests a more transcendent background of meaning.[1] But now the Fourth Gospel proclaims that Jesus as the Son is eventually to share in the omnipotence and absoluteness of God Himself. Thus in the deliberately chosen language of 13^{3}: "Jesus, knowing that the Father had given all things into His hands, and that He came forth from God, and goeth unto God," there is no convincing reason for restricting "all things" to the sphere of perfect revelation, so as to exclude omnipotence in the full sense. Nor is it

[1] *Jesu Lehre vom Reich Gottes*, 118.

easy to grasp the philosophical position of those who quote such a verse in confirmation of the view that in the New Testament Christ is made absolute Lord of the Church merely, not of the universe. We cannot break up reality in unrelated parts. The absolute Lordship of the exalted Christ is the starting-point of all New Testament writers. Some of them refrain from theologising on the matter, but to St. John, as he sought an explanation for his own mind, its reality appeared in complete harmony with Jesus' intimations of His own pre-existence. Why (he felt) should not One who had shared the very glory of God Himself share it once again? He had mediated in the creation of all things from the beginning; He had come to *His own*, though they received Him not (1^{11}); it was fitting, therefore, that He should be their Lord and Master after the resurrection. Hence the Divine power to which Jesus ascends is in no way incommensurate with His nature, overwhelming (as it were) a finite form with an infinite content; still less is it the prize of usurpation. It is the Father's gift, bestowed in consequence of Jesus' fidelity in the work given Him to do ($17^{4.5}$), and fitly answering to His essential being.

But the resurrection is past before the truth of Jesus' greatness has dawned on His followers. The wonderful scene which culminates in Thomas' cry of adoration (20^{28}) portrays the experience of one on whom the discovery has just broken, and whose eyes are blinded with excess of light. In the risen Jesus, fresh with victory from the grave, the apostle discerns the very Lord of glory; and perceiving in a flash of joy and peace that all he had sought for in the Father has been vouchsafed to men in the Son, he grasps the person of Jesus as possessing for faith the value and the reality of God. If his reported words mean anything, they mean an ascription to Christ of Divine prerogatives, they salute Him as the medium and vehicle of that life which is found only in the Eternal. There has been a manifestation of God in human form. Faith in Jesus Christ, aware of its own significance, becomes an explicit faith in His divinity.

Our conclusions up to this point are on the whole confirmed by St. John's usage of the title "Son of man." It is a striking minor detail that, as in the Synoptics, this name is employed solely by Jesus. It occurs some twelve times. But the accent has shifted slightly from His vocation to His person; so that by using the phrase in harmony with his lofty view of our Lord's nature, the evangelist strives to bring out the uniqueness of Jesus' personality. As in the first three Gospels, we can still trace its primitive Messianic sense. Thus in 12^{34}—a question put by the multitude—"Christ" and "Son of man" are used indifferently. In the Synoptics, as we have seen, two types of passage occur in which Jesus speaks of the "Son of man"; they are allusions either (*a*) to His earthly work, and especially to His passion, or (*b*) to the glory of His Parousia. Taking the inverse order, it appears that although the name is nowhere in the Fourth Gospel put in relation to the Second Coming, the majority of passages where it occurs refer quite specifically to Jesus' exaltation (3^{13} 6^{62} etc.) or to His being glorified (12^{23} 13^{31}). It is implied that transcendent glory awaits the Son of man, and befits His person; and this is plainly an expansion of one side of the Synoptic idea.[1] The second type of Synoptic allusion, dealing with Jesus' work on earth and with the passion it involves, is also represented in the Fourth Gospel. It is represented, for example, by sayings which describe the Son of man as giving meat that endureth to everlasting life (6^{27}), or attach eternal life to eating His flesh and drinking His blood (6^{58}), or declare that He must be "lifted up" (3^{14}).

It will be observed that this Johannine usage retains that element of paradoxical contrast which we found to be characteristic and indeed constitutive of the title in the Synoptics, even though the facts are con-

[1] Cf. Ewald, *Die Evangelienfrage*, 43–47.

templated from a slightly different point of view. Certain scholars have maintained that the original significance of the name is well-nigh inverted in the Fourth Gospel, but a careful scrutiny of the data scarcely bears this out. What is undeniable, however, is that in St. John the title "Son of man" seems always to convey the suggestion faintly that for Jesus it is an amazing thing that He should be man at all. He was man indeed, like His brethren; yet in this humanity there resided a Divine content which gave Him a place apart. Or, as it may be put otherwise, the human aspect of His life is not the primary and original aspect; He came into humanity from a higher realm. His disciples may eat His flesh and drink His blood, for He is to pass through death, dying as only man can die; yet only one who was more than man could thus dwell in believers as their inward life. Similarly, it is the Son of man who is to be lifted up, not on the cross merely, but by exaltation. On the one hand, this implies His inherent Divine transcendence, which alone makes such exaltation conceivable; on the other, it presupposes His real manhood, since exaltation comes by way of death. Thus so far from the title, as used in the Fourth Gospel, containing no reference to Jesus' higher claims, it invariably connotes these loftier antecedents as the foil or background against which the fact of His true humanity is placed. We cannot eliminate the duality. As it has been expressed: "In several passages the contrast is expressly marked between the present revelation of Jesus as Son of man and the true glory of His Divine nature. . . . The significance of the name in all these verses lies in the suggestion that the human nature of Christ was united with a higher nature which was present in it even now, and would at last become fully manifest."[1] This note of contrast never seems to fail. The Son of man, in all points authentically human, has heaven open to Him perpetually, and will yet ascend up again where He was before (6^{62}). Hence it is not going too far to

[1] Scott, *Fourth Gospel*, 184 (?).

say that no appreciable distinction can be drawn in the Fourth Gospel between what is predicated of the Son of man and of the Son of God. Both names, originally Messianic, are raised to the highest power. If the one denotes the eternal origin of Christ in God, the other points to His human affiliation but connects it with a higher being with which it is significantly contrasted. This suggestion of a Divine transcendence is the distinctive feature which St. John adds to the Synoptic view.

The Christ-mysticism of the Fourth Gospel has always been regarded as casting a revealing light upon its final interpretation of Jesus' person. We can scarcely overestimate the importance for the evangelist's mind of this conception of mystic union, by which believers are made partakers in the higher life streaming to them from Jesus. The doctrine is central in more than one of the great discourses. "I am the living bread which came down out of heaven; if any man eat of this bread, he shall live for ever" (6^{51}); "I am the vine, ye are the branches; he that abideth in Me, and I in him, the same beareth much fruit" (15^{5}); "I in them, and Thou in Me, that they may be perfected into one" (17^{23}). It is worth noting that this vital fellowship is nowhere described in the Fourth Gospel as being mediated by the Spirit, though in the First Epistle expressions are found which distinctly point that way (3^{24} 4^{13}). At the same time we observe that the idea of life-union with Christ is unmistakably connected with His exaltation.[1] It is not something possible for men while He still lived on earth; rather it forms a substitute, in the future, for His visible presence in their midst. Hence its prominence in Christ's parting words. "Because I live," is His promise, "ye shall live also." The presence of Christ in the believer is a super-

[1] Cf. Titius, *Die neutest. Lehre von der Seligkeit*, iii. 68 f. It does not follow that the historic Jesus could not have spoken of life-union with His followers, as of something to be realised in the future. There is a very fair Synoptic parallel in Mt 18^{20}, the authenticity of which we need not doubt.

natural indwelling, by which they partake in His spiritual life. In 17^{21} and elsewhere this indwelling is explained or illustrated by the analogy of God's indwelling presence in Christ; and as the relation of God to Christ, notwithstanding this mutual interpenetration of life, is wholly personal in character, the communion of Christ with men is also personal; it is a relation of spirit to spirit. And as Christ dwells in the believer, so the believer dwells in Christ, is incorporated or transplanted into the sphere of His supernatural life. This also is paralleled by the abiding of Christ in the Father. "In that day ye shall know that I am in My Father, and ye in Me, and I in you" (14^{20}).

It has however been contended that in the Fourth Gospel this living and spiritual conception is infected with a quite unethical and realistic strain of thought, according to which Christ conveys to men a higher and all but physical essence whereby they partake in the life of God. The union, it is true, is regarded as supernatural; but this in no way precludes an interpretation on ethical and psychological lines. For the vehicle of Christ's self-impartation is His word; His word is as it were the medium or element of the reciprocal possession, as it is put in 15^{7}, "if ye abide in Me, and My words abide in you." And with this it is in harmony that abiding in Christ is represented as being mediated and sustained, on the believer's side, by faith (5^{38}), obedience ($14^{21.\,23}$), and love (16^{27}). St. John has occasionally been unfavourably compared with St. Paul in this matter, and accused of having introduced at a crucial point factors of thought which are less than spiritual, and which prepared the way for later ecclesiastical dogma. It is not necessary to reply to this by urging that St. Paul is the real offender; since for any such counter-charge there is no proper ground. But at least we may point out that the Johannine view lays a deeper emphasis even than the Pauline on the psychological mediation of life-union as a present experience, and that the union itself is everywhere defined as a spiritual relationship of person to person. The mutual immanence, if we may call it so, is the intelligible resultant of Divine grace and human faith. The roots of this Johannine conception may be traced partly no doubt to the doctrine of St. Paul, but in addition the direct influence of Jesus' teaching is apparent.

From this central and characteristic thought we are irresistibly led to one view of Christ's person rather than another. If He is thus one with men, and they with Him, it is impossible to confine His life within the dimensions of normal manhood. But the Fourth evangelist does not leave us to mere inference. Over and over again he represents union with Christ as being, in itself, vital union with God. The analogy of Christ's oneness with the Father is made explicit: "That they may all be one; even as Thou, Father, art in Me, and I in Thee, that they also may be one in us" (17^{21}). This is a conception of which still more is heard in the First Epistle of John. In the Gospel the same practical identity of Christ and God is signalised in those passages which deal with the mission and activities of the Spirit. Not merely is Christ present in the community by the Spirit; He is Himself the object of the Spirit's witness. He is indeed the Giver of the Spirit to His people. But the same predications are made of God. He too is to send the Spirit and come in the Spirit along with Christ. Thus from a fresh point of view the religious equivalence of Christ and God is revealed as the truth from which radiates the whole teaching of the Gospel.

The Christology of St. John, then, may be condensed in the truth that the Father is personally in the Son, the Son in the Father (10^{38} 14^{10}). The most august and profound words of our Lord are simple affirmations of this fact: "I and the Father are one" (10^{30}, cf. 17^{11}); "He that hath seen Me hath seen the Father" (14^{9}, cf. 12^{45}). These utterances and others like them carry our minds in the direction of a simple modalism—Jesus

Christ is God revealed to faith—but no theory of the fact, or of its remoter implications, is anywhere sketched out in the manner of a theological speculation. We are shown that the word of Jesus is the word of God Himself, and conveys a Divine life to the soul; that the Father, exhibited to faith in a historic career, is now fully known in His Fatherhood. Faith is certain of this, and affirms it unconditionally. It is another question how far we can penetrate to the ontological grounds of this modalism and give a speculative or independent account of them which will gain the interest and assent of the philosopher. Even the Logos-conception, which St. John has employed —whether as an implied solution of the problem or as a statement of it in final terms—is incompetent to give us a complete understanding of all mysteries in this transcendent realm. No theory expressible in words, no combination of ideas, even those of an apostle, can after all avail to place us at a point where we see the life of Godhead on its inward side. Nevertheless, we know and are sure that in Jesus' person the God of heaven and earth has appeared among us; that the Son reveals the Father perfectly as being one with Him who is revealed; and that our eyes are enlightened by Him in all knowledge because He dwells within as our inmost life. This is the keynote of the Johannine interpretation. The faith out of which it comes, and which it strives to evoke in other minds, is the great faith that Christ and God are one—the Son sharing the supernatural life of the Father, the Father completely manifested in the Son.

This unity has often been described as if in the last resort it were limited and defective, a unity merely of will and purpose. And the objection is no doubt well taken, provided we agree that will is something less and lower than ultimate reality. If behind all will and thought there exists in God a mysterious incognizable substance, not to be described in terms familiar to human experience, but representing the point through which the threads of cosmic relations pass, and constituting the inmost essence of the Divine life, then indeed the oneness of Christ with God is after all only relative. But the supposition is mistaken. There is in the universe nothing more real than will, the living energy of spirit; nothing more concrete and actual, whether it be in God or man. It is the last home and sanctuary of essential being. We may therefore conclude that the true and inherent Godhead of Jesus Christ, if human words can affirm it, is affirmed unequivocally in the Gospel of St. John. He is completely possessed of those qualities which constitute the proper life of Deity.

Yet even here we encounter that unfailing counter-strain of subordination which we have seen to be present in the New Testament as a whole. It is noteworthy, indeed, that Jesus affirms His personal dependence on God precisely in those passages which deal with His uniqueness. Both ideas are prominent, for instance, in 5^{19-29} So too in 17 the pre-existent glory, which Jesus entreats may be restored, is a gift bestowed by the Father. It is misleading to say that this subordination has reference solely to the life on earth. It is of course manifest during the earthly life in a special degree; Jesus declares that He can do nothing of Himself,[1] that His works, like His knowledge or His right to judge, have been given Him of the Father. But we introduce the distinctions of a later age when we argue that such expressions of dependence are only meant to cover Christ's human nature, or His incarnate life, or what theology designates "the estate of humiliation." For the subordination is quite distinctly predicated of the filial life as such; it characterises Sonship everywhere, always. Even in regard to His exalted life Jesus could say, "I will pray the Father for you" (16^{26}), thus projecting the idea of subordination to the other side of death; and as a parallel to this, relating to His pre-existence, we cannot ignore the statement (10^{36}) that the Father sanctified Him and sent Him

[1] A trait which forbids us to speak of the Johannine Christ as "omnipotent."

into the world. His advent implied, of course, that the dependent nature of the Son became manifest under the new conditions which pertain to a true human life;[1] but St. John suggests that it was because His eternal relation to the Father had been one of filial reliance that He could thus reveal Him perfectly on earth. It is erroneous, therefore, to play off assertions of His Godhead and of His subordination against each other, as if either weakened the force of its opposite, or reduced it to a merely symbolic sense. The evangelist is equally in earnest with both things. For his mind both sayings are essential to the complete truth: "I and the Father are one," and "The Father is greater than I." Sonship is inconceivable without dependence. In the words of Lütgert: "The superiority of God to Jesus does not mean that He reserves anything to Himself; on the contrary, He wholly conveys Himself to Jesus, making Him sovereign of the entire world. What it does mean is that God is everywhere and at each point the Origin, the Giver, the Foundation; while Jesus is the obedient and receptive organ of His will."[2]

We turn now to the special teaching of the prologue (1^{1-18}). It was convenient to defer the Christology of these introductory verses until the general thought of the Gospel had been examined, for after all the subject of the Gospel is not the Logos or Word, but the Divine person Jesus Christ. But with this general exposition in our minds, it is all but impossible to maintain that

[1] It has been maintained that the idea of humiliation is virtually foreign to the Johannine thought, in which the conception of revelation has taken the place which the sacrifice of the cross occupied for St. Paul. Piquant contrasts of this sort have a very real didactic value, but they must not be overpressed. There is sacrifice for St. John in the incarnation as well as in the cross (1^{29}), but also in the intervening life. "Though the greatest stress," Mr. Purchas rightly observes, is "laid throughout the Gospel upon the Son's transcendent dignity, the aspect under which that dignity is invariably contemplated is not that of dignity gloriously won, or dignity brilliantly maintained, but of dignity humbly put aside, and only manifested in pre-eminence of self-sacrifice" (*Johannine Problems*, 104).

[2] *Die johann. Christologie*, 34.

the prologue serves a speculative and not a practically religious purpose. The first paragraph, as Harnack puts it,[1] is a mere preface, not a philosophic programme. Its special ideas are not allowed to intrude upon the record, nor does Jesus ever name Himself "the Word."[2] The prologue on the whole makes the impression of having been written last, in a current vocabulary and mode of thought fitted to make appeal to a quite specific constituency. "The writer desires to avail himself of a conception more congenial to the thought of his readers than to his own, in order to set forth in words familiar to his readers the doctrine he wishes to teach, viz. the uniqueness, finality, and all-sufficiency of the revelation of God made in the person of Jesus Christ."[3] It is no *à priori* philosopheme, by assimilating which the mind was to be prepared to understand and estimate the facts about to be narrated.

To say that St. John derived the Logos-conception from Philo (who may have had it from the Stoics or even Heraclitus) is one of those tantalisingly ambiguous pronouncements which darken a subject almost as much as they enlighten.[4] We cannot indeed hold that there is no mutual relation. But the influence of Philo appears to have acted in a twofold direction. First, by way of antagonism. The evangelist uses Philo's term to deny Philo's thought. In the Fourth Gospel "Logos" means word, not rational cosmic order; uttered revealing speech, not immanent reason; an agency or force dynamic or personal in nature, not static or vaguely ideal. There is nothing answering to this in Philo. It is not merely that in the earlier writer the Logos is probably impersonal; it is also carefully separated from God; as in various Gnostic schools, it is inserted between God and the world to prevent their

[1] *ZTK.* ii. 189–231. [2] As He does in the *Evang. Infantiae*, c. 1.

[3] Burton, *Short Introduction to the Gospels*, 132.

[4] Cf. Harnack's trenchant paragraph, *Dogmengesch.*[4] i. 109. Can we assume "that every presentation of the doctrine of the Logos had passed through the moulding hands of Philo"?

contact, even though in a philosophical point of view it may serve as intermediary; and to crown all, the nature of the Logos is such as to make wholly inconceivable its entrance, by incarnation, upon the real processes of history. But in St. John the Word is personal, is Himself Divine, mediates in the creation of the world, and enters human life by becoming flesh in order that as Jesus Christ, the historic Messiah, He may live and die as man and reveal the very heart of God. Thus even were the evangelist's debt to Philo an ascertained fact, we should still have to acknowledge that the borrowed notion was submitted to changes so radical as virtually to transform it into its opposite.

In the second place, Philo's influence, or at least the influence of a general philosophical atmosphere typified by Philo, may well have decided which of the terms furnished by the Old Testament the evangelist should select for his purpose. Several such terms were open to him—Wisdom, the Spirit, the Angel of the Lord, the Word. In any case, too little allowance has been made for Old Testament associations. The action of the word of God in Gn 1 may well have supplied the first suggestion of the Logos, and at various other points in the older Scriptures the creation and government of the world, as well as the progress of revelation, are traced to the Divine word going forth from God as the active organ of His will.[1]

We hold then that what St. John required and sought for was a term worthy to express the absolute nature of Christ, in whom the eternal, self-revealing God was incarnate; and that this seemed to be furnished by the contemporary religious thought, in which the Logos-conception had become familiarly established. He perceived its extraordinary value for the expositor. More significantly than any other word it gave expression to that aspect of Christ's life and work which he regarded as supreme. In addition to its place in Old Testament thought, it had received

[1] Ps 33^{6} 107^{20} 147^{15}, Is 55^{11}, Jer 23^{29}.

from Hellenism a certain cosmic width of meaning, and thus furnished a point of contact—this every missionary must appreciate—between Christianity and current modes of religious speculation. He chose it therefore as peculiarly fitted to recommend the Light and Life which had appeared in Jesus; but in choosing it he took full precautions to ensure by his exposition that its Christian import should not be overshadowed by former associations. The Word is interpreted by Jesus, not Jesus by the Word. So far from being captured for speculation, the Logos receives a connotation which is fundamentally ethical, personal, soteriological.[1] Its colour and significance are drawn from what the writer has known of Jesus, Son of God and Son of man; it is handled with perfect freedom and without any suspicion of bondage to a phrase. St. John was too near Christ to adopt a really Greek view. In the prologue he but sums up the total impression left upon him by the personality of the Saviour. If we recall the allied doctrine of Hebrews, and the teaching of St. Paul that all things were created by Christ and for Him (Col 1[16]), it will seem very natural that St. John should advance to the explicit identification of the historic Jesus with the creative Word.

A glance at the details of the prologue may illustrate these results. In v.[1] three weighty predications are made of the Logos: (*a*) He was from the beginning, or eternally; (*b*) He existed in a living personal relationship with God; (*c*) His place was within the Godhead. It is next affirmed that He was the medium or instrument of creation. Stress is laid on the truth of His universal relation to humanity; not only was the life in Him the light of men (v.[4]), but it gives light to every man coming into the world (v.[9]). His Divine life had been immanent in the world from the first, though unrecognised; but now He came in person, and to all who received Him He gave the right to become children of God. The commentators point out how v.[14] resumes and care-

[1] This is well put by Schlatter, *Die Lehre der Apostel*, 131–32.

fully corresponds to the first verse of the Gospel. The Word is throughout the subject of discourse, though not named explicitly in the interval; but now in v.[14] the announcement of the Incarnation is laid point for point alongside of the initial statement regarding the absolute eternal nature of the Word. Westcott has drawn out the exact harmony. "'He was God' and 'He became flesh': eternity and time, the Divine and human are reconciled in Him. 'He was with God' and 'He tabernacled among us': the Divine existence is brought into a vital and historical connection with human life. 'He was in the beginning' and 'we beheld His glory': He who 'was' beyond time was revealed for a space to the observation of men."[1] By the phrase of deep simplicity, "the Word became flesh," it appears to be taught that He passed into a new form of existence, a form essentially qualified by human mortality and dependence. Coming forth from God, He took individuality as a man, in unbroken personal continuity with that which He was before.

We may distinguish four stages in the thought thus briefly summarised. There is (1) the Word in His primeval everlasting being; (2) the Lord who comes to His own as Life and Light;[2] (3) Jesus Christ, upon whom the writer's mind has been fixed from the very outset, and who is now further characterised (4) as the only-begotten Son. Minor details, such as the mention of the Forerunner (v.[6]), or the significant phrase, "them that believe on His name" (v.[12]), prove the evangelist's mind to be in vitalising contact with religious experience from first to last. The entire representation is as it were an avenue conducting the mind to a redeeming view of Jesus as an historic person, and the term "Logos," by which the subject

[1] *Commentary, in loc.*

[2] Certain scholars hold that in the recently discovered Odes of Solomon there is revealed a tendency in Jewish thought which has close affinity with the Johannine conceptions of life, light, truth, etc. (cf. Rendel Harris, *The Odes and Psalms of Solomon*[2], p. xiii ff.).

is introduced, is never more than a subordinate element in a special vocabulary, which presents the personality of Christ in a certain aspect and with a special aim.

It is obvious that nothing in the prologue is intended to shed light upon the *mode* of the Incarnation, however distinctly it may assert the fact. Yet when it is read, as it ought to be, with constant reference to the Gospel it has introduced, no one can miss the clear indication of the *motive* which is conceived of as underlying the advent of Jesus Christ. It is the Divine desire to impart life to a perishing and darkened world. No doubt it is characteristic of St. John, in contrast to the Pauline view, to regard the earthly life of Jesus less as a humiliation than as a revelation of Divine glory, the beams of which shine forth clearly in His wondrous works. Nevertheless, he is wholly at one with St. Paul in the conviction that the redeeming work of Christ centres in the sacrifice of the cross (1^{29}). Jesus speaks of His death as the hour of His being glorified ($12^{23.24}$ 13^{31}), and declares that He came into the world to die (12^{27}). But death for Jesus is part of His life as Son. And life and death together make up the perfect revelation. The whole is viewed in the light of eternal fact, the lines of change or temporal distinction being obliterated. All that St. Paul beholds in the exalted Christ is found by St. John, the personal disciple, in the veiled glory of the earthly Life. Thus in the transcendent consciousness of eternal life as an experience generated by the knowledge of the Son, eschatology passes into the background.

The Christology of the First Epistle of St. John is in harmony with the teaching of the Gospel. The first three verses form an implicit commentary on the prologue with which the Gospel opens, and as such they caution us once more against a too theoretic interpretation of the Logos-conception. So complete is the identification of God and Christ that in a series of passages it is impossible to be certain of which the writer speaks. This is the case, for instance, in the great closing verse: "We know that the Son of God is come, and hath given us an understanding that we know Him that is true, and we are in Him that is true, even in His Son, Jesus Christ. *This is the true God, and eternal life*" (5^{20}). What is specially distinctive of the Epistle, however, is the emphatic condemnation of certain active champions of heresy. In the spirit of docetic idealism they had begun very early to disunite the saving word of life from the historic Jesus, and to seek another path to fellowship with God than the mediation of the incarnate Christ. It is possible that they were enthusiastic students of the Alexandrian philosophy animated by the desire to impose the Philonic Logos-conception upon the Christian facts, but in the process dissipating their significance and value. Of these men St. John writes in tones of the gravest indignation. To deny that Jesus Christ is come in the flesh ($4^{2, 3}$), or that He underwent actual death (1^7 5^6), is to abandon the faith for anti-Christian lies. To refute an error so far-reaching the writer falls back on personal testimony, declaring in the first verse of the Epistle that he is proclaiming "that which we have heard, that which we have seen with our eyes, that which we beheld, and our hands handled." The presence of Life among men had been audible, visible, tangible. Christ's advent in the flesh is that on which hangs everything that can be called salvation; victory belongs only to those who receive Him as the Son of God. "Whosoever denieth the Son, the same hath not the Father: he that confesseth the Son hath the Father also" (2^{23}).

BOOK II.

HISTORY OF CHRISTOLOGICAL DOCTRINE.

CHAPTER I.

CHRISTOLOGY IN THE SUB-APOSTOLIC AGE.

§ 1. *Introduction.*—In the *Neutestamentliche Theologie* of Holtzmann we find an interesting passage,[1] in which the writer expresses the conviction that even in St. Paul and St. John there lie the seeds and origins of the later Christological development. This at least indicates that our study of the doctrine in history ought to start from the teaching, not of Jesus Himself, but of the apostles. It

LITERATURE—On the history of Christological doctrine as a whole: Harnack, *Lehrbuch der Dogmengeschichte*[4], 1909 (Eng. tr. 1894); Loofs, *Leitfaden zum Studium der Dogmengeschichte*[4], 1906; Seeberg, *Lehrbuch der Dogmengeschichte*[2], 1908 ff.; Baur, *Die christliche Lehre von der Dreieinigkeit und Menschwerdung*, 1841–43; Dorner, *Entwicklungsgeschichte der Lehre von der Person Christi*[2], 1845–53 (Eng. tr. 1861–63); Ottley, *The Doctrine of the Incarnation*, 1896; Bethune-Baker, *History of Early Christian Doctrine*, 1903; Krüger, *Das Dogma von der Dreieinigkeit und Gottmenschheit*, 1905; Bonwetsch, *Grundriss der Dogmengeschichte*, 1909.

On the present chapter: Loofs, article "Christologie, Kirchenlehre," in *RE.*[3] iv. (to which I owe much); Engelhardt, *Das Christentum Justins*, 1878; Lightfoot, *St. Clement of Rome*, 1890, and *St. Ignatius*, 1889; Zahn, *Ignatius von Antiochien*, 1873; von der Goltz, *Ignatius von Antiochien als Christ und Theologe*, 1894; Rainy, *The Ancient Catholic Church*, 1902; Krüger, article "Gnosis," in *RE.*[3] vi.; Swete, *The Apostles' Creed*, 1894; McGiffert, *The Apostles' Creed*, 1902; Kattenbusch, *Das apostolische Symbol*, 1894–1900; Hatch, *Hibbert Lectures*, 1888.

[1] i. 418, cf. 353.

was from their preaching that the earliest circles of believers received a conception of the Lord. The common faith evoked by the evangelism of apostolic men is the seed-plot of ecclesiastical Christology. To these primitive Christian societies the Gospel of the Kingdom came primarily as a Gospel of Christ—*i.e.* good news about God resting on and revolving round an historic person. This person had revealed God's mind toward men; He had wrought salvation by His death; as Risen and Ascended Lord He was soon to return in glory, and establish the Kingdom in its fulness. He was the Messiah promised from of old, but Messiah in a sense the novelty of which was slowly dawning on the Christian mind.

To speak of an "official" doctrine of Christ in New Testament times is, however, impossible. His Divine uniqueness was indeed acknowledged everywhere. From the first it was felt that He had a universal and eternal meaning, stretching over history and reaching back to the inmost sphere of the Divine. All believers held to Him an attitude of trust and worship. Much earlier than the days told of in Pliny's famous letter they sang hymns to Christ "as though to God." So high a name was but the expression of their new life in Him. But we are not in a position to say exactly how the average believer thought of this uniqueness. Jesus belonged to, if He did not fill, the sphere of God—so much was certain; but men did not question themselves more particularly as to the bearing of this on the axiom of the Divine unity. They were content to have life through His name, and to leave problems of theory alone. The marks of a Christian were, thus far, more practical in kind. Probably the general belief included as its chief items faith in the one God revealed in Christ, a hope in the life everlasting guaranteed by the historic Messiah, and the conviction that after baptism one ought to live in conformity with the example of Jesus.

Do we know of any primitive circle, evangelised by apostolic men, which held a purely "humanitarian" view of Christ? Was there anywhere a group of believers who considered Him to be only an eminent religious teacher, like the prophets, though greater? There appears to have been one such group. In his *Dialogue with Trypho* (cap. 48) Justin writes: "Some there are of your race, who allow that He is Christ, but declare Him to be a man of men; with whom I do not agree." The same party regarded Him as the son of Joseph and denied His pre-existence. But it is noteworthy that even so these were but a section of Jewish Christianity. They formed part of the Ebionite sect, and, like all Ebionites, held that it was by the descent of the Spirit at His baptism that Jesus was endowed for the vocation of Messiah. Certain scholars have argued that this represents the genuinely original Christology, current among the first Christian Jews of Palestine. But the facts are dead against them. St. Paul's teaching as to the Person of our Lord never was, so far as we know, the subject of controversy; which of itself proves that the apostles took the higher view of Jesus' nature. Or, to take another example, the Christological heresy against which St. Paul warns the Colossians contained elements, as Lightfoot has shown, of a Gnostic character. Instances of this kind are sufficient evidence that various types of Christological thought prevailed even among Jewish Christians at the close of the apostolic age, and the effort to make them out unanimously humanitarian is a failure.

Of course, some colour may seem to be given to the mistake by the fact that all types of tradition in the first century lay stress on Jesus' true humanity. From the beginning the Christian mind assumed that Jesus of Nazareth was man. But Loofs points to two considerations tending to show that in primitive Jewish-Christian circles there were no advocates of *mere* humanitarianism. In the first place, to hold, as unquestionably they did hold, that Jesus at His baptism received the plenitude of the Spirit, is to affirm a very great, an absolutely supernatural, thing. It is to assert that a certain individual, at a particular point of history, had vouchsafed to Him the Spirit of the living God in its fulness. Between such a view and that of St. Paul the gulf is not impassable. Secondly, this idea of Jesus as a Spirit-filled man is not, in the strict sense, an expression of their religious estimate of Jesus; it is a theory of the subject, though an incipient one; it is an attempt to explain the uniqueness which that estimate ascribes to Him. Our problem therefore is: What was the prevailing religious estimate of Jesus at the close of the apostolic age?

It is scarcely enough to say that He was held to be the Messiah. That is of course true; but, on the one hand, "Christ" had become for Gentile believers little more than Jesus' surname, while, on the other, for Jewish Christians, the title bore rather on the future than the present, and carried men's minds into the world of eschatology. This being so, we shall find a clearer instance of the practical religious attitude of the Church in the custom of *prayer to Jesus.* That this custom prevailed in the sub-apostolic Church is made virtually certain by the facts to which we can point at either limit of the period.[1] Prayer is addressed to Christ directly in the New Testament (Ac 7^{59}, 1 Co 1^{2}, 2 Co 12^{8}, Rev 22^{20}); and according to the principle *lex supplicandi, lex credendi* we may regard this as the practical "deifying" of Jesus which anticipated a theoretical Christology. Again, in 113 we have Pliny's letter to Trajan, formerly referred to, in which he reports that Christians of his province were accustomed to gather before sunrise on a fixed day of the week, and sing alternately "a hymn to Christ as though to God." In the age of the Apologists the worship of Jesus was viewed by the heathen as a mark of Christian faith, and in the immediately following generations the practice of men like Irenæus and Tertullian does not admit of question. Facts like these, which Loofs enumerates, justify his temperately expressed conclusion that we ought to consider the invocation of Christ "as an inherited

[1] Zahn, *Skizzen aus dem Leben der alten Kirche*², 271 ff.

custom prevailing in all, or at least all non-Ebionitic, churches of the post-apostolic age." "This custom," he adds, "shows more clearly than any incipient Christological speculation, that to the believers of the time from which we have to set out Christ belonged to the sphere of God. And this is the root from which sprang the development of the Christological dogma."[1]

How far this religious estimate of Christ took the shape of ascribing to Him the predicate θεός is uncertain.[2] One gathers generally that the divinity of our Lord, for the most part expressed in practical terms, was a recognised fact among Christians in the second century. For the Christian mind at large He was both God and man, though certain Jewish-Christian groups may have scrupled to use the decided language of their fellows. Many, however, were content to believe in "one God, one Lord," without in the least impairing their monotheism, or pushing reflection beyond the stage of naive faith.

In this transition period of the sub-apostolic age there were, according to Harnack, two main streams of Christological reflection. "Jesus," he writes, "was either regarded as the man whom God has chosen, in whom the Godhead or the Spirit of God has dwelt, and who, after testing, was adopted by God and invested with dominion (Adoptian Christology); or He ranked as a heavenly spiritual being (or the highest after God), who took flesh, and went back to heaven again after completing His work on earth (pneumatic Christology)."[3] Hermas, he argues, is a clear example of the former point of view, which was later declared heretical; Barnabas, Clement, Ignatius, Polycarp illustrate the latter. Harnack himself tends more recently to modify this sharp distinction. Loofs, indeed, had urged that both Christologies, to the limited extent in which they are correctly formulated, go back rather to the

[1] *Op. cit.* 22.

[2] παῖς θεοῦ was a common title; cf. *1 Clem.*, and *Didache*, c. 9 and 10. It at least expressed the belief that His connection with God was of a unique kind.

[3] See *History of Dogma* (Eng. tr.), i. 190 ff.

primitive two-sided estimate of Christ *κατὰ σάρκα* and *κατὰ πνεῦμα*. This he traces to Ro 1[3f.], and considers to be the most ancient and most widely spread of all Christological formulas. It meant that Christ was contemplated alternately on the side of His natural and His supernatural being, without any effort to determine to which the personal subject in Him belonged. There is much that is attractive and illuminating in this suggestion, though it will not cover all the facts. But in spite of the rudimentary character of early Christological ideas, they rested on quite definite convictions. Gospel traditions kept men aware that the self-consciousness of the historic Jesus had been more than human, while His post-resurrection appearances, due to His own direct agency, supplied a final proof of His supramundane nature. Ebionism had little influence in the wider life of the Church. No one of course operated with ideas like the modern "personality"; but it was never doubted that the "Spirit" present in Jesus was essentially Divine and pre-existent, nor would the suggestion that Jesus was a man who had *become* God have been understood at this time. He was always viewed as both things—heavenly Divine Spirit, and true man who had suffered and died. In prayers and hymns He was worshipped along with God the Father.

§ 2. *The Apostolic Fathers.*—We shall gain a clearer view of this common faith by examining data presented in the writings of the so-called Apostolic Fathers, from the year 90 to 140. Ignatius apart, we find that the rest exhibit a striking variety of ideas. All start, as the New Testament does, from the historic Christ, who is identified with the exalted Lord. He is the perfect revelation of God, His servant, His beloved; or again, it is said that God "chose" Him. It is agreed that He existed before His birth in a state of glory and power, and Clement of Rome (about 95) calls Him "the sceptre of the majesty of God," and declares that His coming to earth was a willing self-abasement (c. 16). From the beginning He was Lord of all things, by Him the world was created, God took counsel with Him at the creation of man.[1] On the whole His eternal prior existence was simply assumed, for it was felt that One to whom men appealed in prayer could not be the creature of time. Such ideas of pre-existence must not be confused with those current in Judaism.

One point has caused difficulty. When we read in *2 Clement* (c. 9): "Christ the Lord who saved us, being first spirit, then became flesh," or in *Hermas* (S. 5, 6): "The holy pre-existent Spirit, which created the whole creation, God made to dwell in flesh that He desired," are we to say that the pre-existent Christ is being identified with the Holy Spirit? Baur, Harnack, Loofs[2] and others have maintained this, but in his last edition Seeberg puts forward strong reasons for denying it, and appositely cites St. Paul's identification of the Lord with the Spirit in 2 Co 3[17], although his general practice of differentiating them is quite plain.[3] But in any case we are entitled to affirm that at this stage the dogmatic distinction had not been worked out. Christ is Spirit, or Holy Spirit, by His very essence; as Spirit He is one with God, and of the same nature. It is even said that His sufferings were the sufferings of God.[4] Not that we are to import a Nicæan significance in these phrases. Alongside of the unity of the Son with God goes an emphasis upon His subordination that would scarcely have been possible two centuries later. This was due to inherited ideas about Jesus' Divine mission, His life of obedience and trust, and His return to the Father. Indeed there are parts of *Hermas* where, to secure definiteness of outline, Christ is represented as an angel or lofty spirit, though passages may also be quoted of a different tenor.

When Jesus is called Son of God, in literature of this

[1] *Barnabas*, c. 5.

[2] Loofs calls this Binitarian Monotheism, and thinks that it commended itself by falling in conveniently with the κατὰ σάρκα–κατὰ πνεῦμα formula.

[3] *Lehrbuch d. Dogmengeschichte*[2], i. 98.

[4] *1 Clem.* c. 2.

period, the name "is connected more especially with the human life by which it was manifested."[1] Hence we cannot assume, as we might later, that "Son" *per se* implies a personal relation of the personal factor in Christ to or in the Father. But although speculation was not yet busied with the point, incipient tokens of it are traceable in *Hermas*, who certainly names the pre-existent Christ by the title Son (S. 9[12]). How close the relation between the Son and the Father was conceived to be, may be seen from the opening words of *2 Clement*: "Brethren, we ought so to think of Jesus Christ, as of God, as of the Judge of quick and dead." It was possible, in short, to accentuate either His Divine unity with, or His personal distinction from, the Father.

As regards the entrance of Christ into human life, two streams of reflection are observable. On the one hand, the pre-existent Son of God, it is taught, joined Himself to the man Jesus, making him thus God's Servant, and as Spirit pervading and energising all the workings of the flesh. The man Jesus is but as it were the form and vehicle of the (Christ) Spirit—a view, obviously, with a certain leaning towards dualism. Traces of it may be found in *Hermas* and *Barnabas*. The other line of reflection conceives Christ to have *become* man, exchanging one form of being for another; and this may be illustrated from *2 Clement*, and particularly from the letters of Ignatius. It permitted men to predicate now Divine and now human properties of the one Christ. Certain advocates of the former view, it is possible, held that the union between the Son of God and the man Jesus took place at His baptism—an idea which had been maintained by groups of Jewish Christians, and formed part of the philosophical theory elaborated by Cerinthus in the interests of docetism (Iren. 1. 26). But for this period it would be a mistake to insist on this distinction.

§ 3. *Ignatius.*—When we turn to the attractive

[1] Swete, *The Apostles' Creed*, 29.

personality of Ignatius, the martyr bishop of Antioch, it is to one in whose thoughts and life Jesus Christ formed the inspiring centre. His letters (written before 117) reveal an almost apostolic sense of Jesus' person as a whole, and have left a deep mark on later Christology. "Nowhere else," Dr. Sanday has remarked, "have we the idea of the fulness of Godhead revealed in Christ grasped and expressed with so much vigour."[1] His ideas are Johannine in the main. In perfervid language he sets forth Christ, again and again, as the Revealer of God and the Eternal Head of a race of redeemed men. "Jesus Christ, our inseparable life, is the mind of the Father,"[2] "the unerring mouth in whom the Father hath spoken."[3] He starts from the historic Christ, now exalted and impassible, and dwells with great emphasis on the reality of His earthly career, pointing in turn to His birth, baptism, sufferings, death, descent into Hades, and resurrection.[4] "Ignatius," it has been said, "is the great teacher of the sacramental significance of the incidents of the incarnate life,"[5] and just for this reason his anti-docetism is pronounced. "He suffered truly," he writes to the Smyrnæans, "as also He raised Himself truly; not as certain unbelievers say, that He suffered in semblance, being themselves mere semblance."[6] One or two passages are singularly like the second article of the Apostles' Creed. A strong and keen sense of history comes out. It was because the disciples "touched" Christ that they were able to despise death.[7] Flesh, in the view of Ignatius, belongs to Christ's nature permanently, even in heaven. The whole value of Christianity would perish with the denial that He came into a genuinely human life. This is maintained vehemently against all who professed to give a purer and more spiritual theory. Far from concealing, Ignatius rather glories in the paradoxes and

[1] *Criticism of the Fourth Gospel*, 244. [2] *Eph.* 3. [3] *Rom.* 8.

[4] Cf. *Trall.* 9, where, as Lightfoot says, the word "truly" is repeated again and again as "a watchword against docetism."

[5] Ottley, *Doct. of the Incarnation*, vol. i. 164. [6] 2. [7] *Smyr.* 3.

antitheses of Christ's being; they are cardinal to the salvation He brings. "There is one only physician," he writes in a classic passage, "of flesh and of spirit, generate and ingenerate, God in man, true life in death, Son of Mary and Son of God, first passible and then impassible."[1] Neither aspect can be dispensed with; whatever the verbal tension, the idea must somehow be put in words that God has appeared in, or as, man; the Eternal in time. The union of these two sides, in a vitally indissociable union, is the hall-mark of Ignatian Christology.

It is also implied that the relation of Jesus Christ to the Father is of a unique kind. In Him have been manifested things wrought in the ancient silence of God and perfected in His counsels.[2] Christ is a revelation less of the reason than of the saving will of the Father; for although Ignatius employs the term λόγος, it is scarcely with a technical significance. And this revelation was given, not in His words merely, but in His silent deeds, or, to be more exact, through His inmost self and personality. From this point of view a glance is given to His filial subordination: "the Lord did nothing without the Father," "as Jesus Christ was to the Father, be obedient to the bishop and to one another."[3] Elsewhere He is said to have been an imitator of the Father,[4] and there is a reference to His faith and love.[5] But the writer does not insist on this. The fulness of Christ's relation to God is everywhere expressed by the term "Son." For Ignatius, no doubt, as for St. John, the primary reference of this title is to the historic Lord, now crowned with glory. In virtue of His immaculate birth Christ is Son of Man and Son of God,

[1] *Eph.* 7. The Apostolic Fathers, as Professor Gwatkin has put it (*Studies of Arianism*, 6), "scarcely seem to see the difficulty of reconciling divinity with suffering—for this rather than the Resurrection was the stumbling-block of their time. 'If He suffered,' said the Ebionites, 'He was not Divine.' 'If He was Divine,' answered the Docetists, 'His sufferings were unreal.' The sub-Apostolic Fathers were content to reply that He was Divine and that He truly suffered, without attempting to explain the difficulty."

[2] *Eph.* 19. [3] *Mag.* 7. 13. [4] *Phil.* 7. [5] *Eph.* 20.

with descent through Mary from David and through the Holy Spirit from God. But I am not convinced by Zahn's careful argument that the name "Son" is essentially and exclusively relative to the miraculous birth in the flesh.[1] If we take such phrases as "Jesus Christ, who was with the Father before the worlds,"[2] "Jesus Christ His Son, who is His word that proceeded from silence,"[3] or, still more relevantly, a description like "Jesus Christ, who came forth from One Father and is with One and departed unto One";[4] if we consider that no other designation is available for the pre-existent One, since "Logos" is used quite untechnically, I cannot but feel that—since Fatherhood and Sonship are essentially correlative for him as for the writers of the New Testament—Ignatius also carries "Son" backward into the eternal sphere. His view will then be that "the Eternal Son of God became man, when God created for Him through Mary a human life, namely the life of the historic Son."[5] But however this may be, it is agreed that Christ is presented as pre-existent on the Divine or "pneumatic" side of His being. Not indeed that Ignatius knows anything of the later doctrine of eternal generation, for he uses the epithet "ingenerate" of Christ in His higher being.[6] But the Subject of the historic life had been as God before He "appeared in the likeness of man."[7] We also find in Ignatius the authentically New Testament idea that it was after the resurrection that the Saviour's nature was fully manifested: "our Lord Jesus Christ," he writes, "being in the Father, is the more plainly visible."[8]

In what sense is the predicate "God" applied to Christ in these letters? For it is frequently so applied in moments of deep feeling, even by a writer whose monotheism is emphatic. There are phrases like "Jesus Christ, our God," "the blood of God," and "the pas-

[1] *Ignatius von Antiochien*, 469.
[2] *Mag.* 6.
[3] *Mag.* 8.
[4] *Mag.* 7.
[5] Seeberg, *op. cit.* i. 101.
[6] *Eph.* 7.
[7] *Ibid.* 19.
[8] *Rom.* 3.

sion of my God."[1] The entire content of Ignatius' thought of God is drawn from Christ: he sees the two merged in one. Moreover, functions and honours of a specifically Divine character are ascribed to Christ, such as the knowledge of our secret heart, the power to awaken penitence, to raise up prophets, to care in love for His Church. His relation to the Christian is that of in-dwelling: He is "our never-failing life," union with whom, especially in the Eucharist, is *eo ipso* union with the Father. True, Ignatius makes no effort to construct a set theory of the incarnate person. But it is flying in the face of the actual data to say that for him "God" in this relation is "only a pregnant expression of the fact that in Christ God is grasped and held as eternal salvation,"[2] if by this is meant that he speaks of the Lord's deity merely in value-judgments. The simple fact is that for Ignatius Christ was identical, personally one, with the highest in the highest realm he knew. Christ's life was the human life of God, His coming the renewal of humanity through the union of God with man. He repeats in other words the simple religious modalism of St. John, but he does so without prejudice to more definite formulations of the truth. The one certain thing is that Christ is truly God and man, no less one than the other.

Ignatius nobly represents the living Christological faith of which theology is but the systematised exposition, and the insistent claims of which have ruined many a theory. In a sense, the thread might well be taken up to-day where he dropped it; at all events his pages are extraordinarily modern, and the passion in his words keeps, and will always keep, his thought fresh and vital. In no sense a writer of intellectual power, he cuts his way to ultimate realities by sheer energy of faith. It is because Jesus Christ has mediated to him eternal life through knowledge of the true God that he names Him the Divine Son. Himself little of a theologian, he exhibits the first

[1] Athanasius later rejected such expressions as unscriptural.

[2] von der Goltz, *Ignatius v. Antiochien als Christ u. Theologe*, 25–26.

stirrings of theological interest in the post-apostolic age; and already, it is clear, faith and Christ are bound up together. Belief in God and in Christ are the same thing in different aspects.

§ 4. *The Gnostic Christology.*—Ignatius lived and wrote in full view of Gnostic speculation. More and more it is being felt that Gnosticism—an atmosphere rather than a system—is more easily comprehensible in the light of the general history of religion than as a form of Christianity. Looming on the horizon by the year 60, it became really dangerous in the first half of the second century, striving as it did to capture the Gospel for the philosophy of the age. The Church was to be turned into a mystery-society or a speculative school. At the root of all Gnostic systems—and they are legion [1]—lay the idea of redemption, and the conviction that it was to be won by a rare kind of knowledge.[2] In a way, Christ was made the centre of all. Not only so; at first sight it might appear as if the Gnostics were engaged in a more serious and impressive effort to construe the person of the Lord than their orthodox assailants. But, on the one hand, their Christology was incurably docetic. Partly owing to the accepted metaphysical opposition of spirit and matter, partly through a tendency to see in all things earthly a mystic allegory of great cosmic redeeming processes, His life in flesh was dissolved in unreal appearance. Valentinus says that Jesus did not eat or drink like other men, and that He passed through Mary merely as a channel. By some His birth was totally denied, and of course the same principle, when applied to His death on the cross, robbed it of the value of a real passion. On the other hand, the distinctive feature in Gnosticism was its sharp separation between a Christ who is not truly human

[1] On the many shades of Gnostic Christology, see a valuable note in Seeberg, *op. cit.* i. 238.

[2] What Christ does for men is to reveal transcendent secrets, though there are more mystical suggestions.

and a Jesus who is not Divine. "Christ" is an Aeon who, being "a wonderful concentration of the light and virtue of the Pleroma," or hierarchical Divine cosmos, has come down and joined Himself somehow to the Messiah of the Demiurge, Jesus, that He may infuse a higher mysterious knowledge into receptive souls, thus rescuing for the supernal world nobler elements previously immersed in matter. The union of Christ and Jesus, some held, began at the baptism in the Jordan, and terminated just before death, the precise moment of separation being signalised by the cry: "Father, into Thy hands I commend My spirit." Basilides taught that Simon of Cyrene was crucified in Jesus' room. Thus Christ is to be sought behind, not in, the personality of Jesus.

That Christian ideas enter into this construction is of course not to be denied. The central significance of Christ is vigorously affirmed, and, so far as concerns practical religion, Harnack is probably right in saying that to the majority of Gnostics Christ was a Spirit, consubstantial with the Father.[1] His person, His teaching, His career were recognised as an in-breaking of supreme remedial energies from above. Yet a believing instinct led the Church past the danger. Apart from the docetic taint, apart from the indifference to history as also from the fact that Gnosticism turns on cosmic rather than ethical ideas, it was not even certain after all whether the Redeemer came from the highest God or not. He came out of the Pleroma, but was not His divinity such as might be predicated of many Aeons, all less than God and more than man? Ambiguity on this point disqualified Gnosticism as a substitute for a faith that clung to history, and in that history found very God. At the same time Gnosticism wakened up the Church to more strenuous reflection, and drove orthodoxy from a bare assertion of historic facts, though it cannot be said that the spokesmen of the faith altogether succeeded in avoiding or

[1] *History of Dogma*, i. 260. It is worth noting that ὁμοούσιος τῷ πατρί is originally a Gnostic phrase.

surmounting the dualism which heresy had thus so plainly taught.

Echoes of Gnostic Christology came later from Marcion (died about 165). He maintained that the good God—in contradistinction from the Demiurge who had made the world—took pity upon men, and that in the fifteenth year of the Emperor Tiberius Christ Jesus came down from heaven as a saving spirit (*spiritus salutaris*), assumed a phantasmal body, and, as manifesting the highest God, began to preach in the synagogue at Capernaum. But his doctrine has curious inconsistencies. He may have identified Christ with the good God; in that direction lay all his religious interests. Yet at times there is a clear distinction. And it is remarkable that, with all his docetism, to which the idea of human birth or growth is intolerable, he yet attaches a high value to the crucifixion inflicted on Christ by the Demiurge. Here also the Church felt that the faith of the Incarnation is evaporated in unhistoric fancies.

§ 5. *The Apostles' Creed.*—Moving out into a wider field, let us now observe the profound influence exerted by the earliest forms of what is known as the Apostles' Creed.[1] The present Latin text goes back only to the eighth century, or possibly to the sixth; but its main contents can be traced much farther, and scholars describe it as the Gallican recension of the shorter Roman symbol, that is, the symbol used in the Church of Rome from the third century onwards, and venerated there as an apostolic heirloom. There is virtual agreement that the original Greek text of this Baptismal Creed was in existence before 150; how long before is still disputed. Kattenbusch makes Rome its birthplace about 100, Harnack about 150; Zahn and Loofs, more or less following Caspari, look for its origin to Asia Minor, and date it somewhere in the period 100–130. We are not concerned here with the details of the problem; and interesting as are the variations in

[1] Cf. Loofs, *Leitfaden*[4], 87–88.

the earliest Greek and Latin forms, they are of no religious importance.[1] But we should note the triadic terms in which the Christian faith is henceforward expressed. From this time on the Church professed a knowledge of God, and taught it to her catechumens, which grasps Him as Father, Son and Holy Spirit. Without this the Christian faith in God cannot be put in words; the God of redeeming power and truth is these three in unity.

The second article of the Apostles' Creed, according to our most ancient source, Marcellus of Ancyra, is as follows:—

(Πιστεύω εἰς θεὸν παντοκράτορα·) καὶ εἰς Χριστὸν Ἰησοῦν, τὸν υἱὸν αὐτοῦ τὸν μονογενῆ, τὸν κύριον ἡμῶν, τὸν γεννηθέντα ἐκ πνεύματος ἁγίου καὶ Μαρίας τῆς παρθένου, τὸν ἐπὶ Ποντίου Πιλάτου σταυρωθέντα καὶ ταφέντα καὶ τῇ τρίτῃ ἡμέρᾳ ἀναστάντα ἐκ τῶν νεκρῶν, ἀναβάντα εἰς τοὺς οὐρανοὺς καὶ καθήμενον ἐν δεξιᾷ τοῦ πατρός, ὅθεν ἔρχεται κρίνειν ζῶντας καὶ νεκρούς.[2]

This is obviously a commixture of supernatural and historic facts, with virtually no commentary or interpretation. And history is insisted on because the Church stood confronted with a reasoned docetism, and found its most powerful weapon of defence in a simple recital of the facts of Christ's career. The truth is, we owe the article just quoted, not to any desire to exhibit Jesus Christ as a marvellous Divine being, but to an instinct for the Redeemer's true humanity. Hence the enumeration of the main points of His life, from a real birth—human though miraculous—through passion, death, burial, and

[1] This is true even of the question whether "only" (*μονογενῆ, unicum*) or "our Lord" stood in the original texts of the first clause of the second article. Such details may be studied in Hahn, *Bibliothek der Symbole u. Glaubensregeln der alten Kirche*[3], 22 ff.

[2] Hahn, § 17. The conjectural reconstruction of the Old Roman Symbol (R), given by Professor McGiffert (*Apostles' Creed*, 100), differs from the text given above only in minor details, which do not seriously modify the sense.

resurrection, to His present session in glory and future coming as Judge of the world.

It is illegitimate, however, to suggest that all this human simplicity covers and necessitates no higher implications. Is the term "(only-begotten) Son," for example, applied to Christ merely in an immanent sense, in a heightened mode of the epithet as used in the Old Testament? Or does it carry a transcendent signification, indicative of a Sonship which lies beyond the bounds of time? The latter view is distinctly the more probable. That the name "Son" has its point of departure in the earthly life of Christ is no reason for limiting it to that life. We have seen ground for believing that the wider usage is illustrated in the New Testament; and as regards the Apostles' Creed, there can be no doubt that previous and contemporary writers name God "Father" not relatively to the created world merely, but with special reference to Jesus Christ. In Hermas, in the Epistle to Diognetus, in Barnabas, in Ignatius, God is *essentially* Father. Moreover, belief in the pre-existence of the Divine in Christ, if not universal by the middle of the second century, was very widespread. Finally, there is the verbal arrangement of the Creed itself. The first two articles answer to each other. "Can it be believed," asks Dr. Swete, "that *Patrem* in the first clause of the Creed has no prospective reference to *Filium* in the second?"[1] On the initial mention of the Father follows that of His "Son"; and He, after being designated by His historic name, is first put in relation to God by the adjective "only-begotten," and next in relation to Christians by the title "Lord." Only as supramundane in being could He be worshipped absolutely as Lord of men, and by parity of reasoning only in virtue of a pre-mundane and pre-historic relationship could He be absolutely "Son" of God. After this solemn appellation, the article proceeds to affirm His entrance into human life, and to detail the items of His life-story.

[1] *The Apostles' Creed*, 23.

Son of God from before all time, He became man through the action of the Holy Ghost upon the Virgin Mary. Not even here, as some have thought, is Christ designated "Son" exclusively in consequence of the Spirit's operation. He who was born was the child Jesus, and in Him the pre-existent "Son" became flesh.[1]

We need not here review the specific points which the article cites from the life-experience of Christ. The anti-docetic trend of the whole is manifest. Thus it is the *reality* of our Lord's birth, even more than its unique character, upon which emphasis is laid. The curiously definite statement that the crucifixion occurred under Pontius Pilate goes back, probably, to the early creed of some local church;[2] but its inclusion proves that the primary interest of the authors of the Creed was in facts. Whether the prominent reference to the Ascension is or is not a departure from the oldest teaching (and here Harnack scarcely appears to have proved his case), is a question of no great importance. In any case the transcendent place occupied by Christ is sufficiently indicated by the assertions that He is now at the right hand of God, and will come thence in judgment.

[1] Cf. Seeberg, *op. cit.* i. 180.

[2] Cf. 1 Ti 6[13].

CHAPTER II.

BEGINNINGS OF THE CHRISTOLOGICAL DOGMA.

§ 1. *The Apologists.*—The Greek Apologists of the second century (the most important names are Aristides, Justin Martyr, Theophilus, and Athenagoras) offer a striking contrast to the mental attitude revealed in the Apostles' Creed. Instead of a plain recital of facts, they proposed, as Christian philosophers, to give a rendering of the ideas of the Gospel in the scientific or speculative language of the day. In Christ they possessed what philosophy is ever seeking, and the higher knowledge given by the new faith they now strove to make explicit in a defensive statement of Christianity. And one idea or formula which they used to set forth the dignity of Christ's Person affected later theology to its depths. This was the philosophical conception of the Logos, a speculative deposit of varied systems. The Apologists carried over this elastic idea with them from older studies, and in their writings we see the attempt being made to combine it with the conviction, native to the believing mind, that Christ is θεός, as well as the consciousness that in point of fact they found themselves instinctively paying Him Divine honour.

For the mind of that age, be it remembered, the Logos summed up all the Divine forces energising in the worlds of nature and spirit. It was "a formula capable of

Literature—Engelhardt, *Das Christentum Justins*, 1878; Holland, article "Justinus," in *Dict. of Chr. Biog.*; Flemming, *Zur Beurteilung des Christentums Justins*, 1893; Kunze, *Die Gotteslehre des Irenaeus*, 1891; Harnack, article "Monarchianismus," in *RE.* xiii.; Zahn, *Marcellus von Ancyra*, 1867; Stier, *Die Gottes- und Logoslehre Tertullians*, 1899; Fairbairn, *Christ in Modern Theology*, 1893.

expressing the transcendent and unchangeable nature of God on the one hand, and on the other His fulness of creative and spiritual powers."[1] The current conception of God being utterly abstract and transcendent, a mediator was required to bring Him in contact with the world, and this function only the Logos could fulfil. To the Apologists, then, He is in His distinct or personal being a product of the Father's will (*ἔργον πρωτοτόκον τοῦ πατρός*), though eternally immanent as a principle in God, who has never been *ἄλογος*. In due time He came forth in order to create all things, "begotten from the Father, by His power and will, but not by abscission, as if the essence of the Father were divided."[2] Numerically distinct from the Father,[3] He is yet one with Him in will. In virtue of His origin He is subordinate to the highest God, but He may be called a second God, and ought to be worshipped. Finite in His own being, since there was a time when He began to be, He forms the natural organ of revelation to the finite. Lastly, He has appeared in Christ, not in part merely but completely. In Christ the new law of freedom has been set forth in its entirety, but the Logos had previously been operative in the prophets of the Old Testament and even in heathen sages. He alone is properly to be called Son.[4]

Except Justin, none of the Apologists bestows any particular attention upon the doctrine of Incarnation. The older idea that the union of Divine and human in Christ took place at the Baptism is not found in his pages; instead, he speaks of Jesus the Christ, "being of old the Logos . . . now by the will of God having become man for the human race";[5] and in one passage goes so far into detail as to affirm that "Christ, the whole Logos, who appeared for our sakes, became alike body and reason and soul."[6] This emphasis upon the presence of the whole

[1] Harnack, *History of Dogma*, ii. 207.
[2] Justin Martyr, *Dialog. c. Tryph.* c. 128.
[3] ἀριθμῷ ἕτερόν τι.
[4] *Apol.* ii. 6.
[5] *Ibid.* i. 63; cf. 23.
[6] *Ibid.* ii. 10.

Logos in the Saviour is characteristic of Justin, and forms the implicit ground upon which he goes in declaring roundly that Christ is "God and man." It is a plausible view which finds in him the first faint beginnings of the "two-natures" doctrine, so influential in later centuries; at all events in his contemporary Melito of Sardes there is a clear allusion to the "two substances" in Christ. According to Justin, the Logos (who even as pre-incarnate is designated Christ) came down from heaven as a Spirit [1] and made Himself one with the flesh conceived of Mary. He asserts, indeed, that the Spirit and power of God mentioned by St. Luke is just the Logos Himself, so that Jesus' humanity may be described as the creation or product of the indwelling Logos. Yet Jesus grew up like other men, using the proper means of growth, and assigning to each stage of the development that which befitted it. The risen and exalted Lord will hereafter judge the world; meanwhile His reign from heaven gives victory to His people over demons and all evil powers.

There are indications in Justin that unorthodox views regarding Christ's higher being were not always felt to involve the forfeiture of the Christian name. And this is intelligible when we recollect that for him Christ's Saviourhood mainly consisted in His having taught monotheism and a new morality. "Becoming man according to His will, He instructed us in these things for the conversion and restoration of the human race." [2]

All this has value rather as testifying to the profound impression made by Christ on a mind determined to be philosophic than as a reasoned Christological scheme. In particular, the introduction of the Logos-conception was a dubious expedient, and before long it was to prove itself a weapon which men grasped only by the blade. It is little wonder, indeed, that an idea with so imposing a history should thus have been captured for Christian

[1] Terms are not infrequently employed which seem to identify the Logos and the Spirit.

[2] *Apol.* i. 23.

service. In terms St. John had seemed to authorise its Christian usage; by its suggestion at once of plurality and unity it served to convey the truth that Christ is God, while yet God is one; and its emphasis on the pre-existence of Christ gave credibility to faith's conviction that all things good, fair, and true flow, and have ever flowed, from Him. But in this world fallible men seldom act rightly without mixing their right with wrong. It was so now. In St. John the term Logos is obviously defined by relation to the more fundamental "Son"; it is secondary and interpretative, more particularly for a specific audience, while "Son" is primary, because rooted in the fruitful depths of history. In the Apologists this relation is turned the other way. Here "Logos" comes on the scene with a settled independent meaning of its own; it stands for the vast diffused world-reason; its antecedents are metaphysical, not historical; and from the outset it is capable of being analysed and explicated quite apart from the Jesus of the Gospels. In this case cosmology, not soteriology, gives tone to the discussion; Christ is before all things the Logos, rather than the Son, of God. Thus the mind of the Church, in its Christological reflection, was encouraged to move by *à priori* lines of deduction from the pre-existent Divine Reason downwards to the world, rather than upwards, by intuition, from the experience of souls redeemed through union with a historic person. If Justin could describe the Logos as "a certain rational power," then the personal colour which the believing consciousness insists upon in all categories that concern Jesus Christ vanishes, and the door is opened wide to ideas so mechanical and unethical as to be incongruous with New Testament conceptions of the being and life of God. Further, if the Logos be defined as *caused* by God, it becomes plain that the subordination which, in one sense, is an authentically New Testament idea, is on the point of passing into essential dualism and inferiority. So that in certain ways Justin may be said to have anticipated Arius, as moving too much on the same cosmological plane. And when Athanasius came to the discussion a century later, he was forced to put the Logos Christology aside. On the other hand, it was particularly easy to explain it in a Sabellian sense.[1] Thus a review of the work of the Apologists more than half inclines one to acquiesce in Loofs' verdict: "Their doctrine of the Logos is not a 'higher' Christology than the common one; it falls short of the genuinely Christian estimate of Christ. It is not God that manifests Himself in Christ, but the Logos, a depotentiated God, a God who *as God* is subordinate to God Most High."[2]

But while Justin's formulas thus led him to contrast fatally the Father and the Logos, the conception he was endeavouring to express was in no sense disloyal to Christ. More than once he protests against being accused of worshipping a mere man. Christ, the Logos, is the true Son of God, and has His place essentially in the sphere of the Creator.

§ 2. *Irenæus.*—Irenæus, a native of Asia Minor, and bishop of Lyons at his death in or near 200, wrote a great work, *Adversus Hæreses*, about the year 185. The influence upon his mind of the Asia Minor tradition is shown in a ruling tendency to keep to the *via media* of normal Christian thinking, and eschew bold speculations on the inner life of Godhead. Gnostic or Apologist views of the emanation of the Word, expressed in terms of a material hue, were especially distasteful to him. For no one

[1] On the two wrong roads down which men might be led by the Logos Christology, see a luminous note in Rainy's *Ancient Catholic Church*, 205. Elsewhere he says (203) of the term "Logos": "For the domestic interests of the faith, the use of this word is not indispensable. The Church has framed all her great creeds without employing it." "If Christianity had depended on the Logos," writes Mr. Glover (*Conflict of Religions*, 303–4), "it would have followed the Logos to the limbo whither went Aeon and Aporrhoia and Spermaticos Logos. But that the Logos has not perished is due to the one fact that it has been borne through the ages on the shoulders of Jesus."

[2] *Leitfaden* [4], 129. Dr. Sanday (*Christologies Ancient and Modern*, 14–21) puts the other side persuasively.

understands how the Son is brought forth by the Father; His birth, by the nature of the case, is ineffable (*generatio inenarrabilis*).[1] Gnosticism, in opposition to which Irenæus puts forth all his strength, has made it necessary to reassert the unity and simplicity of God, but though God be inscrutable (here Irenæus agrees with his adversaries), it is His will to reveal Himself savingly to men. As Logos, indeed, He has always been manifested in the world, first through the prophets, finally in Christ His Son. "Through the Word Himself, who had become visible and palpable, was the Father shown forth; all saw the Father in the Son: *for the Father is the invisible of the Son, but the Son the visible of the Father.*"[2] Alongside of the modalism of such expressions are found some faint suggestions of a Kenotic view: "Well spake he," we read, "who said that the unmeasurable Father was Himself subjected to measure in the Son; for the Son is the measure of the Father, since He also comprehends Him."[3] And again: "For this cause the incomprehensible and boundless and invisible One made Himself seen and apprehended and comprehended by those who believe, that He might vivify such as receive and behold Him by faith."[4] There is a revelational identity of Christ and God.

Irenæus starts from the historic Jesus, the God-man, not from the cosmic Logos, and his central problem is: Why did Christ descend?[5] In any case, Christ *is* the Logos in human guise, with an eternal personal pre-existence lying behind His earthly career. But it is fruitless toil to build up theories of His origin from or in God, whether as a preparatory approach to creation or otherwise. To him as to Ignatius the pre-historic One is unbegotten (ἀγέννητος), and in one place he visits with grave censure those "who transfer the generation of a word uttered by men to the eternal Word of God, assigning to Him a beginning of emergence and a genesis."[6]

[1] *adv. Haer.* ii. 28. 6.
[2] iv. 6. 6.
[3] iv. 4. 2.
[4] iv. 20. 5.
[5] ii. 14. 7.
[6] ii. 13. 8.

With equal energy he protests against the Gnostic differentiation of the Logos and the man Jesus. The Redeemer's person is rather the abiding unity of God with man. The Divine in Christ he names "Son," apparently, when it is desired to bring out His relation to the Father, but "Logos," quite in the manner of the Fourth Gospel, when He is contemplated as the great revelation, the Word or Voice of God, making Him apprehensible.

For Irenæus the work of Christ and His person are one organically, and we gain light upon each from the study of both together. Humanity, we are told, lies in sin and death. In Christ this fallen race is saved, not by mere teaching or enlightenment, but in the deeper fashion of what a modern would call personal identification.[1] In His infinite love He was made as we are in order that He might make us to be as He is. Our fleshly and corruptible nature is, as it were, fused or inoculated with Deity, and so made immortal. What we lost in the first Adam, we recovered in Christ the second Adam;[2] for as we become partakers of the Divine nature, union with incorruption confers on us salvation from corruptibility. In other words, Christ saves by gathering the entire race into Himself and suffusing it with His Spirit. Physical terms are used freely, but it would be a mistake to imagine that Irenæus takes redemption to be a purely unethical or material process. On the contrary, for all the weight laid upon the advent of Christ, as in itself redemptorial, it is explained clearly that the Incarnate One had still a *work* to do, which invested His life on earth with real soteriological meaning. He passed through every age of human life;[3] perfect as He was, He became an infant like the rest of mankind, He faced temptation, He bowed Himself to the last suffering of death. Nor is Irenæus without a real interest in our

[1] On the central idea of *recapitulatio* (ἀνακεφαλαίωσις), cf. Seeberg, *op. cit.* i. 325 ff., Bethune-Baker, *Early History of Christian Doctrine*, 333 ff., and Ottley, *Doct. of the Incarnation*, i. 219–21.

[2] iii. 18. 1.

[3] ii. 22. 4.

Lord's moral growth. Doubtless a note of dualism is audible in his statement that the Logos remained quiescent, in order that Christ might be capable of being tempted.[1] Still, incarnation is taken to imply a human soul as well as a body; Christ was no mere human frame inhabited by a higher Divine presence. And on the whole we may say that for Irenæus, as for St. John, the same subject is both Logos and man. "He insists," says Mr. Bethune-Baker, "that it is one and the same person—Jesus Christ—the Logos—the Son of God—who created the world, was born as man, and suffered and ascended to heaven, still man as well as God."[2] He is the meeting-place of Creator and creature: *commixtio et communio dei et hominis secundum placitum patris facta est.*[3] Irenæus is certainly more successful than Justin in getting the idea expressed that in Christ very God Himself has come to us, for with a modalism slightly more conscious and theoretical than that of Ignatius, he tends to construe the Logos not as somehow a portion of the Godhead, much less a second inferior God, but as God Himself breaking forth in revelation.

The main conceptions in this impressive scheme go back, through Ignatius, to the Fourth Gospel. Neither the deity nor the personality of the Son could be dispensed with. But this position naturally raised more questions than it solved. Might this idea of a God-man not imperil the unity of God, not perhaps in a way resembling Gnosticism, but after the debasing fashion of pagan polytheisms? Must not the God who appeared on earth be reckoned a secondary God, somehow numerically different from the Lord of all things? These were salient points of doubt and controversy to which the Monarchians were to call attention.

§ 3. *Monarchianism.*—Can belief in a real incarnation be reconciled with the fundamental Christian certainty that God is one? This, at bottom, was the question

[1] iii. 19. 3. [2] *Op. cit.* 131. [3] iv. 20. 4.

agitated by two modes of thought which began to make themselves felt near the close of the second century, and which resemble the older Ebionism and Docetism on a higher plane. The first of these tendencies endangered Christ's divinity, the second His distinction from the Father; and the conflict lasted rather more than a century. Both go under the name Monarchianism, though of very different types. The name was drawn from their insistence on the unity of principle in God (*μοναρχία*), and it was a cardinal point with them to deny all personal distinctions in the Divine Being. From Tertullian we can see that they were able to make a very strong appeal to simple-hearted members of the Church.

(1) *Dynamic Monarchianism.*[1]—This, the more rationalist of the two views, made its first appearance in the West. Somewhere between 189 and 199 a certain leather-merchant from Byzantium, by name Theodotus,[2] taught Dynamism at Rome, and was excommunicated by the bishop Victor. On the ground that God was strictly unipersonal, he held Jesus to be a man abnormal only in being born of a virgin, though distinguished from others by exceptional holiness and fidelity. At baptism He was filled with a Divine influence or power (*δύναμις*, hence the name Dynamic), and exalted after the resurrection as "Divine." He revealed God the Father, and may therefore be styled His Son and worshipped. But this creed of the Theodoti, Artemon, and their sympathisers is not what we to-day should call humanitarianism. If not a personal and pre-existent Logos, Jesus was yet a man to whom deity was gradually communicated. Seeberg helps us by the remark that what the Church condemned was not their assertions but their denials. These were felt to be perilously retrograde. "Who," says a Church writer of the time, "who does not know the works of Irenæus,

[1] Harnack's proposal to call this group "Adoptian" is perhaps rather ill-advised. See *RE.* iv. 38.

[2] He is to be distinguished from Theodotus "the banker," another member of the group.

Melito, and the rest, in which they proclaim Christ as God and man?" Of course it is possible to say that this party had some externalities of the Synoptic tradition on its side. The idea, for example, that Jesus at His baptism was endowed with superhuman power has points of real contact with primitive belief. But even on their own showing the Lord was in no sense an ordinary man, and some of Theodotus' followers contended that Jesus became God after the resurrection. The majority, however, denied this, and promulgated views which, had they prevailed, would have been fatal to the continued existence of the Christian society. Dynamic Monarchianism, we can see, has certain points of resemblance to modern liberal theories, and is on the whole a tolerably clear example of how often they are not the best theologians who profess to dispense with theology.

(2) Others, however, felt that a more Christian way might be found to preserve the Divine unity, and one which involved neither a ditheistic Logos doctrine nor a view of Christ that reduced Him to the plane of bare humanity. This was the party of *modalistic Monarchians*,[1] or, as they were sometimes named, not altogether unnaturally, *Patripassians*. Numerous in Egypt, for almost a generation they held the field in Rome. They knew that Christ was God, but they were equally sure that God is one. No subordinationist theory would suffice. Hence, in the full belief that they had Scripture on their side, they represented Christ as being just the Father Himself, an appearance or modification of the one God. None other than He was born, suffered, and died. Noetus and Praxeas, both from Asia Minor, where a naive form of modalism was very old, Epigonus, Cleomenes, and (in a sense) Callistus, bishop of Rome, are the most prominent names. Tertullian wrote against Praxeas, Hippolytus against Noetus and the Roman bishop. The movement

[1] For a subtle estimate of the tendencies which might lead men from one form of Monarchianism to the other, see Rainy, *Anc. Cath. Church*, 215–16.

was at its height in the second and third decades of the second century.

The theory, then, was as follows: Christ is the one God, only in a specialised mode or aspect making revelation possible. Johannine sayings like "I and the Father are one," or "He that hath seen Me hath seen the Father," are meant literally, and imply a unity of person as well as of essence. Support may also have been found in principles of the Stoic philosophy for holding that Father and Son are but two *names* for one reality. According to Hippolytus, it was the teaching of Noetus that "in so far as the Father is not made, we rightly call Him Father. But in so far as He was pleased to subject Himself to birth, He is as engendered become His own Son, not the Son of another."[1] As invisible, ingenerate, impassible, He is Father; as visible, generate and mortal, He is Son. And this one God was nailed on the cross, rendered up His spirit to Himself, died, yet did not die, and on the third day raised Himself from the grave. In Noetus' own words. "If now I confess Christ as God, He clearly is the Father if He is God at all. Now Christ, who Himself is God, has suffered; hence the Father has suffered, for He was the Father." This is the theory in brief. To the objector who quoted the prologue to the Fourth Gospel, it was answered that when St. John appears to speak of Christ as pre-existently separate from the Father, he is really using the language of allegory. Praxeas, a "confessor" of Asia Minor, is specially explicit. *Post tempus*, he is represented as saying, *pater natus et pater passus, ipse deus, dominus omnipotens Jesus Christus praedicatur.*[2] This drew from Tertullian the biting phrase that one of the two jobs Praxeas had done for the devil at Rome was to crucify the Father.[3] Elsewhere he remarks that the God of Praxeas' creed is a "turncoat" (*versipellis*).[4] Sometimes an effort was made to avoid the conclusion that the Father suffered by distinguishing in the Lord's

[1] *Rep.* ix. 10.
[2] Tert. *adv. Prax.* 2.
[3] *Ibid.* 1.
[4] *Ibid.* 2.

person between the flesh, which is Son, and the spirit, which is Father: *filium carnem esse, id est hominem, id est Jesum, patrem autem spiritum, id est deum, id est Christum*;[1] *filius patitur, pater vero compatitur*.[2] But this clearly gives up the point of Modalism.

There are heresies and heresies; some erring in the statement of the faith, others denying it outright. And it is impossible not to feel that Monarchianism of the modalistic type is of the more venial kind. It attracted many earnest and devout men. Noetus' exclamation, as reported by Hippolytus—"How can I do harm by glorifying Christ?"[3]—is significant. Patripassianism indeed, though it resulted from the application of an imperfect scheme of conceptions to the older and purely religious modalism of Ignatius and Irenæus, was from one point of view no more than a vigorous affirmation of the basal certainty that in Jesus Christ we find God Himself personally present for our salvation. However mistakenly, it aimed at serving the interests of faith. For many who resented the subtleties of theological debate, it must have offered itself as an effective working theory. But the equilibrium of the doctrine was peculiarly unstable. In Praxeas' hands it came very near to Docetism. He recognised no human soul in Jesus, and the flesh which with him did duty for complete human nature can hardly have been more than a bare selfless vesture of the indwelling God. Already there are faint anticipations of Apollinaris.[4]

The classic representative of this species of Modalism has been found by later times in Sabellius, a native of Egypt who lived in Rome about 220. But in reality Sabellius was only unusually frank. A comparison with Noetus shows that scarcely anything was new in his teaching save the inclusion of the Holy Spirit in the

[1] Tert. *adv. Prax.* 27. [2] *Ibid.* 29.

[3] τί οὖν κακὸν ποιῶ, δοξάζων τὸν Χριστόν;

[4] On the Monarchian movement as a whole, see an informing article by Professor Warfield in the *Princeton Theological Review* for Oct. 1905.

modalistic scheme. For him also the Divine in Christ has no personal subsistence, but is a mere passing phase of the one deity, who is denoted by the name *υἱοπάτωρ*. Three phenomenal aspects—Father, Son, and Spirit—are referred to a transcendent Godhead which remains immutable behind them all. In the *prosôpon* of the Father, God acted as Creator and Lawgiver; in the *prosôpon* of the Son as Redeemer, from the birth at Bethlehem on to the ascension; thenceforward as the Holy Spirit. Epiphanius relates that Sabellius used to compare the Father to the orb of the sun as we see it, the Son to its light, and the Spirit to its heat; while Athanasius adds that he described the Father as being *expanded* into the Son and the Spirit.[1] These three Divine phases, then, correspond to three periods of revelation—the Old Testament, the New Testament, and the subsequent history of the Church; the entire development making up the unified history of God's self-manifestation. But what is of first-rate importance in the system is Sabellius' explicit declaration that these revelational aspects of God are *successive and temporary*. For him God is not Father, Son, and Spirit simultaneously; only as one aspect ceases to be does another rise into existence. This is a far-reaching divergence from the Church's doctrine of the Divine "economy," to which otherwise it approximates. From certain indications Sabellius appears to have modified the rigour of his logic so far as to hold that after all the Father predominates throughout the entire process of revelation; in the Son and Spirit He is still somehow operative, as the Godhead *par excellence*, revealing itself in temporary forms. But on one point he stood firm—neither Son nor Spirit has personal subsistence.

The point of view was admirably simple in its logic. Sabellianism is only Modalism quite conscious of itself, and formulated in such a manner as to bring out glaringly some of the defects of the Logos doctrine held by Origen

[1] *Or. c. Arianos*, iv. 25

and Tertullian. And it is not difficult to assign one reason for its oft-repeated failure to win the Church's confidence. This is its definite negation of the existence of the Divine Christ after His ascension. In His earthly life He was God; at its close He was again absorbed, like a sunbeam retracted once more to its native source in the sun. This was more than a dubious Trinitarian theory; it was an attempt upon the immediate certainties of the Christian mind, and would in itself have been enough to discredit explicit Sabellianism with believers. And in point of history, many theories which critics have described as Sabellian really lack the distinctive feature of authentic Sabellianism; they ignore the successiveness of the phases, and what is in consequence the merely temporary being of the Divine Christ.

The extremer views of Sabellius, however, must not be charged upon the Modalists generally. Indeed, there is ground for holding that, as compared with the Logos Christology, they had a truly concrete view of the historic Christ, and stood for a conception that did more justice to religious faith. Reflective modalism was initially only a one-sided statement of the unity of nature subsisting between the Son and the Father. As against this, Tertullian had an easy task in proving that the New Testament implies the distinct personality of the Son. And Athanasius and Hilary press home the objection that writers like Praxeas dissolve the whole redemptive economy. "In his view," writes Athanasius, "the Father becomes the Son, and with the absorption of the Son the Father also is no more—which means a Christianity without Father and Fatherhood, hence also without Divine Sonship. On the other hand, the Son remains a mere name, and disappears along with the Spirit once His mission is accomplished."[1] It was felt that Sabellius had fallen back into the hard monotheistic abstractions of Judaism. Basil, indeed, makes this charge directly. At a Synod in the year 261, Sabellianism was condemned.

[1] Cf. Thomasius-Bonwetsch, *Dogmengeschichte*, i. 189 f.

§ 4. *Tertullian.*—In Tertullian, the passionate and inexhaustibly energetic Western, whose literary activity may be placed between 195 and 220, we encounter a form of Christology whose main features took shape in the heat of the Monarchian controversy. A Stoic by philosophic training, Tertullian was converted and ordained at Rome. His theory of the Logos, at which we must first glance, is in great measure an inheritance from the Apologists, but expanded and deepened. First existent in God, as it were anticipatively or in potentiality, the Logos arose out of God as Son by generation before all worlds, being thus projected, or invested with independent being, with a view to the creation of the universe. Thus He had a beginning: *fuit tempus, cum filius non fuit.*[1] Pr 8^{22} fills a large place in these speculations. The process of the Son's coming to be is actually described as one of emanation, and the old figure of the sun and its beam reappears in illustration.[2] Father and Son constitute the one Divine substance, the one as it were overlapping and embracing the other: *pater tota substantia, filius derivatio et portio totius*[3]—a famous sentence. They are differentiated as persons, not by division or separation, but rather in virtue of an economic distinction. The lines of subordinationism are strongly marked.[4] In the Father resides the plenitude of deity, in the Son so much only as is consistent with His derived position (*pro modulo derivationis*).[5] Things which may not be ascribed to the one are predicable of the other. This subordination holds even of the pre-existent Logos. On such terms, since a sharp distinction is made between the Divine existence now and before the generation of

[1] *adv. Herm.* 3.

[2] Cf. the threefold simile in *Apol.* 21.

[3] *adv. Prax.* 9.

[4] Mr. Bethune-Baker surely oversteps the mark in saying that "there is no suggestion or thought of subordination, in any other sense than in regard to origin, and even that is merged in the unity of substance" (*op. cit.* 142). This is to forget Tertullian's dependence on a traditional Logos doctrine.

[5] *adv. Prax.* 14.

the Logos, the Trinitarian life is drawn into the processes of time and history. It is a form of subordinationism, so far, which, owing to the cosmological entanglements of the Logos doctrine, and the persistence of the quasi-philosophic assumption that God's essence lies in mystery and abstract isolation, and cannot therefore be communicated, goes near to wreck the validity for faith of the work of the historic Christ. At the same time even Tertullian's most emphatic statements of subordination are intelligible enough as expressing a criticism of the Monarchian theory. There can be no question as to his religious estimate of Christ. He was true God, only in a real and independent personality, which, although never characterised as "created," yet issued from the Godhead at a distinct point in the past, and in due time will finally be abdicated, that God may be all in all.

Tertullian, who expressed Christian ideas in the natural language of a Roman, is the first to speak of the Godhead as *una substantia, tres personae.* Loofs rightly refuses to see in these terms a deposit of the great divine's training as a jurist. *Substantia* was a familiar word in philosophy, and *persona*, though it originally signified in law a "party" or "individual" with legal rights, had passed into common speech. Much more baffling than Tertullian's use of legally flavoured terms is a marked predilection for mechanical and even crudely physical images.

The pre-existent Logos or Son, then, assumed flesh for our salvation, this being the last stage in the coming of the Logos to full personal existence. He was born of a virgin, for as Son of God He had no need of human fatherhood. The incarnation, prompted by God's redeeming love, was an act of His unconditioned power and freedom, since unlike creatures He can take a new form while yet remaining what He is. Thus Tertullian does not scruple to say that God was born and was crucified. The resultant person, we are told, was compound of two substances (this rather than "natures" is his term),

—spirit and flesh, Divine and human respectively. In one place, indeed, the soul of Christ and His flesh are represented as two substances making up His humanity, the Divine Logos thus being a third.[1] But his more usual practice is to speak of two substances as united in one person. He holds with decision that incarnation is not a metamorphosis into, but an assumption of, flesh; and there is nothing against which he contends more vigorously (so far anticipating the Monophysite controversy) than the view which blends spirit and flesh together in a new hybrid mixture. "If the Logos became flesh," he says, "by a transfiguration and change of substance, it at once follows that Jesus must be substance composed of two substances, like electrum compounded of gold and silver. At this rate Jesus cannot be God, for He has ceased to be the Word; nor can He be Man incarnate, for He is not properly flesh."[2] This may be regarded as Tertullian's genuine conviction, though phrases occur now and then, like *homo Deo mixtus*,[3] or *filius Dei miscens in semetipso hominem et Deum*,[4] which look the other way. He insists trequently on the permanence in Christ's one person of both substances; not only so, each substance acts independently and by itself, according to its own character. *Salva est utriusque proprietas substantiae.*[5] The substances of flesh and spirit are conjoined, not confused. *Videmus duplicem statum, non confusum, sed conjunctum, in una persona, deum et hominen Jesum.*[6] It is worth noting that for Tertullian Christ is certainly an individual man, not mere impersonal humanity.[7]

The paradoxical character of the Christian doctrine, when squarely faced, so far from being toned down, is proclaimed in exulting antitheses. *Natus est Dei filius; non pudet, quia pudendum est. Et mortuus est Dei filius; prorsus credibile est, quia ineptum est. Et sepultus resurrexit;*

[1] *de carn. Christi*, 13.
[2] *adv. Prax.* 27.
[3] *de carn. Christi*, 15.
[4] *adv. Marc.* ii. 27.
[5] *adv. Prax.* 27.
[6] *Ibid.*
[7] The orthodox view a century or two later was different.

certum est, quia impossibile.[1] Yet, having once chosen his formulas, Tertullian could scarcely avoid a certain dualism, which not seldom threatened to dissolve the union of God and man in Christ. The God in Jesus, he argues, needed no baptism; nor may God suffer or die, any more than dishonour done to a stream can touch the parent fountain. Hence the cry of desolation on the Cross "was uttered in order to prove the impassibility of God, who forsook His Son while giving the man in Him up to death."[2] To balance this, stress is laid upon the eternal nature of the union, and it is declared that even in His glory Jesus wears both the form and substance of human flesh and blood. The thought is in a sense an inheritance from Ignatius,[3] though it has a new definiteness.

Harnack has called Tertullian the father of the orthodox doctrine of the person of Christ. That he should be so, in spite of the hampering inadequacies of the Logos Christology bequeathed to him by the Apologists, with its suggestions of a reduced deity mediating a transcendent Absolute, is the best evidence of his amazing power. In fact, the issue of his work was to put in terms of the Logos conception a religious and doctrinal view of Christ so rich and full as ultimately to break through its own limitations. It is too much to say, with Dorner, that Tertullian marks the transition from the Logos Christology to a Christology interpreted by Divine Sonship (this applies rather to Athanasius); yet it is true that he prepared the way for the beneficent change. His great phrase, *nihil tam dignum Deo quam hominum salus*,[4] involving an ethical rather than a purely ontological idea of God, might, had it been followed out, have supplied a worthy background even for his boldest Christological assertions, in which he sought to laud and magnify the grace of the Redeemer.

The Christology of Tertullian was disseminated in the West chiefly through the *de Trinitate* of Novatian, a

[1] *de carn. Christi*, 5.
[2] *adv. Prax.* 30.
[3] Cf. *Smyr.* 3. 1.
[4] *adv. Marc.* ii. 27.

book which Harnack describes as a dogmatic *vade mecum* for the Latin Churches. A vehement adversary of both types of Monarchianism, he taught, particularly as against Sabellius, at once the real Deity of Christ and the personal distinction of Father and Son. Christ is true man and true God. Yet so far is Novatian from commingling both, that he posits two Sons in the theanthropic Person—one *filius natura*, the other *filius ex adoptione*. The manhood could be put on and off like a garment. He re-echoes the subordinationist strain of his master, prophesying the future cessation of the Son's independent being, even though, strange to say, he appears to hold the existence of the Son to have been eternal in the past. The *vis divinitatis*, "having been sent forth, and also given and directed to the Son, circles back to the Father in virtue of the communion of substance."[1]

[1] *de Trin.* 31.

CHAPTER III.

THE ASCENDANCY OF THE LOGOS DOCTRINE.

§ 1. *The Alexandrian Theologians*: (*a*) *Clement.*—As we turn to the Christological work of the great Alexandrian Fathers, it is needful to realise the conditions of thought and feeling in view of which they wrought out their systems. On the threshold of the third century began a striking revival of the religion of Mithras, a primæval god of the Aryans, which affected virtually the entire Roman world. Thenceforward for more than a hundred years Mithraism and Christianity struggled for mastery, each professing to satisfy man's craving for blessedness and eternal life. Christianity won because it is a faith grounded in history. The authentic and concrete revelation in the historic person of Jesus proved stronger than all the mysteries. Meanwhile the religion of educated men was growing eclectic and syncretist. A sort of monotheistic worship of the sun; the adoration of great men of the past, as Pythagoras and Apollonius of Tyana—these may illustrate the prevailing tendencies; and it is a fair question whether the biographies of these men did not owe something to the wish to present a heathen Christ superior to our Lord.

Nor must we overlook the philosophic movements

LITERATURE—Bigg, *Christian Platonists of Alexandria*, 1886; Bonwetsch, article "Clemens von Alexandrien," in *RE.* iv.; Preuschen, article "Origenes," *RE.* xiv.; Westcott, *Religious Thought in the West*, 1891; Hatch, *Hibbert Lectures*, 1890; Redepenning, *Origenes*, 1841–46; Gwatkin, *The Knowledge of God*², 1908; Bonwetsch, *Die Theologie des Methodius*, 1903; Routh, *Reliquiae sacrae*², 1848; Pfleiderer, *Gifford Lectures*, 1895; Allen, *The Continuity of Christian Thought*, 1885; Liddon, *Bampton Lectures*, 1866.

of the time. Two of the biographers of Pythagoras were Porphyry and Iamblichus, distinguished leaders of the Neo-Platonic school, which had been founded by Ammonius Saccas, a teacher of Platonic philosophy at Alexandria. The system of which he was the expositor received its most perfect expression at the hands of his pupil Plotinus, whose life extended from 205 to 270. It may be described as a kind of dynamic pantheism. There are three great cosmic principles.[1] Primal being resides in the One, the Infinite, the Good, which is beyond and above all attributes, whether of thought, will, or energy, and yet is the uncaused and moveless source of all existent things. Next comes the Nous, its exact emitted image and the archetype of lower being, embracing in itself likewise the supersensible world (*κόσμος νοητός*). And lastly the Nous gives forth, as its product and copy, the Soul or Psyche, related to the Nous in turn as the Nous is to the One. Placed between the Nous and the world of phenomena, it shares in some degree the character of both. Material nature is meant to be subject to Psyche. But in actual existence this intended harmony of subordination is displaced by strife, the result being that the entire phenomenal system is shot through with illusion and vanity. Something in the very essence of matter condemns it to be a principle of darkness. Hence to be born into corporeality signifies that the soul has fallen into the toils of sensuality, though redemption is not impossible. Each soul must leave the material behind and rise to the region of Divine knowledge, and even in the present life we may approximate to this, above all through the medium of passive intuition. In perfect receptivity and repose the soul is able to touch and grasp God directly, losing itself in the Divine with a silent rapture or ecstasy of unutterable feeling. Porphyry relates that to his own knowledge Plotinus tasted this supreme bliss on four distinct occasions.

[1] To each of these potencies the name *ὑπόστασις* is given, indicating that they represent the Divine in specific forms or modes of existence.

It is customary for historians to deny that Neo-Platonism is dualistic, and to contrast it in this respect with Gnosticism, against which Plotinus wrote vehemently. Yet the idea of matter which Neo-Platonists assumed, as of something indefinite, formless, evil, came very near to pure dualism. We learn that Plotinus was ashamed of his body.

A system of this kind, obviously, would act as a foil to Christianity, rather than as its intellectual model. The influence of Neo-Platonism on Church thinkers has been much exaggerated. Doubtless, like the writers of the New Testament, the Fathers may not have disdained to borrow from their rivals this or that technical expression, without prejudice to its new Christian meaning, or to learn something of the art of formal ratiocination. But men like Tertullian and Origen were after all seeking to theologise upon a faith anchored to historical realities; the Neo-Platonists, on the other hand, were bent on a metaphysical cosmology. Their trinity and the Trinity of Church writers have scarcely anything in common but the number three. Furthermore, their idea of matter barred out incarnation from the first as inconceivable. To Porphyry, Christ was a pious sage who may well have risen to immortality after death, but one whose place is distinctly beneath Pythagoras. His followers, it was argued, had mixed His doctrine with falsehood, and abandoned His toleration of other faiths.

It is in a world filled, or being filled, with religious and philosophical influences of this description that we must picture Clement of Alexandria, and especially Origen, at work. The Gospel had to be stated defensively in an extremely difficult situation. The task of the Apologists must be resumed, and the adversary beaten with his own weapons. And Christ had to be set forth, not as the Saviour of the world merely, but as One in whom lay hid the treasures of wisdom and knowledge; for men felt there was a specifically Christian gnosis, and neither the name nor the idea could be dispensed with.

Clement is said, with much probability, to have been a native of Athens. A pupil of Pantaenus, one of the best teachers in the institution known as the Catechetical School of Alexandria, he was himself a member of the staff more or less from 190 to 216. The faith of Irenæus and Tertullian he too shared with conviction; evidently, however, he regarded himself as free to construe its elements with a certain speculative liberality. He describes himself as a scholar of Tatian, and there are frequent traces of the influence of Justin. With all his admiration for Greek philosophy and intense sympathy with its noble and inspiring characteristics, he never wavers in the conviction that Christ has brought to men the best and highest revelation of God.

This revelation, naturally enough, Clement interprets by means of the Logos doctrine, with the result, at all events partially, of depersonalising the historic Saviour. The timeless content for which He stood, rather than Jesus Christ in His concrete actuality, holds the central place. Through the Eternal Logos is revealed God most high, who is seated far above all distinction; and from the Logos comes "all that there is upon earth of beauty, truth, goodness, all that distinguishes the civilised man from the savage, the savage from the beasts."[1] He is freely named Son, and in that character separated by an absolute gulf from things created. Precisely how Clement means us to conceive the relation of the Logos to the Father it is difficult to say.[2] He uses contradictory modes of expression, according as the Logos is viewed from the side of humanity or of God Himself.[3] From below He appears as the fulness of the Godhead concentred in an independent life; from above He is the highest next to the Almighty, the minister of God, mediating all created life, and at a certain distance from the Father as the

[1] Bigg, *Christian Platonists of Alexandria*, 72.

[2] It is at all events an essential relation. "If God is a Father, He is at the same time Father of a Son" (*Strom.* v. 1. 1).

[3] Cf. Redepenning, *Origenes*, 110–14.

absolute monad. But in a writer who asserts both the full equality of Father and Son, and the Son's subordination, we are bound, I think, to hold that the idea of subordination is secondary. It is a result of the effort to posit distinctions in the Godhead.

It has been maintained that Clement makes an important difference between the Logos as in God, and the Logos-Son, to whom it has been given to become incarnate. But the theory, tempting as it is, appears to depend on a single passage of doubtful interpretation.[1] The Word, we are told, came into the world, fashioning His own humanity; and "this Logos, the Christ, the cause both of our being at first (for He was in God) and of our well-being, this very Logos has now appeared to men, He alone being both, at once God and man."[2] The continuous identity of the Subject is put quite clearly; the Logos "put on a man," and was "God in the form of man, stainless, the servant of His Father's will."[3] A tendency to think of our Lord's humanity as but a garment brings Clement repeatedly to the verge of docetism. Christ's body was superior to physical needs; "He ate, not for the sake of His bodily frame, which was held together by a holy energy, but lest His .companions should think about Him otherwise."[4] He knew no pain, or grief, or emotion, and had no need to learn. Theories which start, not from the historical Christ, but from the pre-existent Word, and proceed by way of deduction, will always be in grave hazard on the side of docetism, and Clement is no exception. But when it is contended by some writers that for him "the Lord's descent into flesh" was no real incarnation, but only an extreme case of Divine inspiration or possession, we must demur. Not only is Christ's full Godhead vital for Clement, as furnishing a guarantee that the revelation He brought was perfect, but there are

[1] The question is argued by Mr. Bethune-Baker, *op. cit.* 134 f.

[2] *Protr.* 1. [3] *Ibid.* 2.

[4] *Strom.* vi. 9; *i.e.* to refute docetism by anticipation. Cf. Glover, *The Conflict of Religions in the Early Roman Empire*, 299.

too many passages whose meaning is quite explicit. Thus, for example, He speaks of Christ as "a God in human form,"[1] and elsewhere says that "assuming the character of man, and having been fashioned in flesh, He enacted the drama of human salvation."[2] But he cannot be quoted as teaching the Two Natures doctrine; for the unity of Christ is assumed by him rather than demonstrated; and indeed he scarcely inquires at all regarding the exact relations which obtain between the Divine content of Christ's person and its phenomenal human form.

§ 2. (*b*) *Origen.* — Origen (185–254), a pupil of Clement, and his successor in the mastership of the Catechetical School of Alexandria, is the supremely great name among the divines of the Christian East. An Egyptian by race, he was the child of Christian parents. His width of interest, his learning, his fabulous industry, not least his devoutness and fine simplicity of nature, make him a noble and memorable figure. As an exegete, in spite of a tendency to allegorise, his services to theology were vast. His troubled yet unceasingly studious life cannot be recounted here; but the secret of his wonderful influence is revealed in the farewell eulogy pronounced upon him by his pupil, Gregory Thaumaturgus, bishop of Neo-Cæsarea. Later ages, even those which disowned his heresies most bitterly, paid tribute to his power. "It was Origen," says Harnack, "who created the dogmatic of the Church, and did more than any other man to win the Old World to the Christian religion." He was leader in the campaign of Christian theology against the varied forces of pagan thought, and the thirst for knowledge felt by the loftier spirits within the Church found its satisfaction mainly in his innumerable works. To his tireless intellect, theology was very life and happiness. Though conscious of a staunch fidelity to the historic faith, he felt it essential that the contents of the creed should at

[1] *Paed.* i. 99. [2] *Protr.* x. 110.

the same time be sublimated by the methods of reverent speculation, provided only that the limits of ecclesiastical and apostolic tradition were recognised. Within these limits free discussion must have its way.[1]

We turn first to his doctrine of the Logos. God the Father—this is, as so often, the point of departure—is immutable and absolute Being, self-conscious Mind throned above all mind and all substance. As being perfectly good, He must communicate Himself, and it is in the Logos that He is first made apprehensible. This Logos or Son (the two names are freely interchanged), being the most eminent of the Divine powers or ideas, embraces within Himself the whole contents of the intelligible world; and for us, indeed, it is a higher thing to view Him in this light than to dwell only upon the Christ incarnate and crucified. Very emphatically Origen insists that the Word is personal, as well as eternally and intrinsically Divine. Both aspects are vital. "For him and the men of his time," says Dr. Bigg, "the great object was to establish the true Personality of Christ, to show that though God He yet was not the Father."[2]

As Son, then, the Logos proceeds from the Father; not, however, by way of partition, but as the will does from spirit, or, as he elsewhere expresses it in a great phrase which has lodged itself in the Church's mind, by an *eternal generation.* The exact words are: *est namque ita aeterna ac sempiterna generatio, sicut splendor generatur ex luce.*[3] The nature of this generation is ineffable; we only know that "it denotes no finite act either temporal or pre-temporal, but an eternal or intemporal process or relation." Hence to say that a time was when the Son was not, is an error (*οὐκ ἐστιν ὅτε οὐκ ἦν*).[4] As an independent subsistence, then, the Son is numerically distinct from the Father, but withal they are in substance absolutely one. In essential content the Son is *ὁμοούσιος* with the Father, as vapour is with water or children with

[1] Cf. the opening words of the *de Principiis.*

[2] *Op. cit.* p. 166.

[3] *de Princip.* i. 2. 4.

[4] Cf. *ibid.* i. 2. 9.

their parents. They are two ὑποστάσεις, not one, as the Monarchians said. It is quite in harmony with this homousia that Origen should elsewhere describe the Son as "begotten of the Father's will," for in the spiritual realm no contrast exists between will and substance.[1]

Our first impression is that by this decisive assertion of the homousia the co-equality of the Son with the Father has been secured. But it is not so. Origen shares, in a real measure, the subordinationism of the Apologists. Regarding the Son as "the most ancient of all the works" of God,[2] he does not hesitate to speak of Him as a κτίσμα.[3] The Son is the second God, but not immutably or intrinsically good, as the Father is. The Father's will is wiser than the Son's; at creation the Son was the Father's servant, executing His commands. Most remarkable of all, while practising prayer to Christ as Divine, and indeed insisting on it as a duty, Origen proclaims that there is a still higher object of invocation. "In the supreme moment of adoration, when the soul strains upward to lay itself as a sacrifice before the highest object of thought, we must not stop short of Him who is above all."[4] Here, accordingly, there is a wavering use of terms. If the result is contradictory, it is surely due to a difficulty from which the Christian theologian cannot escape; for the Son may be viewed from above or from below. Seen from above, He appears as the first step towards man, and, in addition, the content of the word "Son" must, for us, be drawn from our knowledge of the Incarnate Life; seen from below, He is the object of religious faith, and *ipso facto* on one plane of being with God. In Origen's case the difficulty was intensified by his desire to construct a theory including both Christ and the universe. Christ the Son is not merely Saviour; He is the World-Reason, pervading and moulding all things. Hence He stands

[1] Loofs, *Dogmengeschichte*, 194. [2] *c. Cels.* v. 37.

[3] On such expressions the Arians fastened, though with only superficial plausibility.

[4] Bigg, *op. cit.* 186.

midway between the Uncreated and His creation, between the One and the Many, partaking in the nature of both. Allusions to the Spirit are even more subordinationist in tone.

In spite of his assertion that the Logos incarnate is not of first-rate importance for "gnostics," or Christians of the intellectual rank, Origen's sketch of Christological doctrine[1] was such as to exert later a profound influence. Faced with the difficulty of conceiving how the creative and all-permeating Logos could gather Himself into an earthly life, his solution was to make the human soul of Jesus a mediating bond uniting the infinite Logos to finite flesh (*substantia animae inter Deum et carnem medians*).[2] Like all souls, the soul of Jesus was pre-existent. But alone of all it had kept its purity, and thus, quite apart from the Incarnation in time, had become one spirit indissociably with the Logos; the two being fused in a union that "may be compared to a mass of iron glowing for ever with a white heat." In their unity they passed into an incontaminate human body, born of a virgin. Thus was constituted the God-Man (θεάνθρωπος); and since the Eternal Son is the chief partner in the resultant complex being, it is fitting that the Incarnate person as a whole should likewise be designated "Son," and that the Son of God should be said to have suffered death. But though Jesus was, in Origen's view, a real man, the normality of His body is not quite beyond suspicion. True, it is no phantasmal appearance; there is no docetism in the strict sense; but neither is it composed of coarse matter: rather it is of ethereal purity and celestially fair, with a glorious brightness that shone forth even upon earth, and was manifested completely after death. Moreover, the union of the Divine and human in the one Christ is represented as permitting an equally real separation. The taunt of Celsus about a crucified God is pointless; for of God it is impossible to predicate such things, and the man Jesus

[1] Cf. Harnack, whose pages on this subject are particularly brilliant.
[2] *de Princip.* ii. 6. 3.

alone suffered and died. "The Word, still remaining essentially the Word, suffers none of those things which are endured by the body or soul; but, condescending occasionally to one who is unable to gaze upon the splendours and brightness of deity, He becomes as it were flesh."[1] In the light of His cosmic functions the Logos cannot be thought of as confined to the human life of Jesus; even while appearing thus in a form suited to our capacities, He yet manifested Himself everywhere as before.

Christ, then, is a single complex being; and in strong contrast to the aspect of his teaching just noted, Origen insists that between the two phases or elements of His constituted life there obtained not a communion merely, but a gradual merging and commingling, with the result that the humanity of Jesus is itself deified (*deificavit quam susceperat humanam naturam*).[2] In terms of a later age, we may speak of a *communicatio idiomatum*. So far did this go that in the end, after the resurrection, the body was completely absorbed in the Divine spirit. The ascended Lord has ceased to be man.[3] But from another point of view Origen felt himself justified in declaring that Jesus' humanity still persists, though His body has been transmuted into a higher form. For His soul still preserves its being, merged in the Logos by an inner mystical union wrought by its perfection of holy love. As God-Man, we are told, Christ offered the sacrifice which atones for sin, and paid the ransom by which the devil's power has been shattered. This, it is true, is always balanced by the assurance that His crucifixion is of value only for those who cannot rise to the apprehension of ideal truth. "To know Christ crucified is the knowledge of babes." But to such as need Him not, or need Him no longer, in the capacity of Physician and Redeemer, Christ is Divine Teacher and Leader, who opens the door of the Holy Place of sacred mysteries. Of love to this Christ, Origen speaks with the most intense feeling.

[1] *c. Cels.* iv. 15. [2] *in Matt. Serm.* 33. [3] *in Luc. hom.* 29.

There is no trace in Origen of sympathy with Monarchian ideas, against which he directs various passages of strong polemic. But he uses freely all other views about our Lord's Person which were current in the Church, dovetailing them into each other with amazing skill, and adapting to his purpose not a few conceptions which later times banned as heretical. His main conception, according to which the personal Logos united Himself to the personal soul (and so to the body) of Jesus, differs noticeably from the tendency of earlier writers, like Irenæus, to say rather that the Logos *became* man. This insistence on the personal being of Christ *qua* man is a conspicuous merit in his system. Even Clement had spoken of the direct union of the Logos with a human body, and later thinkers were apt to surrender the position Origen had gained by his clear perception of Jesus' soul as truly human. Yet in Origen's hands the result was an obvious dualism. If in Christ we have a human subject which, as a free moral personality, cleaves inseparably to the Logos, and is ultimately lost in Him, the total outcome, as Harnack puts it, is not so much a doctrine of two natures (though the phrase "two natures" does occur) as rather that of two subjects which gradually become amalgamated with each other.[1] The human personality of the Saviour finally disappears, leaving only its Divine content. Still, we cannot forget that the unity which Origen strove to bring out between God and man in Christ was a unity so ethically mediated that it could also be designated "essential" or "substantial." He felt how great was the condescension of the Eternal Son in being born, and by conceiving His advent as a real self-exinanition he makes room for a truly human development. "Ignorance and learning," he writes, "pertain not to the Eternal Wisdom in itself, but as it is in flesh; for Christ had to learn to stammer and speak like a child with infants." This condescension of God to human life is met and ratified by a capacity on the part

[1] *History of Dogma*, ii. 373.

of humanity to receive the essential life of God; and it is probably in the main as a real effort to illustrate this position that the thought of Origen marks an epoch in Christology.

§ 3. *The Correspondence of the Dionysii.*—If Tertullian dominated the West, in the East the influence of Origen was supreme. But trouble was sure to result from the inconsistency of his views—his assertion of the homousia, for example, coupled with a distinct subordination of the Logos. How easily he could be misinterpreted we see in the brief significant controversy of Dionysius of Alexandria with Dionysius of Rome, about the year 260. The former had received his training in the school of Origen, and, in fulminating against the Sabellians of Egypt, had been unfortunate enough to exaggerate the subordinationism of his master. Accentuating the distinction of Father and Son, he declared that the Son is the Father's creature, and was not before He came to be. He has a different *οὐσια* from the Father, as the vine has from the vintager or a ship from its builder. This was of course utterly to misconceive Origen, who had taught clearly enough that as begotten by the Father the Son is absolutely separate from all creatures. Complaint was promptly made by the orthodox to Dionysius of Rome; the eternity of the Son had been denied, and suspicion cast upon His unity of essence with the Father. Thus they pled the doctrine of Origen against his erring follower.

The bishop of Rome dealt with the matter on the lines of Tertullian and Novatian. He urged that in zeal for the three distinctions in the Godhead the unity must not be overlooked. Tritheism is the deadliest of foes. Hence, appealing to the Baptismal Creed, he was content to say that faith accepts the being of one God, the Almighty Father, of Christ Jesus His Son, and of the Holy Spirit. In particular, the Logos must have been ever in the Father, for He is no product of time, not having been made, but begotten in a Divine and ineffable manner. The Roman bishop appears even to have laid stress upon the term ὁμοούσιος, and Seeberg points out that this is the first occasion upon which the historic adjective figures as a definitely orthodox expression.[1] The tone of his answer to the Eastern complaint is judicial, not speculative, as was natural in a man not attempting originality, but seeking a wise and tested *via media*. Dionysius of Alexandria, protesting meanwhile that some of his expressions had been misconstrued, showed himself very ready to make amends. It was true, he said, that no time had ever been when God had not been Father; the Son, as the radiance of Eternal Light, was Himself eternal. To say, however, that he rejected the homousia was false, though he had felt a delicacy in using a term not to be found in Scripture. Thus the correspondence ended, with apparent agreement on all hands as to the unity of essence. What is mainly of interest to the modern student is to observe how one part of Origen's system has already begun to be set in opposition to another, and also to note how practically-minded Rome, clinging to the Creed, and deprecating additions to it, stands in uneasy contrast to the Eastern love of speculation.

§ 4. *Paul of Samosata.*—A few years after the death of Origen, theological attention was drawn sharply to the opinions of Paul of Samosata, the ablest expositor in the ancient Church of Dynamic Monarchianism. Paul was bishop of Antioch from 260 to 269. With considerable knowledge of the world he combined striking gifts of exposition, and could hold unfriendly synods at bay by the sheer skill of his dialectic. Starting with a purely Old Testament idea of God, he taught that in the man Jesus there dwelt the Divine Sophia or Logos. But the Logos is no personal subsistence (ἀνυπόστατος); it is simply the Spirit of God, and exists in the Deity as a man's reason

[1] *Op. cit.* i. 468.

does in himself, and this essential impersonality renders it unthinkable that it should manifest itself personally in a human life. It is present in Christ, therefore, only as a power or influence, like the indwelling of wisdom in the prophets. What is unique in Jesus is the inhabitation of the Logos *sensu eminenti*; the man is as a temple for the higher presence. Thus the historic Jesus while superior to other men in all things, is strictly "from beneath" (*Χριστὸς κάτωθεν*); Mary bore a man our equal, who is the only personal subject in the case, and whose existence began at the nativity. But the Logos from above inspired Him, and wrought in Him as a quality, though not in essential or personal form (*οὐκ οὐσιωδῶς ἀλλὰ κατὰ ποιότητα*). Apparently Paul made a good deal of the Baptism, as marking the point at which the Logos was communicated. Thus endowed, Jesus kept Himself by obedience in the love of God. Between God and Jesus, as two distinct persons, there subsisted a relationship of perfect unity in disposition, based on perfect love, a bond which is best described as ethical, not natural, since it is constituted by mutual knowledge and communion between a Father only in heaven and a Son only on earth. Finally, in virtue of His transcendent merit, Jesus attained to such a permanent union with God as qualifies Him to be Saviour, and confers upon Him the name that is above every name.[1] Subsequently to death and resurrection He was invested with Divine power, and may fitly be designated "God (born) of the Virgin." As Harnack expresses it, "He became God through Divine grace and His constant manifestation of goodness."[2]

Clearly enough this scheme has some connection with Origen, though whether of misinterpretation or revolt is not so easy to say. Origen too had said much of the ethical development of the man Jesus, and of His possession of the Logos. Yet the difference is obvious that to Origen the Logos existed hypostatically before all time, while for

[1] Paul was fond of arguing from Ph 2^{5-11}.

[2] *History of Dogma*, iii. 43.

Paul the hypostatic factor is purely human. Curiously, although Seeberg calls him the first Unitarian, and declares that he is the only thinker among dynamic Monarchians whom the name really fits, Paul nevertheless persisted, with whatever inconsistency, in speaking of the Godhead of Christ, and this after he had stopped the singing of hymns in public worship which affirmed Christ's essential divinity.

Harnack praises Paul warmly, almost as if he were an early Ritschlian of the left wing. Thus, for example: "Paul's expositions of nature and will in the Persons, of the essence and power of love, of the Divinity of Christ, as only perceptible in the work of His ministry, because exclusively constituted by unity of will with God, are almost unparalleled in the whole dogmatic literature of the Oriental Churches in the first three centuries."[1] He also commends him for having fixed upon Jesus' will, not His nature, as the element of Divine uniqueness, and in general for his refusal to plunge into speculation. The authenticity of the fragments on which Harnack bases part of this eulogy has been questioned; but in any case we may well permit the Samosatene to remind us that a mere opposition between will and nature is unsound. Nature certainly may mean "substance," and on that understanding it is obviously a category unequal to the task of interpreting supremely personal and spiritual realities, so that Paul's protest will seem in place as a warning that "nature" can only be usefully employed to mean the whole personal being, whether of God or man, as a living unity of knowing, feeling, and will. Beyond this terminological concession, however, we cannot go. If we have to choose between a Saviour who was God by original and inherent life, and one who, as now suggested, *became*[2] God, we shall scarcely hesitate. The conception of a Godhead which came to be, although not unknown in

[1] *History of Dogma*, iii. 44.

[2] ὕστερον αὐτὸν μετὰ τήν ἐνανθρώπησιν ἐκ προκοπῆς τεθεοποιῆσθαι, Athanasius, *de Cogn*. 26. 45.

nineteenth-century thought, is sheer mythology. It is simply a mistaken expression of the perfectly legitimate demand that the human aspect of Christ must not be sacrificed or suppressed.

It is interesting to observe that the Council which condemned Paul, in 268 or 269, explicitly censured the term *ὁμοούσιος*. This was done, according to Athanasius, because Paul had contended that if Christ is *ὁμοούσιος* with the Father, their two identical *οὐσίαι* must be derived from a still higher *οὐσία*, as the ultimate source or fount of Deity, which would imply that in reality three *οὐσίαι* exist. But Hilary's account is much more probable. The word was rejected, he says, because Paul had used it to cover his doctrine of the impersonality of the Logos. For as yet *οὐσία* and *ὑπόστασις* were synonyms; and the assertion of one essence was taken to imply one personality. Henceforth no Christology could hope for a hearing which did not make room for the hypostatic pre-existence of Christ, and affirm His divinity as eternal in the past no less than in the future.

CHAPTER IV.

THE ARIAN CONTROVERSY.

§ 1. *The Heresy of Arius.*—Before the commencement of the Arian strife, the Church appeared to have reached three fixed truths respecting the Lord's person, as the fruit of previous controversies. These points were (*a*) the Son's unity of essence with the Father; (*b*) His eternal generation; (*c*) His personal distinction from the Father. Suddenly, however, new conflicts broke out round the first and second of these, and raged for near a century.

Arius, through whose intervention the question became acute, was a presbyter of Alexandria, of whose birth and early life we know nothing. One of the churches of the city was under his care, and he appears to have discharged his responsibilities with exemplary diligence and piety. Of ascetic aspect and winning manners (so it is said), his faults were vanity and ambition. Nevertheless, albeit the most detested heretic in history, it seems likely enough that when in advanced years he began to urge his peculiar theories, it was without any clear consciousness that he was deserting from the traditional view of the Church.

Previous to his residence in Alexandria, Arius sat at

LITERATURE—Gwatkin, *Studies of Arianism*, 1882; Newman, *The Arians of the Fourth Century*[2], 1854; Loofs, articles "Arianismus," *RE.* ii., "Christologie," *RE.* iv., and "Kenosis," *RE.* x.; Schultz, *Die Lehre von der Gottheit Christi*, 1881; Gore, *Dissertations*, 1895; Voigt, *Die Lehre des Athanasius*, 1881; Rainy, *The Ancient Catholic Church*, 1902; Zahn, *Marcellus von Ancyra*, 1867; Curtis, *History of Creeds and Confessions of Faith*, 1911; Moberly, *Atonement and Personality*, 1901.

the feet of Lucian of Antioch, a contemporary and follower of Paul of Samosata, who had fallen out of Church fellowship, but presided over a famous exegetical school. Lucian had made certain modifications in Paul's Christology, which Arius took over from his teacher. They involved an approximation to the left wing of the Origenistic school, a representative of which we have already encountered in Dionysius of Alexandria. For the most part Arius only repeated the views of Lucian. The occasion of the decisive outbreak, according to the historian Socrates (i. 5), was a doctrinal address given to his presbyters by Alexander, bishop of Alexandria, probably in the year 318. Thus the controversy was Eastern in origin. In the West, owing to the influence of writers like Tertullian, the mind of the Church had been satisfied with formulas which combined the deity of Christ with the oneness of the Godhead. So Dionysius of Rome had insisted on the homousia, going back to the *una substantia* of Tertullian. Prior to the controversy, therefore, the West had virtually pronounced judgment.

Arius sets out from a baldly transcendent monotheism.[1] God is abstractly perfect and infinite, one and unbegotten, which means that the idea of a Divine emanation or προβολή cannot be entertained; "the unity of God," in short, "excludes not only distinctions inside the Divine nature, but also contact with the world."[2] Hence the Son, although pre-existent, is not unbegotten; for anything else would make the Father composite and divisible, and the second "unbegotten" were Brother of the first. Accordingly the Son had a beginning. Before all time He came into existence, out of nothing, by God's will, His primary function being that of mediator of creation. So that He is a creature, even if the first of creatures, as is proved by Pr $8^{22ff.}$. Before His generation

[1] So much is God a mystery that Arius says He is inscrutable to His own Son.

[2] Gwatkin, *The Arian Controversy*, 6.

or production He was not. "God was not Father eternally; on the contrary, there was a time when God was alone, and was not as yet Father, though later He became Father. The Son did not exist eternally; for, all things having come to be out of that which was not . . . the Logos of God also Himself originated out of things that were not (ἐξ οὐκ ὄντων), there was once when He was not, and He was not prior to His becoming (ἦν ποτε ὅτε οὐκ ἦν, καὶ οὐκ ἦν πρὶν γένηται)."[1] This means, of course, that there is no identity of essence between the Father and the Son (ξένος τοῦ υἱοῦ κατ' οὐσίαν ὁ πατήρ). There is indeed a Logos immanent in God, but it is not the Son; and the Son, like all other creaturely beings, participates in this inherent Logos, and is Himself named Logos only by way of grace. Arius was willing to call Christ "God" on occasion, and in fact went so far as to employ the orthodox-sounding phrase, "fully God, only-begotten, immutable."[2] But this was an evasion, as he virtually concedes in the more popular *Thalia*:[3] "Even if He be styled God, yet is He not true God, but only by the participation of grace, even as all others." At this point a startling corollary comes into view. If the Logos is not unbegotten, neither is He immutable. "The Logos Himself is changeable (τρεπτός); it is by His own choice that He remains good, so long as He will; but when He wishes, even He can change, just as we can." God, knowing in advance that He would be perfect, gave Him anticipatively the glory won by His human virtue. Such things had been said before, by Paul of Samosata, regarding the historic Christ; but it is noteworthy that Arius, following Lucian, affirmed them definitely of the pre-temporal Logos, possibly influenced by his belief that Christ had no human soul. its place being taken directly by the Logos.

Schultz has pronounced the Arian theory of the Lord's

[1] *Thal.* in Athan. *Or. c. Ar.* i. 5.
[2] In his Epistle to Eusebius of Nicomedia.
[3] A collection of songs "for sailors and millers and wayfarers."

person to be "inwardly the least stable and dogmatically the most worthless of all the Christologies to be met with in history."[1] Few will question the justice of this verdict. For Arianism introduced a mythological element into Christianity, strangely reminiscent of the heroes and demigods of pagan legend. Proofs, no doubt, might have been quoted as to this or that point from older writers, for both the Apologists and Tertullian had taught that the Son had a beginning in time; but there is a difference between the casual phrases of pioneer exploration and the clear-cut terminology of deliberate system. The completeness with which Arius missed his mark is one of the ironies of history. Starting with a desire to clear the worship of Christ from a charge of polytheism, he led the way straight back to heathen idolatry. After proclaiming that Christ's humanity is fundamental, he ended by denying Him a human soul. Above all, he made it fatally certain that on his terms our Lord is no true mediator, no daysman "who can lay a hand upon us both." God stands outside the world, and the chasm cannot be bridged. The Church refused, on purely religious grounds, to be put off with a Saviour who turned out on examination to be only an inferior cosmological principle. And from the first it was an ominous characteristic of Arianism that it strove to render the Gospel into the terms of common sense, and took pride in having so banished all mystery that the problems of Christology are child's play to any fairly intelligent outsider.

Our business is with the progress of doctrine, not the struggles of parties, and we cannot follow the windings of the sixty years of controversy. Yet it should be said that Arius pled his case before the world with singular political dexterity. His influence was not confined to Alexandria. Bishops and virgins of Egypt favoured him, and he had champions among the episcopate of Palestine and Syria. Shallow and thoughtful men alike were

[1] *Gottheit Christi*, 65.

attracted by his views, at least to begin with; but most of all he was assisted by the prevailing fear of Sabellianism. It was only after an immense expenditure of intellectual and ethical resources that the Church as a whole was brought to see how the specious simplicity of his theories was totally subversive of the fundamental realities of the Christian faith.

§ 2. *The Nicene Creed.*—The first to stamp the doctrine of Arius with churchly disapproval was his bishop, Alexander. Probably in 321, he passed sentence of excommunication on the leader and a few of his chief followers. Alexander's own statements on Christology are opaque, and not devoid of superficial contradictions, but his drift is quite clearly to maintain the essential unity of Father and Son, and the inherent divinity of the Redeemer Christ. To Arius he replied that if Christ is the effulgence of the Father's glory, to deny His eternity is to deny that in God there is light eternal. God, as such, is Father, and this He cannot be without a Son. On the other hand, Alexander holds that the Son is generate of the Father, though in no material sense or by way of actual division. At the same time, as an Origenist of the right wing he can speak of the Logos as "a mediating only-begotten nature,"[1] set between the unoriginate Father and created things, and his distaste for Sabellianism manifests itself in the phrase that the two natures in the Divine substance were not one, but like in all points. It is even explained that the Father, who alone is unbegotten, is anterior to, as well as greater than, Christ; on which Harnack well remarks that evidently "the real point in dispute [with Arius] was not as to subordination and co-ordination, but as to unity of substance and difference of substance."[2] But an irreconcilable hostility to Arius' doctrine is expressed in his insistent claim that the resemblance of the Son to the Father is an essential

[1] μεσιτεύουσα φύσις μονογενής.
[2] *History of Dogma*, vol. iv. 23.

one. If the Arians suspected Alexander of Sabellianism, his phrases were more to blame than his ideas.

By this time Constantine had become aware of the dispute. Perceiving how detrimental bitter controversy must be to the unity of his empire, he resolved to bring it to an end, and summoned all Christian bishops to assemble at Nicæa in Bithynia (325). It was the first ecumenical Council, and something like 300 bishops attended, mostly from the East. Two presbyters came from Rome, and Hosius of Cordova was the Spanish deputy. In the Council itself we can distinguish three parties, shading off into each other—the Arians, led by Eusebius of Nicomedia, and comparatively few in number; a still smaller group who sided with Alexander by conviction; and between these, the great majority of the bishops, either too indifferent to theology to appreciate the issue, or disposed by conservatism to rest content with Origen as usually interpreted. Of this middle party the spokesman was Eusebius of Cæsarea, by far the most learned member of the Council.

First of all the Arians presented a creed shaped to their mind, only to see it torn fiercely in fragments. On this Eusebius of Cæsarea brought forward the baptismal creed of his own church, "a short and simple document, admirably recommended to conservative feeling by its scriptural language and prudent evasions of the question before the Council."[1] It was Origenist in general type, speaking of Christ as the Logos of God, "the first-born of all creation, begotten of the Father before all ages," and, in short, had the good and bad features of a compromise. The bulk of those present would have accepted it without discussion; but men like Athanasius and Marcellus of Ancyra, who realised the danger, were resolved not to be put off with ambiguities. They felt that phrases like "first-born of all creation" gave a loop-hole to Arianism, and that the mere statement that the Son "was made flesh" affirmed nothing vital as to

[1] Gwatkin, *Studies of Arianism*, 39.

His possession of a true human soul. Possibly in the end it was Hosius of Cordova who urged the Emperor to include the pregnant words *ὁμοούσιος τῷ πατρι*, as a bulwark against equivocation. Hosius, as a Western, may have overlooked the difficulties in the phrase of which the Easterns were conscious, and which had led them, fifty years before, to reject it in their condemnation of Paul of Samosata. Further, *ὁμοούσιος* agrees with the Western tradition as stated by Tertullian. Once the Emperor had indicated his approval, nothing remained for the majority but to submit; and ultimately the creed of Eusebius was remodelled in a spirit of stern and resolute opposition to all Arianising views. The text, as passed with virtual unanimity, is as follows:—

Πιστεύομεν εἰς ἕνα θεὸν πατέρα παντοκράτορα, πάντων ὁρατῶν τε καὶ ἀοράτων ποιητήν. Καὶ εἰς ἕνα κύριον Ἰησοῦν Χριστὸν τὸν υἱὸν τοῦ θεοῦ, γεννηθέντα ἐκ τοῦ πατρὸς μονογενῆ, τουτέστιν ἐκ τῆς οὐσίας τοῦ πατρός, θεὸν ἐκ θεοῦ, φῶς ἐκ φωτός, θεὸν ἀληθινὸν ἐκ θεοῦ ἀληθινοῦ, γεννηθέντα, οὐ ποιηθέντα, ὁμοούσιον τῷ πατρί, δι' οὗ τὰ πάντα ἐγένετο, τά τε ἐν τῷ οὐρανῷ καὶ τὰ ἐν τῇ γῇ· τὸν δι' ἡμᾶς τοὺς ἀνθρώπους καὶ διὰ τὴν ἡμετέραν σωτηρίαν κατελθόντα καὶ σαρκωθέντα, ἐνανθρωπήσαντα, παθόντα, καὶ ἀναστάντα τῇ τρίτῃ ἡμέρᾳ, ἀνελθόντα εἰς οὐρανούς, καὶ ἐρχόμενον κρῖναι ζῶντας καὶ νεκρούς. Καὶ εἰς τὸ ἅγιον πνεῦμα. Τοὺς δὲ λέγοντας· ἦν ποτε ὅτε οὐκ ἦν, καὶ πρὶν γεννηθῆναι οὐκ ἦν, καὶ ὅτι ἐξ οὐκ ὄντων ἐγένετο, ἢ ἐξ ἑτέρας ὑποστάσεως ἢ οὐσίας φάσκοντας εἶναι, ἢ κτιστὸν ἢ τρεπτὸν ἢ ἀλλοιωτὸν τὸν υἱὸν τοῦ θεοῦ, ἀναθεματίζει ἡ καθολικὴ ἐκκλησία.[1]

[1] "We believe in one God the Father Almighty, Maker of all things both visible and invisible. And in one Lord Jesus Christ the Son of God, begotten of the Father, only-begotten, that is, of the substance of the Father, God of God, Light of Light, true God of true God, begotten not made, of one substance with the Father (*homoousion*); through whom all things were made, both things in heaven and things on earth; who for us men and for our salvation came down and was made flesh, was made man, suffered, and rose again the third day, ascended into the heavens, and cometh to judge quick and dead. And in the Holy Spirit. But those

The main desire of those who framed this creed was obviously, as has been remarked, to exclude Arianism. At all costs it must be affirmed that the Son is not a creature, and that He is of one essence with the Father. This explains the alterations introduced into the Eusebian Creed, of which a brief account may be given. To begin with, Christ is designated, not as Logos, but as Son; and the two phrases, "the first-born of all creation" and "begotten of the Father before all ages," are dropped. Arians could have accepted both. Next, there are additions pointing in the same direction: (1) "only-bégotten" has attached to it the explanatory clause, "that is, from the essence of the Father"; (2) two phrases are inserted, "begotten, not made," and the famous "of one essence with the Father"; (3) the creed ends with unmistakable anathemas. According to these decisions, the Divine Sonship of Christ is set forth as no accident of time, but an eternal, and, as it were, organic relation within the Godhead. The distinction between Father and Son and their unity are equally stated and balanced over-against each other by the two phrases "from the essence" (distinction) and "of one essence" (unity). Finally, by adding "was made man" to "was made flesh," the Arian tenet that Christ had a real body, but no human soul, was definitively barred out; the Council, with remarkable self-restraint, laying down no other finding as to the constitution of the theanthropic person. Two curious facts are worth mention, as indicating that the Council had no leaning to Origen, and was more concerned to insist on the unity of Father and Son than the distinction. In the first place, there is no reference to "eternal generation"; in the second, the anathemas employ *ὑπόστασις* and *οὐσία* as synonyms. The latter usage almost entitles a thinker like Marcellus

who say that 'there was once when He was not,' and 'before being begotten He was not,' and 'He came to be of things that were not,' or contend that the Son of God is of a different substance or essence, or created, or (morally) alterable or mutable—these doth the Catholic Church anathematize." For the Greek text, see Hahn, § 142.

of Ancyra to read ὁμοούσιος in a Sabellian sense. The Sabellian associations of the word, at all events, are the most natural explanation of Athanasius' long reluctance to adopt it.

In the end only a few refused to sign; some perhaps, like Eusebius of Nicomedia, subscribing their names with secret reservations; others feeling, in their own bitter phrase, that "the soul is none the worse for a little ink." In point of fact, the views of Athanasius had been forced on half-convinced men, and reaction came inevitably, with the result that the Council of Nicæa opened a new stage in the controversy it was designed to close. This brings us to the man who now fought for truth in the front rank, and through whose instrumentality the Church was enabled to keep the faith.

§ 3. *Athanasius.*—Athanasius (*c.* 297–373) comes into view at the Council of Nicæa, to which he accompanied his bishop, Alexander. Probably a native of Alexandria, and doubtless trained in the grammar, logic, and rhetoric of the time, he appears early to have won the regard of the bishop, who employed him as his secretary. By the opening of the Arian controversy he was deacon, and in 326 succeeded Alexander in the bishop's chair. Although technically ineligible, he is considered on good grounds to have played a leading part in the Nicene debates. Though not erudite like Origen, he exhibits a clear and disciplined intelligence, as well as a searching religious power, and a courageous loftiness of spiritual temper, which make his vast influence no mystery. Statesman, saint, thinker, he gave his life as a long sacrifice for truth, with hardly one lapse from consistent greatness.

His fundamental ideas may be gathered from his tract, *On the Incarnation of the Word of God,* written before Arius had broached the new theory. Its leading thought is that God Himself has entered human history. Through the fall sin had invaded earth, bringing upon guilty man the fate of corruption and mortality. A higher power must interpose, since repentance on man's part would have been insufficient remedy; and hence in His infinite love God did the wonder of wonders. "The immortal Word took human flesh, and gave His mortal body for us all."[1] He wrought deliverance by receiving the principle of death into Himself, so permitting it to wreak all its might and terror on His nature, and annulling its power for all who are one with life in Him. By resurrection He vanquished the powers of corruption for ever, in a triumph which is the surety of our glorious return to God. To use the very words of Athanasius, "He was made man that we might be made God."[2]

His piercing criticisms of the Arian doctrine are only an application of these principles, from which he never swerved.[3] Arius, he said, taught pure polytheism; for if the Father is not Father everlastingly, and if in time a Son emerges, as the finite progeny of Godhead, and afterwards a Spirit lower still, who can answer for it that this is the end? Only if the Son is identical in nature and essence with the Father is it possible to speak of the Divine unity, and that this is the Son's true place is settled by the fact that Christians pray to Him. Again, the theory of Arius takes all certainty out of salvation. For how can it be certain if the Logos is morally alterable; how in that case can we see the unchanging Father in the Son, or regard the Son as the Father's image? In short, given the Arian view of Christ, it is idle to talk of our attaining to real union with God, or the forgiveness of sins, or immortality. If the Son has a created nature, His becoming man leaves us still at a distance from God, for no one who is a creature like ourselves could raise us to oneness with the Creator. He could never give us what He had not for Himself. A Godhead not original, but derived, could not be passed on to

[1] Gwatkin, *Arian Controversy*, 10.

[2] On the rendering "God," rather than "gods," see Robertson's note, p. 54 of his translation of Athanasius (*Nicene and Post-Nicene Fathers*, vol. iv.).

[3] Cf. Seeberg, *Dogmengeschichte* (1te Aufl.), 162 f.

others. Accordingly, "He had not promotion from His descent, but rather Himself promoted the things which needed promotion; and if He descended to effect their promotion, therefore He did not receive in reward the name of the Son and God, but rather He Himself has made us sons of the Father, and deified men by becoming Himself man. Therefore He was not man, and then became God, but He was God, and then became man, and that to deify us."[1] This is an idea which perpetually recurs; to partake of the Son is to partake of God Himself.[2] And once more, the idea of a cosmological mediator is superfluous. God is not too proud to touch the world, and needs no intermediary to bring Him in contact with finitude. Such a notion is immeasurably more unworthy of Him without whom not even a sparrow falls to the ground, than a clear assertion of His creative activity. Indeed, with a surprising divergence into pure logic, Athanasius in one passage[3] urges that if God needs a mediator to create, and the Logos is a creature, yet another mediator must have been required to create *Him*, and so on to infinity. Arius therefore satisfies reason as little as he does religion.

Thus, if Arius held Christ as part of the created world, Athanasius contended still more resolutely that His place is within the sphere of essential Godhead. Carefully maintaining that Divine unity to which Sabellius had borne confused witness, he set forth the being of the Son as Divine in the absolute and eternal sense. "Whatever that manner of existence is which differences God from all creatures, that is to be ascribed to the Son as well as to the Father."[4] His is no mediating nature, as Origen had taught, between the increate and the created; "the Son is different in kind and different in essence from things originate, and on the contrary is proper to the Father's essence and one in nature with it."[5] At the same time His independent personal being is secured. What binds

[1] *Or. c. Ar.* i. 38–39 (Robertson's translation).
[2] *Ibid.* 16. [3] *Ibid.* ii. 26. [4] Rainy, *op. cit.* 335.
[5] *Or. c. Ar.* i. 58; cf. 13.

Father and Son together is unity of essence (ἑνότης τῆς οὐσίας); the Word is generate from the essence of the Father. Still, at first Athanasius shows a certain avoidance of the word ὁμοούσιος, which occurs but once in the *Orationes contra Arianos.* He speaks indeed of the Son as "having with His Father the oneness of Godhead indivisible,"[1] and refers to "the identity of the one Godhead"[2] which Son and Father share. He can even express his meaning adequately by the term "like," in a variety of combinations; as "like in essence" or "like in all things." And, in agreement with the Nicene Creed, he employs ὑπόστασις and οὐσία as synonyms. But it has been pointed out that a change took place during his second exile, part of which was spent in Rome (339–346). For whatever reason, Athanasius went back to Alexandria a more convinced advocate of the term ὁμοούσιος, which the Nicene Council, he remarks, had inserted to check the Eusebians, "by way of signifying that the Son was from the Father, and not merely like, but the same in likeness."[3] It is characteristic of him that in such a case he would not decline the newer phrase.[4]

The Son, then, comes forth from the Father by birth or generation; and by generation Athanasius means simply the Son's complete participation in the whole essence of the Father. The idea of an efflux or emanation is inapplicable: "God, being without parts, is Father of the Son without partition or passion; for there is neither effluence of the Immaterial, nor influx from without, as

[1] *Or. c. Ar.* iv. 41. [2] *Ibid.* iii. 4. [3] *de Decr.* 20.

[4] When Athanasius says (*de Decr.* 27) that "the Word is not of another essence or subsistence (ἐξ ἑτέρας οὐσίας ἢ ὑποστάσεως), but proper to the Father's," he is obviously hampered by having so far no settled term for the distinctions in the Godhead. "Hypostasis" and "ousia" are used interchangeably. The West had *personae* for the three aspects of Deity, but the Greek equivalent (πρόσωπα) was suspect owing to its Sabellian associations. This lack of terminological unanimity and clearness was extremely awkward; and at times we can see that Easterns and Westerns who felt themselves at variance were really in agreement, but got to cross-purposes through the ambiguity of terms, and especially owing to the fact that the technical words in Greek and Latin did not correspond. Something was done to clear up the confusion by the Council of Alexandria in 362.

among men; but, being uncompounded in nature, He is Father of one Only Son." Again and again it is insisted that this generation is not of the Father's will (ἐκ βουλήσεως) but of His nature, for the Son is not to be reduced to the offspring of arbitrary volition. Athanasius' favourite symbol of the relationship is the familiar one of radiance in its unity with the parent light.[1] So the Godhead, which exists in the Father, belongs to the Son also in the totality of its essence; "the same things are said of the Son which are said of the Father, except His being said to be Father."[2] Finally, the generation is an eternal one, for "as the Father is always good by nature, so He is always generative by nature."[3]

An argument of this kind, based not so much on logic as on permanent religious considerations, really meant that the philosophical doctrine of the Logos, as interpretative of the Lord's person, had been replaced by the conception of the Divine Sonship. Experience had proved that the term Logos too easily lent itself to cosmological theories with no bearing on salvation, and tended to denote a mediating Being, essentially distinct from God. In such ideas Athanasius could have no interest. The Saviour must be God, if a world perishing in death was to be renewed in Divine immortality. Being very God, however, and having put on human flesh, the Son became liable to suffering; nay more, He submitted to be put to death in the body, that by His risen power He might quicken all men. In Him, as the Second Adam, we have gained what was lost through the first, for whatever happened to Christ's flesh happened to us also mystically. Loofs has justly remarked that this doctrine of redemption, which goes back through Asia Minor tradition to the Fourth Gospel, is the most important element in the Athanasian theology. Not only was central significance given thereby to the historic Christ, but the religious interests at stake in the Arian controversy were placed in their true light, and the ultimate triumph of the Nicene doctrine assured.[4]

[1] Cf. *Or. c. Ar.* iii. 4. [2] *Ibid.* [3] *Ibid.* iii. 67. [4] *RE.* ii. 18–19.

Looking back, we can perceive that a strongly monotheistic tendency gave tone to Athanasius' mind, and lent irresistible force to his conflict with the followers of Arius. His unfaltering conviction that the Son has His being within the one Godhead was also in line with immemorial Christian instincts, and was expressed, besides, with such resolute and persistent energy that after his time neither Sabellianism nor a doctrine of subordination affecting the intrinsic nature of the Son could make headway. But withal Athanasius never wavered in the belief that the Father is the source and fountain of deity. These two aspects of theory, the one identifying the Son with the Father's essence, the other representing the Son as somehow caused by, or derived from, the Father as the Divine Monad, are both present in his writings, and neither can be ignored in an estimate of the whole. Animadversions, no doubt, may be made upon this or that defect in his teaching. We should put differently his point that God is Father "by nature, and not of will," for to the modern mind will is the very core and essence of personality. And the Lord's humanity is referred to with ominous frequency in terms which might seem to make it consist only of the flesh. Nor will Athanasius' exegesis always bear inspection, though he has an instinct for the really important passages of the New Testament. His power lay in his possession of the truth, and in his worthy representation of a great cause. His phraseology is by no means sacrosanct, and we should often apply a different mode of argument; but with the New Testament in our hands it is impossible not to acquiesce in his main conclusion. Even the word "consubstantial" (ὁμοούσιος), so fiercely assailed both then and now, is but the assertion of the real deity of Christ in terms of the philosophy by which it had been denied.[1]

[1] Cf. Illingworth, *Reason and Revelation*, 123. "The place of Athanasius as a great religious leader has been obscured by his position as a theologian; but when we turn to his writings, where do we find less of what is commonly called dogmatic theology? There is argument, reason-

§ 4. *Marcellus of Ancyra.*—At Nicæa, we have seen victory being snatched by a resolute minority in face of an immensely larger but divided party. The great mediating group—often called Eusebians, or later Semi-Arians, though this term really belongs to the later party of Homœans—quickly recovered themselves, and a reaction ensued. The belief of the churches was against Arius, yet not definitely for Nicæa. This at all events holds true of the East, where conservative feeling inclined strongly to the indefinite Christological formulas of an older time. Two objections were made. In the first place, ὁμοούσιος was a new word, and it was an unheard-of thing thus to put an unscriptural expression (and one previously condemned) into a creed—not the creed of a particular bishop, but a symbol or definition constructed by a general Council, and meant for the whole Church. To this Athanasius rejoins that "if the expressions are not in so many words in the Scriptures, yet they contain the sense of the Scriptures."[1] Secondly, the Nicene doctrine was denounced as Sabellian. Some colour, it may be admitted, was given to this accusation by the teaching of Marcellus of Ancyra, than whom the Nicene Creed had no more ardent champion. His is a curiously modern type of theory in certain aspects, and will repay a brief examination.[2]

ing, searching for proofs and their statement; but all that belongs to the outworks of his teaching. The central citadel is a spiritual intuition—I *know* that *my* Saviour is the God Who made heaven and earth. He took his stand firmly and unflinchingly on that personal experience, and all else mattered little compared with the fundamental spiritual fact. It was not his arguments, but his unflinching faith, that convinced his generation" (Lindsay, *History of the Reformation*, vol. i. 433). Athanasius felt less interest in the problem of the theanthropic Person, and can hardly be said to recognise the distinction of *person* and *nature*. Cf. Scheel, 102.

[1] *de Decr.* 21.

[2] A clear, if rather unsympathetic, account of the Christology of Marcellus is given by Gwatkin, *Studies of Arianism*, 75–82. See also Moberly's valuable note, *Atonement and Personality*, 208–15; and Sanday, in *HDB.* iv. 579. A modern writer who resembles Marcellus is the celebrated Moses Stuart of Andover; see some interesting pages in Foster's *History of the New England Theology*, chap. x.

His main interest in the unity of God was exhibited in an energetic antipathy to the ditheism he felt to be encouraged by, if not immediately derived from, the teaching of Origen. But he was not consciously a Sabellian. Instead, he went back, as he not quite unnaturally believed, to the authentic doctrine of the New Testament. Holding with the Arians that generation carried with it the inferiority of the Son, as neither co-eternal nor co-equal with the Father, he rejected the term "Son" as a designation of the pre-existent One. "Logos" is the proper term; the Son, on the other hand, said Marcellus, was generate at His birth "four hundred years ago," at which point of time the Logos —*i.e.* the eternally inherent power of God, which emerged before time to create the world—came forth into personal subsistence. The original emergence of the Logos being "an active extension of the Godhead,"[1] the relative distinction implied in it was augmented by the incarnation; the incarnate Logos, as he puts it, is "separated from the Father by the weakness of flesh," yet without change in His previous relation. In fine, "the Word as such is pure spirit, and only became the Son of God by becoming the Son of Man."[2] In the same way, the Spirit exists only since Christ breathed it on His disciples. "We see the Monad being expanded into a Triad."[3] At the Parousia, Christ will appear in flesh once more; thereafter the relation of Sonship will terminate, "the Logos being merged in God as He was before the existence of the world." What will then become of His body, unworthy of God in any case, it is impossible to say.

If not Sabellian, the theory was at least Sabellianising. That its author was acknowledged by the great bulk of the Homousians proves how sincerely they held the Divine unity, and took the threefold historic revelation as the point of departure. Marcellus met them here. The Christ of the Gospels is *κατὰ πνεῦμα* the eternal

[1] *πλατύνεσθαι ἐνεργείᾳ.* [2] Gwatkin, *Arian Controversy*, 54.
[3] *ἡ μόνας φαίνεται πλατυνομένη εἰς τριάδα.*

Logos, and, until His final abdication, partner in the throne of God. But the scheme was at once rejected as involving a merely transitory incarnation; and unquestionably, so far as language goes, the Son of God is in Marcellus' view a mere phenomenon of time. He came into collision with Christian feeling even more violently by the suggestion that the Lord's humanity itself is but a temporary vesture, a servant's form to be laid aside when the servant's work is done. But in justice we should remember that his refusal of the name "Son" to the pre-incarnate Christ appears not to have been quite definitive after all. He fought passionately for the Nicene Creed, in which the pre-existent One is Son, not Logos; and when in 371 his followers presented a creed to Athanasius, it was found to contain a distinct acknowledgment of the eternal Sonship, with anathemas upon those who held the contrary. At all events, Athanasius never disowned him publicly, though he tacitly refutes him in the *Fourth Discourse against the Arians.* Not till 380 was Marcellus condemned in the West. "Of whose kingdom there shall be no end," in the so-called Nicæno-Constantinopolitan Creed, is aimed at him.

§ 5. *Movements of Semiarianism; the Cappadocian Divines.*—Under Constantine, who died in 337, and especially in the reign of his successor Constantius, the mediating party were high favourites at court. In 351 his brother's death left Constantius sole Emperor. At once his will became law in religion. Many of the noblest Westerns, including Hilary of Poictiers and Hosius of Cordova, endured exile for the sake of the Nicene faith. In 356, Athanasius fled to the desert for the third time, not to return for six years, and the triumph of Arianism seemed complete. Under the leadership of Ætius of Antioch and Eunomius of Cyzicus, men came forward to revive the teaching of Arius in its most objectionable form. Only logic is wanted, and logic tells us that if God is unbegotten and His essence simple, there is no mystery in His being; on the other hand, and with equal obviousness, if the Son is begotten He cannot be God as the Father is; nay, in strictness, He cannot be like the Father at all, for He is a mere creature. Euzoius only put this Anhomœan position bluntly when at Antioch in 361 he carried the position that the Son is *κατὰ πάντα ἀνόμοιος τῷ πατρί.* The next step was explicitly to condemn the Nicene Creed; and this was duly done in the Sirmian manifesto (357), an overtly Arian document in which it was declared that the words essence, of the same essence, or of like essence, ought not to be used, because they do not occur in the Holy Scriptures, and because the matter passes human comprehension.[1] Even the veteran Hosius was compelled to sign, though he would not condemn Athanasius. This seemed to make an end of the Nicene doctrine for good. But the policy of huddling up difficulties in silence rarely prospers, nor was the situation cleared by the sedulous evasiveness of the definition promoted by the new Homœan party soon after at the conference in Sirmium (359): "We say that the Son is like the Father in all things, as the Holy Scriptures say and teach."[2] In the capacious ambiguity of a phrase like this, even the punctuation of which was uncertain, all sorts of opinion were at home. Meanwhile, these minimising tendencies made little or no headway in the West.

Throughout the East also they were opposed strongly. In 358, Basil presided over a council at Ancyra, which affirmed very emphatically the Son's similarity of essence, and formed the turning-point of the contest by giving rise to the Homœousian party. Rejecting the Nicene "consubstantial" as Sabellian, they declined the Anhomœan position still more vehemently.[3] Gradually they began slowly to approximate to the Nicene theology, feeling that with it lay the future of religion. Athanasius returned once more to Alexandria, and held out a conciliatory hand. He recognised (*de Synodis*) that the

[1] See Hahn, § 161. [2] *Ibid.* § 163. [3] *Ibid.* § 162.

Homœousian formula "of like essence" was distinctly meant both to affirm Christ's true Sonship and to deny His creaturehood; and though preferring his own terms, he was willing to discuss the matter. Two points are worth noting. When Basil and his friends urged that *ὁμοούσιος* should be replaced by *ὅμοιος κατ' οὐσίαν*, they meant no casual resemblance, but rather specific identity; Christ is *essentially* like God as a human son is like his father. And again, it was among these Homœousian writers first that *οὐσία* and *ὑπόστασις* began to be distinguished clearly; the one being used to designate the Divine essence (Lat. *substantia*), the other to denote a personal distinction within the Godhead (Lat. *persona*). They felt that if this useful differentiation of the general from the individual were adopted, all danger of taking the Nicene formula in a Sabellian sense would be gone. The understanding on these points attained between Athanasius and the Homœousians at the Council of Alexandria in 362, ensured the ultimate fall of Arianism, and issued in the formation of the younger Nicene party. The same Council repudiated the view that the Holy Spirit is "a creature," or distinct from the essence of the Son, a tenet which had been maintained by a group led by Macedonius of Constantinople.

This younger Nicene party was headed by three remarkable men, Basil of Cæsarea (died 379), his friend Gregory of Nazianzus (died 389), and his brother Gregory of Nyssa (died after 394). They were enthusiastic students of Origen—in spite of the growing tendency to rank him as heretical—who revered Athanasius as the father of orthodoxy. By interpreting his theology in an Origenistic sense, they lent to it a colour considerably different from the original. But their influence on the doctrine of the Trinity was profound. Assuming the three hypostases in the Godhead, they strove to bring out the unity of the one Divine essence, and to fix their results the significance of the principal terms was defined with a new sharpness. "'*Ουσία* now received a significance midway between the abstract 'essence' and the concrete 'individual,' yet so that it inclined very strongly to the former; ὑπόστασις was placed in meaning midway between person and quality (accident or 'mode'), yet so that the personal idea was the stronger."[1] Starting as they did from the threeness in the Divine, with the unity as a mysterious problem, it was particularly difficult for the Cappadocians to avoid the semblance of tritheism, and this was an accusation long current in the West.

In Christology, their work largely resulted in a revival of the idea of the Logos, as mediator of creation. And yet they ring out clearly the believing certainty that only through God Himself is fellowship with God accessible to man. This determines their view of the Lord's person. But they lay the emphasis otherwise than Athanasius. Basil, for example, argues that the revelation of the Image of God in flesh gives us that knowledge of God which makes us like Him, and that only He who is the essential Good can perfect us in goodness. Gregory of Nazianzus contends that none can deify our spirits save He who is Spirit essentially, and that only the death of the Son of God can atone for the sins of the whole world. Gregory of Nyssa looks back more eagerly to the historic Christ, pointedly naming Him, however, "the only-begotten God," wholly identical in essence with the Father.

In 381 the Emperor Theodosius convoked a general Council at Constantinople, and there, in addition to the condemnation of the Sabellians and the various types of Arian, the Nicene Creed in its original form was ratified. No new creed was set forth. For centuries tradition held that the creed now commonly known as the Nicene[2] (technically the Nicæno - Constantinopolitan) had been promulgated at this Council, which is certainly an error. It came into existence earlier, and has close resemblances to a creed which, as Epiphanius relates, was used by the Church of Salamis in Cyprus. Others connect it with

[1] Harnack, *Grundriss*, 182; cf. Loofs, in *RE.* iv. 46.
[2] Hahn, § 144.

the baptismal creed of the Church of Jerusalem. In the acts of the Council of Chalcedon it is ascribed to the 150 bishops who met at Constantinople, and put on a par with the original Nicene Creed, which thenceforward it virtually displaced. Its phrasing and order are distinctly inferior to those of its predecessor. "The elaborate framework of Nicæa is completely shattered, and even the keystone clause 'of the essence of the Father' is left out."[1]

The Arian conflict was now over, and the East could lay aside its fear of Sabellianising definitions.

[1] Gwatkin, *Arian Controversy*, 160.

CHAPTER V.

CONTROVERSIES AS TO THE FULL HUMANITY OF CHRIST.

§ 1. *Apollinarianism.*—It was now an axiom that the Divine manifested in Jesus Christ was one in essence with supreme Godhead. His real humanity also had been assumed from the first, and explicitly defended in opposition to Gnostic docetism. But men had scarcely reflected on the question how two natures could unite in one personality, or how room could be made, in a life thus dual or composite, for human nature as a whole. Tertullian had spoken of "two substances in one person"; but this was a Western formula. The instinctive feeling of the Church was of course that in order to save man Christ must Himself be man. But if God and man are actually disparate and incommensurable, how shall this deep craving of the believing consciousness be satisfied? The problem could not be resolved by the merely figurative declaration that the humanity of Jesus is in the Logos as glowing iron in fire.

We have seen that in the Nicene Creed "made flesh" was explained by the added phrase "made man," in order

LITERATURE—Voisin, *L'Apollinarisme*, 1901; Lietzmann, *Apollinaris von Laodicea und seine Schule*, 1904; Holl, *Amphilochius von Ikonium in seinem Verhältnis zu den grossen Kappadoziern*, 1904; Swete, article "Theodorus," in *Dict. Chr. Biog.*; Harnack, article "Antiochienische Schule," *RE.* i.; Bright, *History of the Church 313–415*; Loofs, articles on "Nestorius," *RE.* xiii., and "Eutyches," *RE.* v.; Rainy, *Ancient Catholic Church*, 1902; Krüger, article "Cyrill von Alexandrien," *RE.* iv.; Loofs, *Leontius von Byzantium*, 1887; Krüger, *Monophysitische Streitigkeiten*, 1884; Curtis, *History of Creeds*, 1911; Hefele, *Conciliengeschichte*, iii.

to exclude the Arian tenet that Christ had a human body but no human soul. Eudoxius of Constantinople had put the Arian view unambiguously in the creed known by his name: "He took no human soul, but became flesh. . . . Two natures there were not, but instead of the soul was God in flesh, the whole one composite nature."[1] Not even Athanasius had grappled with the interior problems of the theanthropic Life. He was accustomed to speak of the Logos as having assumed a human body, or simply flesh; and while the Saviour was for him—at least in his earlier phase—an individual man, he frequently operates with the conception "flesh" as denoting an impersonal vesture or instrument, to which it was natural to refer the phenomena of suffering, progress, and exaltation. But he never worked out a clear view. An extraordinary variety of opinion prevailed as to the relation of Christ's manhood to ours. Harnack points out that docetism, of a finer or coarser shade, was almost universal. Few ascribed to Christ a genuinely human soul, and by many His flesh was conceived as heavenly in character, as a transmuted form of the Logos, or simply as a garment. "No one in the East really thought of two natures. *One* eternal Divine-human nature, *one* Divine-human nature that has come to be, a Divine nature temporarily changed into the human, a Divine nature inhabiting the human or clad in a veil of humanity—these were the dominating ideas."[2] If the Church was to pronounce on the connection between the Divine and human in Christ, she had first to clear up her mind as to the significance of His humanity.

Apollinaris of Laodicea (died about 390) was the first to raise the question in an acute form. A theologian of the first rank, he set the problems at which after-centuries laboured. His dominating aim was to secure the complete unity of Christ's person without sacrificing His real deity, or representing Him, with Paul of Samosata or Photinus, as a mere ἄνθρωπος ἔνθεος. But he considered the Arians were right in objecting to

[1] Hahn, § 191. [2] *Grundriss*, 191.

the current doctrine that it predicated of Christ two personalities; to quote his words, "if perfect God were joined to perfect man, they would be two—one, Son of God by nature, one by adoption" (θετός).[1] A man-God is really as unthinkable as a centaur. We must apply the fundamental axiom of logic that two perfect entities cannot become one. Besides, how can we ascribe freedom of will to the man Jesus, without such risks as faith dare not accept? Where complete manhood is, there is sin. For these reasons Apollinaris was obliged to deny the entirety of Christ's human nature. At first he held that the Logos had taken merely a human body; later, in a defensive statement of his position, he developed the view—resting on a trichotomic pyschology (cf. 1 Th 5[3])—that the body and soul in Christ were human, whereas the place of the human spirit was taken by the Logos. Thus he attained his supreme object; the human spirit, source and seat of mutability, is replaced by the immutable Divine Word. The danger is removed, not by curtailing the Divine nature, which would be heresy, but by leaving out that element in man's being which means a perilous fallibility. As a further advantage, the fatal deficiencies of Arianism are vetoed, for the Logos contemplated in this scheme is no mere creature, but eternally and inherently one with God.

These difficulties surmounted, Apollinaris was able to describe the Logos and the abridged human nature as having been fused in "a single nature," "a single essence." Instead of two natures, which imply two self-conscious and self-determining subjects, what exists is an essential union of God and man. There is but one incarnate nature of God the Word (*μίαν φύσιν τοῦ θεοῦ λόγου σεσαρκωμένην*).[2] Apollinaris took this so literally as to affirm an actual deification of the flesh of Christ, thus furnishing a reasoned basis for the physical doctrine of redemption current in the Greek theology. "His flesh," we read, "makes us alive through the Deity now become one essence with it, for

[1] *Fragm.* 81. [2] *Ad Iovian.* 1. Hahn, § 195.

the flesh is Divine, having been joined to God."[1] On his special presuppositions, however, the outcome of Apollinaris' argument could scarcely fail to be docetic; and we are not surprised that at last he should venture upon the statement that Christ's flesh is not consubstantial with ours, since it is the very flesh of God. It is even in a sense pre-existent. It may be that in speaking of the pre-temporal reality of Christ's flesh Apollinaris meant to indicate the belief that the Logos, as such, is archetypal man, "not foreign to that human spirit which is in His likeness, but rather the true perfection of His image." But in that case his expressions have an unfortunate obscurity.

Scholars are on the whole agreed in acknowledging the singular intellectual brilliance and power of Apollinaris' work. Indeed, his theory of the person of Christ has with some reason been declared by certain modern writers to be the most consistent and successful application known to us of the psychological presuppositions and speculative categories of his time. It is a question whether even Athanasius had greater gifts for pure theology. The fact is all the more remarkable—may we not say, the more providentially significant?—that, notwithstanding the marked strain of docetism in previous Christologies, the Church at this point definitely refused to follow a daring thinker who seemed only to regularise and make logical her own docetic tendencies. Her reasons for this refusal are convincing. In the first place, it was felt that Apollinaris taught no real incarnation after all. In becoming man, the Son of God took possession only of a partial or mutilated humanity. Not only so; that very constituent of human nature was left out which is intrinsically akin to God and capable of vital relations to Him, and God is conceived as "uniting Himself only with that in man which he shares with the beasts that perish."[2] Doubtless by maintaining that the Logos can thus replace the principle of intelligence and moral action in man, Apollinaris so far

[1] *Fragm.* 116. [2] Caird, *The Fundamental Ideas of Christianity*, ii. 156.

brings out the close relationship of the Divine and the human, for only related things can be substituted for each other; but this furnishes no compensation for so grave an omission. Again, sin is primarily an affair of man's spiritual being; it is the spirit that is corrupted, misguided, estranged from God: hence the salvation we require must be applied to and take possession of that focal point of human life, and this, according to the theory of Apollinaris, is precisely what cannot be. As Gregory of Nazianzus put it tersely: "that which is unassumed is unhealed" (τὸ γὰρ ἀπρόσληπτον, ἀθεράπευτον). The very part of man in which sin resides gains nothing from the redemptive powers of Christ, and consequently falls short of eternal life. And yet again, owing very much to his use of categories which are more physical or metaphysical than ethical, Apollinaris tends to define God and man as absolute contraries which cannot on any terms be truly one. God is immutable, man is mutable; God is essentially self-moving, man is wholly passive; from which it obviously follows that a living unity of the two is inconceivable. We have to choose between a human and a Divine spirit in Christ. The sublime thought that Christ is perfect in His humanity just because of the personal indwelling of God, and thereby becomes the Head of a new redeemed race, has completely fallen out of sight. Nevertheless, in spite of these grave defects, which prepared the way for Monophysitism, Apollinaris quickened the mind of the Church and forced an interest in vital questions. In particular, he made it necessary for those who rejected his conclusions to admit into their view of Christ a real belief in His spiritual experience as man, lived out "not under unnatural or supernaturally guarded conditions, but under strictly human conditions of growth, trial, dependence, and freedom."[1] It was a lesson the Church took centuries to learn.

The task of combating the Apollinarian positions fell chiefly to the two Gregories, who were themselves perhaps

[1] Dykes, in *Expos. Times* for Nov. 1905, 56.

too near the heresy to strike at it with effect. Gregory of Nazianzus rightly finds that the death of Christ is an atonement only as it is the death of One who is true man as well as God, and we have already seen how unerringly he laid his finger on the central weakness of the novel theory. For both thinkers, however, the subject or Ego in Christ was the Logos, His human nature being no more than the sphere in which deification should take place. Gregory of Nyssa compares the relation of the Divine and human to that between a drop of vinegar and the sea in which it is swallowed up,[1] and affirms that even Christ's body in which He suffered became identical, because commingled, with the Divine nature that assumed it.[2] Man's weakness and mutability disappear in the life of God. Along with this, it is true, went a strong assertion of the two natures. It was the manhood that wept at the grave of Lazarus, the Godhead that raised him up. But these two natures mutually interpenetrate, and Gregory of Nyssa threw out the valuable idea that in Christ's person we see a *growing* unity, in which the humanity comes fully to partake of the qualities of Godhead only after the passion and the resurrection.[3] Thus he was able to make room for the human life of Jesus.

In 381, at the Council of Constantinople, Apollinarianism was explicitly condemned; but neither in the Church nor outside was a period then put to its influence.

§ 2. *The School of Antioch: Nestorius.*—If the criticism of the Cappadocian thinkers occasionally lacked force, it was not so with the theologians of Antioch. Diodorus, founder of the exegetical school of Antioch, had had as his most famous pupil Theodore of Mopsuestia (died 429). Theodore came to the problems of Christology with a mind preoccupied with thoughts of the immutability of God, the freedom of the will, and the reality of Jesus' human life. We must gain a point of view from

[1] Cf. Dräseke, *op. cit.* 175.
[2] *contra Eunomium*, c. 3.
[3] Cf. Bonwetsch, *Grundriss d. DG.* (1909), 89.

which His ethical career is seen as exemplary for ours. Hence no more can be affirmed than a relative moral union of Godhead and manhood; the Saviour's person consists of two independent natures, each complete within itself, but united in one personality by means of an ethical bond (συνάφεια). God is present in Jesus as He was in saints or prophets, only in complete fulness, not substantially but by way of grace or favour (κατ' εὐδοκίαν, not κατ' οὐσίαν), and in a union which is perfected at the ascension. There is a oneness accordingly for the spectator, a oneness of name, worship, honour; but the unity so affirmed is imported into the object by the mind, not resident in its actual constitution. The passion, for instance, does not touch the Godhead. Theodore could even speak of two "hypostases," or persons, united as it were by a moral league.

This mode of interpretation, beyond all doubt, held within it elements of value. To it the Church owed a vivid realisation of the earthly career of Jesus, with all its richness of ethical experience, and that human individuality of life which means so much for us to-day. "Probably," as Dykes has put it, "Theodore's best contribution to the subject lay in his insistence that the development of our Lord in knowledge and virtue could be no θέατρον, but a genuine human progress culminating in genuine human virtue; and that this human life and character, with its free self-determination and moral victories, was essential to His work of redemption."[1] And yet there was not a little in the rational supernaturalism of Antioch to awaken the misgivings of faith. While Theodore himself fulminated against Paul of Samosata as an *angelus diaboli*, many others believed that lines of connection could easily be traced from Samosata to Antioch, and that the advantages of consistency and clearness were entirely on the side of the older writer. Theodore and his group, it goes without saying, were convinced adherents of Nicæa, and

[1] *Op. cit.* 55.

in all sincerity acknowledged the presence of the Eternal Word in Christ. But in point of fact it was difficult for them to call Jesus more than a supremely inspired man. He is man side by side with God, man in alliance with God, not God in and through and as man. There is concord of will and purpose, not the oneness of a single personal life. Now, only those could be content with this, whose conception of salvation had declined from the New Testament level. It was not merely that the Antiochenes repudiated the physical doctrine of redemption, for so far they were on right lines; it was rather that they scarcely felt the necessity for pardon and regeneration. Christ to them is the Leader and Perfecter of faith rather than a Redeemer who quickens and restores the soul by inward grace. The same tendency to emphasise the ethical more than the religious aspects of the Gospel is shown by the fact that the qualities of manhood they fixed upon for Christ, and vindicated as essential, were abstract moral freedom and the capacity to suffer.

But here, as in the Arian controversy, it was found that views which might be held quietly in schools of doctrine woke the sounds of strife when proclaimed in the Church at large. A liturgical phrase began the war. Nestorius, patriarch of Constantinople in 428, had received his theological education at Antioch. Offended by the application of the epithet θεοτόκος to the Virgin Mary, he vehemently took sides with a presbyter who had assailed the word as inaccurate and extravagant. It was a popular term, and even Theodore had used it. But Nestorius pronounced it heathenish. "Mary," he writes, "did not bear the Godhead; she bore a man who was the organ of Godhead." Not θεοτόκος but Χριστοτόκος is the right name. As Mr. Bethune-Baker has expressed it: "What he feels must be guarded against at all costs is, on the one hand, the idea that the Godhead itself was born of a woman, wrapped in swaddling-clothes, suffered and died; and, on the other hand, the idea that the manhood of the incarnate Word was not real manhood like our own."[1] To understand the fierce resistance he met with, we must consider that the word now assailed had come to be a testimony against the Unitarian theories of the day. It goes back at least to Athanasius and probably to Origen. And that Nestorius' dislike of it was not unreasoning, or the product of mere negation, is clear from the fact that he later conceded the word, provided only it was not held to make the Virgin a goddess.

But in general he remained true to the Christological traditions of Antioch. God the Word is sharply distinguished from the man Jesus. The Holy Spirit did not create the Word, but formed a temple for Him from the Virgin, which He should inhabit. "For His sake who wears I worship Him that is worn; for the sake of the hidden One I adore Him that appears. From Him who appears God is inseparable: for this reason I do not separate the honour of Him who is inseparate. I sever the natures, but I combine the worship."[2] The man Jesus was not deified, but He was taken into a unique personal conjunction with the Logos, and after the resurrection lifted up to a share in His universal power. Loofs has pointed out[3] that it was easier for Nestorius

[1] Mr. Bethune-Baker has published a brief work in which he endeavours to clear Nestorius' reputation for orthodoxy (*Nestorius and his Teaching*, Cambridge, 1908). He comes to the conclusion that Nestorius was in reality no "Nestorian," since "he did not hold the belief commonly attributed to him that in Jesus Christ two persons, the person of a God and the person of a man, were mechanically joined together, one being Son by nature and the other Son by association, so that really there were two Sons and two Christs. He is as explicit as possible on this point" (82). And again: "He did not think of two distinct persons joined together, but of a single Person who combined in Himself the two distinct things (*substances*), Godhead and manhood, with their characteristics (*natures*) complete and intact though united in Him" (87); "he had had all through the weary years of the struggle 'one only end in view—that no one should call the Word of God a creature, or the manhood which was assumed incomplete'" (197). It is indeed a question whether dualism can be charged upon Nestorius in any sense that would not also hold against the Creed of Chalcedon.

[2] Serm. 9 (Loofs, *Nestoriana*, 262).

[3] *Leitfaden*, 290.

than for Theodore to emphasise the unity of Christ's personality, because, like Marcellus of Ancyra, he regards the terms "Son," "Lord," and even "only-begotten" as terms proper to be used of the Incarnate, rather than "God the Word" or "Man." For they express the duality of nature in Him, the created nature and the increate. It is the historic Christ, single though duplex in nature, that forms his real point of departure.

§ 3. *Cyril of Alexandria.*—Nestorius had the misfortune to be opposed by one of the most powerful and most unsympathetic figures in Church history. Cyril (376–444) had been bishop of Alexandria since 412. A master of diplomatic intrigue, unscrupulous in his methods, ambitious, proud, and violent, he was nevertheless a really great divine, and to this day has a place of special honour among the teachers of the Greek Church.

The Christology of Cyril in its essential features is a continuation of the theory held by Athanasius and Gregory of Nazianzus. Like them, he chiefly aimed at supplying a theoretical basis for the physical theory of redemption, according to which humanity is imbued or saturated with deity through the incarnation; and the militant opposition which this involved to the theologians of Antioch, who denied the real union of the natures in Christ, was the predominant influence in his doctrinal activities. Starting from the eternal being of the Logos, as a hypostatic distinction in the Trinity, he teaches that He not only assumed but became flesh, and formed the personal subject in the God-man.[1] Christ, be it noted, was not an individual man. On the contrary, the Word,

[1] Ottley well remarks that Cyril gives no consistent answer to the question what is meant by the "unity" of the Divine person. At one time it appears as an *original* unity, being constituted by the one unchangeable Logos "who remains even after the Incarnation what He was before it." "Sometimes, on the other hand, Cyril speaks of the person of Christ as if it were a *resultant* unity," issuing from the amalgamation of the two natures. But the former point of view is more typical. (*Doctrine of the Incarnation*, vol. ii. 82.)

having passed into human nature, as constituted by rational soul and body—which now are *His* soul and body indissociably—yet remains the one indivisible subject He was prior to incarnation. The two natures are in no way confused or mingled—"the flesh is flesh and not deity, even if it has become flesh of God"—but their union has produced a permanent essential state or fact; it is a *ἕνωσις κατ' οὐσίαν καὶ καθ' ὑπόστασιν*, a *ἕνωσις φυσική*. Manhood has been taken up intact into the unity of the Divine essence. But we may speak of a certain interchange of the properties, in this sense that the person being one, all qualities of either nature can be predicated of the one Christ. Thus, for example, the Logos is visible and tangible, and the suffering is the suffering of God. The natures are distinct, yet when we see them most truly we see them in a mysteriously intimate cohesion, all that properly inheres in the one passing over to, and becoming the possession of, the other. There are no doubt occasional infidelities to this point of view, as when Cyril declares the Logos to be as little affected by suffering as fire in glowing steel by the smith's hammer-strokes, and replaces the recorded limitations of our Lord's knowledge by what is really a prudential affectation of ignorance.

A favourite mode of expression with Cyril is the phrase that Christ is "one out of two natures" (*ἐκ δύο φύσεων εἷς*). In other words, before the incarnation two natures existed, thereafter only the one Divine-human nature of the Lord. Indeed, we encounter once again the older Apollinarian formula, "one incarnate nature of God the Word," which Cyril mistakenly believed to be Athanasian. The phrase is an epitome of his polemic against Nestorius. The Logos had not united with Himself the person of man; He had become flesh, and the Virgin had borne the incarnate Word "according to the flesh." As soul and body are one in us, so Godhead and manhood were made the one Christ. Hence the Nestorian assertion of a mere "conjunction" or "contact" is to be utterly rejected; nothing but a hypostatic union will serve.

"If the Word did not suffer for us humanly, He did not accomplish our redemption Divinely; if He who suffered for us was mere man and but the organ of deity, we are not in fact redeemed."[1] One detail of historical importance should be noted. Since the person in the God-man is but the prolongation of the one life of the Eternal Word—not the effect of incarnation—it follows in Cyril's view that Christ's human nature is impersonal (*ἀνυπόστατος*). This much resembles the theory of Apollinaris, but Cyril escapes the danger, at least verbally, by his emphatic insistence on the completeness of the human nature assumed by the Logos. At the same time, while he does not enter explicitly on the question—even he can still use *φύσις* and *ὑπόστασις* as synonyms—Cyril really heads the list of writers who have held that the human nature of Christ possesses no independent personality of its own, and is personal only in the Logos.[2] In itself it is reduced to unconscious and impersonal elements. The step, in a multitude of ways, was a singularly unfortunate one. It broke decisively, as we have seen, with earlier and better patristic views. And it added enormously to the difficulty of recognising in the Christ of Church dogma the historic Saviour who had long been enshrined in the inmost heart of faith, for no real meaning could be attached to a human "nature" which is not simply one aspect of the concrete life of a human person.

Nevertheless it is a merit in Cyril not easily to be overestimated, that he strove with such persistence to bring out the living and organic unity of Christ's person. And here he was guided by a genuinely religious interest. "This school of Greek theology was right," it has been said, "in the stress it laid on the closest possible union of God with Man in order that the dynamic power of the

[1] Quoted by Bonwetsch, *Grundriss*, 90.

[2] His account of Christ's human knowledge is unconcealed docetism. There was really no ignorance, and could be none, in a nature physically united to the Logos. When Christ said that He was ignorant of the day of judgment, "He usefully pretended not to know."

Christ-life might operate upon the race whose new Head He is come to be."[1] That is at all events a thoroughly sympathetic verdict on its deepest motive, and it explains much even in Cyril's view of the *communicatio idiomatum*, or interchange of qualities between the natures, which was later to become fertile in so many unedifying artificialities.

Harnack says roundly that Cyril's theory is pure but unintentional Monophysitism. Loofs, with more prudence, remarks that the question whether the Christology is to be called Monophysite is after all a matter of words. "There were many Monophysites who thought just as he did. But if we reserve the name for the view that Christ's humanity was raised above humanity even before the resurrection, and that the *μία φύσις* of Christ was, so to speak, the result—by mixture or addition—of the *ἕνωσις*, Cyril must be acquitted of the charge."[2]

From his point of view Cyril naturally attacked Nestorius with vehemence, and they hurled anathemas at each other. Cyril exerted all his powers to bring out the irreligious consequences of Nestorianism. How could the sufferings of a man save us; and in the Eucharist was it no more than human flesh that we received? Rather at every point manhood is blended with Godhead. By thus insisting on "one incarnate nature" Cyril was unquestionably faithful to the instinct of Greek Christianity. Ere long he succeeded in gaining the adhesion of Celestine of Rome (430). The West, alike by tradition and temperament, occupied a middle position between Antioch and Alexandria, but, having been long accustomed to phrases like *deus natus, deus crucifixus est*, it now leant to Cyril's emphasis on the unity of the Redeemer's person.

Nothing would serve but the meeting of another Council. It was held at Ephesus in 431, and takes rank as the third Ecumenical Council of the Church. Suffice it to say that the Cyrillians first deposed Nestorius, before the arrival of his friends, to which they replied by deposing

[1] Dykes, *ut supra*, 57. [2] *Leitfaden*, 293 f.

Cyril and Memnon of Ephesus. The Emperor confirmed both sentences, but that on Cyril was soon reversed. By 433 court influence had driven both parties into outward harmony, and Cyril accepted a creed drawn up in great part by Theodoret of Cyrus—whose Nestorian sympathies were strong—while Nestorius was dropped by his old supporters. The terms of this creed paved the way for Chalcedon, but its excessively ambiguous tenor has led Harnack to speak of it as "the saddest and most momentous event in the history of dogma since the condemation of Paul of Samosata."[1] It declared that Christ was "consubstantial with us in His humanity, for there has been a union of two natures; wherefore we confess one Christ, one Son, one Lord."[2] Nothing was decided as to whether two natures existed in Christ *after* the incarnation. But Loofs says truly that the arrangement in no way mitigated the differences between Cyril and Nestorius on the question whether Christ was, or was not, an individual man. For Cyril, it was not the person of *a* man that the Logos had assumed, but man, *i.e.* the qualities and attributes of human nature. This shadowy abstractness of conception was only too certain to lead men away from the historic life portrayed in the New Testament.

Henceforth the strength of the Nestorians lay in Persia. The pious barbarism of the monks flung them ever more violently on the side of Cyril.

§ 4. *The Eutychian Controversy; Chalcedon.*—Cyril's death in 444 seemed to bring peace, when suddenly the flames of war shot up again. They were kindled by Eutyches, archimandrite of Constantinople, a keen but limited and ill-balanced nature, whose piety gave him influence, and who had been one of Cyril's most ardent followers. At a council in his own city he was accused of heresy by Eusebius of Dorylæum. He had certainly used imprudent phrases. "My God," he said, "is not of like essence with us"; the body of God could not be a man's

[1] *History of Dogma*, iv. 197. [2] Hahn, § 170.

body, but only like it; and so forth. Opponents of the Cyrillian theology at once exclaimed that Eutyches was only blurting out what Cyril had held secretly. In 448 a synod held at Constantinople, under the presidency of his bishop, Flavian, condemned the old man on the charge of denying the consubstantiality of Christ's human nature with ours. In the circumstances, Eutyches drew back upon the Christological positions of his old leader, and expressed his own view thus: "I confess our Lord to have become out of two natures before the union. But I confess one nature after the union." But he refused to concede the orthodox belief that two natures existed in Christ after the incarnation had taken place. He found a powerful advocate in Dioscurus of Alexandria, an ambitious and coarse-grained ecclesiastic who felt that the championship of Eutyches might help him to a kind of papacy in the East. On the other hand, he was opposed not merely by Flavian but by Leo of Rome, who had chosen his side with some hesitation. At this point the Emperor, with whom Flavian was no favourite, commanded him to hand in a confession of faith justifying his evil opinion of Eutyches. The document he prepared is of great interest, as an anticipation of the Formula of Chalcedon.[1] It proved that men were beginning to make distinctions between "nature" and "hypostasis," on the basis of which a reconciliation might be hoped for between Alexandria and Antioch.

Dioscurus, however, was not to be restrained, and, having persuaded Theodosius to summon a new council at Ephesus (449, known later as the Robber Synod), he presided over it, and forced through both a rehabilitation of Eutyches and a condemnation and deposition of the Antiochene leaders. The Roman deputies were refused a hearing. Under cover of an appeal to a resolution of the Council of Ephesus in 431, forbidding the addition of a new creed to that of Nicæa, the Union Symbol of 433 was summarily put aside. Anathemas were pronounced

[1] Hahn, § 223.

against all who should teach that in Christ there were two natures subsequently to the incarnation. And it is a very arguable position that Dioscurus faithfully represented the view really held by the majority in the East.

It was to this Council that Leo of Rome sent his famous Dogmatic Epistle, which, though left unread, grew every month in importance. It revived Christological formulas which Tertullian and Augustine had made familiar. "Two substances or natures in the one Christ" is the keynote. The substances in the Incarnate remain what they were, but are combined in the unity of the person. Each nature preserves intact its own characteristics, the lowliness and infirmity of man being assumed by the Divine majesty and eternity. Not only so, but in the Divine-human life of the one person each nature performs its own proper function in alliance with the other, a basis being thus found for Biblical expressions which imply a *communicatio idiomatum*, or interchange of qualities; as when it is said that the Son of Man came down from heaven or that the Son of God was crucified and buried. Leo is also emphatic as to the integrity of our Lord's manhood, and makes severe animadversions on the criminality of Eutyches in denying it and so casting the shadow of unreality on the passion which had been endured for our salvation.[1]

The Epistle is written with great practical wisdom and insight, the positive and negative results of previous discussions being lucidly set forth and sagaciously balanced over against each other. Fine shades of theological distinction are avoided, and no effort is made to follow the

[1] The following are the most significant phrases: Salva proprietate utriusque naturae et substantiae et in unam coëunte personam suscepta est a majestate humilitas, a virtute infirmitas . . . impassibilis deus non dedignatus est homo esse passibilis et immortalis mortis legibus subjacere; . . . qui enim verus est deus, idem verus est homo . . . agit utraque forma cum alterius communione, quod proprium est . . . propter hanc unitatem personae in utraque natura intelligendam et filius hominis legitur descendisse de cœlo . . . et rursus filius dei crucifixus dicitur ac sepultus. Cf. Loofs, *Leitfaden*, 299.

Greek divines in subtle or elaborate speculative theories. On the whole, Leo comes a good deal nearer to the view of Antioch than of Alexandria. Still it is impossible to claim him for either. There is no direct refutation of Nestorius, only of Eutyches.

Theodosius died in July 450, and in 451 his successor Marcian convened the synod Leo had asked for, not, however, at Rome, but at Chalcedon. It was the fourth Ecumenical Council of the Church. About six hundred bishops came, and from the first the guidance of events lay in the hands of the Western deputies. Leo's Epistle was recognised as the norm of orthodoxy; Dioscurus deposed; Nestorianism and Eutychianism condemned. Shouts were heard from the assembly: "We all believe as Leo does." The inviolability of the creeds of Nicæa and Ephesus was reaffirmed, and thereafter the Council set forth the following definition:—

Ἑπόμενοι τοίνυν τοῖς ἁγίοις πατράσιν ἕνα καὶ τὸν αὐτὸν ὁμολογεῖν υἱὸν τὸν κύριον ἡμῶν Ἰησοῦν Χριστὸν συμφώνως ἅπαντες ἐκδιδάσκομεν, τέλειον τὸν αὐτὸν ἐν θεότητι καὶ τέλειον τὸν αὐτὸν ἐν ἀνθρωπότητι, θεὸν ἀληθῶς καὶ ἄνθρωπον ἀληθῶς τὸν αὐτόν, ἐκ ψυχῆς λογικῆς καὶ σώματος, ὁμοούσιον τῷ πατρὶ κατὰ τὴν θεότητα καὶ ὁμοούσιον τὸν αὐτὸν ἡμῖν κατὰ τὴν ἀνθρωπότητα . . . ἐν δύο φύσεσιν ἀσυγχύτως, ἀτρέπτως, ἀδιαιρέτως, ἀχωρίστως γνωριζόμενον· οὐδαμοῦ τῆς τῶν φύσεων διαφορᾶς ἀνῃρημένης διὰ τὴν ἕνωσιν, σωζομένης δὲ μᾶλλον τῆς ἰδιότητος ἑκατέρας φύσεως καὶ εἰς ἓν πρόσωπον καὶ μίαν ὑπόστασιν συντρεχούσης.[1]

[1] "Therefore following the holy fathers we all with one consent teach men to confess one and the same Son, our Lord Jesus Christ, the same perfect in Godhead and the same perfect in manhood, truly God and the same truly man, of a rational soul and body, co-essential with the Father according to the Godhead, and co-essential with us according to the manhood . . . to be acknowledged in two natures, without confusion, without mutation, without division, without separation; the distinction of natures being by no means taken away by the union, but rather the property of each nature being preserved and concurring in one person and one hypostasis." For the text, see Hahn, § 146.

In the main this was a document approximating closely to the theology of Cyril; but the phrase "in two natures" proves that at a critical point Western influences had triumphed, for as it now stood the clause satisfied only the Antiochenes and a few friends of the Union Symbol of 433. Still, both Cyril and Leo had been acknowledged as authoritative. Obviously the framers of the definition wished not so much to formulate a theory of Christ's person as to bar out extreme statements on either side. Hence the famous four adverbs, fixing the two natures relatively to one another, are all negative. At the same time the unity of the person is positively emphasised, as may have been done already in the Athanasian Creed (which is perhaps earlier): *unus Christus, non confusione substantiarum, sed unitate personae.*[1] In the last resort a clearly felt soteriological interest is behind the careful phrases, and enables us to interpret the whole as a combination of the vital elements which faith has always insisted on combining in its view of Christ the Saviour. Thus the reality and integrity of each nature, of Godhead and of manhood, is upheld; the incarnation has not issued in a being that is somehow neither Divine nor human, or either exclusively. On the other hand, the theanthropic Life is a personal unity not severed into two independent subjects, but hypostatically one. Thus the decisions of Chalcedon may reasonably be viewed as a great utterance of faith, aware of the wrong turnings which theory may take so easily. They have been well compared to buoys anchored along a difficult estuary, on the right and left, to guide the ship of truth. With the religion of the Creed, accordingly, we have no quarrel.

But with its theology it is otherwise. As Dorner has remarked, it is mere short-sightedness to imagine that the Christology of that age, which could operate with ideas of God and man only in the form in which they were then current, took shape in determinations which need no amendment, and admit of none. As a theory or doctrine,

[1] Cf. Bonwetsch, *Grundriss*, 93.

therefore, the formula of Chalcedon is susceptible of criticism. Thus it may be pointed out that Christological relations which, in essence, are ethical and personal, have been too much expressed in terms imbued with a certain mechanical and even material flavour. This is particularly true of the term "nature" (φύσις), which is not an ethical word at all. Now non-ethical realities admit of no true unity; hence we are not surprised to find that Godhead and manhood are contemplated here as being in essence so disparate, so utterly unrelated and heterogeneous, that a miracle of sheer omnipotence is needed to unite them. Love, it is true, is behind the incarnation, and gives it its significance, but the methods by which this love accomplishes its purpose are not sufficiently conceived as spiritual, with the result that from the first Christ's true humanity is overshadowed, if not indeed seriously curtailed. So that objections may be raised to the resultant doctrine from two quite opposite points of view. In the first place, it awakens suspicion by its dualism, by its blank unrelieved insistence upon the eternal parallelism of two "natures" set in a relation to each other which after all is ethically unmediated—scarcely less so than in the theory of Nestorius. God and man are yoked together, not exhibited in the singleness of personal life. That this was the preponderating tendency of Chalcedonian Christology is proved by the Dyophysite and Dyothelite findings of the next three hundred years, and against this tendency Monophysitism offered a valuable protest, so far, by contending that all that is Divine in Christ is human, and all that is human, Divine. Nothing else represents the unity of impression made by the historic Jesus. Secondly, the unity which Chalcedon nevertheless affirms is a purely marvellous one—a mere wonder, a thing inexpressible in genuinely spiritual terms, the humanity so reduced to a mere selfless "organ" of the Divine Word that it becomes impossible to think this Christ as the Head of a new redeemed race of men and Himself the Patterr

Man. From this point of view the strictures of Principal Dykes are hardly too severe. "A Being," he writes, "who combines in an inscrutable fashion Divine with human properties, and of whom consequently contradictory assertions can be made, whose single Person is Divine, while His dual natures hold an undefined relation to one another: this is not a scheme to satisfy either head or heart. It is but the bare skeleton of a dogma, in which one cannot readily recognise either the Jesus of the Gospels or the Christ of the Church's worship."[1]

Thus the Council did not so much reconcile or synthesise the opposing theories put before it, as conceal their opposition under extremely careful phrases. But when the Creed had to be interpreted, would it be read in the light of Cyril's teaching, or Theodoret's, or Leo's?[2] All three were grammatically possible; which should rank as correct was to be the problem of the next century.

§ 5. *The Monophysite and Monothelite Controversies.*—In point of fact the Chalcedonian decisions had at first a nearly fatal influence on the Eastern Church. Instead of peace the Council brought a sword, for Dyophysites and Monophysites counted each other the worst of heretics. There were risings in Egypt, Palestine, and Syria. The monks refused to take their theology from Rome. We cannot pursue the details of this miserable conflict, but we note one or two landmarks which obtrude themselves on a rapid survey. Krüger has adverted to a curious parallel between the course of Arianism and Monophysitism, utterly unlike as the two movements were in religious motive. If Lucian was father of the one heresy, Apollinaris was father of the other. If the Arians appealed to Origen, the Monophysites appealed to Cyril. And as it required a race of thinkers trained by Origen to secure the triumph

[1] *Expository Times*, October 1905, 10. On the whole subject, cf. Dorner, *Entwicklungsgeschichte der Lehre von der Person Christi*, ii. 144–49.

[2] Loofs, *Leitfaden*, 301.

of Nicæa, so too it was only by the efforts of men who had gone back to the Christology of Cyril that permanent recognition was gained for Chalcedon, in so far as it was gained at all.[1]

The watchword of the Monophysite party was the Cyrillian formula, *μία φύσις τοῦ λόγου θεοῦ σεσαρκωμένη.* Starting from the concrete unity of the Divine-human Christ, within which two natures can be discriminated only in theory, they contended like the Nestorians that "nature" and "person" are equivalent, or at all events coincident ideas. And since the general (Godhead, manhood) exists only in the form of concrete personality, never merely in the abstract, it follows that to say "two natures" is tantamount to saying "two persons," that is, to pure Nestorianism. What has offended the Church in Monophysitism has not been so much these presuppositions,—in which from one point of view there is nothing objectionable—as rather the docetism which Monophysites from Cyril to Julian never succeeded in shaking off. The following points are important:[2]—

(*a*) In the Monophysite Christology two diverging tendencies appeared. These are represented by the Severians and the Julianists, so named from their leaders, Severus of Antioch and Julius of Halicarnassus. It was the aim of the Severians to distinguish Godhead and manhood ideally within the one Christ. So they accentuated the unmingledness of the natures, together with the creaturely and mortal character of our Lord's humanity, and even drew attention to limitations in the knowledge of Jesus. At the same time they repudiated the Chalcedonian *ἐν δύο φύσεσιν*, and especially Leo's insistence on the (so to speak) private and independent activity of each nature, an interpretation which they judged to be no better than Nestorianism. Their real interest lay in affirming a single Divine-human subject, a *φύσις καὶ ὑπόστασις θεανδρική*. On the other hand, the Julianists, while

[1] *Das Dogma von der Dreieinigkeit*, 230.

[2] Cf. Harnack, *Grundriss*, § 43.

denying that the manhood of Christ was totally absorbed in the Godhead, still maintained that His human nature was not as that of other men. Transmuted by its contact with deity, it was incorruptible, glorified, and even uncreate, not merely after the resurrection, but from the very moment of assumption. Hence the passibility of Christ is no mere natural attribute of His being man; it rests at every point on His free will.

(*b*) In order to maintain the unity of the Empire, repeated attempts of a political kind were made to suppress the Chalcedonian Creed. Thus Basiliscus the Usurper cancelled it by his Encyclicon in 476, and in 482 the conciliatory Zeno attempted in his famous *Henoticon* to evade its terms, declaring that while the Son of God was co-essential with the Father in deity and co-essential with us in manhood, yet He was one, not two, the miracles and the sufferings being predicable of the same subject. This was a direct blow at the authority of Leo, and a thirty-five years' schism with Rome was the result. But in 519 the *Henoticon* was once more cast aside, and the Creed of Chalcedon, which had come meanwhile to be invested with the sanctity of tradition, was restored. The so-called Theopaschite controversy, which sprang up over the phrase ὁ σταυρωθεὶς δι' ἡμᾶς, inserted by Peter the Fuller in the Trishagion, showed how unwilling the West even now was to interpret Chalcedon in a Cyrillian sense, whereas the East would hear of no other. It was the strong hand of Justinian (527–565) that lifted the definition of 451 into permanent supremacy. To please the Monophysites, Theodore of Mopsuestia and Theodoret were condemned.

(*c*) In the sixth century the defenders of Chalcedonian orthodoxy are obviously men of marked intellectual power. Aristotelian metaphysic supplied good weapons. The most conspicuous name is that of Leontius of Byzantium (*c.* 485–543), forerunner of John of Damascus; a lover of severe philosophic categories whose influence on the Christological evolution is of real historic importance. Retaining the distinction between "nature" and "person," he took the Formula of Chalcedon on the whole in a Cyrillian sense. The human nature of Christ is not strictly impersonal, nor on the other hand does it possess, as the Antiochenes held, an independent personality or centre of the conscious moral life; it is ἐνυπόστατος, *i.e.* it has personality only in and through the Logos. By the aid of this finer species of Apollinarianism, Leontius was able to maintain both that an exchange of qualities obtained between the two natures and that each nature has its own "energy," as Leo had affirmed in his Epistle. Harnack well names Leontius "the father of the new Christological orthodoxy, as the Cappadocians had been fathers of the new Trinitarian orthodoxy."[1] He is the first scholastic. His conception of the "enhypostasia" or impersonality of Christ's manhood was new only in formula; but as a formula it *was* new, and in theological history the power of formulas has been immense.

(*d*) At last, in 553, when the fifth Ecumenical Council met in Constantinople, victory rested with the orthodoxy which read Chalcedon in the sense of Cyril. The decisions now formulated were meant to make an Antiochene interpretation of the Creed for ever impossible. Christ is one; and of this one Christ both miracles and sufferings must be predicated. The two natures are distinguishable only in theory. The Logos was also man, but in the historic Christ there existed no human personality. "Here in Constantinople the Christology of the Ancient Church reached its conclusion."[2] But the triumph of Cyril, though it satisfied the instincts of Eastern faith, failed to reconcile the Monophysites. Their Churches remain to this day.

The two parties, as Dorner observes, were not in the last resort so far apart as they supposed. "The Monophysites only represent the effort to attain a more inward unity of the natures than the Chalcedonians, but

[1] *Grundriss*, 207. [2] Loofs, *RE.* iv. 52.

can do as little as their opponents to prove the inner cohesive affinity of the Divine and the human. The Chalcedonians, on the other hand, represent the effort to secure a true and relatively independent humanity, without confusion or conversion; but fundamentally—although declining to admit it—they really fail to transcend the Monophysite view that the human becomes hypostatic only in the Divine."[1]

It remains to treat shortly of the Monothelite controversy, the ethical sequel of that which we have just surveyed, and due to political attempts at union. Thus far nothing had been determined as to volition in Christ, and the terms of Chalcedon could be read either way. Harnack says that in point of fact nobody had spoken of two wills in Christ prior to the sixth century, not even the Antiochenes.[2] The question now became a burning one. Sergius, patriarch of Constantinople, advised the reigning Emperor Heraclius to issue the formula (about 630) that the one Christ had wrought all things by a single Divine-human energy (*μίᾳ θεανδρικῇ ἐνεργείᾳ*). This was meant as a sop to the Monophysites, and met with considerable success in Egypt. But opposition came from Sophronius, afterwards bishop of Jerusalem. The consequence was a second royal edict (the *Ἔκθεσις πίστεως* of 638), inspired by Sergius and Honorius of Rome, and affirming the existence of a single will in Christ. The minor question of one or two "energies" was brushed aside as unscriptural. On this the West blazed up in revolt, and even in the East divines like Maximus Confessor flung themselves ardently into the defence of a position which they held to be only a corollary of the two natures affirmed at Chalcedon. Two natures implied two faculties of volition. Fearing a revolution, the Emperor Constans II. issued in 648 the notorious rescript entitled *Τύπος τῆς πίστεως*, prohibiting all discussion of the subject. But its influence proved small, and feeling was intensified by cruel measures taken

[1] *Entwicklungsgeschichte*, ii. 189. [2] *Grundriss*, 209.

against Martin of Rome. The Emperor was murdered in 668, and after some years his successor Constantine Pogonatus saw his way to combine with the Pope in taking a more conciliatory position. In 680 the sixth Ecumenical Council gathered at Constantinople; and there, on the basis of a communication from Agathon of Rome obviously modelled on Leo's Epistle, the Dyothelite position was explicitly affirmed. The exact terms by which the relation of the natures had been defined at Chalcedon are now carried over to the relation of the wills. In Christ, it is declared, are two natural wills and two natural energies (modes of activity), the human will not being opposed to the Divine, but rather obedient and subordinate to its omnipotence. Thus the dualism is asserted in its sharpest form, as implying two parallel series of volitions and activities, while yet it is added, with seeming inconsistency, that the almighty will of the Logos so conditions the will distinctive of the humanity as wholly to absorb its independence and self-motion. Maximus had tried to bridge the gulf between the two wills by suggesting that the pure human soul is in itself godlike, akin to the Logos ethically and in essence; but his suggestions came to nothing. In the East the Monophysite habit of thought persisted; for even if the Western interpretation of Chalcedon had triumphed formally, yet the ideas of Apollinaris and Cyril retained vitality, and held a place firmly in the now official conception of the impersonality of Christ's manhood.

So much for the outward features of the conflict; let us glance at the theological motives operating beneath the surface. Both sides of course started from the accepted doctrine of two natures in one person. But within this complex whole the Monothelites began from the unity of the person, the Dyothelites from the duality of the natures. If one party referred the will to the personal Ego in Christ, the other held with equal conviction that it forms part of each "nature." The

Monothelites feared Nestorianism—the combination of a fallible with an infallible will—and preferred to think of Christ's humanity as being related to the Logos as the body is to the soul. For them the unity of will had a vast religious significance. "We conclude," writes Theodore of Pharan, their leading representative, "that *all that which we hear from Christ and believe is the work of God* . . . from beginning to end the whole incarnation is one truly high and Divine activity."[1] At this point, however, our sympathy is checked by Theodore's inveterate tendency to docetism, manifested, for example, in the statement that our Lord's sense-experience at each moment was evoked by no natural necessity but by His Divine volition. It was this docetism which lent power to the Dyothelite counter-argument. Over and over again it is insisted that a nature without a will is nothing; that if Christ was man, He must have been man willing and active. One *composite* will is inconceivable. Only through His human will could Jesus finish the work given Him to do. Faith, love, hope and all the virtues are only possible for one in whom they are the outcome of real spontaneity; unless He were endowed with a human faculty of volition, and were thus humanly free, Christ could not be our pattern. Here also a true religious interest is at work.

Each party, it is manifest, had taken possession of one aspect of the truth. As the question was then stated, each had much to say for itself, and had no need to fear the other's refutation. The philosophic reader will be apt to say that no advance was possible till the relation of the will to the personality, the centre of conscious moral experience, had been thought out more clearly, and the idea of personality itself submitted to a more exact analysis. On the other hand, the basis of doctrine in past facts had been virtually abandoned, and it was necessary to recover vital touch with the historic Jesus. "What this Christology handed over to the Church was not a finished result but a problem—that

[1] Baur, *Dreieinigkeit*, ii. 109.

God Himself should have lived and walked here, a man like to us."[1]

Finally, a brief reference is due to John of Damascus (died probably before 754), to whom the theology of the Greek Church owes its definitive systematic form. He taught that the two natures in Christ interpenetrate each other like fire and iron (περιχώρησις), with an ensuing exchange of qualities. He laid stress, moreover, on the "Enhypostasia" of the manhood,[2] thus perpetuating, in spite of the Dyophysite and Dyothelite creeds, a view that has many points of affinity with Apollinaris. The Logos is placed as head on the mere trunk of humanity. But in neither respect was he original. What he offers us is rather a scholastic elaboration of results attained by the Cappadocians and by Leontius of Byzantium. Development had stopped with the Council of 553, and John was merely "the registrar of Greek orthodoxy." And thus by degrees the Church's memories of the human life of Jesus faded into oblivion. Men lost the sense of history. Nothing had happened at the incarnation save that Godhead assumed a new relationship, took a new organ, began to work at a new place. Nor was the situation bettered by the bravely persistent instinct of revolt against dualism, for this only meant that one aspect of the double Life is swallowed up indistinguishably in the other. Christ's deity is seen as "loosely attached to His human nature, yet overbearing it, and reducing to little better than a phantasm the moral victories and pathetic conflicts of His earthly career."[3]

[1] Seeberg, *Lehrbuch d. DG.* (1895), i. 231.

[2] Since the Logos forms the personality in Christ, He prayed not for Himself but as an example to us.

[3] Dykes, *ut supra*, 59.

CHAPTER VI.

LATER CHRISTOLOGY IN THE WEST.

Augustine and the Middle Ages.—Henceforward we shall be engaged solely with Western thought, for in the East theology had sunk into petrified inaction. Even of the Latin Church it may be said that it was more occupied with the means of salvation than with the person of the Saviour.[1] The creed functioned as a legal mystery, which no one outside the great Church could understand. Speculation, accordingly, was kept within narrow bounds. From the eighth century to the sixteenth not a single contribution of real importance was made. As in earlier times, Western divines proved skilful rather to register and formulate the ecumenical decisions than to serve as pathfinders in new fields of truth. One exception may be named in Hilary of Poictiers (d. 367), who developed an impressionist view which has been interpreted as akin to modern Kenotic theories, but its influence on the course of thought is negligible.

Even Augustine (354–430) is scarcely to be designated an original or creative mind in the realm of Christology; he impresses rather by the amazing verbal

LITERATURE—Scheel, *Die Anschauung Augustins über Christi Person und Werk*, 1901; Gottschick, article "Augustins Anschauungen von der Erlöserwirkungen Christi," *ZTK.* 1901; Möller, article "Adoptianismus," *RE.* i.; Ritschl, *History of the Doctrine of Justification and Reconciliation*, 1872; Schultz, *Die Lehre von der Gottheit Christi*, 1881; Foley, *Anselm's Theory of the Atonement*, 1909; Neander, *Church History*; Seeberg, *Die Theologie des Joh. Duns Scotus*, 1900.

[1] Réville, *History of the Dogma of the Deity of Jesus Christ*, 158.

and dialectical ability with which he reproduced the accepted doctrines of the Church.[1] Biblical and orthodox ideas gradually mastered him, but he never quite flung off the early influences of Neo-Platonism, and these inclined him, at each stage of his development, to define the Son as identical with the Neo-Platonic *νοῦς* or Wisdom; yet without any of the subordinationism to which a similar path had conducted Origen. In his mature period, however, he insists that the man Jesus had been conjoined with God the Logos in such a unity, "that it is the same Son of God who is Son of Man, the same Son of Man who is Son of God."[2] The conception by which he resolves all difficulties is the distinction—in reality very old—between the *forma Dei* and the *forma servi*; a distinction not to be hastily equated with that between the two natures. In terms, of course, this contrast of "forms" is taken from Ph 2; but while St. Paul describes our Lord as having abandoned the one mode of being for the other, Augustine regards them as co-existent (*non formam Dei amittens, sed formam servi accipiens*). It is curiously hard to say whether Augustine's sympathies were more with the East or West. On the one hand, his tendency is to conceive Godhead and manhood as self-evidently exclusive of each other, thus keeping the two natures apart, and in this view, which on the whole predominates, he follows Ambrose. This made it possible to regard the humanity of Christ as constituting an independent moral subject, genuinely human in its growth and progress, and Augustine did not even shrink from declaring that Christ's humanity—like the elect everywhere—was the object of Divine predestination. His Mediatorship rests on His participation in manhood (*mediator non quia deus sed quia homo*). It is perhaps a one-sided estimate of this element which leads Harnack to remark that

[1] On the whole subject, cf. Scheel's full and able monograph, *Die Anschauung Augustins über Christi Person und Werk* (Tübingen, 1901).

[2] *Enchir.* c. 40.

Augustine's profoundest interest "centred in the human soul of Jesus."[1] On the other hand, his more explicit statements are in line with Athanasius, and share in the Cyrillian docetism. In the God-man the personal factor is supplied by God the Word; the assumed human nature is deified, while the Word remains metaphysically unchangeable, and nothing like a *commixtio* is really possible. But for the ends of popular exposition, he is accustomed to say that Jesus Christ is man and God in one person, as each of us is flesh and spirit. Obviously this analogy, if pressed, would have led straight back to Apollinarianism, of which Augustine was a lifelong and passionate opponent. But the phrase is none the less a symptom. It fits in with the increasing Western tendency to speak of Christ's "flesh" or "body," rather than of Christ the man. Most of these ideas received symbolic expression later in the so-called Athanasian Creed, which first comes into view near the end of the seventh century.

In Spain the older Augustinian tradition lived on for centuries, in contrast to the semi-Monophysite reading of Chalcedon, which had become orthodox by the lapse of time. Westerns used and loved the phrase *Christus deus et homo*; and it hardly seemed inconsistent with this that in the eighth century Elipandus of Toledo and Felix of Urgel should have begun to teach that the human nature combined with the deity of the Redeemer was not at once taken up into the essential unity of the Divine person, and consequently had no direct share in the Divine Sonship, but was only Son of God *adoptively*. Thus a line in the Spanish liturgy speaks of the *passio filii adoptivi*. Hence, too, the name Adoptianism. In the fight with Arianism it had been customary to maintain that Christ was Son *natura, non adoptione*; and the new view, ill-informed as its phrases were, was meant as a corrective of orthodox extravagances which might overshadow the real humanity. Elipandus may well have felt the old influence of Antioch. But Charlemagne inter-

[1] *Hist. of Dogma*, v. 128.

posed, and Adoptianism was condemned at the Synod of Regensburg in 792 and twice later, Alcuin being its keenest foe. It was urged that, like the Nestorians, the Adoptianists held a double personality in Christ; but it is worth noting that in refuting their errors Alcuin went so far as to say, *in adsumptione carnis a deo persona perit hominis, non natura.* This *persona perit hominis* left even the orthodoxy of Cyril behind, and meant that the strict two-nature doctrine was consistent with, not to say demanded, a wholly impersonal conception of what manhood in Christ is. The formula of Chalcedon was in fact ill adapted to express the Western idea of redemption, and Adoptianism proved it. One who in His true humanity should be the normal subject of moral life, and should atone by a real passion for sin, as Head of the Church and Brother of the redeemed—this, and nothing less, was felt to be indispensable if guilt were to be abolished and holiness made a possibility. Adoptianism was easy to refute, but it betokened grave defects in the received doctrine.

The dogma of transubstantiation, now rising into view, was a new and powerful influence tending to annihilate the true humanity of Christ. One can discern a certain parallelism between the view that the human factor in our Lord had as such no personality, but was personal only in and, as it were, under the Logos, and the later controversy as to whether in the Eucharist the substance of bread and wine continues to exist, or is so merged in the higher essence that only its phenomenal accidents remain. In both cases the simple perceptions of faith were turned upside down by theory.

The dialectic activities of the Middle Age added little to the Church doctrine of our Lord's person.[1] In proportion as the historic Life grew dim and the exalted Saviour receded in the distance, the interval was filled with other mediators, highest of all being the Virgin Mary. The *anhypostasia* was steadily maintained. But Scheel

[1] See an important note by Loofs, *Leitfaden*, 531–32.

observes with great point that "outside the topic of the person of Christ, where the impersonality of His human nature is asserted, Catholic dogmatic has in the doctrine of His work emphasised the humanity so strongly that its impersonality seems to be forgotten."[1] Practical piety kept a firm grasp on the full manhood of Jesus, as is proved by the immense literature on the Imitation of Christ, yet without affecting Christology proper. Above all, the great mediæval theories of Atonement, to be intelligible, required a genuine humanity, animated and energised by the personal life of a Brother. Anselm's words as to the "merit" of Christ have no meaning, if Christ the man had no personality. In essence this is true also of Abelard and St. Bernard. The later scholastics, without exception, build the argument on Augustine's great maxim: *in quantum homo, in tantum mediator*; so especially Peter the Lombard. The deity of Christ came into view rather as the infinite co-efficient raising human action and passion to an infinite value. Yet these teachers, in the Christological section of their work, set forth a view which was simply docetic. Indeed, the Lombard did not scruple to say that in respect of His humanity Christ was nothing at all (*Christus secundum hominem non est persona, nec aliquid*), but at this Nihilianism the Church took fright, and he was censured in 1170. Here can be traced the malign influence of the pseudo-Dionysius, that unknown Christian theosophist of (probably) the sixth century, whose Neo-Platonic and more than half-docetic conceptions did so much to colour mediæval religious thought, and to infect it with a mysticism which had nothing Christian about it save the name.

No writer of this time approaches Bernard of Clairvaux in the intensity with which he realised the manhood of Jesus. Besides the mysterious and half-unknown Christ of the sacrament, he grasps and clings to the Man whose mind and deeds and passion are the medium of Divine life to the world. In the historic Christ God is personally

[1] *Op. cit.* 274.

present to redeem. *Cum nomino Jesum,* he says in a beautiful phrase, *hominem mihi propono mitem et humilem corde . . . eundemque ipsum deum omnipotentem.*[1]

Like other thinkers of the period, Thomas Aquinas (d. 1274) and Duns Scotus (d. 1308) also did homage to an idea of God well-nigh excessive in its remote transcendence. In Christology it was felt that at all hazards a confusion of deity with finite forms of life must be avoided. Hence Aquinas teaches that the Logos takes impersonal—though somehow individual—human nature into unity with itself; the counterstroke immediately following, however, to the effect that after all the union is real not in the Divine nature, but in the human nature only. Or, to put it otherwise, the natures are not so much united, as brought into a common relation to the Logos. At bottom, the theory is Monophysite. It means that the incarnation is to be constructed merely in a relative sense; for, while God is present in the manhood of Jesus, it is only in such a fashion that He might equally be present in more than one man, and other instances of God-manhood are quite thinkable as well as the historic Saviour. Nowhere else is the error so apparent of regarding Christology as an abstract problem in the combination of Infinite and finite, with the inevitable result that on each side of the equation impersonal categories are inserted, and the discussion has practically no relevance to the Jesus of the Gospels. How true this is we see from Thomas' declaration that from the conception of the Virgin onwards the person of the God-man is absolutely complete and perfected; in Christ, accordingly, there exists neither faith nor hope, since both are excluded by His perfect vision of God. The forms of human knowledge and volition remain, but all is really determined by the will of the Word. Even so the unity for the sake of which the humanity has been curtailed is not achieved. For Thomas concedes in the last resort that Christ's human

[1] *in Cant.* 15. 6; quoted by Loofs.

mind, as being created, is, unlike His deity, incapable of grasping the Divine essence. His soul knows all that is or will be; not, however, that which is possible. So, too, with the omnipotence which, as Son of God, He possessed wholly, but as Son of Man only in part, and as far as the measures of humanity permit. But Aquinas has much to say that is noble regarding the man Christ Jesus as the recipient of grace.

Perhaps the most disconcerting notion in this theory as a whole is an allusion to the possible plurality of incarnations, for a shadow is thus cast upon the essential uniqueness of Christ as Saviour. It is an idea with which the believing mind can make no terms. The period was one that hardly felt a distinctive interest in Christology. Men were content to prove the logical connections of the traditional scheme. They had learnt nothing, and also forgotten nothing.

Duns Scotus, a generation later, was scarcely more successful in lifting the debate to a truly moral plane. And yet, though Thomism conquered, he does exhibit a deeper appreciation of Jesus' human experience, and faintly indicates the limitations of His knowledge as man. Even so much as this, however, was gained only at the cost of distinguishing very sharply between the two natures, for Duns wholly agreed with Thomas in affirming that neither suffering nor merit could be predicated of the Divine essence. The union of the natures is at best a relation of dependence whereby the humanity is subsumed under the divinity; a relation comparable to that between substance and accident, and imposing on the Godhead no limit of any kind. Jesus has no human personality or independent being. His humanity exists in the Logos only as my foot exists in me. The man alone *became*, not the Logos in any sense, for deity cannot become that which is not eternal. Still, the instinct for a true manhood was ineradicable, since only through the merit of Jesus is the world redeemed.

CHAPTER VII.

THE CHRISTOLOGY OF THE REFORMATION CHURCHES.

§ 1. *Luther.*—It is not too much to say that with the Reformation, and especially with Luther, there came into the world a deeper understanding of the person of Christ than had prevailed since the apostolic age. "The attitude towards Jesus which Luther consciously held," says Herrmann, "marks a step forward in the development of the Christian religion."[1] This was due to religious interest being now simply concentrated on Christ, and no longer dispersed vainly over a multitude of mediators and spiritual exercises. What emerges in consequence is a distinctive type of Christian piety. The Gospel is in the historic Saviour, and it is all there. Theology and Christology are no longer independent aspects of doctrine; they coincide. The Reformers, writes Dr. Lindsay, "knew no other God than the God who had manifested Himself in the historical Christ, and made us see in the miracle of faith that He is our salvation."[2]

Luther's system of belief, if system it may be called, rests on and revolves round the person of Jesus Christ. To him faith in God and faith in Christ are

LITERATURE—Bruce, *Humiliation of Christ*[2], 1881; Th. Harnack, *Luthers Theologie*, 1862–86; Köstlin, *Luthers Theologie*[2], 1901; von Kügelgen, *Luthers Auffassung der Gottheit Christi*[2], 1901; Lindsay, *History of the Reformation*, 1906; Herrmann, *Communion with God*, 1906; Hastings, *Dict. of Christ and the Gospels*, 1908; Bensow, *Die Lehre von der Kenose*, 1903; Haering, *Der christliche Glaube* (*Dogmatik*), 1906; Schaff, *History of the Creeds of Christendom*, 1877.

[1] *Communion with God* (2nd Eng. edition), 148.

[2] Hastings, *DCG*. ii. 862.

one and the same thing. "I have no God," he exclaims, "whether in heaven or in earth, and I know of none, outside the flesh that lies in the bosom of the Virgin Mary. For elsewhere God is utterly incomprehensible, but comprehensible in the flesh of Christ alone." And again: "Wilt thou go surely and meet and grasp God rightly, so finding grace and help in Him, be not persuaded to seek Him elsewhere than in the Lord Christ. Let thine art and study begin with Christ, and there let it stay and cling." Hence the problems of the Trinity and the two natures ceased to be mere enigmas of speculative dialectic, providing the *theologia gloriæ*, as Luther called it, with a field for keen intellectual play; at every point they remained in living touch with religion. Christ is for sinners the one mark on which saving trust must fix; elsewhere God is known only as an angry and devouring fire, whereas in Christ He is a very ocean of love unspeakable.

It was among the rare excellences of Luther's Christology that he fastened an indissoluble bond, as St. Paul had done, between the person of the Redeemer and His redeeming work. Any view of Christ, therefore, which may be developed in abstraction from what He actually did for men, in His life, death, and resurrection, is but a formal and delusive play of words. To start not from metaphysical presuppositions as to what Godhead and manhood are, and the possibility of uniting them, but from Jesus' cross and victory and the working of His Spirit in the heart—this is the only true way. These two, the person and the office, are an organic unity, neither being intelligible apart from the other. Both are asserted when faith says "our Lord." As the work is eternal, so must the person be. On the other hand, none but such a person could have accomplished a work so great. Therefore even in contemplating the passion we ought "mostly to consider the person, and study well *quis, qualis, et quantus* Christ is."

From all this Luther derives an intuitive certainty

that to understand Christ we must begin with the knowledge of His human life. To him the manhood of Christ signified more than to any post-apostolic teacher. The foundations of faith are to be laid in the recorded facts of our Lord's career as man, and anything else would be to start building from the roof. "The Scriptures," he says, "begin very gently, and lead us on to Christ as to a man, and then to one who is Lord over all creatures, and after that to one who is God. So do I enter delightfully, and learn to know God. But the philosophers and doctors have insisted on beginning from above; and so they have become fools. We must begin from below, and after that come upwards."[1] Otherwise we miss Him who is the ladder that guides us upward to the Father, the lowly glass in which we see God. Luther is quite conscious of a difference in accent separating him here from the scholastics and even from many of the Fathers; it is indeed his complaint against the Roman Church, that she never dreamt we ought to learn to recognise God in Christ.[2] Too often the Fathers fled from the manhood of Christ to the Godhead, pleading that the flesh profiteth nothing. Whereas the fact is that except as man Christ could never have redeemed us by His cross and triumph. Sinners are *guilty*; hence none but the proper and true God could "purge sin, destroy death, remove the curse," and only in flesh could even God Himself do it. Thus it is impossible to draw Christ too deeply down into nature and the flesh. We cannot make Him too human. The mere juxtaposition of Godhead and manhood, as Luther never tires of repeating, is of no avail; we must have the Son of God fused and inwoven with humanity, and one person therewith. If Christ were not God, there were no God at all, but in Him God has entered into a bond with sinners closer even than a brother.

Very plain words, accordingly, are used regarding the reality of Jesus' earthly life as one of limitation,

[1] *Werke* (Erl. ed.), xii. 412. [2] Herrmann, *op. cit.* 157.

growth, and trial. The apocryphal stories of His youth are "mere folly." "He ate, drank, slept, and waked; was weary, sad, joyous; wept, laughed; was hungry, thirsty, cold; sweated, talked, worked, prayed." In the days of earth He was no almighty man. So far from remaining in a different order of being, "there was no difference between Him and other men save that He was God and without sin." Luther wavers slightly on the question as to the *necessity* of a virgin birth for sinlessness, but regarding the fact alike of sinlessness and of birth from a Virgin he has no doubts at all. Always the motive of this unprecedented insistence on our Lord's humanity is religious and practical. We are undone if we cannot say, "This *Man* is God."

But if Christ was true man, faith is equally assured that He was not mere man. It is the very corner-stone of Luther's theology that none other than God could avail to atone for human sin. Athanasius himself could not speak more plainly than he as to the absolute centrality of the Godhead of Christ. "If Deity be wanting in Christ," he writes, "there is no help or deliverance for us against God's anger and judgments"; and again, "if it could not be held that God died for us, but only a man, then we are lost." Without this God who died and rose again, we dare not draw near in worship. The mystics come far short in representing Him as only an example, for that turns Him in reality into "an angry judge and a horrible tyrant." But the principle that the person is as the work guides us aright, for "since no one can give eternal life but God alone, it follows inevitably that Christ must be truly and naturally God." Strong words come to Luther's pen as he thinks of the Zwinglian conception of *Alloiosis*, according to which it is only by a figure of speech we can assert an interchange of qualities between the natures—manhood and Godhead thus being ultimately kept apart. This, says Luther, is sheerly false, "for if I believe that the human nature alone suffered for me, then is Christ worse than no Saviour to me." The objection that Godhead cannot suffer he grants as an abstract proposition, but one overruled by the actualities of the Scripture record. To repeat it yet once more, he knows no God except the child on Mary's bosom and the Man upon the cross. In Dr. Lindsay's suggestive phrase, "Christ fills the whole sphere of God."[1]

These two sides, the deity and the humanity, were held or rather fused together by Luther with a kind of passion. "Since Cyril," writes Harnack, "no teacher has arisen in the Church, to whom the mystery of the unity of the two natures in Christ was so deep a consolation."[2] Christ as daysman, as Mediator, must by the very constituents of His person have standing-ground on both sides, so binding God and man in unity. We are saved through soul-union with Christ, a union so personal and vital that our sins become His and His perfect righteousness ours; and this mystic unity is itself possible only because in Christ God is one with manhood. The doctrine grows sharper in the sacramental controversy, but Luther had grasped its import long before. To quote the luminous words of Principal Dykes: "The traditional Christology of the schools, which so coldly held asunder the finite and infinite natures, seeing in the incarnation no more than a mere clothing of unchangeable Deity with a garment of mortal flesh to be its medium of self-manifestation, could no longer satisfy. Rather Luther saw in the incarnation (1) the attainment by God of what He has always longed for in His love, namely, humanity as His own form of existence, and (2) the reception by Man of what he was made for, namely, Divinity as the very contents of his spiritual life; a union, in brief, real and vital, by which two disparate, yet allied or kindred, natures coalesce for good and all into one single indivisible personality."[3]

The basal article of faith once settled, Luther was pre-

[1] Hastings, *DCG.* ii. 862. [2] *Dogmengeschichte* (1te Aufl.), iii. 695.
[3] *Expository Times* for Dec. 1905, 105.

pared to give and take with respect to inherited technical phrases, provided only facts were secure. He could even say, in a well-known passage, that his soul hated the word "homoousion," and that he preferred not to employ it.[1] Modern critical theologians, however, are scarcely accurate in regarding Luther as a forerunner of their own view that the Gospel is quite independent of Christology. It is indeed the fact that acceptance of the deity of Christ had ceased, for Luther, to be a doctrinal preliminary of saving faith; but this is so because Christ, so far from counting for less in personal religion, now counts for infinitely more, and stands in the very centre of the religious experience itself. Belief in His Godhead, in other words, is no mere theoretic approach or avenue to faith; it was a living constituent *in* faith, to be afterwards analysed out and made explicit by the theologian. Here in Christ, Luther cries, I have the Father's heart and will, coming forth in love for my salvation; and the heresy of heresies is that which separates the mind and disposition of God from that of Jesus. We must not make "a Christ apart by Himself and a God apart by Himself," but reckon the two all one. Now it was this great evangelical intuition that God and Christ confront us as a single Divine redeeming cause that moved Luther to argue with such intensity that the two natures are so united that they cannot really be looked at apart. There had been a time, he admits, when he thought he did well to distinguish them; and if the efforts failed by which he later strove to rectify this error, we can see that it was because the condition of human thought in his time supplied no categories but such as were intrinsically unequal to the task. For Luther, as for Augustine and Athanasius, "Jesus is a Man in whom God dwells, and who is God";[2] but this is a faith which it is impossible to express worthily by saying that in Him a Divine nature and a human nature are conjoined, or that a Divine substance underlies the

[1] Cf. Th. Harnack, *Luthers Theologie*, ii. 186.

[2] Lindsay, *ut supra*, 860.

human life of Jesus. The experience of the man who finds in Christ the saving presence of very God is, as Herrmann protests, "not so much expressed as concealed by the formula that combines a Divine nature with the human nature of Jesus."[1] This, after all, does no more than reproduce the content of one of the Reformer's most characteristic passages: "Christ is not called Christ because He has two natures. What is that to me? That He is by nature God and man is for Himself. But what gives me comfort and blessing is that He so applies His office and pours forth His love and becomes my Saviour and Redeemer."[2]

Thus new thoughts of Christ are struggling in Luther with old forms. In terms, to take one instance, he subscribed to the old dogma of the impersonality of Christ's human nature, but in point of fact he felt no genuine interest in the idea, and it had only the faintest influence on his argument. What he gives to the world, as Loofs has excellently remarked, is not new dogmatic ideas but new religious intuitions. By a vitalising innovation he drew the mind of a whole age back to the historic Christ, declaring with tremendous power that faith possesses its proper object solely in the person of the crucified and exalted Lord. So passionately did he preach the unity of Christ and God, that a parallel has naturally been pointed out between his naive modalism and that which we have discovered in primitive writers like Ignatius. And Herrmann has done a service by bringing out the fact, so significant when closely scrutinised, that for Luther the right confession of Christ's deity is possible only for a redeemed man. As he puts it, quite in Luther's spirit, "when Christ redeems us from ourselves, then we see God working upon us in Christ's person."[3] It is true, of course, that Luther often fell beneath the level of these glorious thoughts. The exigencies of controversy at times seduced him into old mistaken paths. The two-nature

[1] *Communion, etc.*, 151. [2] See Erlangen edition, xii. 244.
[3] *ut supra*, 167.

doctrine hampered the free expression of his mind. Yet in nothing was his greatness as a Reformer more clearly manifested than in his rediscovery of the historic Saviour, who redeems sinful men by drawing them into union with His own wondrous person as disclosed in the New Testament. This apostolic Gospel was not new in religion, but for long it had been banished from theology. In this man it rose from the dead once more, and by claiming to revolutionise men's conception of our Lord's saving work, claimed also to reconstruct their ideas of His person. And to this hour the Church is occupied with the problem essentially as it was stated by Martin Luther.

§ 2. *The Lutheran and Reformed Christologies.*—The Reformers, alike in Germany and Switzerland, had made it plain that they took over without reserve the orthodox Christology of the ancient Church, as set forth in the three so-called Ecumenical Creeds. Melanchthon indeed declared, in a famous sentence, *Hoc est Christum cognoscere, beneficia eius cognoscere non . . . eius naturas, modos incarnationis contueri*;[1] but the pregnant suggestion was not yet developed, and the Protestant scholasticism which rose to its height in the seventeenth century was led into other paths, in the first instance by the pressure of sacramental controversy. A dreary formalism took possession of the official views of Christ. Dialectical refinements, with minute distinctions intended to veil minute concessions, or to avoid the more glaring self-contradictions of too omniscient and undaunted hypotheses, revived the intellectual methods of the Middle Ages, and went far to stifle the fresh and life-giving intuitions of the Reformation. The main interest of this uninspiring age, so far as our subject is concerned, lies in the revival of that old dispute as to the relation of Godhead and manhood in Christ, which had prevailed between Alexandria and Antioch. Now it came up freshly, in a modi-

[1] *Loci* of 1521, Introduction.

fied form, as between the Lutheran and the Reformed Churches, having been stimulated into detailed expression rather than initiated by a divergence of view regarding the Lord's Supper. Consubstantiation and the ubiquity of the Body and Blood of Christ went hand in hand, and shaped the Lutheran reading of the two-nature doctrine. At one in the conviction that the eternal and pre-existent Son had become man by assuming human nature in its entirety, the two Churches differed in their interpretation of the composite unity thus created.

The official Lutheran Christology at the close of the sixteenth century is to be found in the Formula of Concord of 1577 (Art. 8), behind which lie domestic controversies of scarcely more than pathological interest. It must be said that the theory of Christ's person here set forth attaches itself, often, to Luther's least happy suggestions, and even petrifies as dogmas what were, for his own mind, only so many vivid metaphors. A compromise had to be found between the views of Brenz and Chemnitz.[1] According to Brenz, the unity of the Divine-human person is such that from the moment of the incarnation Christ's manhood shares in the glory and power of His deity. He did not renounce the use of this power and glory even in the days of His flesh, though for the most part He exercised it only in a hidden manner, and Brenz feels himself justified in saying that the living Christ in His majesty governed heaven and earth while He yet lay dead in the sepulchre. On these terms our Lord's humanity is ubiquitous in the fullest sense. Chemnitz, on the other hand, pleads for what is designated the *multivolipræsentia*, *i.e.* the power of being present at will simultaneously in many places. This power, he holds, resides in Christ's manhood in virtue of its having been absolutely suffused by the Divine nature, which ever after works in, with, and through the other. At the same time, though on earth Christ in His humanity

[1] Brenz was at the head of the Swabian school, while Chemnitz led the Lower Saxons.

possessed all the fulness of the Godhead, He *chose not to use or manifest it*, but suspended its exercise temporarily. The Formula of Concord, on the whole, leans to the side of Chemnitz. There is a real communication of qualities from one nature to the other, the deity participating in the passion of the humanity, the humanity in the majesty of the Divine. Yet it is insisted that no transformation of the qualities of one nature into those of the other is to be supposed; what took place was not an essential transfusion, but a permanent communication; and withal there is an explicit statement to the effect that no addition to or diminution of the attributes of the Divine nature resulted from the incarnation of the Word.[1]

Turning to the contrasted Christologies held by the Lutheran and the Reformed Churches, let us note that the Lutherans, in the endeavour to give fuller expression to the religious content of faith, were mainly eager to bring out the unity of the Divine-human life. Hence they went back to Luther's underlying axiom, "that human nature has been created for participation in the life of God, and is destined to reach it to a degree of which we can form no conception save from the exemplary instance of Jesus Christ, our Head."[2] *Finitum est capax infiniti.* Insisting that the inseparability of the two natures must be taken seriously, they worked

[1] That the matter was after all left ambiguous is proved by the seventeenth-century controversy between the Tübingen theologians and those of Giessen (1616–27). They long debated the question: Did the God-man, in the days of His flesh, actually renounce the use of Divine powers, in respect of His humanity (both sides agreed that these powers were in His possession), or did He merely employ them secretly? The first view is that of Giessen. Tübingen took the second, holding that in secret the child Jesus ruled the universe *qua* man, and that He later exhibited at times both omnipotence and omniscience. Gradually the opinion of Giessen prevailed, though illogically enough on the strictly Lutheran premises; and in Quenstedt, at whose hands the doctrine received final shape, the presence in the manhood of Christ of strictly Divine powers had become a mere potentiality. Cf. Haering, *Der christliche Glaube*, 434; Schmid, *Doctrinal Theology of the Lutheran Church* (Eng. tr. by Hay and Jacobs), 396 ff.; and see Index of Bruce, *Humiliation of Christ*.

[2] Dykes, *ut supra*, 104.

out a theory in rather unprofitable detail. First of all comes the *unitio*, or incarnation, the actual combination, that is to say, of deity and humanity in one person; and this is strictly an *act*. The permanent result, on the other hand, is a *state*, the perpetual conjunction with mutual possession of the two natures now subsisting in the one person of the Son; this state being technically known as the *unio personalis*. It is not that a part of the Logos is united to a part of the flesh. Rather the whole Logos and the whole flesh form one indissoluble Life, the hypostasis of the manhood, which in itself is impersonal, being constituted or replaced by the pre-existent Divine personality. So closely joined and, as it were, coextensive, are the natures, that the Logos has no existence outside the flesh, nor the flesh outside the Logos (*Logos totus in carne*). In short, it is no mere verbal or ideal or relative union, but one which is wholly reciprocal and personal. Finally, from the personal union, and the resulting communion or mutual permeation of natures, there flows the *communicatio idiomatum*, a peculiar and original tenet for which appeal was made to Col 2[9]. In two ways, it is true, the ancient Church had taught a mutual transference of qualities in the Saviour's person. First, qualities of either nature may be ascribed to the Divine-human person, as when it is said, "Christ is of the seed of David," or "The Son of Man is from heaven" (*genus idiomaticum*); secondly, redemptive qualities or actions of the theanthropic person as a whole may be ascribed to one or other of the natures, as in the propositions, "The Son of God was manifested to destroy the works of the devil," or, "The blood of Jesus cleanses from sin" (*genus apotelesmaticum*). But the Lutherans went further, and became responsible for what was really a theological innovation, by definitely teaching that Divine attributes may be predicated of the human nature, since there is a real transference of properties from the one side to the other; they exchange something of their substance as if by a process of endosmosis (*genus majestaticum*).

Even in His human nature Christ is almighty and omnipresent, and a basis is thus found in strictly Christological doctrine for the tenet of the sacramental ubiquity, or multipresence, of the Saviour's body. The fourth possible class of propositions, asserting the conveyance of human properties to deity, was summarily put aside, no one being found to question the immutability of Godhead.[1]

A little reflection is enough, I think, to prove that this dogmatic Lutheran Christology has swung round eventually in a direction exactly opposite to that in which primarily it had sought to move. For the inspiring motive of the whole had been a passionate desire to vindicate for faith the possession of a Divine Christ, whom we can grasp and hold. It was for the sake of this that Luther put forward the stupendous conception of a humanity which is omniscient and almighty. Now in all probability Luther's mind, in affirming that the manhood received and used the properties of Godhead, was chiefly occupied with the exalted Lord in His risen majesty; yet further reflection was sure to suggest that if this intercommunication of qualities was a fact, and an essential outcome of the personal union of the natures, it was impossible that it should date merely from the ascension. Rather it must belong to the earthly Jesus from the first moment of incarnation. And at once this evoked two objections. First, it might be said, the Gospels present us with no such Figure—a man who yet is omniscient or omnipresent; on the contrary, He exhibits the natural and accustomed limitations of humanity. To meet this difficulty, the older Lutheran divines took a somewhat novel line as to the "states" of Christ and the *Kenosis* which Scripture declares Him to have undergone. They drew a sharp distinction between incarnation and humiliation. The subject of humiliation or self-emptying is not the Logos, for in becoming man the Logos surrendered

[1] It is at this point that modern Kenotic theories have interposed, asking whether that which is commonly said to be inconceivable is so in fact.

nothing of His Divine majesty. The subject of humiliation is the God-man in respect of His human nature; and for Him humiliation consisted solely in this, that while retaining possession of the Divine qualities conveyed to His humanity by its union with the Logos, He yet made no habitual use of them. He usually dispensed with them, and only at times did His real powers flash through the veil.

But this naturally provokes a second criticism. Apart from the fact that the scheme still impairs the full manhood of the historic Christ, is there not, one feels, something curiously mechanical in a conception of deity and humanity, and their mutual relations, which first combines them absolutely in order to secure a personal unity of life, and then cancels the reality of the combination lest its effect should be to submerge the lesser of the two united factors? Thus Lutheran dogma spoke of the infant Jesus ruling the universe, but only secretly; and both the leading statement, and still more if possible the added qualification, leave an impression of being completely alien to the thought of the New Testament. Further, it is doubtful whether the goal aimed at, even as regards the Atonement, could really be attained this way. It was axiomatic indeed that the blood of Christ has infinite expiatory value, as being the life-blood of the God-man; but if Christ in order to be capable of death must disengage His humanity yet once more from the Divine properties conferred on it by incarnation, loosening anew the formed union, could it be said that His blood any longer possessed that infinite worth which derives from personal oneness with the Divine? For now it is not the God-man who dies, but a humanity disengaged from the higher unity.[1]

If the Lutherans prolonged the line of Alexandrian reflection, the Reformed Christology, on the other hand, maintained the traditions of Antioch, holding the formulas of Chalcedon as sacrosanct. The Lutheran maxim they

[1] Cf. Haering, *ut supra*, 434.

met with a direct negative: *finitum non est capax infiniti.* In consequence they held the Divine and human natures rigidly, not to say coldly, in separation. It is true that in Christ the Infinite nature and the finite co-exist in a personal union mediated by the Holy Spirit, for the person of the former, *i.e.* the eternal Logos, has assumed the latter, and henceforward is the God-man Jesus Christ. But the special teaching of the Lutherans as to the communication of qualities they rejected, as leading to the deification of the Lord's manhood. Each nature retains the attributes properly belonging to it; the hypostatic unity, therefore, is of an indirect kind, being placed wholly in the person, which singly rules over and combines two entities in themselves separate. Of this oneness the best illustration or analogy is given in the mystic union of Christ with the believing soul. In harmony with this, the Reformed divines put forward a different interpretation of the *Kenosis.* The subject of humiliation in Ph 2, they rightly held, is not the incarnate God-man, but the pre-incarnate Son; and for the apostle's mind humiliation is simply the incarnation. Closer inspection, no doubt, reveals the fact that after all the Logos is considered not to have divested Himself of His Divine glory, but only to have conjoined the human nature in personal union with Himself. Nevertheless, the Reformed writers insisted with tenacity that this manhood was veritably human, of one essence with our own; and in great measure the strength and religious value of their construction lay in this persistent effort to do justice to Jesus' experience of growth and trial, as recorded with concrete detail in the Gospels. Sinless and infallible, He yet grew in knowledge, holiness, and power. Not even in the exalted state does His human nature cease to be separated from the Divine by an impassable gulf. Perhaps it was by a certain instinct of compensation that this insistence upon the sublime and absolute transcendence of the Divine Logos, even in relation to His own manhood, came to have alongside of it so marked an emphasis on the ethical reality of Jesus' human life. Be that as it may, while the Lutherans had taught that the whole Logos was present in Jesus, the sharp distinction of Infinite and finite in the Reformed scheme made this impossible. It was decided, therefore, that the Logos, truly present in Jesus' manhood, is none the less existent outside it—*totus extra carnem* as well as *totus in carne*—governing the world simultaneously from a different centre of life and consciousness, so to speak, from that at which He dwelt incarnate in Jesus.[1] It is not surprising that opponents should at once have rejoined that on these terms the incarnation was made of none effect, since the relation of the Logos to Jesus now resembled that which He bears to other men alike in degree and in kind.

If the Lutherans had made the reality of Christ's human nature dubious, equally natural was the charge that Reformed writers destroyed the unity of the person. It was argued that for them the two natures present in the theanthropic life are glued together "like two boards," with no living interpenetration. They had accused the Lutherans of being Monophysites or Docetics, and now they had to hear themselves styled Nestorians and Ebionites. The relative justice of these unhappy recriminations we cannot stay to canvass, but at least we ought not to miss the great religious motives operating in the expressed convictions of both sides. If the Lutherans had made a nobly conceived effort to formulate the truth that Jesus is Immanuel, God with us, the concrete presence of God in perfect manhood, the Calvinists in

[1] This is what is meant by *illud "extra" Calvinisticum*, of which Lutheran divines speak with an approach to horror. Calvin formulates it with his usual clearness: "Although the boundless essence of the Word was united with human nature into one person, we have no idea of any enclosing. The Son of God descended miraculously from heaven, yet without abandoning heaven; was pleased to be conceived miraculously in the Virgin's womb, to live on the earth, and hang upon the cross, and yet always filled the world as from the beginning" (*Institutes*, bk. ii. chap. 13, *ad fin.*). This view can unquestionably appeal to the general trend of ancient and mediæval Christology, but it may well be doubted whether it does justice to the religious interests bound up with the idea of incarnation.

turn proclaimed no less truly the reality of Jesus' human life, as a religious and ethical experience, striving to regard the Incarnate One "as He regarded Himself—as the Son of Man, the Man of sorrows and acquainted with grief."[1]

These two Christologies offered an easy mark to the polemic of the Socinians. The leader of these theological insurgents, Faustus Socinus (1539–1604), had proclaimed that if religious doctrines are to be believed, they must be amenable to the strict rules of logic; and accordingly he had denied the doctrine of the Trinity, of the pre-existence of Christ, and of His two natures. Jesus is a mere man, but He was sent into the world by a benignant God, and only through Him can salvation be secured. Yet to this mere man wonderful things have happened, and it is hardly an exaggeration to say that Socinus could have accepted every article in the Apostles' Creed. For Jesus is distinguished from all other men by His birth of a virgin, by His sinlessness, and by a special baptism of the Holy Spirit, endowing Him with miraculous power; not only so, but as a reward for the perfect obedience of His earthly life He has been raised to heaven and constituted God's viceroy over the whole universe.[2] In this capacity, we are expressly told, He ought to be worshipped, for, though not in Himself possessed of the Divine right to worship, special permission has been accorded to believers by God sanctioning His adoration; and Socinus went so far as to hold that the exalted Jesus might properly be called God. Nevertheless to these far-reaching Christian affirmations there were appended the most singular negations. God, in the last resort, is

[1] Bruce, *ut supra*, 132. On the whole subject of the Lutheran and Reformed Christologies, see his fine chapter.

[2] "Even the critical spirits of the Reformation period, the Socinian Unitarians, made no real headway till they had elevated the creaturely Jesus, by resurrection, to a heavenly world-papacy" (Kähler, *Angewandte Dogmen*, 132). They are the clearest instance in history of the theory which ascribes to Christ a *gewordene Gottheit*, a Godhead which once was not but now is.

not present personally in Jesus, and His position as glorified and in a sense Divine Lord can be justified only by a species of what we must call deification. One feels that neither orthodox nor heretics were so placed as to comprehend each other, and that already the conditions of the problem were passing into a new phase, of which it may be the final issues have not yet emerged. "This Socinian doctrine," Professor Dick Fleming has said, "rests on the same presuppositions as the orthodoxy of the day, namely, that the supreme and essential characters of deity are omnipotence, omniscience, unchangeableness; but by applying this conception logically to the person of Christ, Socinians emptied their Christology of all religious value. For union with God is the need of the human heart; and the doctrine of the God-man, contradictory as it was, held a truth for which Socinianism found no expression." [1]

We turn now to the modern phase of the Christological question, as reconstituted by two centuries of untiring historical research. New questions begin to be asked, and new combinations set on foot.

[1] Hastings, *DCG.* ii. 867; cf. Bovon, *Dogmatique Chrétienne*, ii. 151.

CHAPTER VIII.

CHRISTOLOGY IN THE NINETEENTH CENTURY.

§ 1. *Theocentric and Anthropocentric Conceptions.* — Two hundred years ago a striking change of attitude took place in serious students of the person of Jesus Christ. Till then the point of departure had prevailingly been *theocentric*, as it may be called: that is, men engaged in Christological construction set out from the Eternal Word or Son, the Second Person of the Trinity, and at times it almost seems as if we were being summoned to watch the incarnation taking place through the eyes of God Himself. Somewhere near the beginning of the eighteenth century, pioneer minds began to feel that this cannot be the right path for human intelligence. We must start from a point closer to ourselves. So the great modern movement of research, of which the outcome has virtually been a rediscovery of the historic Jesus, who is now better known than at any period since the apostolic age, represents an ever-growing volume of devout study of the Life pictured in the Gospels, inspired

LITERATURE—Faut, *Die Christologie seit Schleiermacher*, 1907; Günther, *Die Lehre von der Person Christi im XIXten Jahrhundert*, 1911; Weinel, *Jesus im XIXten Jahrhundert*, 1903; Bleek, *Die Grundlagen der Christologie Schleiermachers*, 1898; F. H. R. Frank, *Geschichte und Kritik der neueren Theologie*[4], 1908; Frommel, *Études de Théologie Moderne*, 1909; Pfleiderer, *Development of Theology in Germany and in Great Britain in the Nineteenth Century*, 1890; G. Frank, *Geschichte der protestantischen Theologie*, Bd. iv., 1905; Herrmann, "Christliche-protestantische Dogmatik," in Hinneberg's *Kultur der Gegenwart*, I. iv. 2, 1909; Fairbairn, *Christ in Modern Theology*, 1893; Bruce, *Humiliation of Christ*[2], 1881; Bensow, *Die Lehre von der Kenose*, 1903; Orr, *Christian View of God and the World*, 1893; Tulloch, *Movements of Religious Thought*, 1885; Ecke, *Die theologische Schule A. Ritschls*, 1897; Garvie, *The Ritschlian Theology*, 1899.

by the conviction that, whatever more, it is at all events genuinely and completely human. The point of view, in other words, gradually became *anthropocentric.* These adjectives need imply no serious difference of opinion as to ultimate conclusions; "anthropocentric" must not be confused with "humanitarian." It is less a question of antagonism than of order. For both sides Christ is God manifest in the flesh; indeed, as a recent writer has remarked, modern preoccupation with the historic Christ "has had the effect of making the old problem of His Person stand out with a quite fresh sharpness of outline." For it is precisely the unique human characteristics, the transcendent traits and personal pretensions plainly exhibited in the record that send us back, for reasonable explanation, far and beyond the possibilities of normal manhood. If previously the movement of Christian thought had been from above downwards, its direction was now imperceptibly reversed, and, as was natural in an inductive age, came to be upwards from below. And the problem confronting the modern mind may, therefore, be said to be: Given the fact that Jesus is thus true man, proposing indeed unheard-of claims, equally separate from sinners and distinct from saints, yet nowhere transgressing the limits of perfect manhood as it moves within unique and inimitable conditions, what is the relation between this Life, in which God is personally present, and the inner being of the Godhead? And further, what is the relation, in the person of Christ Himself, between the Divine content of His being, and the specific form it assumed in Him of a perfectly revealing human consciousness?[1]

Round this question, then, the Christological work of the moderns has in the main revolved, although its orbit has occasionally swung out very far from the centre. During the nineteenth century a varied but rewarding debate went on. Not since the age of the Cappadocians has the person of our Lord so held the focus of Christian thought as in the nineteenth century.

[1] Cf. Haering, *Dogmatik*, 428.

The background of the modern movement is furnished by the uninspired Rationalism of the *Aufklärung*. Röhr, a characteristic exponent of its temper, declares that Christology has no place in the system of Christian doctrine, since we are concerned not with a religion for which Jesus is object of faith, but only with that which Jesus taught. Hence the *Aufklärung* dispensed with Christology because first it had virtually dispensed with faith in Christ as Saviour. Jesus is indeed the Teacher of a perfect morality, and the pattern of character for all time; but there is nothing supernatural about Him. To call Him in any metaphysical sense God's Son is irrational, for His personality was the product of natural gifts directed by an energetic will. Even Kant failed to transcend these meagre conclusions. To him Christ was but the abstract idea of ethical perfection, of moral unity with God; and what saves is faith in this ideal, not in Jesus as a person. Church doctrine, he said, has committed the error of applying to Jesus epithets and conceptions which rightly belong to the ethical ideal, of which He is but the symbol. Thus, for example, it is true that the idea of perfect humanity has hovered before the mind of God from the beginning, and, as an effluence from His being, may even be designated His Son; but to speak of the pre-existence of Christ is mythology. The connection of faith with historical events is purely fortuitous, and the phrase "historical revelation" can only be interpreted as meaning that throughout the course of ages the eternal truths of Reason have been rising into the clear light of knowledge. This is tantamount to the assertion that Christ has no permanent place in the religion known by His name. The principle of Christianity and the person of Christ were distinguished sharply—a familiar phenomenon in the ensuing century, and even now not quite obsolete, though it is easy to see that it implies the disappearance of the Gospel of the New Testament. It implies that Jesus is not, in any legitimate sense, the object of saving trust. His significance for religion is only casual, chronological, indirect. Our business is solely with the rational faith of which Jesus was the most eminent preacher and pioneer; and all truth about God, virtue, and immortality proclaimed by Him may be appropriated, and will save us, quite apart from a personal relation of dependence on Christ Himself. We have the seed, and can ourselves grow the flowers. We shall see that in the speculative movement which sprang from Kant the same principle is regarded as axiomatic; as when Fichte, for example, contends that unity with God is the great matter, but the path to it wholly immaterial. If Christ were to return to earth He would set little store by our recognition of His place as Redeemer, provided only Christianity itself were dominating the minds of men.

Much of the interest of this period lies in its close affinity with a widely spread tendency of the present day. Recently a prominent writer of the advanced wing declared, with grave emphasis, that if historical investigation were to decide that Jesus had never lived, he should not as a religious man feel himself seriously impoverished or disconcerted. We have the ideas of the Gospel, and may neglect its facts. But if our personal relation to Christ, as believers, is put in abeyance as an illegitimate and unscientific prejudice, then, be it in the eighteenth century or to-day, purely historic investigation will yield a conception of His nature which living faith never can accept. "It is no mere accident," Ritschl once observed, "that the subversion of Jesus' religious importance has been attempted under the guise of writing His life."[1]

§ 2. *Schleiermacher.*—It was in view of the situation just described that Friedrich Schleiermacher addressed himself to the problem of Christology. His qualifications for the task were unrivalled. Apart from a sub-soil of warm Moravian piety, and of reverent love for Jesus, his

[1] *Justification and Reconciliation* (Eng. tr.), 3.

mind had been enriched by fruitful conceptions of the profound significance of religion in human life. He saw that religion is a thing *sui generis*, not to be swamped by morality or confused heedlessly with mere knowledge. He saw, too, what the older Rationalism had failed to see, that Christianity is anchored to facts of the past, and that here lies its secret. Never was man more alive to the value of the Christian fellowship for living and authentic Christian faith. He it was, as an American theologian has finely said, "who led the German Christianity, in its returning course, to our Lord." The absoluteness of the Christian religion is the key to his view of its Founder.

Here we shall confine attention to the Christology of Schleiermacher's great dogmatic work, *Der christliche Glaube* (1821–22; second edition, greatly altered, 1831), neglecting his cursory treatment of the topic in his *Reden*, issued more than twenty years earlier. There, while acknowledging our vast debt to Jesus, he had declined to recognise Him as the only Mediator. His view of Christianity as the fleeting expression of an eternal ideal debarred him from assigning a central and permanent importance to the historic Lord. And Christology is obviously out of the question for one to whom Jesus is but *primus inter pares*. At this point Schleiermacher temporarily approaches the position of his later antagonist, Hegel.

Far otherwise is the tone of his epoch-making treatise on dogmatic. For here Christianity is defined at the very outset as a teleological monotheism, the unique characteristic of which is this, that in it everything is directly related to the redemption accomplished by Jesus. No longer is He *a* Mediator, adapted to the form which the religious sentiment assumes in Christianity; He is *the* Mediator, final, supreme, transcendent. Salvation is indissociable from His person. "There is no other mode," he writes, "in which one can come to have part in the Christian fellowship than through faith in Jesus as the

Redeemer." And progress will consist, not in separating from Him, but in ever assimilating His work more completely.

This position is defended by an argument which, at least in intention, is purely experimental. Here as always, he reminds us, the point of departure is the Christian mind, and our problem takes this form: Who and what must Christ have been, to explain the state of a redeemed soul? What are the dimensions of His being, if He is the sufficient reason of the salvation we now enjoy? It is undeniable that there is given to us, as Christians, a continuous invigoration of the sense of God which is accompanied by a rising consciousness of bliss and of victory over the world. This experience of redemption, which cannot have been generated accidentally, and which is found only within the Christian Church, must have a cause capable of producing it. Thus, going back by inference from the specifically Christian consciousness to Him who evoked it, from effect to cause, we are able to determine the quality of Jesus' person.[1] He is the living and self-communicative Saviour, the inexhaustible fount and *creative Type* of new life and freedom conveyed to all who trust Him. From Him flows a stream of vital and vitalising power.

On the basis of these experiential facts a worthy doctrinal superstructure may be raised. If Christ redeems man, it must be in virtue of redemptive forces resident in His nature; if, within the Christian Church, our religious sense is progressively triumphing over our lower impulses, it is because that triumph was realised in Jesus absolutely. His consciousness of God was such that it is properly described as a unique presence of God in Him, an original entrance of the Divine into human life. In this modified sense, Schleiermacher accepts the ecclesias-

[1] Theologians, of course, use this argument by instinct, but no one else has employed it with Schleiermacher's clearness and tenacity. Whether it ought to rank as primary is another question. J. H. Skrine gives an attractive modern statement of the principle, *Creed and the Creeds*, 167 ff.

tical doctrine of incarnation. And in that doctrine he selects for peculiarly warm and intense devotion the sinlessness of Jesus. Jesus was perfectly and absolutely holy. "Not holy, however, with a holiness merely acquired (which would have made Him but a model, and a model incapable of effecting man's redemption), but with a holiness acquired—or rather conserved—on the basis of inherent holiness (only this last gives Him the creative power of a type). This absolute and primary perfection of Jesus is simply the complete and perpetual triumph in Him of the God-consciousness over the sense-consciousness. Thus it excludes alike every moral fault and every religious error, and constitutes His divinity."[1] As the Archetypal Man (*Urbild*) He is a perfect union of the historical individual and the ideal personality, crowning the creation of our race, Himself creating a new race, determined in personal life, as He was, by God. Type and history coincide in Jesus; all that is historic is typical, and all that is typical has become historic.

Schleiermacher is also convinced that the advent of this unique and archetypal Figure cannot be explained, on the principle of uniformity, by His human *milieu*. Rather it is due to a creative Divine act; it is a stream rising from the deepest fount of all spiritual life—a second Divine creation, as it may be called, which completes the first, though transcending it, because it forms part of the same original Divine idea. Thus the appearance of Christ in our world is positively miraculous (*eine wunderbare Erscheinung*). Although the Virgin Birth is rejected, a supernatural conception is strongly affirmed in the spiritual sense that the powers of the race were unequal to the task of producing this unparalleled Life. On the other hand, it has been maintained that for Schleiermacher the being of our Lord is supernatural only in a relative sense, inasmuch as the resident powers of human nature, the receptivity of man for God-consciousness in perfect measure, is

[1] Gaston Frommel, *Études de Théologie Moderne*, 172 f.

regarded as the second and equally important factor in His origin.[1] This, however, is an objection which it is scarcely possible to sustain except on grounds which would involve a denial of the ethical affinities of God and man. There is more justice in the criticism which points to the grave diminution of the contents of New Testament faith in Schleiermacher's categorical assertion that the resurrection and ascension, as well as the prediction of Christ's return to judgment, form no real part of the doctrine of His person (§ 99).

Apart from the supernatural character thus generally predicated of Jesus' origin, His nature was precisely similar to ours, and underwent a precisely similar development.

A light is cast on Schleiermacher's deeply Christian conception of the Saviour by his mystical view of His redeeming work, on which we may not dwell. Its cardinal idea is that of vital union with Christ. It is by taking us up into the energies of His God-consciousness and the fellowship of His perfect blessedness that He reconciles and saves.

The influence of this great thinker in leading Christologians to start from a present experience of the new life as immediately dependent on Jesus was closely akin to that of the Reformers, and its depth and value can scarcely be overestimated. If, as so often happens, he himself gained less than might have been hoped from the new point of view, and failed to satisfy some deep Christian instincts, this was owing to defects inherent in his theoretic notion of what salvation is. Its relation to the world too much predominates. Redeemed men are men liberated from the oppression of finite causes, and dependent solely on the Absolute Causality, rather than forgiven sinners, living in fellowship with God the Father. The idea of religion present in the *Reden* still persists. Thus, while Schleiermacher asserts—no one more emphatically—the central

[1] Cf. Mulert, *Schleiermachers geschichtsphilosophische Ansichten*, 66 ff., 84 ff.

and redeeming place of Christ, it is doubtful whether his speculative presuppositions permit him to hold such a person as either real or possible. As long as religion is defined in impersonal terms—as long as it is not seen to be communion with a personal God—it has not been made clear that its perfected stage can arrive only through a personal Mediator. A principle may suffice. Moreover, though he preferred to wreck his system as a monistic structure rather than tamper with Christ's absolute immunity from sin (for a miracle *is* a miracle though its sphere be the soul), he yet has left a certain shadow upon the genuine humanity of the Sinless One. Can we say that a Christ from whose inner life even the minimum of moral conflict is excluded[1] is our Companion in temptation, our Brother and Captain in victory; is not what appears in Him, as it has been put, "merely the natural predominance of a higher principle"?[2] This also flows from the romantic pantheism which haunted Schleiermacher from first to last, and leads him to represent Jesus' consciousness of God more, on the whole, as the natural play of temperament than as perfect reciprocal fellowship with His Father. Finally, it is difficult to concede that Schleiermacher has been able to preserve the religious truth of incarnation. Christ's humanity, in his view, is no doubt God-possessed; still, a God-possessed humanity is one thing, and may have degrees; God manifest in the flesh is quite another.[3] And it makes a difference to theology when it falters in repeating the words of St. Paul: "Ye know the grace of our Lord Jesus Christ, that, though He was rich, yet for your sakes He became poor." The *religious* importance of Christ's eternal being has too much been ignored.

On the other hand, the invaluable service of Schleiermacher to the Christological thinking of three generations

[1] *Sendschreiben* (ed. Mulert), 22.

[2] Haering, *ut supra*, 437.

[3] Christ is exhibited as the objective ground of faith, but in the last resort He is shown to us still more clearly as *the first believer*. Later liberalism has attached itself to this element in the whole. Cf. Loofs, *RE.* iv. 56.

may be summed up in the statement, first, that he proclaimed the advent of Christ as a supernatural interposition, redeeming and Divine; secondly, he once more placed the figure of Jesus at the centre of His own religion. To men bred in the Rationalism of the eighteenth century this came as a revelation, as life from the dead. It opened to them a new world. Christ the focus of Christianity—the watchword was never forgotten. And Schleiermacher's were the lips from which it pealed forth with the persuasive charm imparted to it by a great personality. In the words with which Dr. Fairbairn closes a finely judicious estimate: "In his religious system Jesus held the same place as God held in the practical system of Kant; in the one case God was a necessity to the conscience, in the other Jesus was a necessity to the consciousness; but while the former had all the severity of an inflexible moral law, the latter had all the beauty and all the grace of the Redeemer and Saviour of mankind."

§ 3. *Hegel and his School.*—In point of speculation Hegel and Schleiermacher are contrasted and antipathetic types; yet it would be easy to prove a close relation between their conceptions of the essence of religion. Both in fact represent a view of life and the world inherited from Goethe. Whereas for the exposition of this romanticism, as it may be styled, Schleiermacher chose terms of feeling, Hegel construed it in the severer categories of pure thought. Taking up in a higher sense the tradition of eighteenth-century Rationalism, according to which Christianity is doctrine, he welcomed the Christological dogma as embodying the true philosophy under the forms of imaginative intuition, and setting forth the ontological unity of God and man, which philosophy defines by ideas, in the music and poetry of the heart. Man, he held, is finite spirit, and ultimately identical as such with Infinite Spirit; not only so, but, according to the fairest exegesis of Hegel's words, it is in the finite spirit that the Absolute, or God, first attains to self-consciousness. History is God's self-realisation in and through the processes of human experience; in yet more general terms, reality is definable as the evolution of Absolute Reason mediated by nature and history. There is no more lofty truth than that God and man, so far from being disparate in essence, are a rational and intrinsic unity. Religion, inferior to philosophy as an exponent of this unity, still does its best to get it expressed, and in pictorial fashion the thing is accomplished in the ecclesiastical dogma of the God-man.

On these terms Hegel showed himself more than ready to maintain friendly relations with the Church's creed. He saw his way to put such a meaning upon doctrines like our Lord's deity or atonement as would admit them to an important and even an essential place in his highly speculative construction. Of course there was a price to pay. The significance of the historic Jesus has been misconceived, and readjustment is essential. What the Church predicates of Him is, properly, a symbol; but a symbol of a vast metaphysical idea. It is through its aid that faith in the God-manhood has arisen, and the world been educated to perceive the truth of racial or universal incarnation, according to which the life of man is God's life in the form of time, and the Divine and human natures, being related as universal and particular, realise themselves only in organic unity with each other. The death, resurrection, and exaltation of Jesus are grand pictures of ontological ideas; they speak to us of the fact that man, viewed merely in his alienating finitude, is the prey of negation and dissolution, whereas if envisaged in his proper unity with the Infinite he takes high rank in the total process of the world. "This essential unity must be presented to the consciousness or interpreted to the experience of man by a manifest fact or sensuous reality in order that he may through knowledge attain to union. In other words, in order to save man from his state of division and estrangement, God must 'in an objective manner' enter this empirical or sensuous present as man's equal or fellow, and so cause it to appear—and appearance is always for another, and the other is here the Church or the society of faith—that the Divine and the human natures are not in themselves different, but really alike, akin, able to be in the unity of a person."[1] At times, indeed, it seems as if Hegel's attitude to the Church doctrine were genuinely positive; yet the progress of the discussion unfailingly brings out the fact that he was much less interested in Jesus than in what was believed about Him. And these beliefs are but man's stammering utterance of metaphysical theorems. Human history is the process of God's becoming, the self-unfolding of Reason under conditions of space and time; and in this sense, but no other, the Word became flesh and dwelt among us. "The history of Christ is the visible reconciliation between man and the eternal. With the death of Christ this union, ceasing to be a fact, becomes a vital idea—the Spirit of God which dwells in the Christian community."[2] It is from this side that Hegel contemplates the doctrine of the Trinity. The Son of God is the finite world of nature and man, which is estranged from its Father, and must be again resumed into essential harmony.

It would be unfair to say that in this scheme Jesus is deprived of all importance, for He is held to have been the first to realise the great speculative principle for which the Christian religion stands. If not Himself the God-man, He first perceived that God and man are one. Thus far Hegel transcended the unhistorical naivété of the eighteenth century. But it is clear that, apart from this casual chronological relationship, Christian doctrine, in its revised and sublimated form, has no longer any particular connection with the historic Christ. Christianity receives absolute rank, but at the cost of its tie with history. For only the world-process as a whole, and no single point or person in it, can be the true manifestation

[1] Fairbairn, *Christ in Modern Theology*, 220.
[2] W. Wallace, *Encyclopædia Britannica*, art. "Hegel."

of the Absolute. Hence, to quote Hegel's unequivocal language, "Christology affirms simply that God comes to be Spirit (*Geist wird*), and this can take place only in finite spirit, in man; in whom there arises the consciousness of the Absolute, and who then is likewise the Absolute's consciousness of itself." Thus, when Hegel has waved his wand, and uttered his dialectical and all-decisive formula, a change comes over the spirit of the believer's dream; everything appears to be as Christian as before, yet instinctively we are aware that nothing specifically Christian is left. Doctrines which as translated into the language of the notion show as high philosophical truths, and have the air of exhibiting the Christian as an imperfectly self-conscious Hegelian, turn out to have no relation, other than one which is accidental, to facts of the past. All we need say is that to believe this does not matter is a departure from Christian ground. When once the Gospel has been severed from a historic person, and identified with a complex of metaphysical ideas, what it ought to be called is scarcely worth discussion; that it is no longer Christianity is clear.

At the same time, a philosophical achievement of such real magnitude as Hegelianism could not but leave a deep permanent mark on theology. Certain minds, it is true, became so intoxicated by the new system as to find it scarcely credible that the world could ever get beyond it. Men like Daub, Marheineke, Goeschel and Rosenkranz handed on the Hegelian tradition with ardour, the result in some cases being—not unnaturally, if we recollect what in one sense was the strongly conservative bent of Hegel's mind—to bring to the surface once more the pure intellectualistic orthodoxy of a former age. Even those who maintained a critical attitude, however, made sincere though timorous efforts to demonstrate the necessity for the supreme idea of God-manhood having actualised itself in a single personal life. It was urged that Incarnation must take the form of incarnation in one person, if it was to be more than an abstract conception.

"The idea that in humanity we see Christ," said Rosenkranz, "receives its full truth only through the mediation of God's absolute incarnation in the person of Jesus." But Marheineke revived the master's tendency to substitute "humanity" for Christ in all propositions asserted by the Church of her Lord. "In the Ascension," he writes, "we are taught that religion, originating as it does in God, has no abiding place here on earth, but necessarily and eternally returns again whence it took its rise." Evidently this is a mode of thought already trembling on the verge of a Rationalism hardly distinguishable from that older type on which Hegel had earlier poured his indignant scorn. Sooner or later, then, some one was bound to speak out, and expose the hollow and precarious alliance which had been proclaimed between the Christian faith and dialectic pantheism. The word which broke the spell came from Strauss.

According to Strauss the received Gospel history is in the main a collection of myths gradually accumulated in the early Christian society, a wreath set on the Master's brow by reverent and loving fancy. Little of a historical kind is ascertainable about Jesus Himself, and that little is in any case totally incapable of sustaining the weight of Christological dogma. In point of fact, not scientific thought but religious imagination is responsible for the identifying of a Divine humanity with the person of Jesus; for while Jesus was unquestionably the pioneer who first grasped the thought that deity and humanity are in essence one, yet the Christ of faith (by which is meant not the historic actuality of incarnation but the abstract notion) is in no sense coincident with any specific individual. In words that soon became famous, Strauss declared that "the Idea loves not to pour all its fulness into one example, in jealousy towards all the rest. Only the race answers to the Idea."[1] What was meant for mankind must not be narrowed into a monopoly.

In spite of these brave words, Strauss felt himself

[1] *Leben Jesu* (1835), § 147. This formula has made a profound impression.

compelled by the critics of his *Leben Jesu* to make large concessions in regard to the creative power of the historic person whom we name Jesus Christ. If he had tended previously to contemplate Him as no more than the vehicle of an idea, something of Jesus' actual greatness now seemed to break on him, at least temporarily; and he commits himself to the statement that in religion Christ is not merely unsurpassed but unsurpassable, so that we have no option but to regard Him as in fact the founder of the Christian religion. Great personalities stand at the source of all new religious epochs; can Christianity be an exception? These admissions may strike us, perhaps, as grudging and unimportant; but, as Faut remarks, "what is interesting in this confession is, first, the argument from effect to cause, which had been decisive for Schleiermacher's Christology, and next the acknowledgment that a person, not an idea, must have been the source of Christianity." But even this admission was wrung from Strauss at the sword's point; and he followed it up with explanations which clearly proved, if proof were needed, that he was still as far as ever from the Christian attitude to Jesus.

Though we can no longer believe in Jesus, he continues, it is vitally important that we should retain the Christological dogma, provided only we explain to ourselves carefully what it means. Worthless for history, it has all the greater value for speculation. Thus many items in the gospel narrative—the supernatural birth of Jesus, His miracles, His resurrection and ascension—remain as eternally valid truths. They remain, in other words, as timeless symbols of a metaphysical idea. "Conceived as in an individual, a God-man, the attributes and functions which Church doctrine ascribes to Christ are mutually contradictory; in the idea of the race they harmonise." "Humanity is the union of two natures, the incarnate God, the Infinite Spirit reducing itself to finite measures, and the finite Spirit recalling its infinity. Humanity is the child of the visible mother and the invisible Spirit; it is the Sinless One, inasmuch as its evolution-story is without spot or blemish, and the impurity that always clings merely to the individual is sublated in the race and its career. Humanity is the Dying One who rises again and ascends to heaven, inasmuch as it draws an ever-higher life from the negation of its natural existence."[1] Christianity, in brief, is the final refutation of all dualism, the perfect expression of pure monistic immanence. Moving always within the ideal world, it is superior to history.

The only thing to be done with most of this is to deny it firmly. It ought to be clear by this time that the proposed identification of the Christian faith with the ontological theory that God and man are one—God the essence of man, man the actuality of God—is an utterly hopeless enterprise, which the scientific historian cannot take seriously. For it conflicts with the elementary fact that the Church existed, and knew itself to be redeemed by Jesus, long before the Christological dogma thus metaphysically canonised by Strauss had come to be. Faith was the parent of dogma, not its child. The truth is that the very idea of religion as consisting in personal fellowship with God had faded from Strauss' mind, and with its disappearance went also in large measure the power to sympathise with, or appreciate, essential Christian piety as it existed from the first.

We turn now to the systematic theologian in whom we see Hegelianism at its best, Biedermann of Zürich. Actuated by a sincere and positive interest in Christianity, he desired to construct a theological system which faith might safely accept; but he meant to do so exclusively with materials drawn from, or at least coloured by, the monistic philosophy he had learnt from Hegel. Religion as such he conceived, in opposition to Strauss as an objectively real interrelation of God and man, the Infinite Spirit and the finite; a view, he considered, equally antagonistic to dualism and pantheism. And while

[1] *Glaubenslehre*[2], ii. 740.

faith has its own real place, and is not to be unworthily defined as inferior to pure thought even from the point of view of religion itself, the task of theology is to raise it to the plane of completely self-conscious knowledge, so reducing its naiver utterances to philosophic and permanently valuable terms. We may be briefer in our account of Biedermann, because, with that monotony of phrase which afflicts so much Hegelian writing, he is perpetually recurring to one or two speculative axioms, which have already come before us. The keynote of his Christology is the explicit distinction between the principle of redemption and the person of the Redeemer. Strauss, he holds, was justified in his complaint that the Church wrongly predicates of Jesus what in point of fact is true only of Divine-humanity. But a dogma which, as interpreted of Jesus, is logically self-destructive, is nevertheless grandly true of the ontological unity of God and man. God and man are distinct in nature, but they are one in existence; one, as the Chalcedonian Creed puts it, without confusion, without mutation, without division, without severance. To speculative thought, accordingly, the incarnation is no single event, capable of being assigned to a specific time; it is an eternal fact, an unbeginning and unending factor in the life of God. Similarly, the atonement is no temporarily performed act, but God's timeless process of self-reconciliation, while the resurrection and ascension represent the eternal regress of Absolute Spirit to itself by way of finite being. In short, the Christ-principle, as it may be called, is but the religious expression of the fact that Infinite and finite Spirit, although distinct in essence, exist in a vital metaphysical reciprocity. With this alone dogmatic is concerned. On the other hand, dogmatic proper has nothing to do with the Christ-person, the historic Jesus. As the Founder of the Christian religion He belongs to the sphere of history; He is subject, not object, of the Christian faith.[1]

[1] The position taken by Dr. Edward Caird, in his *Evolution of Religion*, is very much that of Biedermann. Thus he writes: "By Him (Jesus) as

None the less, Biedermann makes a persistent and in some ways a deeply impressive effort to combine principle and person in a more living unity. If not identical with the principle of redemption, Jesus was yet the first to become conscious of it, and to make it known. Hence the relation between principle and person, though at first defined loosely enough, is not after all outward and accidental; it is inward and abiding, for without the mediation of Christ the principle could not have realised itself in fact. Biedermann never succeeded in overcoming this inconsistency between his initial separation of principle and person *in abstracto,* and his later admission that in concrete fact they are indissolubly bound up together. He was also hampered by an imperfect conception of the personality of God, and of the resulting nature of religion, for in his pages the Divine sonship which it was Christ's function to reveal hovers ambiguously between the idea of personal and ethical communion with the Father and a purely ontological relation of finite to Infinite Spirit.

In general it may be concluded that Hegelianism tended to commit a grave offence against history by construing Christianity as a system of ideas which is intelligible and effective apart from Jesus Christ. Strauss took this position frankly, but its influence is seen even in the more moderate theories of Biedermann. On the other hand, Hegel rendered the Church an easily forgotten service by stimulating an intenser reflection upon Christological problems in their universal aspect.

§ 4. *The Kenotic Theories.*—In the first quarter of last century, a union of the Lutheran and Reformed Churches in Germany was projected in connection with which arose a novel and remarkable type of Christological doctrine.

by no other individual before, the pure idea of a Divine humanity was apprehended and made into the great principle of life; and consequently, in so far as that idea can be regarded as realised in an individual,—and it was a necessity of feeling and imagination that it should be regarded as so realised,—in no other could it find so pure an embodiment" (quoted by Dr. Forrest, *Christ of History and of Experience*, 305).

From the well-known passage in Philippians, which figured prominently in the discussion, these theories came to be styled Kenotic,[1] and their differential feature, as it has been put, is that they seek "to do justice to the truth that the Incarnation of the Son involved a *real* self-limitation of His Divine mode of existence." I think the origin of the name has occasionally been forgotten by those who profess to explain the motives by which the authors of these views were actuated. The suggestion has frequently been made that the object of the Kenotic theories was to signalise the reality and integrity of our Lord's manhood, and obviously this is one of the fundamental principles of their method. Like other moderns, they had been taught by recent study of the Gospels that Jesus, whatever more, was truly our fellow-man. But, over and beyond this, they were also bent on bringing out the wondrous nature and subduing magnitude of the Divine sacrifice; and in this connection they wished to throw into strong relief the exceeding greatness of the step downwards taken by the Son of God when for our sakes, though rich, He became poor. It was as if they said, not merely, This is what in love He came to be; but, Even this which He became is unintelligible except by contrast with what He had been. He did not remain all that He was in the pre-existent glory, but stooped down, by a real surrender and self-impoverishment, and took a lower place. In the light of that renunciation we gain a new glimpse of the lengths to which Divine love will go for man's redemption. This I believe to be the profoundest motive operating in the Kenotic theories—this sense of sacrifice on the part of a pre-existent One; and it is a

[1] Dr. Forrest has justly pointed out that the word Kenotic must not be taken as implying that "the truth in this matter rests on a particular exegesis of this single passage in Philippians (2^{5-11})." Its basis in the New Testament is in reality far wider. "The Pauline expressions as to the self-emptying or self-impoverishment (2 Co 8^{9}) of the Son only emphasise what the narratives of Christ's life suggest, and their elimination would leave the problem as presented in the Gospels precisely where it was" (*Authority of Christ*, 98).

conception notoriously absent from the Christological arguments of not a few who have criticised these theories with great severity.

The Kenotic theologians, one and all, proceed upon orthodox assumptions as to the Trinity and the two natures present in the one person of our Lord. Their object is to show how the Second Person of the Trinity could so enter into human life as that there resulted the genuinely human experience which is described by the evangelists. To this problem they are unanimous in replying—of course with individual variations—that the eternal Logos by a wonderful suspension or restriction of His Divine activities reduced Himself within the limits and conditions of manhood. Somehow He laid aside His Divine mode of existence in order to become man. Thomasius of Erlangen, the greatest name of this school, followed the earlier hints of Sartorius in rejecting the traditions of Lutheran exegesis as to the Philippian passage in so far as he maintained that the self-emptying there affirmed has relation, not to the incarnate, but to the pre-existent Christ. The Logos, he writes, renounced the fulness of His Divine being in all those relations in which He reveals Himself *ad extra*, lowered Himself to become the substratum of a real human personality, exchanged His Divine consciousness for one that was human, or rather Divine-human; and thus became capable of forming the centre of a single personal Life. Further, we may construe this Life as undergoing a veritably human development, inasmuch as the Logos had voluntarily contracted His life to the form and dimensions of human existence, submitting to the laws of human growth and preserving His absolute powers only in the measure in which they were essential to His redeeming work; and at the close of His earthly career He resumed once more the glory He had laid aside. Thomasius was at one with previous Lutheran Christology in holding that there is no presence or activity of the incarnate Son outside of His human nature; and he argues that by the addition of the *genus tapeinoticum*—according to which the attributes of the humanity were transferred to, and imposed limits upon, the divinity—completeness was for the first time given to the older theory of the *communicatio idiomatum.*[1] He replied to the objection that his view conflicts with the doctrine of the Divine immutability[2] by insisting on an important distinction between the essential or immanent attributes of Godhead, which cannot be held in suspense, namely, truth, holiness, and love, and attributes—such as omnipotence, omnipresence, omniscience—which are relative to the world and so far external. These last, lacking in the historic Christ, do not in strictness belong to the essence of God, but are evoked by His relation to the world; holiness, love, and truth, on the other hand, constitute the very being of deity, and it is precisely they which are incarnate in our Lord. This may be taken as the classic form of the Kenotic theory,[3] but it appears in a still more thoroughgoing shape in Gess, who extends the *kenosis* to immanent attributes also. The self-depotentiation of the Logos is absolute: "He reduces Himself to the germ of a human soul." He suffered the extinction of His eternal self-consciousness, to regain it after many months as a human, variable consciousness, subject to the processes of gradual development, and sometimes—as in childhood, sleep, and death—involving no self-consciousness at all. Step by step Christ came to know who He really was. Nay, Gess does not shrink from adding that the incarnation affected the internal relations of the Trinity, for during the

[1] Cf. Loofs' article 'Kenosis,' *RE.* x. 246 ff.

[2] Dorner especially took this point.

[3] It was expounded by Thomasius first in his *Beiträge zur kirchlichen Christologie* (1845), but the fullest and most attractive statement is his *Christi Person und Werk* (1853–61), particularly the second volume. His main principles were accepted by Lutherans like Kahnis, Luthardt, and Delitzsch, and by Reformed divines like Ebrard and Godet, while in this country they have won a modified approval from writers like Fairbairn, Gore, and Forrest. The most valuable English account and criticism of the chief writers and their views will be found in Bruce's *Humiliation of Christ*, Lecture IV.

period covered by the earthly life we must conceive the eternal generation of the Son by the Father, and the cosmic functions of the Son to have undergone a temporary interruption. Godet, in his commentary on the Fourth Gospel, takes much the same line. In respect of the incarnate life he draws a sharp distinction between Christ's filial *consciousness*, which re-awoke at His baptism, and the filial *state*—*i.e.* the Divine "form of God," the mode of existence answering to His true being—which He only regained at the ascension. And the problem of the cosmic functions of the Son, *ex hypothesi* suspended for a time, he solves by the statement that "when the Logos descends into the world, there to become one of the beings of the universe, the Father can enter into direct relation to the world, and Himself exercise the functions of Creator and Preserver, which He commonly exercises through the mediation of the Word."[1]

The theory of Gess in a special measure drew forth vehement and often scornful condemnation. This conception of a human soul-germ which gradually evolves into identity with the Logos, of the second Person of the Trinity first denuded of all the properties of Godhead, save its bare essence, but ultimately restored to the plenary possession of all His attributes, was contemptuously described as pure mythology, which it required "a kenosis of the understanding" to believe.[2] To the objection of orthodox critics, however, that what we reach in Jesus on Kenotic principles is a *merely* human conscious life, the answer may reasonably be given, that on any terms the experience of Jesus transcends that of other men in so far as He is aware that once He was more than man and will some day return to His former high estate. "It is the paradox of His unique consciousness that He who exists as man knows Himself to be God, and remembers the time when He exercised the attributes of power and knowledge which for the time being He has laid aside."

While admitting that on the whole ecclesiastical

[1] See his *Commentary* on St. John, i. 358 ff., 394 ff.

[2] Biedermann.

decisions in the early centuries were against him, Thomasius nevertheless maintained that in such writers as Ignatius, Tertullian, Origen, and Hilary he found so many points of real contact with his own theory that Kenoticism might in a sense be described as the long-delayed fulfilment of ancient tendencies. In an important article Loofs has scrutinised the justice of this claim.[1] It must be conceded that he destroys the case for regarding the Kenotic theory as the logical climax or consistent outcome of past Christological development. No one would dream of saying that the Fathers had even begun to look in the direction of a Kenotic *theory*. At the same time I am not convinced that writers like Ignatius, Irenæus, and Hilary did not give intermittent expression to great religious intuitions which, if consistently developed, would have led them more or less in the direction of the modern view, though in point of fact they at once neutralised the force of these expressions by counter-statements of a more traditional cast. Whenever they shake off the haunting docetism that pervades so much of their reflection on the historic Christ, and take the idea of incarnation seriously, it is to this side that their best thoughts incline. But in truth it is of comparatively slight importance whether the Kenotic writers at first exaggerated their claim to historic orthodoxy, provided they can appeal to the recorded facts and believing witness of the New Testament, not, of course, for the details of a theory, but for the great religious idea they have striven to set forth. It is only in the eyes of those who deem patristic Christology wholly superior to revision or amendment that the alleged defective orthodoxy of Thomasius and his adherents will seem a grave offence.

At a later stage of this work I shall attempt to deal

[1] *RE.* x. 246 ff. The subject is discussed also by Harnack, *Dogmengeschichte*[4], i. 215; Thomasius, *Christi Person und Werk*, ii. 160–76, and *Dogmengeschichte*[2] (ed. Bonwetsch), i. 374–75; Bethune-Baker, *History of Doctrine*, 297 ff. On the Kenotic elements in Luther, see Th. Harnack, *Luthers Theologie*, ii. 204 ff.

more at length with the general import and religious value of what may be called "the Kenotic principle"; there is space here only to notice one or two of the more usual criticisms. The most frequent and at first sight the most damaging objection to the Kenotic doctrine is that it contravenes the fundamental axiom of the Divine immutability. The doctrine of the Divine immutability, however, when used in *à priori* fashion, is apt to prove a weapon we grasp by the blade. If we hold with conviction that Jesus is one in whom God Himself enters humanity, then He does so either with all His attributes unmodified, or in such wise as to manifest only those qualities which are compatible with a real human life; and which of these alternatives we shall adopt is of course settled for us by the actual facts contained in the historic record. To say that we cannot think away a single Divine attribute without destroying God is not only a statement so abstract as to be inapplicable, at least directly, to the concrete problem before us; it is a principle which only needs to be rigorously enforced to discredit *every* view of incarnation. But if we find reasons in the Gospel narrative for hailing Christ as the incarnate Son of God—reasons which have nothing to do with any supposed possession on His part of *all* the Divine prerogatives in their fulness—we must repel the objection that He cannot be God because He is neither omniscient nor omnipresent.

It is a more recondite form of the same criticism to urge that a temporary cessation alike of the cosmic functions of the Son and of His participation in the eternal life of the Godhead, as implied in the theory of Gess or Godet, is inherently unthinkable. I have no wish to minimise the seriousness of this; but there are two considerations which, I think, may reasonably be held to mitigate the difficulty. In the first place, the Trinitarian assumptions which lie behind the objection are too often of a kind that go perilously near the verge of tritheism, in so far as it is presupposed that the

Divine relation to the universe can only be sustained by the Son in His distinct being, and is threatened with collapse by His withdrawal. A more Christian view of the unity of Godhead largely modifies the gravity of the problem. Secondly, those who hold that the self-limitation of the Son in becoming man was real are in no way bound to provide a solution of remoter questions. We are free to believe, on the evidence of history, that the life of the incarnate Son was in harmony with the conditions of a genuine manhood, without being compelled to go on to speculate on subjects as to which the New Testament furnishes no data. There is in theology such a thing as a wise agnosticism against which the traditional Christology, just at this point, has grievously offended. And if Kenotic writers have employed language which appears to threaten the unity of God, and brings confusion into our conceptions of the interior life of deity, the defect is due very much to their sharing the erroneous metaphysical assumptions of their orthodox opponents.

The service which the Kenotic Christology renders has been well summarised by Dr. Forrest. "(1) It represents an advance on the Chalcedon symbol, in that it gives a truer impression of the New Testament facts and teaching as to the Divine *sacrifice* involved in the Incarnation, and thus emphasises the very quality that endues the Incarnation with its power of moral appeal. (2) By insisting that the Divine elements in Christ's character are not metaphysical, but ethical and spiritual, it reminds us that the deepest qualities in God and man are akin, and that humanity is grounded in and reproduces the eternal sonship in God."[1] Like all other theories, Kenoticism must be allowed the full benefit of the cardinal distinction in logic between a principle and the details of its application. It will not do to reject as mythology[2] an idea which, *in its inmost meaning,*

[1] *Christ of History*, 203.

[2] Ritschl, *Justification and Reconciliation*, 409–11.

is inseparable from the New Testament conception of our Lord—the idea, namely, that in whatever fashion God in Christ brought His Divine being down to the measures of our life, and became poor for our sake.

§ 5. *Christology of the Mediating School: Dorner.*—Beside the speculative and confessional theologies which flourished in the nineteenth century stands another group, various in character and composition, and for that reason difficult to describe by any less vague epithet than "mediating." The members of this group strove to mediate, first, between the Lutheran and the Reformed confessions, in the interests of union; and secondly, between Church doctrine and philosophy. Rothe, Ullmann, Julius Muller, and Dorner are some of the most distinguished names. We select Dorner as the best known and probably the most influential thinker of the party, and present those features of his Christological work which are on the whole most interesting and distinctive.[1]

A fundamental presupposition of Dorner's theory is the principle—equally religious and speculative—that God and man are not mere opposites, but are spiritually of kin. Man has in him that which is infinite, at least in the form of receptivity for the Divine; and it is this receptiveness of humanity for God, when raised to its highest, absolute power, which provides a real basis for the existence of Jesus as "the adequate personal organ of Deity." We may even say that since it is God's nature to communicate Himself to man, and man is closely allied to God, the idea of the God-man, in whom both are perfectly united, is demanded antecedently by reason. Not only so; the organism of humanity craves a Head, a central representative Individual, infinitely susceptible of God; so that from yet another point of view we are guided to the thought that religion requires for its consummation and absolute expression not the idea of incarnation merely, but

[1] On what follows, see Kirn's article "Dorner," *RE.* iv. 802 ff.

the fact. This transcendental necessity, as it may be called, which is rendered still more poignantly urgent by the fact of sin, is finally confirmed and sealed to us in the actualities of history. The real Jesus more than fulfils the postulates of pure thought. Nor is it sufficient to explain His central place in humanity by the dynamic immanence of God in Him. Nothing less than a personal self-communication on the part of God is adequate to the human need, for only He can perfectly reveal God who *is* what He reveals.

Dorner's supreme interest in the unity of the theanthropic Person leads him to argue that the true path to the elucidation of this unity is to start not from either of the natures separately but from their union as a given fact, as a spiritual life-process the outcome of which, owing to the inherent organic affinity of both, is the creation of a specifically Divine-human consciousness. The Logos, antemundane principle in God of revelation and self-bestowal, joins Himself to human nature, not, however, in its empirical quality of sinfulness and defilement, but as a new humanity, destined to be the Head of a race of redeemed men. It is at this point that we come upon the differential feature of Dorner's theory. The unity of the Divine-human life is not to be conceived as complete from the beginning. "Since Christ exhibited true humanity in an actual human life, a truly human growth pertains to Him. Since, on the other hand, God can only be perfectly manifest in Christ when the whole fulness of the Divine Logos has also become the proper fulness of this man in knowledge and volition, and therefore has become Divine-human, with the growth of the human side there is also necessarily given in Him a growth of the God-humanity; and the incarnation is not to be thought as at once completed, but as continuous, nay augmentative, seeing that God as Logos ever apprehends and appropriates such new aspects as are generated by the true human development, just as, conversely, the growing actual receptiveness of the humanity combines consciously and voluntarily with ever new aspects of the Logos." The anticipated objection that this view yields no more than a human Ego in ever-deepening personal fellowship with God is met by the statement that "the Logos is from the beginning united with Jesus in the deepest bases of being, and the life of Jesus was Divine-human at every point, inasmuch as a receptiveness never existed for the Deity without its fulfilment."[1]

This general conception is already present in Dorner's great work on the historical development of Christology;[2] but in the later *System of Christian Doctrine* his statement of the Trinitarian presuppositions is modified at an important point. He insists that if we are to escape the perils of tritheism in our construction of the Trinity, and of Nestorianism, or the assumption of two separate personalities, in Christology, a distinction must be drawn between hypostasis and personality. The Logos, he declares, "is of Himself neither a person in the same sense as the absolute Divine personality, nor as an individual man."[3] And what He does is not so much to constitute the personality of the incarnate One as rather to supply the basis of it, in His character as the eternal principle within the Godhead of freedom, movement, and revelation.

I should single out two points in regard to which the foregoing theory has proved suggestive. First, it lays a needed emphasis upon the affinity of the Divine and human natures, which earlier thought had too much tended to define as consisting in attributes so unlike as to be wholly disparate and incompatible. There was a real need that theology should recur to the instinctive assurance of the New Testament writers that between God and man there is no real incongruity, but rather an essential kinship. Secondly, the conception of an incarnation which is gradual, not mechanically and unethically complete from the beginning, is one which merits the closest scrutiny, and in a later part of this work we shall have occasion to

[1] *System of Christian Doctrine*, vol. iii. 328 (Eng. tr. slightly modified).
[2] First edition, 1839; second, 1845. [3] *Op. cit.* vol. iii. 293.

return to it. Frequently in past systems the person of Christ has been displayed in a light which suggests that its initial completeness is a matter of principle, but the conviction that the coalescence of the Divine and human life in our Lord was somehow a growing and advancing fact is one from which it is difficult to escape if we look closely at the historic data. Of course it is another question whether Dorner's theory, based as it is on certain metaphysical assumptions in regard to the "natures," can be defended against the criticism urged amongst others by Kirn, that the immanence of the Logos, which according to one part of the argument is the *basis* of the entire Divine-human process, is, according to another part, no more than its climax and consummation.

§ 6. *Christology in Britain and America.*—Apart from the Unitarian positions defended with so much dignity and impressiveness through a long series of years by the late Dr. Martineau, we do not find in the theology of the English-speaking races much that need be chronicled, whether in the way of external criticism or interior expansion of traditional Church doctrine. A series of brief allusions must suffice. Coleridge poured a stream of fresh life into English divinity, but he had relatively little to say regarding the theory of our Lord's person. On the whole he inclined to a Platonising view of the inherited dogma, loving to speak of Christ as the Logos, or Redemptive Reason, whom he describes as "the living and self-subsisting Word, the very truth of all true being, and the very being of all enduring truth; the reality, which is the substance and unity of all reality."[1] The Broad Church school, which served itself heir to many of Coleridge's best ideas, was too closely occupied with the Christianising of social life to have leisure for sustained doctrinal reflection on our subject. Erskine of Linlathen scarcely touched Christology. McLeod Campbell did much by his noble book on the

[1] *Notes on the Book of Common Prayer* (published 1838–39).

atonement to promote more spiritual conceptions of our Lord's inner life, and to exhibit the vital unity of incarnation and atonement for sin.[1] Maurice, like Coleridge, showed a Platonic tendency to speak of principles or ideas rather than of persons; and it would probably be a fair criticism on certain expressions in his works to say that they have the effect of depersonalising Christ, and of representing Him almost as a vague spiritual atmosphere or element, rather than as an historic Figure with specific qualities revealed by His career on earth. Thus it is a favourite line of reasoning with Maurice that every man, simply as man, is joined to an Almighty Lord of life, One nearer to him than his own flesh. "The truth," he declares, "is that every man is in Christ . . . except he were joined to Christ he could not think, breathe, live a single hour." Christ the essential and all-embracing ground of human life; every man in Christ whether consciously or not—these may be called the root-principles of the theology of Maurice, which he vainly contends are derived from the express teaching of the apostles.

We may recur for one moment to the controversy evoked between 1828 and 1830 by the Christological tenets of Edward Irving, whose life was one of the greatest and saddest of the century. He was charged in ecclesiastical courts with holding "the sinfulness of Christ's humanity"; but the expression is really unjust, and no reader of the history of the case will deny that more than one argument on which his ecclesiastical condemnation rested was gravely docetic in its implications. Irving clung with his whole soul to Christ's sympathy with the tempted, His veritable brotherhood with man; and to secure this he felt it his duty to affirm that the Son of God in

[1] Cf. his words in the Introduction to *The Nature of the Atonement*: "My attempt to understand and illustrate the nature of the atonement has been made in the way of taking the subject to the light of the incarnation. Assuming the incarnation, I have sought to realise the Divine mind in Christ as perfect Sonship towards God and perfect Brotherhood towards men, and, doing so, the incarnation has appeared developing itself naturally and necessarily as the atonement" (p. xvii, Sixth Edition).

incarnation took upon Him *fallen* human nature, with the possibility of sin, though, by the indwelling omnipotence of the Holy Spirit, sin never for one moment touched Him actually. In his own words: "The point at issue is simply this, whether Christ's flesh had the grace of sinlessness and incorruption from its own nature, or from the indwelling of the Holy Ghost; I say the latter." Elsewhere he inveighs against two main errors: the belief that Christ's nature was intrinsically better than ours, or that it underwent a physical change before its assumption into the person of the Son. "It was manhood fallen which He took up into His Divine person, in order to prove the grace and the might of Godhead in redeeming it." So the humanity was without guilt, but with everything else that belongs to man, and was "held like a fortress in immaculate purity by the Godhead within." "Christ was holy in spite of the law of the flesh working in Him as in another man; but never in Him prevailing."[1] And on these premises Irving built up a theory of salvation according to which our Lord, thus maintaining His personal sinlessness, and enduring to the uttermost the penalty due to His sinful human nature, achieved the reconciliation of God and man in His own person, the thing done in one portion being done, virtually, in the whole.

Of this eccentric though touching view it may be said, briefly, that the oneness of our Lord with us in the moral conflict, which was for Irving the heart of all things, is indeed a great fact; yet a theory of it is not to be purchased at the price of asserting that His humanity

[1] Irving was not quite original in this view. Cf. Ullmann, *Die Sündlosigkeit Jesu* (7te Auflage), 101; and Bruce, *op. cit.* 250, who points out that the same theory was simultaneously advanced by Gottfried Menken, of Bremen. A writer in the *Encyclopædia Britannica* (9th edition), vol. xiii. 372, says curiously that Irving was condemned "for publishing doctrines regarding the humanity of Jesus Christ now generally held by the broad school of theologians." This statement, if read at all strictly, is absurd. No modern thinker with whom I am acquainted could be said to hold Irving's position.

was corrupt, with a corruptness which only the Holy Spirit could hold in check. Misled probably by the patristic habit of using "flesh" as a synonym of "manhood," Irving confused the idea of "corrupt" with that of "corruptible" (in the sense of liable to corruption or decay), and hence from the fact that Christ was liable to decay and death, as being capable of dying, deduced the rash conclusion that His humanity was fallen. Certainly he held strongly that only a fallen nature could be tempted, and that to deny this is to deny Christ's manhood. There can be no doubt that Irving passionately repudiated the idea of Christ having *actually* sinned; but it is after all only a loose idea of sinlessness which takes it as compatible with the existence in Christ of a potential fault and strong efficacious germ of evil, divergent even as undeveloped from the Divine standard of perfect righteousness; which is the connotation of "fallen human nature" and "original sin" in all other cases.

The influence of the eminent American divine, Horace Bushnell (1802–1876), is in many ways comparable to that of Ritschl. On the whole he deprecated unprofitable curiosity, peering into impracticable questions. "Christ is not given," he writes, "that we may set ourselves to reason out His mystery, but simply that God may thus express His own feeling and draw Himself into union with us, by an act of accommodation to our sympathies and capacities." The deity of Christ, he repeats again and again, is in, not outside or apart from, what He does in bringing us to God, but we must be content with ignorance as to the nature of God's indwelling in Him. Not in metaphysical but in ethical conceptions can we best set forth the highest truth about His person.

§ 7. *Ritschl and the Ritschlians.*—The work begun by Schleiermacher was taken up fifty years later by Albrecht Ritschl (1822–1889), who strove even more persistently to vindicate for the historic Christ the central place in

His religion. Ritschl, we can see, had a deeper sense of history than his predecessor, whose view of redemption, he considered, represented it too much as acting on men like a natural influence rather than as mediated by those ethical and spiritual motives which alone are operative in Christianity. Also he laid stress on the supreme blessing of the Gospel as consisting in personal fellowship with God, which is brought to the individual by the influences of the Christian society, is based on the forgiveness of sins, and sent home to heart and conscience by the sight of God's love revealed in Jesus. If we know God as Father, it is because we know Him through the Son.

Ritschl would not have claimed to teach any Christology in the older sense of the word. Many traditional problems, he held, such as that of the two natures and the Trinitarian relation of the Son to the Father, have no bearing on experience and lie outside the range of theology. Like every other doctrine, our view of Christ must be stated in judgments of value or appreciation (*Werthurteile*), which affirm His significance for the soul; or, to put it otherwise, we see the Divine quality of Christ's person in the Divine character of His work. The impression He makes is most fitly expressed by saying that He has for us *the religious value of God.* He redeemed men by fulfilling perfectly the vocation given Him to establish the Kingdom of God, and patiently enduring all things even to death: and on the basis of this achievement the society gathered round Him is forgiven, has imputed to it the position or relationship towards God, which Jesus held for Himself inviolably to the end, and is raised "above the iron law of necessity" into the freedom and joy of God's family. Since the functions of Jesus—uniting in Himself, as He does, absolute revelation and ideal humanity—are thus Divine, He is Himself Divine in character. If He inaugurated a new relation between God and man, realised it in His own life, and now produces it in all believers, then to call Him Divine is, in

Herrmann's striking phrase, "only to give Him His right name." But it is useless to try and *explain* the significance of Jesus; instead of being explicable by other things, He explains everything else. He is known by faith in a unique and unapproachable relation to His people; to go behind this, and interpret it by ideas like the Absolute or the Logos, is to define the clear in terms of the obscure. No confession of His Godhead has any value save as generated by experience of His grace.

Every one must feel the truth of much of this. Christ's person seen in the light of His work is a principle fixed once for all by Luther and Schleiermacher. But one may reasonably doubt whether Ritschl does actually let this fundamental axiom carry him all the way. The argument is that Christ is Divine just because His gifts—pardon, liberty, life—are so; but does Ritschl after all push home the inference? That he assigns to Christ an absolute uniqueness for religion is unquestionable; but passages also occur in which he declares plainly that the Godhead of Christ must be capable of imitation by His people, and protests that the dogma of His pre-existence confers on Him a solitary greatness in which the believer can have no share. There can be no doubt at all that in defining the content of Christ's deity he omits altogether the idea both of pre-existence and of exaltation. We have no concern, he argues, with the pre-existent One, who exists for God only; our faith is asked for the historic life that began at Bethlehem. In the same way nothing can be known about the exalted Lord save from His recorded history. It is easy to see that this exclusive insistence on a past which is growing ever more remote tends to the representation of Christ, semi-deistically, as absent and far away, rather than as ever-present in the sovereign power of His resurrection. And as regards the conception of pre-existence, Ritschl steadily declined to acknowledge its religious meaning and importance. No one could possibly wish to censure a mere refusal to embark on empty speculation in this region, or to forsake the indications of concrete believing experience; but it is another thing when theology, at the instance of a mistaken philosophical positivism, grows blind to the infinite self-surrender of God in becoming man for our redemption.

In the further progress of the Ritschlian movement, as might be expected, many varieties of opinion came gradually to light. Thus it was debated whether on the principles of the master it is permissible to speak of the Godhead of Christ; and sides were taken on the question, though to some extent parties differed only about a word. Some discussion has also taken place regarding the precise elements in the New Testament picture of Jesus to which faith is directed. Is the resurrection, for example, part of the ground of faith, a vital factor in the message that evokes faith; or is it not rather the object of a conviction in which faith is already presupposed? Along with this there has gone a general consent that while faith rests upon the historic personality of Jesus, as revealed in His actual words and deeds, this must not be construed into a statutory dependence on particulars of the Gospel story.

§ 8. *The Modern Radical School.*—A few concluding words may be said respecting the positions maintained, with so much vivacity, by members of the radical party which has sprung into prominence in the last ten years, and which, speaking broadly, represents the extreme left wing of Ritschlianism. They form the so-called *religionsgeschichtliche Schule*, and their aim is without fear or favour to determine the place of Christianity in the religious history of the world. Of this school Dr. Sanday has said with justice that "the writers cut themselves adrift from the universal verdict of the Church and from traditional Christianity. They make no attack upon the Creeds, but they deliberately ignore them, and in one or two places where this important question would naturally come up, they in set terms deny what the Creeds affirm.

As a rule, the central doctrine of all is not so much contested as quietly put aside. The constructive view of primitive Christianity is built up without it."[1] The following is a characteristic statement by Wernle. "We know," he writes, "that above the general level of mankind rise the prophets and mediators, men who stand in an especially close relation to God and have an especial sense of being called by Him, whose souls are full of the mysterious and wonderful, who breathe the air of eternity and behold visions of the world that lies beyond this outer world of phenomena. Amongst them we see Jesus. That which distinguishes Him and places Him apart from the others cannot perhaps be expressed theoretically at all, but we can express it practically by entering into His service and by doing God's will as He bids us do it. So . . . we testify to men, in Jesus' own way, that He is our Master and that He has made us at one with God. He who will may call this a practical Christology. The dogmatical, certainly, lies behind us."[2] These sincere and moving words suggest one or two observations.

First, the category under which Jesus is subsumed is that of hero or religious genius. It is a conception introduced into theology by Strauss, and largely accentuated by Thomas Carlyle; and by these writers it is explicitly held to embrace more than Jesus. They tell us that in the primitive age adoring believers inevitably came to deck Jesus with all conceivable names of honour, and to declare in retrospect that He was God's unique gift to man, a creative vehicle of revelation, a point at which heaven touched sinful earth. But this is poetry, out of which theology has made prose. In sober truth, Jesus is not the object of faith; like us, rather, He *has* faith, and we come to share it.

Again, these writers are well aware that their views run directly counter to the apostolic doctrine. Formerly it was customary for those who rejected the traditional

[1] *Outlines of the Life of Christ*, 263.
[2] Quoted in the *Review of Theology and Philosophy*, i. 278.

Christology to appeal to the New Testament, but this is now given up. It is perceived that in most important respects the Church has the New Testament on its side; not of course for each detail, or for the intellectual categories employed in after days, but in essence. Accordingly men like Wernle and Bousset now repudiate the apostolic view of Christ quite as sharply as that of the fourth century. St. Paul, St. John, and the writer to the Hebrews are equally wrong with Origen and Athanasius—not so far astray, perhaps, but as really. Christology has been a blunder from the first. It is worth while to note the fact that the apostolic convictions about Christ are admitted to have been the very centre of their message. Nor is it denied that our religion has never assumed a form in which it did not rest mainly on a Christological basis. But the writers I have in mind would say that all this is owing to an unfortunate misconception, which would very likely have been avoided if men had left dogmas alone and kept close to facts. And for the modern intelligence, it is held, nothing can be made of the person of our Lord till we distinguish clearly between the historic Man of Nazareth and the dogmatic Christ of the apostles. Jesus' place in the doctrinal system is not at the centre, but among the "means of grace." In a certain loose sense it may be fitting to say that we find God "in" Jesus, but the time has gone past for speaking as if God had received us "for Christ's sake," or for bowing to the absolute claim: "No man cometh unto the Father but by Me."

Finally, these writers profess to be able to show how the primitive but mistaken view of Jesus came to exist. Virtually every ingredient in the New Testament conception of our Lord can be traced to its proximate origin in the ideas of some other faith. A vague Messianic ideal was then current in the world; a kind of redemption-myth circulated in a thousand pious minds over the Roman Empire in myriad forms, and these yearning dreams of eternal life, in all their pathetic intangibility, were in due time deposited on the idealised name of Jesus.[1] It was felt that all things expected of the coming Saviour had been fulfilled in Him. The fermenting thought of the time supplied a fruitful soil for an imaginative and mythological growth of doctrine, which can be traced, nearly without remainder, either to oriental Gnosticism or to Judaism of the syncretistic type.

This modern form of what may fairly be called the Higher Unitarianism will occupy us repeatedly in this book; and at present I will only pause to offer one criticism. It is that little has yet been done by writers of this party, save by vague allusions to the mystery of personality, to shew why Jesus drew to Himself these wonderful epithets of religious trust and adoration. Why should this Man be chosen to have such things said of Him as that in Him all things consist, that in Him dwells all the fulness of the Godhead bodily, unless He had indeed made such an impression on the apostles that no lower terms would serve? It is surely a question of sufficient gravity how we are to account for the worship given to Him, then or now, except on the supposition that His nature was such as rightly to evoke and to retain it. To suppose the contrary is at variance with the one certainty on which faith builds, which all testimony supports, and which serious Christian reflection instinctively assumes—the certainty that Jesus drew a clear distinction between Himself and all the children of men, and that alike in His own mind and that of the Church universal He is not one of a class, or even first among His compeers, but in a solitary and unshared sense the Lord and Redeemer of the world.

[1] If this be so, how comes it that no trace exists in Judaism of the myth of a dying and rising Saviour? Cf. *supra*, p. 75.

BOOK III.

THE RECONSTRUCTIVE STATEMENT OF THE DOCTRINE.

PART I.

PRELIMINARY QUESTIONS.

CHAPTER I.

THE INTELLECTUAL NEED FOR A CHRISTOLOGY.

THE Christian religion is acknowledged to consist in or involve a certain spiritual attitude to the person of Jesus Christ. Historically it is in this way that Christianity has defined itself, both in experience and in theory; from the first it has been a spiritual movement in which He is assigned the central place and becomes the object of explicit faith. No branch of the Church has enjoyed a strong or contagious life which has ceased to look to Jesus with adoring trust and to find in Him the abiding way to the Father. And the proposal to reconstruct Christianity by displacing Jesus from this position is one which leaves the firm ground of fact by surrendering continuity with the past and adopting the visionary programme of a

LITERATURE—Dorner, *System of Christian Doctrine*, 1890; Kaftan, *Zur Dogmatik*, 1904; Garvie, *Studies in the Inner Life of Jesus*, 1907; Caird, *Fundamental Ideas of Christianity*, 1899; Simpson, *Fact of Christ*, 1900; Kähler, *Wissenschaft der christlichen Lehre*[3], 1905; Forsyth, *Person and Place of Jesus Christ*, 1909; Frank, *System der christlichen Wahrheit*[3], 1894.

religious life worthy to retain the rights of the Christian name while yet renouncing the fundamental Christian conviction.

In a later chapter we shall inquire in more detail what is meant by the statement that Christ is, in the proper sense of the word, the *object* of religious faith. At present we assume the fact. And from it we derive the immediate inference that for reasoning men it is impossible to refrain from a theoretical interpretation of this Person in whom they believe. If we put faith in Jesus, and if, as Luther used to say, faith and God belong together, we must seek an explanation of One who so far at least occupies a position in the Christian consciousness on that side of reality which we call Divine;[1] we must ask whether He has the reality as well as the religious value of God. The apostles, who had been prepared for the Gospel by the profoundest religion of antiquity, felt that the conception of God had been radically modified by their experience of Jesus; and those who share that experience, in its regenerating power, must like them be conscious of an irrepressible impulse to search out and construe to intelligence the implicates of Christ's redeeming influence, and in particular of His personal relationship to the Father. Not merely, that is, ought Dogmatic to include a Christology as one of its integral constituents, but the task of Christology is prescribed *ab initio* by the specifically Christian experience. Silence on the matter is an avowal that we feel no need of Christ as mediating our personal possession of God. Kaftan puts the truth not a whit too strongly when he asserts that Christology is either the doctrine of Christ's Godhead, or it is nothing at all.[2] The one real question before us is how the man Jesus is God for the believing mind, but this question we may not shirk.

To this contention that the modern theologian has no choice but to "christologise" there are, however, two

[1] Cf. Denney, *Jesus and the Gospel*. [2] *ZTK.* (1904), 181.

possible objections, both widely current and each diametrically antagonistic to the other. On the one hand it is said: Christology cannot be essential, since it is in fact superfluous; on the other hand it is said, with equal emphasis: Christology is no longer essential, since the work was all done long ago.

Christology is held to be superfluous by all those modern writers to whom it comes naturally to describe Jesus by the category of genius or hero. For this mode of thought, at bottom a significant reaction against Naturalism, Jesus is the sublimest of great men. He is the man in whom faith in God, virtue, and immortality is seen in unsurpassed and victorious power; He is the most inspired of the prophets of God's love. But in the last resort He takes His place beside us over-against God, content to struggle and pray like His human brethren. We are summoned, therefore, not to put faith in Him, but to share the faith He had. It is merely a venial exaggeration to call Him the one Mediator between God and man. A new and superior revelation may yet be given.

It is unnecessary to say that on such terms theology cannot long retain a serious doctrine of Christ's person. Something might still be said regarding Him, doubtless, under the rubric of "the means of grace"; but in no sense could we be said to believe in God *through* Him in such wise that He forms an integral and organic part of that in which we believe. His relation to the new life of grace and freedom is at best fortuitous. He was the first Christian; into that phrase we may put what depths of meaning we choose, but to transcend it is forbidden. All Christology based on the hypothesis that He was more is only dead matter too long harboured within the system of religious truth.

The question whether this is a position compatible with Christianity may be answered in two ways. It may be answered alike by reference to history and by an examination of ideas. As concerns history, it will not be denied that from its most primitive origins the Church adored

Jesus Christ and set Him in the highest place. For the apostles Christ filled the whole sphere of God, and the settlement of fundamental issues between Divine holiness and human sin rested on what He was and had accomplished. Not less for us to-day faith in God means faith in Jesus. In this naive and experimental sense, it is not too much to say that the Godhead of Jesus is *de fide* for the Christian mind. Thus only can the vital continuity of the Christian religion be preserved. It is an open question, of course, whether the terms anciently employed to define Jesus' unique transcendence will not bear amendment; but the spiritual attitude they witness to is the essence of religion as we have learnt it from Christ Himself. To alter this is to alter the religion; and why in that case the old name should be retained is something of a mystery. Once abandon the New Testament conviction of Jesus' relation to men, and theirs to Him, and while doubtless for a time it may be difficult to restrain our hearts from going out to Him as of old in adoring worship, the lapse of time may be trusted to do its fatal work. We shall cease to trust Him; for One who is simply human to the mind cannot remain adorable to the conscience and the heart.

Turning now to the proposed new category, let us note how impossible it is to accept hero or genius as a satisfying designation of Jesus Christ. For one thing, it has no relation to the singular self-consciousness mirrored in the Gospels. If language has a meaning, this is a framework into which Jesus' thought of Himself, as the unique Son of the Father and therefore the unique Deliverer of man, simply cannot be compressed. If we call Him hero, it is only because at the same time He reveals Himself as infinitely more. And that no man *can* be more is an unprovable *à priori* dogma, resulting from a violent application of the abstract principle of Uniformity. Along with this, however, we can see that the ethical quality or constitution indicated by the two suggested words is inapposite to the case. The powers of a genius, and their active exertion, have reference properly to his own self-centred will. His supreme aim is to realise himself, to express his nature perfectly, to develop and unfold the abnormal powers pent up within him. He has no sense of an entrusted mission; men are there for him to use in the process of his self-manifestation, and whether the outcome will be to bless or curse them is a question of relatively slight importance. Jesus, on the other hand, is the Christ. He is come not to do His own will but the will of God who sent Him. Not to develop or glorify His own nature is His first care, but to serve; to serve the Father, primarily, but a Father who is best served by the redemptorial service of man. In other words, there is nothing in Christ's aim or personality which is not religious; genius need not have any religious quality whatever. A second consideration is that genius is after all only a question of degree. It transcends the ordinary bulk of mankind to an extent which can approximately be measured, and there is a class or group of men to all of whom the title can be applied with tolerably equal justice. But the Christ is solitary. Hero-worship therefore—and hero is simply genius in the sphere of will—must always be separated by an impassable gulf from the believing worship of Christ. To adore a hero is, in the subtlest way, to adore humanity and therewith ourselves as part of conceivably heroic mankind; but when we worship Jesus the Christ we implicitly worship God in Him. I do not deny that an attitude towards Jesus is possible—an attitude of romantic or æsthetic admiration in which conscience has no part—which is not felt as altering or indeed touching our relation to God; but whatever be the proper name for this attitude of mind, it has at all events no connection with religion. It centres after all in the human Ego, not, as religion must, in God.

One point more may be noticed. In the presence of a genius we are acutely and disablingly conscious of our distance from him, of his cold and remote transcendence of other men; and it is therefore in no way surprising that with enthusiasm for genius there should often be combined, in the devotee's mind, a pessimistic contempt for mankind as a whole. Admiration of the superman is made a refuge from disgust at the common crowd. His wealth of being is some meagre consolation for the universal poverty. But these are feelings which cannot breathe in Jesus' presence. His sublimity does not put us far from Him; instead, it gives us courage to draw near and receive out of His fulness. He is nearer to us, more by far our fellow and our kinsman, than the greatest names in human story; and in this connection it is noteworthy that His overwhelming influence on the disciples never had the effect of obscuring their instinctive sense of His real manhood. But if we are personally conscious of His subduing power, we know by the same experience that His gifts are for others also. One who loved us, in our unworthiness, could not despise any. He could not regard men as things to be handled, and utilised, and cast away. He could not transgress the high ethical law which enjoins that persons must always be treated as ends, never as merely means.[1]

Whatever then be the scope or value of the category "hero," it is useless for the purpose of formulating the Christian view of Christ. To guide ourselves by it is to make an initial irretrievable mistake. Now as in the beginning faith consists in taking to Jesus the attitude which He Himself invited. Now as in the beginning the name of God has the final meaning Jesus gave it, and part of that meaning is Himself. But if Jesus is a hero and no more, even if the greatest of all heroes, Christology is but a waste of labour. We need not strive to bring out the implications of His supreme religious value if that value is in the end merely relative.

A recent writer has observed that "the idea that for a new object we might have to create a new concept,

[1] Cf. with the foregoing two admirable pages in Schlatter's *Das christliche Dogma*, 305–6.

perhaps a new method of thinking, is deeply repugnant to us."[1] He is speaking of philosophy, but it is not in philosophy alone that this form of intellectual inertia has been exhibited. It has been conspicuously manifest in the interpretation of Jesus. *Entia non sunt multiplicanda praeter necessitatem* is a good rule, but it may result in spurious simplification, and thus hide from us the impossibility of getting the facts into the ready-made frames of our old concepts, or fitting the new reality with some one of the familiar time-honoured categories. This comes of the wilful assumption that one of the old concepts, already known, *must* suit; that there can after all be no surprises for the mind. Applied to the person of Jesus, this illicit axiom has meant that various writers, forming by actual inspection of the race a notion of what manhood is and can do, are accustomed to insist that His experience and action shall in no way transcend the empirical outline thus drawn. Hero is a familiar category of greatness; hero, therefore, He at most can be. Nothing could be more certain than that this is the way to miss the truth. Nature, we shall all concede, can only be understood if we are prepared to accept her originalities equally with her commonplace; and in like manner, if we wish to know God's supreme will for our salvation we must listen in lowliness to the supreme voice He speaks in; the voice that finds us at greater depths of our being than any other. We know comparatively little as to the possibilities of the world, and an intellectual experience which is sometimes painful reveals the perpetual necessity of remaking our science and philosophy to the measure of quite unexpected realities. The wholly unprecedented fact of Jesus, therefore, in its Divine and absolute significance, is not to be rejected off-hand as something which the very structure of the human mind forbids it to recognise. His solitary and all-determining character must be looked at as a quite conceivable reality; and we must in candour

[1] Bergson, *Creative Evolution*, 51.

be willing to acknowledge that a new conception, not hitherto called for, may be required to describe Him. We must not force Him, so to say, to be the mere hero or genius He has no interest in being. To-day as of old He hides Himself from those who would take Him by violence to make Him king.

This, then, is the first method in which modern theology has tended to put Christology aside. It places Jesus wholly on the side of reality we call human, and then denies consistently enough that Christology is part of Theology as the doctrine of God. To the faith inspired by the New Testament, on the other hand, this is a method excluded by the single consideration that we cannot state the Christian thought of God except as we include Christ in our statement. He is an integral constituent of what, for us, God means. The richness of significance present in the word Divine as a fruit of the Christian experience of redemption, is not capable of being expressed save by reference to the Son as really as to the Father. This fact renders a Christology essential.

The second point of view from which modern Christological thinking may be deprecated as superfluous is that of literal fidelity to the definition of Chalcedon. That definition may be regarded as at once complete in theory and legally binding on all later ages. It is true, no serious mind will affect indifference to the Fathers' long labour in this domain; we can never overestimate the value of their unflinching witness to the incarnation, or the resoluteness with which, in spite of great temptations to error, they affirmed in symbolic documents the perfectness and integrity of our Lord's manhood. Nicæa is a position gained once for all. Chalcedon, on the other hand, betrays a certain tendency not merely to define but to theorise. It embodies, even if faintly and as it were by allusion, a particular form of interpretation which it is no real gain but a distinct loss to carry back in our minds to the study of the Gospels. It is one thing to hold that in returning to the Synoptics we must bring with us the light of the Epistles, for this means simply that the testimony of the apostles to Christ is a prolongation, as well as a consequence, of Christ's testimony to Himself. It is quite another thing to hold that in reading, say, St. Mark we ought to keep the Chalcedon formula in the background of our minds, and interpret what we read in view of its authoritative terms. That is to ignore the scientific history of dogma.

At the outset of our independent study, then, it is well that we should consider certain reasons which preclude a simple or literal acceptance of tradition. It is not merely that the influence of the Logos idea upon tradition was immense, and not at all times salutary. It is not merely that there are more avenues than one by which the mystery of our Lord's person can be approached, and that of these possibilities tradition chose one that offers immense difficulties to a history-loving age. These are minor questions. For modern thought the chief defect in strictly traditional Christology has been its insistence, not accidentally but on principle, upon what for brevity is called the doctrine of the two natures. Let us take this doctrine in a convenient form supplied by the Westminster Confession: "Two whole, perfect, and distinct natures, the Godhead and the manhood, were inseparably joined together in one person, without conversion, composition, or confusion." The sense of the important word "distinct" is to be gathered from a later dictum in the same chapter: "Christ, in the work of mediation, acteth according to both natures, by each nature doing that which is proper to itself."[1] This view of the Divine-human personality, present even in the *invicem* of Leo's Epistle, is that in which tradition came to rest, but which now fails to satisfy the great bulk of evangelical theologians. We need not at this point recall the scholastic subtlety and artifice of the *communicatio idiomatum* developed with an

[1] c. viii. 2.

ever-increasing complexity in post-Reformation days, and issuing in an abstractness of conception sadly unlike the mobile realities of Jesus' life. Neither is it simply that the term "nature" turns out to be insufficiently ethical for its purpose, and is in some ways peculiarly unfitted to serve as a designation of Godhead. For here, it is possible, a compromise may be effected. Discarding its technical and rigid sense, we may hold that human "nature" means everything pertaining to man's proper constitution, the whole sum of his spiritual and bodily endowments; while on the other hand Divine "nature" is equivalent to all that forms part of the true being of God. If these two be put together, we may then say that Jesus Christ, the God-man, is Himself a living unity of both. But apart from this (it may be) not insurmountable objection, two fatal difficulties remain.

First, the doctrine of the two natures, in its traditional form, imports into the life of Christ an incredible and thoroughgoing dualism. In place of that perfect unity which is felt in every impression of Him, the whole is bisected sharply by the fissure of distinction. No longer one, He is divided against Himself. It has always been perceived that a dualism of this kind, if more than a form of words, annuls the very thought of redemption by means of God's self-manifestation in flesh. Divine and human alternately vitiates the truth of incarnation. The simplicity and coherence of all that Christ was and did vanishes, for God is not after all living a human life. On the contrary, He is still holding Himself at a distance from its experience and conditions. There has been no saving descent. Christ executed this as God, it is said, and suffered that as man. It could not be otherwise, since in the last resort deity is impassible. Now this leaves a profoundly disappointing impression of unethical mystery and even, in a sense, duplicity. It means that the reader of the Gospels has constantly to be on guard against his own instinctive intuitions. The self-consciousness of Jesus, as depicted by the evangelists, we may call

Divine or human as we please; to express the whole truth we must call it both at once. But it is a single consciousness after all; it moves always as a spiritual unity; and separatist or divisive theories do a grave disservice not merely to clear thinking, but to religious truth and power. Always the result has been that deity and humanity in Christ are joined in ways so external that either may be contemplated and (so to speak) analysed in abstraction from the other. It is an unquestioned merit in the ecclesiastical Christology that it brings out emphatically the basal oneness of Christ with God, insisting further that this oneness is, in ultimate character, mysterious; it is a grave fault, on the other hand, that it should so construe this mystery as to get wholly out of touch with the actualities of the New Testament. Briefly, the doctrine of the two natures, if taken seriously, gives us two abstractions instead of one reality, two impotent halves in place of one living whole. It hypostatises falsely two *aspects* of a single concrete life—aspects which are so indubitably real that apart from either the whole fact would be quite other than it is, yet not in themselves distinctly functioning substantialities which may be logically estimated or adjusted to each other, or combined in unspiritual modes.

In the second place, there is a difficulty concerned with the person in which the two natures are held to be "inseparably joined together." Once more we are obliged to report unfavourably on the term "nature," this time from a rather different point of view. The ancient dogma proceeds on the definite assumption that, in both God and man, there exists a complex whole of attributes and qualities, which can be understood and spoken about as a "nature" enjoying some kind of real being apart from the unifying or focal Ego; whereas nothing is more certain than that it is within personal experience, and only there, that all the varied factors of our human life — intellectual, moral, emotional, social — have any proper existence or reality. To put it frankly, when we abstract from personality—the spirit which gathers the manifold particulars into unity and suffuses each with the glow and intimacy of specifically conscious life—what we vaguely call "human nature" is not human nature in the least. It is at most hypothetical raw material, which, if taken up into and shot through with self-consciousness, becomes an organic factor in a real human experience, but in separation, as untenanted or by itself, it is no more human nature than hydrogen by itself is aquatic nature. We must not be tempted into the obvious mistake of regarding one element in a living unity as being the same thing outside the unity as within it. Now in tradition human nature *is* thus taken (even if it be only provisionally) as real apart from personality. According to the technical phrase, the manhood is anhypostatic. What constitutes the person is the Ego of the pre-existent Logos, who assumes into union with His own hypostasis that whole complex briefly described as "human nature," conveying to it the properties of His divinity. Certain teachers of the Church, who felt keenly the unreal character of an impersonal humanity, strove to redress the balance by asserting that our Lord's manhood is personal separately or in its own right, with the unavoidable result that two personalities came only too plainly to be predicated of the one Christ. A twofold personality, however, is not merely something that we fail to understand; it is something we see quite well to be impossible. In fact, a being in whom now the God acts, now the man, is equally repellent to faith and theory. It implies that to reach the Godhead we must pass out beyond the manhood, and *vice versa*—the two being so utterly heterogeneous and disparate that no true union is conceivable.

This dilemma, then—the Scylla of a duplex personality and the Charybdis of an impersonal manhood—has invariably proved fatal to the doctrine of two natures. If it takes Jesus' manhood seriously, as the New Testament of course does by instinct, it makes shipwreck on the notion of a double Self. If, on the other hand, it insists on the unity of the person, the unavoidable result is to abridge the integrity of the manhood and present a Figure whom it is difficult to identify with the Jesus of the Synoptic Gospels. For tradition the unity of the person is always a problem, and to the last a mystery; for the New Testament it is the first reality we touch. For tradition it appears as a hypothetical conclusion tentatively posited at the close of intricate processes of reasoning; for the New Testament it is given in a direct and original impression. For tradition the question is that of uniting two abstractions which have been defined in bare contrast to each other; for a mind which takes its religion from the New Testament the problem is to investigate the grounds which have led Christians in every age to confess this concrete historic person, Jesus Christ, as God. If objection be made to this ever-renewed work of re-interpretation, as impeaching the final truth of Chalcedon, two considerations, I think, may be urged by way of answer. First, it is impossible to believe that the human intelligence has made no progress, since the fifth century, in the precision or delicacy of its instruments, or that this progress is in no way to the advantage of Christian thought. Secondly, each modern writer, whatever his orthodoxy, does in fact put a more or less modern construction upon the categories of the ancient Church. It must be so, unless he is content merely to repeat the conciliar phrases. No history at all can be written, or any exposition of truth historically received, the writing of which is not linked to present experience by a secret bond, freshening the point of view, and thus importing novel and valuable elements of truth. Only a deeply felt interest in the present gives power to reanimate the past.

Furthermore, it is necessary to redress the balance which had been disturbed by the partial absence from the patristic mind of a steady regard for the manhood of Jesus. No modern reader can be unconscious of the docetic strain present in much early writing. Too often, perhaps most typically in Cyril, the humanity of Christ is set forth as little more than semblance; and we have seen how this bias more and more pressed on mediæval thought, and at last virtually obliterated in the mind of the Church expositor the significance of New Testament words as to Jesus' liability to temptation, infirmity, and every wholesome human feeling. Distinct statements about His growth in wisdom and the like were ignored or twisted in a false direction. It seemed as though union with the Logos had denaturalised His experience as man. How a corrective movement set in with the Reformation—a movement anthropocentric in the sense that it took human facts as point of departure—and how vast gains accrued thereby to the modern religious estimate of Jesus, we have endeavoured to explain. The Church received a new impression of His actual career and of the significance of His Messianic consciousness. Not only so; but it is now impossible for us to adopt—as is done in much traditional Christology—a minimising tone respecting the immensity of sacrifice made by God in becoming man, with a life lived in flesh and defined by the limits of mundane experience. A partially de-ethicising tendency of the kind just noted was naturally accompanied by a less than moral view of sacraments, and of their mode of action in the soul; and it is worth noting that when the Reformers turned back resolutely to the historic Christ, as God's only Son and our Redeemer, they revived also the primitive apostolic conception of Baptism and the Lord's Supper, as conveying to men no magical grace or semi-physical influence or blessing, but the Lord Jesus Christ in His whole saving power. At each point a fresh view of Christ quickened their sense of historic fact.

We conclude, therefore, that faith in Christ is not to be confused with adhesion to a particular Christological formula, and that the doctrine of two natures, in the rigid abstract shape given it by tradition, is detachable from the believing estimate of our Lord. If this be so, the effort to reinterpret the premises and implications of faith in Him is no mere venial exercise of intelligence, but a duty to the evangelic mission of the Church. Where the Spirit of the Lord is, there is liberty. As Kähler puts it, "He who finds the essence of the traditional dogma in its sharp rejection of heresy, or its scholastic form, commits the blunder of mixing up theology and faith. On the other hand, he who regards it as but the historic form apart from which believing witness to the living God—as distinct from metaphysical traditions—could not have been saved for later ages, may well join hands with a fellow-worker who pleads that we need another and a new dogma." [1]

But if a mere verbal acquiescence in tradition is out of the question, since it lends no aid to the modern student, a distaste for certain particulars of the ancient dogma is by no means equivalent to a renunciation of all Christology. We cannot appeal to men not to think. They do not leave their intelligence behind them when they become Christians. Hence we may anticipate that now, as in the early centuries, constructive principles are being slowly worked out, in the hope that by their means we may attain to a deeper understanding of Him in whom God has drawn near to us. In every age minds which have been quickened and inspired by Christ will continue to pour forth new thoughts concerning His person and His work. It will always be felt that "difficulties which are themselves the creation of the intellect must be intellectually disposed of." It is not an objection to this that in due time our interpretations likewise will become obsolete and insufficient. It must be considered that for an ever larger proportion of earnest men there is virtually no middle course between holding a doctrine on grounds which can be really even if imperfectly apprehended by the mind, and discarding the

[1] *Angewandte Dogmen*, 137.

doctrine in question altogether. A Christ whom they cannot place luminously in relation to life or thought is a Christ with no reality for them. Moreover, it is vain to speak as if ours alone were the responsibility of agitating these great issues. Already various definite modern theories of Christ have been placed before the world; some of them, it may well be, are of a kind we have no option but to reject; and we cannot suppose that it is possible to deal with them satisfactorily save on principles which appeal to the Christian mind of our own time—principles which are consistent with each other and would find their place in a positive and constructive statement. The fact that each reasoned view of Christ should call for criticism and modification at the hands of later ages, so far from being an embarrassment, is a profound testimony to the magnitude of the theme. Christological theory is in truth like the great cathedral. "It is ever beautiful for worship, great for service, sublime as a retreat from the tumult of the world, and it is for ever unfinished." The Christ whom any mind or group of minds can reproduce is not the infinite Redeemer of the world.

Further, it will scarcely be denied that the task of thus interpreting Christ afresh is a vital part of our religious service. He is to be loved with the heart, but also with the mind. It is all but impossible for a thoughtful man to adore Jesus Christ, finding in Him blessedness and eternal life, and not be conscious of a powerful desire to reach coherent views of His person. What we already know of Him has led us to faith and worship; may not (he will ask) a deepened knowledge, if it be attainable, add a yet profounder significance to our confession of His name? Is it not unworthy that in an age when men are prepared to spend time and power lavishly in the investigation of the properties of matter, and each new step towards the conquest of nature is saluted with a proud and eager gratitude, Christian thinkers should flag in the effort to reach lucidity and truth of judgment as to the person of our Lord? Why should we turn from these problems so easily with the sad confession: *Ignoramus et ignorabimus?* Such words—though they are often taken so—are no proof of a peculiar susceptibility to the overwhelming power of Christ—the mind being as it were dumb before Him; they suggest, rather, that the very soul of the Gospel—Immanuel, God with us—has so far left us unimpressed. Many writers on doctrine at the present moment are either dubious as to the value of systematic thought or afraid of their own minds; Ritschlianism, with all its service to faith, has a little disparaged the use of reason in theology; and of nothing are we more in need than a wise and instructed courage. We require the brave heart that will launch out into the deep. Principles and methods may yet be gained, based alike in faith and reason, by means of which a real and positive command of the great verities of Christology may be secured for the intelligence of our own time. The question is ripe for re-examination, not merely from the point of view of the apologist, keen to win the outsider, and tempted by this very keenness to attenuate the unspeakable gift in his search for the minimum of truth a normal contemporary can be induced to accept. Still more urgently it needs to be freshly scrutinised from the point of view of the Christologian proper, whose part it is to formulate, if that be possible, all that Christ is to the fully surrendered mind; not permitting the poor average of faith to set itself up as criterion, but asking insistently who Christ must be if He is indeed the Mediator, the Advocate with the Father, the person who has availed as a propitiation for the sins of the whole world. We have to catch on our minds, not the lowest form of belief compatible with a profession of Christianity, but something of the incredible wonder of the Jesus who ransomed us with His blood. A recent writer on some cardinal elements of the Gospel has insisted on "the demand they make for an enlargement of human faculty to take in the unimagined greatness newly revealed in them by God"; and this sense of dilation, of infinity, of inexhaustible and unending magnitude, is the element we are most of all bound to pass into our theoretic statements. It may be taken as certain that the student of Christology will undergo in the field of theory the same experience of perpetually renewed effort to grasp a transcendent object as he encounters in the realm of devotion. In both spheres, of doctrine as of faith, it transpires that each new conception of Christ we form, only to dismantle and reshape it later on the score of inadequacy, gives place to one always more broad and deep and high.

One point still remains: Shall we aim at a metaphysical view, or shall we rest in an ethical Christ, asking no hard questions that may lead out over the seas of thought? Are transcendent problems to be discounted from the beginning as irrelevant or at all events quite subordinate? What is our duty—to think things out, even if this should mean a speculative interpretation of Jesus, or in reverent agnosticism to deprecate intrusion into such high matters and stay safely within the frontiers of a verifiable experience? Advocates of the less ambitious plan are now more numerous than ever. Doubtless, too, so far as it goes, their guiding interest is a positive one. It insists on redemption as a boon appreciable mainly through conscience and feeling; it dwells on the self-consciousness of Jesus as the very mirror of God's heart; and these profoundly evangelical positions merit and will receive wide sympathy. In less commendable fashion, its tacit plea that faith is a necessity but Christology a luxury makes appeal to the distaste for systematic thought so curiously common in our time; and the appeal which is primarily meant for all who distrust speculation may also be welcomed by the indolent. In certain cases, moreover, an exclusive emphasis on what is called the moral view of Christ may cover negative conclusions as to His real transcendence.

In this general contention much, of course, is undeniable. Dr. Forsyth has shown us that the moralising of dogma is an essential of all modern Christian thought.[1] The conception of Divine omnipotence, for example, must be transposed from the key of barely ontological ideas into that of ethical relations as between persons. The almightiness of God is exerted not *in vacuo*, but in a moral universe and under moral conditions; a fact with an obviously direct bearing on the question of what God may do for man's salvation. It is more than possible that by this ethicising of the Divine attributes we may relieve some of the gravest problems of the incarnation, particularly those which are due less to ascertained facts of history than to the physical and all but mechanical thought-forms employed by the early Church. Thus far, then, the plea for ethical categories is abundantly justified. Conceptions which have lost all relation to the conscience are of no more use for our purpose. The re-statement of Christology in fully personal and spiritual terms may be a long and exacting task; but it is unavoidable, and if carried forward on sound lines may well hope for results of a permanently valid character.

At the same time, it is clear that a metaphysic of the conscience is none the less metaphysical. Guided as it is, like all knowledge, by an interest more vital than speculative, it is at the same time an interpretation of the real. The moral certainties of redeemed men bring them in touch with the last and highest facts in the universe. There is no incognizable Absolute, no more authentic or final realm of being, from the apprehension of which they are in the last resort debarred, nor is faith thus morally conditioned subject after all to the appellate jurisdiction of philosophy. By all means let us recognise the truth that it is through the medium of conscience that Christ is known in His ultimate and universal significance and His relation to God and man; but let us also recollect that the Christ thus ethically known pertains ultimately to the sphere of reality with which the metaphysician is concerned, and that there exists no legitimate point of

[1] *Person and Place of Jesus Christ*, Lects. VIII. and IX.

view in which He appears as a merely relative phenomenon. Moral perception, in fact, is our best guide to the nature of true being; if we distrust the utterances of the moral faculty, there seems to be no reason why we should ever trust our minds at all. Between the ethical and the metaphysical view of Christ, then, there is no final antagonism. The ethical, when taken as ultimately true, *is* the metaphysical; it is metaphysical in the only sense relevant to a moral intelligence. The phenomenon of moral worth is reality appearing to our minds. The reality is not behind the worth, or within it as a secret core; it is the Will, the self-conscious activity, of which the worth is a living attribute. Hence if we are inspired by Christian faith to affirm that Jesus Christ is identical with God in will—a Will manifested in His achievement—we have reached a point beyond which no advance is possible; for in ethical terms, the highest terms available, we have affirmed His ontological unity with God in a sense generically different from that which is predicable of man as man. Intelligent will is the organic centre of personality; and the will of Jesus fixes His absolute status in the world of being. In every conceivable sense in which this is a *true* estimate of His person, it also is a metaphysical estimate.

No escape then is possible, in this field or any other, from the obligation to think things out persistently to the end. If we are conscious of the spiritual supremacy of Christ—His unique position in religious history, His unique significance for each soul—we have no choice but to ask what conceptions of His person are guaranteed by this impression. Once these conceptions have been gained, they take their place as among the truest and most adequate of which the human mind is capable. If Christian experience counts for anything, then it counts here. It is in touch with reality; the being which our mind apprehends in Jesus is real being. A right doctrine of His person, therefore, is not dealing with ideas which are only counters—useful metaphorical expressions ultimately unredeemable by fact. It is dealing with ideas necessitated by Jesus' witness to Himself and the confirmation of that witness furnished by the story of the Church. These true ideas it is unnecessary to clothe in the formulas of conciliar theology. The language, the categories, the intellectual forms of earlier days are in certain respects not such as we can use. None the less our final thought of the Redeemer has the same meaning as of yore. The coinage of far-off ages may doubtless be defaced and soiled; the inscriptions set upon it may be in part undecipherable. Yet the ore from which the ancient currency was struck is still in our possession; and the task of modern Christology, as we believe, is to stamp the mintage freshly, sending it forth for the service of a new generation.

CHAPTER II.

CHRISTOLOGY AND THE HISTORIC CHRIST.

AMONG modern theologians there is a general disposition to agree that if Christology is to be valid for the modern mind, its point of reference and of departure must be fixed in the Jesus Christ of history. This was in fact the new Reformation gospel. In Western Catholicism the idea had become regnant that Christianity is the Church, while the Church in turn is Christ, the perpetual incarnation of God in the world. Official doctrine made no attempt to control Christology by recorded fact. Jesus was hidden by a crowd of saints. Conceptions of God prevailed which had little relation to the Son who alone makes known the Father. But the Reformers insist that God is sphered and embodied for us in Christ; that only there is He displayed as Redeemer; and that a preacher's duty is to make men see in Christ "the work of God and His Fatherly heart towards us," not to "talk much of God in the heathen manner." Schleiermacher too rang out this note subsequently to the *Aufklärung*; and Ritschlianism, be its faults what they may, has rendered an invaluable service by holding the Church's mind close to the actual person of our Lord. Its influence has coincided significantly with the ever-

LITERATURE—Forrest, *The Christ of History and Experience*[4], 1903; Herrmann, *Communion with God*, 1906; Kirn, *Glaube und Geschichte*, 1900; Sanday, *Christologies Ancient and Modern*, 1910; Kähler, *Der sogenannte historische Jesus und der geschichtliche biblische Christus*[2], 1896; Wobbermin, *Geschichte und Historie in der Religionswissenschaft*, 1911; Gordon, *The Christ of To-day*, 1895; Ritschl, *Justification and Reconciliation*, 1900; Simpson, *Fact of Christ*, 1900.

increasing tendency to put aside convention and look at the reality of things.

It is because it is a religion for the sinful that Christianity is indissolubly implicated with historic fact, and specifically with the fact of Christ. It is a religion of atonement. God has reconciled us to Himself through His Son, attesting His gracious will by Jesus who lived and died and rose again. Whatever satisfaction Christianity may render to the intellectual or æsthetic needs of mankind, is due to its having first met and satisfied the need of salvation. But the need of salvation cannot be satisfied by a bare idea. Not mere ideas but facts are indispensably vital; facts which have existence in the same field of reality as we ourselves, *i.e.* the field of history. Nature may indeed reveal a power indefinitely great and a wisdom indefinitely wide, but as regards *forgiveness* it is silent. That is a transcendent word; sun, moon, and stars cannot utter it, nor can earth and sea. It is in history, and only there, that the infinite love of the Eternal is put within our reach and we are made certain of it as a personal and inalienable possession. Nor is it in the course of the world at large that we encounter God thus; for history in general is filled with dubious voices, with warring currents of tendency which cross and mingle. God's Fatherhood, in the loftiest and most subduing sense, is known only in Jesus. He is indeed present in all events, ruling past and future ceaselessly; but yet in one unique tract of reality the veil upon His working grows diaphanous, and we behold His very heart. It is as with life-blood circulating through the whole body, yet here or there so near the surface that by a touch we feel the pulsing flow. Only in the fact of Jesus does a basis for religion exist not made by man, but given by God Himself. Apart from this Redeemer, Christianity is not redemption in the least; it is but one more impotent abstraction.

Nevertheless to urge this conviction will to-day almost certainly provoke the retort that to base faith on history is the most shortsighted of mistakes. Faith demands a Christ who has absolute value for our relation with God, but can anything absolute emerge in the conditioned series of time-events? How shall the absolute appear in time and place? Has not religion itself displayed an inveterate tendency to lift what it reckons holy out of the shifting stream of change into the region of the eternal, the immutable?

The objection may be put from two points of view and buttressed by two kinds of argument. On the philosophical side, it derives ultimately from the Greek view of things, which set out from the study of physical nature, not of man—who is made for history, and is "a creature of days and years and also of generations"—and which tended to disparage the succession of human events as something proper only to the realm of γένεσις, the sphere of change and incalculable variety, which can never satisfy the properly metaphysical interest. No one raised the problem of what progress means, or human history as a whole. No one inquired whether conceivably it has been "assigned to man to have history for the manner in which he should manifest himself,"[1] and whether accordingly in our search for the meaning of the world we are bound not to stop short with principles, truths, laws because what we seek is given only in facts, events, historical transactions. In modern times, the same objection has never been expressed more powerfully than in the famous word of Lessing: "Contingent historical truths can never afford proof of necessary truths of reason." No absolute verity can be mediated through events of time. Between the two lies an ugly broad ditch. This has been called by far the strongest blow yet struck at Christianity. Spinoza argued on similar lines; and Kant, notwithstanding a willing admission that the ideal took shape and form in the historic Jesus, does not hesitate to assert that the question whether Jesus' fulfilment of the ideal was complete is relatively unimportant.

[1] See *Life of Principal Rainy*, by P. Carnegie Simpson, i. 204.

Faith and history live in disparate worlds which never intersect. Fichte crowns the series by the declaration that it is contrary to the Christian religion to demand faith in the historic Christ. If a man is in fact united to God, his duty is not to be perpetually going back upon the *way* to such union, but to live in the thing. Anything else invades true spirituality. God is revealed in conscience and in the main march of events; this is all we know on earth, all we need to know.

The answer to Lessing plainly is, in the first place, that history is not contingent. At all events for the Christian mind, sure of God and of God's government, bare contingency is meaningless. Curiously enough, it was Lessing who did more than all his contemporaries to lift men above the strange and arid prejudice that history is only a Wirr-warr of beings, happenings, relations, and to exhibit it as the workshop of life both for nations and persons. The education of mankind, regarding which he spoke many deep words, is in fact an education by way of historical media, moving upward from limited and meagre origins, yet attaining in due time to a heritage defined and enriched through the bygone experiences of man. Again, the Christian message does not in any case consist in necessary truths of reason. It is not, for instance, a necessary truth of reason—a truth, that is, which rises with self-evidencing clearness in the mind of every normally intelligent adult—that God is so truly love that He interposed to bless and save mankind. For certainty here, we must have the record of definite phenomena accrediting themselves to conscience and heart. Unless faith, like Antæus in the legend, stands firm on the mother-earth of fact, it must come to be spun sentimentally out of the inner consciousness; uncorrected, uncontrolled, uninspired by great actualities. Again, if it be said the Gospel as involved in history must consent to be equally relative with other facts of the time-series—that it has to choose, in short, between historicity and finality—the answer is that this is pure assumption, and assumption which must be changed if it conflicts with real phenomena. It may well be even bad metaphysics; it is so, if, as not a few philosophers have begun to think, life is an eternal creation of novelties, a scene not of self-identical persistent objects with unvarying mutual relations, but of the incessant uprising of the new and imprevisible. For in that case the fatal presupposition of mechanism as an exhaustive conception of the real vanishes, and the only remaining question is whether the novelty emergent at a specific point in history was an absolute and all-sufficient Redeemer. Once more, it is obvious that the religious life of man has always moved upward, not by the influence of abstract conceptions, however rich or versatile, but by the power of great personalities. Each vast movement starts with a man. It rises into strength because an idea and a mind have become fused in one—the thought embodied in a soul, the soul dedicated to the thought and acting only in its service. This is unquestionably how concrete history has proceeded from phase to phase; it has moved by incessant new departures; and if the axioms of a mechanical psychology break down helplessly before a Paul, a Luther, or a Wesley, acknowledging their inability to deal with the original and inscrutable factors these names represent, it is hard to see how they can expect to cope with the incomparable life of Jesus. Finally, it is found that *à priori* notions of historic relativity are extinguished in Jesus' presence. They are broken by redemption as an experience as of old Samson broke the restraining withes. The men who followed Christ in Palestine and learnt to name Him Lord, those who in every time have felt the sweep of His power and the renewing impulse of His Spirit—no one of them all but is aware that in Jesus we touch the supreme moral reality of the universe.

On the historical side, however, the objection to binding up faith with history takes the form of asking whether criticism of the New Testament may not have destroyed for good and all the possibility of touching the real Jesus. It has been argued that His personal existence is a myth. Even if the more judicious smile at this, can we regard the situation as satisfactory which makes Christianity dependent on imperfectly attested narratives of the past? Is not this ultimately to condemn the faith of simple believers to permanent insecurity as the satellite of scholarship—a tyranny quite as insupportable as that of any papacy? Or, to turn the whole matter round, may not our exact knowledge of Jesus prove, religiously, our fate? After all, He belongs to the first century. Assume for the moment that His disciples were able to transmit His message without falsification; must He not have been, in a real measure, the child, the creation, of His own time and land? His teaching follows the methods practised by His prophetic forerunners, His beliefs are drawn largely from the Old Testament, and His conception of the universe was that current in His day. Can His thought of God have escaped quite unharmed?

Our answer to this must begin with the admission that nothing in the past can be so certain for the historian, *purely as an historian*, as that it will bear the weight of personal religion. Historical research can no more give us a Saviour Christ than science can give us the living God. Even if Christ were the Redeemer of the world, and knowable as such, it is not in fact by way of scholarly investigation that He could be thus known. There are matters, in short, which history by itself is incompetent to treat of; for, as Professor James once put it, "a rule of thinking which would absolutely prevent me from acknowledging certain kinds of truth, if those kinds of truth were really there, would be an irrational rule."[1]

That, however, is but a preliminary point. The really important thing is that no man is a mere historian, even if he tries to be. For no man is without a conscience—the sense of unconditional and infallible obligation; hence none can be guaranteed against the risk of finding himself

[1] *The Will to Believe*, 28.

in the presence of One who deals with us in ways which we know to be God's ways. It may happen to any man, at any time, given the witness of a living Church, to be inescapably confronted with a Person who convicts him of moral ruin yet offers him the saving love of God. And if this should happen, he will then know, with a certainty which no history can give or take away, that in this Jesus he has touched and met with God. The Gospel picture of Jesus carries with it the demonstration of its own veracity. It is not so much that we argue consciously that this Man could not have been described had He not been real; rather He makes His own overmastering impression and subdues us to Himself.[1] He is beheld as the last and highest fact of which moral reason takes cognizance.

It thus appears that the ground and content of Christian faith is eventually superior to the shifting results of historic criticism. Not only so; the conviction of Christ's power is ultimately unaffected in its central import by the progress of investigation. All investigation derives its data from the New Testament itself, and has therefore no option but to assume the truth of certain main elements in the apostolic representation of Jesus, which yield the sole criterion of reality. If Jesus is cognizable at all, He is cognizable in the Gospels and Epistles; no other source exists. Besides, it is not putting it too strongly to say that the Christ depicted in every part of the New Testament is *radically* the same Christ. There is a close similarity, for instance, between the Christology of St. Mark and of St. John. The Christ of St. Paul, like the Christ of all the Gospels, is a crucified and risen Lord; throughout, the attitude of faith to Him is identical. After a book like Dr. Denney's *Jesus and the Gospel*, this position may be taken as established. Scientific inquiry, therefore, may and does force theology to reform its methods of Scripture proof; it cannot touch the Saviour held forth, in every

[1] Cf. a vigorous sentence from Jonathan Edwards: "The Gospel of the blessed God does not go abroad a-begging for its evidence so much as some think; it has its highest and most proper evidence in itself" (*Works*, v. 178).

part of the New Testament, to repentant faith. The final outcome alike of scholarly exegesis and of simple Bible reading is a more lucid apprehension of Jesus Christ as in the sovereign power of His resurrection He fills the primitive believing consciousness. This is not to say that the whole task of verifying the Christian religion may safely be thrown upon the experience of the individual believer, confirmed by past centuries of faith.[1] The truth about Jesus cannot be read off the believing mind *simpliciter*. For it *is* a believing mind only as it has been quickened by contact with the revealing history. The regenerate soul is no more real independently of the historic Christ than a child is real, not to say intelligible, apart from his parents. The experience of being saved and the knowledge of what God did to save us form one indivisible unity, and it does not help intelligence in the least to put asunder, even provisionally, what in fact is joined together. That faith should manufacture its own data, or do anything but apprehend that by which it is created, is inconceivable.

The position here sketched in outline must not, however, be hastily identified with a different view superficially resembling it. Especially the venerable Kähler of Halle has set forth impressive arguments to the effect that in the last resort we must simply be content with the witness of the apostles to Jesus, and that it is idle to seek, behind their testimony, a scientifically reconstructed picture of Jesus as He was. The records, he points out, do not even establish the order in which the narrated episodes took place, much less the course of Jesus' spiritual development. In these circumstances, any one who aims at a biography of Jesus is compelled to fill up the meagre outline with private fancies, based on psychological analogies which really are irrelevant to a sinless life. And since the evangelists in any case are not chroniclers but preachers, the effort to disentangle "the historic Jesus" from their

[1] As is done in the well-known argument of Dale, *The Living Christ and the Four Gospels*, Lects. I. and II.

account must be fruitless, because perverted by illegitimate dogmatic considerations. It was by the apostles' preaching of Christ that the Church came into existence; their preaching, accordingly, must remain the vital soil of her life and the final court of appeal by which the truth of her message is sanctioned.[1]

In much of this we shall all acquiesce gratefully. Nevertheless it does not meet the question whether after all the Gospel can rest for us simply on the faith of other men. If, as Luther reiterates, faith and God belong together, we cannot really believe in anything but God as He makes Himself known *to us.* Even to a New Testament evangelist it is possible to say, in the language of the Samaritans: "Now we believe, not because of thy speaking; for we have heard for ourselves, and know that this is indeed the Saviour of the world" (Jn 4[42]). The grounds of faith accessible to apostles are open to us also. For one thing, the impression made on them is itself an index of its cause. Jesus revealed what He was not merely—indeed not mainly—by what He said, but by the way in which His personality told on others, fixing itself indelibly in their minds. This picture of Jesus, moreover, once we have apprehended it, can be employed to control the evangelical narratives themselves. The gradual outcome of reverent familiarity with the Gospel portrait of Jesus is to put us in possession of a conception of His person, so luminous, authentic, and self-consistent as to release us from dependence on peripheral details. The Christ shining out upon us from the sources is a fact so real and sure that it tests and attests its own constituent elements. And the susceptible reader of the Gospels simultaneously begins to find in the Christ thus known a Redeemer who both evokes the longing for God and satisfies the longing He evokes. Thus the apostles' faith is for us a mirror reflecting the actual Jesus, and enabling us to know Him for ourselves.

[1] *Der sogenannte historische Jesus und der geschichtliche, biblische Christus*[2] (1896).

The historic Christ, then, is the criterion alike of faith and of the Christology inspired by faith. But what is the precise content of this phrase, "the historic Christ"? How much does it cover? No present-day answer to this question has been more influential than that of Herrmann. He points out that the saving revelation of God cannot be a mere multiplicity of facts, which could only distract the mind. It must be a unity, collected round a fixed centre with which faith can have immediate relations. And this fixed centre is "the inner life of Jesus." Whatever else may be in doubt, this at all events is incontestably real. "The one thing which the Gospels will give us as an overpowering reality is just the inner life of Jesus Himself. . . . Whenever we come to see the Person of Jesus, then, under the impress of that inner life that breaks through all the veils of the story, we ask no more questions as to the trustworthiness of the evangelists." This picture of Jesus subdues us; it is, as he finely adds, a "free revelation of the Living to the living."[1] At this point, however, there emerges a distinction to which Herrmann clearly attaches great importance. It is the distinction between the ground of faith (*Glaubensgrund*) and convictions generated by faith (*Glaubensgedanken*). The ground or basis of faith, we have seen, is the inner life of Jesus, a moral ultimate behind which criticism cannot penetrate and in virtue of which Jesus comes home to us as the personal manifestation of a redeeming God. Contrasted with this unanalysable datum, however, are beliefs or thoughts which do not create faith but are created by it, beliefs which express truth sooner or later felt by the Christian to be involved in his fundamental trustful response to Jesus. Such beliefs are the affirmation of His Divine origin, His resurrection, His sovereign and universal power. Is this contrast valid? In particular, are we justified in narrowing "the historic Jesus" into what Herrmann has designated His "inner life"?

[1] *Communion with God*, 74–75.

He is undoubtedly so far right that no legitimate development in our conception of Christ can be a bare external addition to our incipient believing view. All true elements of an evangelical Christology must be implicit from the first; points to which they can be fastened when unfolded later, and which really demand the more complete statement, are given, though latently, in the initial confession, "Jesus is Lord." Belief in the resurrection is a case in point. To grasp or acknowledge worthily the risen Lord, a man must have been impressed with Jesus in a certain way. Our faith in the resurrection, though it finds occasion in the Synoptic narratives, draws its intensity and passion from our sense of Jesus' greatness; we so trust the power and glory of the Christ depicted in the Gospels, that the apostolic witness to His triumph wins our free assent. What would be fantastic if asserted of another, clearly is predicable of Him. But a principle of this kind, however sound, does not cover Herrmann's position.[1] In point of fact, belief in the resurrection of our Lord is not on a par with various doctrinal affirmations of which theology avails itself for the interpretation of Jesus as Mediator. For the resurrection is itself part of the revelation to be interpreted. It is an integral element in the whole presented datum in which the love of God has become manifest for our salvation. Our faith stands upon the entire fact of Christ and His experience, as that through which God's saving power has been revealed and made effective. But Jesus' experience did not end in death. It embraced resurrection also, and this can be ignored only by a violent effort of abstraction. Remove the experience of Easter morning, therefore, and the revelation of God to which we are called to respond is altered, because the quality and value of Jesus' whole career is altered. Something great has been withdrawn from the Pauline climax: "It is Christ that died, *yea rather* that was raised from the dead, who is at the right hand of

[1] Cf. Häring and Reischle, *ZTK.* (1898), 129–133.

God." Diminish the revelation, and perforce the faith which reacts on revelation is also diminished. A Christ whom we know to have been raised out of death, and to have shown Himself to His disciples as the Living One, and a Christ of whom we are not quite certain whether He is risen or not, are obviously so different that they must evoke a quite different religious interest. If our view of God, therefore, is to be fully Christian, if we are to believe in Him as omnipotence no less than love, we must hold that the resurrection enters vitally into the creative ground of faith. It is part of the Gospel in which Jesus is held forth. Or, to put it otherwise, the "historic Christ" is not the carpenter of Nazareth merely, the Hero of humanity, the ancient religious genius; He is the Lord who rose again to the glory of the Father.[1]

To sum up, then, the Christ entitled to be called historic is the Christ mediated to us by the testimony of apostles; so mediated, however, that in their witness we are able to perceive and know Him independently. No line of demarcation can be drawn prohibiting us, in our assertions regarding Him, from passing beyond the hour of His crucifixion. The limits within which Christ is revealed are not fixed between Bethlehem and Calvary. He is revealed also in His rising from the dead. Hence the Fourth Gospel follows a true and irrepressible believing instinct, when it envisages the whole earthly ministry of Jesus as already charged with the consummated significance of His exaltation. For this means simply that the historic Jesus and He in whom faith sees the last and all-sufficient manifestation of God are one and the same. We cannot read the Gospels and not feel that this Man is destined for resurrection; and what the writers of the New Testament have done is not to overlay the concrete facts of history with confusing and irrelevant

[1] Niebergall's declaration on behalf of modern radical theology is significant. "We need," he says, "something else which will serve as well as the old doctrine of the exalted Christ" (*Hilligenlei*, 34). Has this substitute been found?

mythology, but with profound spiritual insight to construe Jesus' whole career in the light of its stupendous issue. There has never been a Christianity in the world which did not worship Christ the Lord as personally identical with Jesus of Nazareth. A criticism, therefore, which, after repudiating His exaltation, strives to disinter the real Jesus from the mounds of untrustworthy legend, is reduced for lack of matter to constructions of a subjective and imaginary character. These constructions proceed on lines which almost by definition make valid results impossible; for, resting as they do on partially naturalistic assumptions, they are led to argue, first, that no transcendent Person such as the Christ of faith could possibly exist, and secondly, that even if He did, it is inconceivable that a subsequent age should be credibly informed of His reality.

But if the earthly Jesus and the exalted Lord are one, and are both of them aspects of what we ought to mean by "the historic Christ," in the sense that the resurrection is part of the historical revelation which evokes faith, this implies further that the historic Christ is identical also with the Lord present in experience now and always. "The resurrection," it has been put, "constitutes the great point of transition in the Christian faith, at which He who appeared as a single figure in history is recognised as in reality above historical limitations, the abiding Lord and life of souls."[1] In every age His influence has continued to reconcile men with God. And these effects of His person, in touching hearts and changing lives, must be taken account of in our estimate of Himself, for the capacity to do these things in humanity must have originally been resident in His being. The final proof of the Gospel, indeed, lies in the living interrelation and correspondence between the New Testament picture of Christ and our experience of His redeeming energies. Now as then, He convinces men of sin yet assures them of forgiveness, judges them in

[1] Forrest, *Christ of History and of Experience*, 158.

righteousness yet restores their soul; and this in virtue of a personality uniquely and inseparably one with God. If the pictured Christ be the die, the impression within the Christian consciousness answers to it part for part. Both reveal the actual Jesus. As He imprinted Himself on the disciples' mind, He imprints Himself to-day on ours; and in both cases harmonious effects flow from a single real cause. The transcendent Christ, active "all the days unto the end," guarantees the Jesus of Palestine, for ever anew He grants to men the very experiences undergone by the primitive group of believers.

It is therefore a principle of cardinal importance that Christology, at each point, should be animated and controlled by what we know of the historic Christ; but, like other excellent principles, it must not be applied in any narrow or legalistic spirit. Without this constant reference to fact, this instinctive recurrence to the self-consciousness of Jesus and the impression made by Him on the first Christians, we launch ourselves upon the wide uncharted sea of mysticism. But it does not follow that every doctrinal statement about Jesus must be sanctioned verbally by a word from His lips or by a distinct apostolic utterance. What is required rather is that the New Testament picture as a whole should be truthfully reflected in our construction as a whole. Let the portrait of the historic Christ, contained in primitive testimony, be brought to bear directly upon our mind, saturating it through and through; and thereupon let us proceed to give free systematised expression to the thoughts which arise within us. This is, as a fact, what has happened whenever theologians have spoken worthily of Jesus Christ, and it is clearly the procedure which harmonises with the native freedom of the Gospel. And if it be said that this appears to commit the Church to the vagaries of individual feeling, and the cry be raised for some inflexible rule by which to measure the correctness of opinions, it must be replied that no *legal* guarantee for unchanging orthodoxy can be given. Nothing in Christianity, let us be thankful, can be guaranteed in that way. But there are better sureties within our reach. We have the promise of the Spirit, to lead the Church into all truth; we have the Word of God, which liveth and abideth for ever, and to which the Spirit bears witness perpetually in the hearts of men. These are the real—these, when we speak strictly, are the only and the sufficient—guarantees that the mind of the believer, working freely on its data, will reach conclusions that are in line with the great faith of the past. Wherever sincere thinkers are impressed by Christ as those were impressed who gathered round Him at the beginning, there the truth will be.

CHAPTER III.

CHRIST'S PERSON IN RELATION TO HIS WORK.

It is a feature of the best modern Christology that the person of our Lord has come to be exhibited as interpretable only through the medium of His redeeming work. There is an all but universal feeling that to know what He has done and does will reveal to us what He is. Nature is relative to function; the work, as philosophers say, is the *ratio cognoscendi* of the Worker. In a former chapter Schleiermacher was found to be the pioneer of this inductive method, but it goes back really to Luther, whose words are very strong. "Christ," he says, "is not called Christ because He has two natures. What does that signify to me? He bears this glorious and consoling name because of the office and the work He has undertaken."[1] A kindred spirit, Athanasius, had used it long before, speaking in the *de Incarnatione* of an inquirer who "sees Christ's power through His works to be incomparable with that of men, and comes to know that He alone among men is God the Word."[2] The forms in which this principle of regress from work to person may be applied we shall examine presently; here it is enough to note how essential and convincing it is to study the Redeemer not *à priori* but

Literature—Kähler, *Das Kreuz, Grund und Mass der Christologie*, 1911; Gore, *Bampton Lectures*, 1891; Frommel, *Études morales et religieuses*, 1907; Haering, *Der christliche Glaube*, 1906; Wendt, *System der christlichen Lehre*, 1907; Denney, *Death of Christ*, 1902; Garvie, *The Ritschlian Theology*, 1899; J. Drummond, *Studies in Christian Doctrine*, 1908; Walker, *The Spirit and the Incarnation*[2], 1901; Cairns, *Christianity and the Modern World*, 1906.

[1] *Werke* (Erlangen ed.) xii. 244. [2] c. 45 (Bindley's trans.).

in the medium of redemption, of which as believers we have direct or experimental knowledge. To pass on from first-hand data to more remote inductions and hypotheses, from fact to explanatory theory, is the method of all sound investigation. Not that we are limited to this mode of thought. On the contrary, when we have reached an hypothesis, we go on to test it in a new way by inquiring how it serves for the inverse process of deduction. Hence we shall find that Christ's person casts light on His work as well as gains light from it.

The mutual bearing of person and work is strikingly illustrated by the main drift of Christology in its great historic phases.[1] An intimate connection has existed at each point between conceptions of our Lord's saving influence and His intrinsic being. Take first the Greek view of redemption. It was felt in the East that man needs primarily to be saved from that radical corruption which may be summarily described as "death." Sin has enslaved us to decay. Death, then, is the great evil; the loss of fellowship with God, though deeply realised, is of second-rank importance at this point. Athanasius' words about sin are fairly typical: "If indeed it had only been a trespass, and not a consequent corruption, repentance would be well enough."[2] But, as he proceeds to argue, corruption necessitated the more thorough cure of incarnation. This fixed the outline of Christology. Salvation is to be freed from death and decay; the Saviour, accordingly, was conceived as the ineffable and transcendent mystery in which immortal deity is combined with mortal manhood, the whole lump of humanity being thus leavened with the impassible and uncorruptible powers of Godhead and raised into what appears to have been thought of as a physical or semi-physical union with the Divine. Man universal is deified in Christ by the living amalgamation in Him of human nature and the eternal Logos. Doubtless this irradiation of humanity is fully manifest only in the resurrection and ascension of the Incarnate One, but in

[1] Cf. Haering, *op. cit.* 374 f.

[2] *de Incarn.* 7.

principle it is real from the first moment at which the Word took flesh. No doubt also the Incarnate is the object of faith; yet this faith, in its turn, is likewise conceived as a mysterious participation in His secret Divine nature, conveyed most characteristically in the sacraments, which act for the most part in non-moral ways. Thus the Redeemership of Christ is expressed in categories which could have only a temporary sway. It is set forth in terms more than half corporeal; salvation has at times the look almost of a substance which it is possible to assimilate physically. Christ Himself is an incomprehensible mystery in whom the indefinable essence of Deity is combined with that of manhood, and the mystery so indicated lies rather below than above what we know as ethical and personal realities.

Of course this is not the whole truth about the Greek Christology,[1] but it is a real and influential part of the truth. And it exemplifies the maxim that conceptions of Christ's work and of Himself vary together. If what He does upon us is to effect a quasi-physical change in our essential manhood—primarily in the essence of humanity as such, a real universal in which we participate—we are naturally led to define His person in terms of substance, not spirit. For reasons which are both religious and psychological or philosophical, this is out of touch with the modern mind. But we are in accord with these great thinkers in the fundamental conviction which inspired them. We also believe that the dynamic power of Christ is operative in the organic life of mankind, and that He interposed in loving power to regenerate by Himself descending into the bosom of humanity as a redemptive force.

Take now the Christology of the West. As St. Augustine lays bare his soul before God, what we see is chiefly an impassioned longing for righteousness, for deliverance from the guilt of sin. To be saved is to be

[1] The place of knowledge (*i.e.* a truly spiritual element) in the Greek view of salvation must not be overlooked.

made righteous; and the mode of salvation consists in the secret infusion of supernatural grace, bestowing power to do meritorious works. There is an influx of grace as charity whereby men are enabled to deserve higher grace. This determines the thought of Christ. He is not merely as God-man the ineffable mystery the East had found Him; in His Divine humanity He makes full satisfaction for the infinite sin of man. To the Western mind religion is in large measure a thing of law, and Christ a legal person. Having purchased forgiveness by His passion and obedience, He is perpetually operative within His Church—defined as the institute of grace—above all in the mass and the sacrament of penance, which distribute the energies of His Divine life. As the source of life He is indeed object of faith, but here also faith has lost its New Testament significance. It is now become the acceptance of Church dogma and of religious precepts. Hence if in Greek thought the person of our Lord had been interpreted by predominantly physical conceptions, the Western terms are rather those of jurisprudence; and when Latin theology took its most characteristic form, unmodified by the deeper motives of religion, the living personality of the historic Christ was apt to vanish in the rigid and mechanical actings of a non-human lay-figure.[1]

In this case also the conceptions of what Christ has done and of what He is are correlative. His work is that of a legal intermediary, and it fixes the constitution of His person. A dualistic combination of deity and humanity sufficed. Anselm puts it frankly. "To this end," he writes, "was efficacious the diversity of natures and unity of person in Christ, that if human nature were not able to do what must needs be done for the restoration of mankind, the Divine nature might do it; and if it were

[1] In one point of view Western writers did much to sustain a sense of our Lord's true manhood. Their profounder grasp of the atonement implied an Atoner who, as a real ethical subject, was capable of accepting vast responsibilities. Thus if in the traditional Christology His manhood ranked as impersonal, its full personality was virtually assumed in the doctrine of His saving work.

hardly suitable to the Divine nature, the human might effect it."[1]

Finally, the Reformers gave back to the Christian thought of salvation its properly religious tone. If in the East the categories had been too much formed on a physical analogy, and in the West on the procedure of the law-court, for Luther and Calvin redemption once more became simply personal—a relation, historically mediated, between God and the soul. God is Holy Love, and salvation is fellowship with Him. It rests on the forgiveness of sins, it is appropriated by faith as grateful self-surrender to an infinite object. And Christ is conceived in forms suitable to and worthy of this function. He is the Revealer of God; He is man's Surety and Representative. In Him the eternal Divine truth and love touch us; in Him we are led to the Father; and these two sides of the relationship—God in Him for us, we in Him for God—at each point condition and harmonise with one another. Thus the great problem re-appears in spiral fashion one stage higher—How must we think of His intrinsic nature in the light of this new conception of His work? Who is Christ, if He thus embodies to sinful men the redeeming grace of the Eternal? There is one principle, then, countersigned by history, which is fundamental to all profitable debate. It is the principle that our thought of what Christ has achieved will fix and delimit that which we can know of Himself. As the redemption is, so by necessity is the Redeemer.

This general truth has been or may be developed in various related ways. We may single out these four conceptions as offering us the best sort of inductive guidance when we try to clear up our minds regarding the person and place of Jesus—(1) ethical supremacy, (2) atonement, (3) union with Christ, (4) revelation. Contemplating these central matters we find that Christ's work is such as to lead our thoughts spontaneously in the direction of a quite

[1] *Cur Deus Homo*, ii. 18.

distinct view of His position. His work is but His person in movement.[1]

(1) Christ is the supreme moral authority of human life. He inspires a new ideal of character and conduct, which it has been found impossible to realise except by His aid. We are not now concerned with the ways in which this influence is mediated, but solely with the fact itself, its harmony with Christ's own mind, and its implications for Christology.

As regards our Lord's mind, it is obvious that He asked from men a personal obedience more absolute than normal man may ask from his fellows. It was an obedience covering the entire field of human life. The persuasion of men to trust Him was His one chief aim. On loyalty to Himself He insisted in a manner resembling the jealousy of God in the Old Testament. It is impossible to add anything to the words: "If any man come to Me, and hate not his own father, and mother, and wife, and children, and brethren, and sisters, yea, and his own life also, he cannot be My disciple."[2] To the ancestral code of Judaism His attitude is one of sovereign liberty; by the inherent right of the legislator He cancels the past and enacts new ordinances for His kingdom. When announcing these higher laws He makes no appeal to Divine sanctions. To His own consciousness He is the representative of the Father, privy always to His purpose in all its scope and able to declare His mind as the Son to whom all things are delivered. His verdict on great life-issues is uttered in a tone of complete finality. Whether it be the character of an individual, or seeming conflicts of duty, or the call for renunciation, or fitness to receive pardon, the truth lies clear before Him. He reviews, condemns, forgives, commends, enjoins, with a decision from which there is no appeal. Never do we read of His solving an intellectual problem, but at

[1] With a true instinct, early religious art invariably represents Jesus as *acting*.

[2] Lk 14^{26}.

each step He disposed of questions greater by far. That He took this place intentionally, with the consciousness of being called to a unique task and of possessing for it unique powers, is evidenced by His stupendous claim to be the final Judge of the world. This assertion He made unequivocally, and from the Epistles we can see that it was never forgotten. In principle it was of course not new; for by assuming the right to forgive sin Jesus professed to fix the destinies of men; yet at least there was affirmed a new universality and timelessness of moral jurisdiction. In His own mind, therefore, Jesus' authority over mankind is not merely absolute in the sense that it is valid eternally; it is valid in the sense that it goes down to the depths of personality and represents the last verdict of Love and Holiness on all that we have been.

On the other hand, this astounding claim—not usurped or snatched at, as we have seen, but simply presupposed—has been acknowledged by all Christian believers. In every age those who call Jesus Lord have rejoiced that He should exercise an unshared control over life and conduct. Whether we can or cannot explain it—and the thing may be as ultimate as the consciousness of right and wrong—they are somehow made aware that He is highest in the moral sphere; that is, not merely that His precepts are unsurpassed in power and clarity, or that His own life is their perfect illustration, but that He confronts us as One who is on the throne of conscience, who has a right to interfere with us, and through submission to whom alone we obtain victory in the moral strife. The right of Jesus to rule has been often canvassed; its limits have been sought for; the terms in which it is to be defined have been keenly scrutinised: but for the Christian it is still true that the moral supremacy of Christ, in its majestic gravity, covers the length and breadth and depth and height of human experience, and subjection to it is not a question of less or more, but a question of life and death. "As the result of growing familiarity with our Lord," it has been said, "conscience becomes surer of Him than of itself; finds in His will the same awful obligation that it finds in the law of Duty; His will, *because it is His,* whenever we are certain that we know it, is supreme."[1]

Now the fact of Christ's overwhelming authority, which it thus is freedom to obey, is a fact calling for interpretation. For it is not only that we cannot conceive a limit to His authority; by degrees it becomes clear to us that there *is* no limit. We search in vain for an exception to the rule that His will represents the highest form of obligation. It is a remark of Mr. A. C. Bradley that "we cannot apprehend an object as sublime while we apprehend it as comparably, measurably, or finitely great. Let the thing be what it may—physical, vital, or spiritual—the moment we say to ourselves, "It is very great, but I know *how* great," or "It is very great, but something else is as great or greater," at that moment it has ceased to be sublime."[2] This unmeasured greatness, this sublimity, pertains to Jesus as our Lord. His power to rule passes understanding. And our feeling of this is strikingly confirmed by its antagonism to immediate impulse. When the authority of Jesus first breaks upon a man, he is conscious of a certain suspense or hesitation; there is a sense of being checked, or baffled, or even stupefied, or possibly even repelled or menaced, as though something were affecting him that he could not receive, or grasp, or stand up to. But once he has ceased to feel that his personality is being invaded, there succeeds, at a long or short interval and with mounting gradations of intensity, a sense of being borne out of himself and carried away into the dominion of very Goodness, with an adoring homage which is more than strongly tinged with awe and self-abasement. No man has ever complained that Jesus' will misled him, or deprived him of that which is, in the absolute sense, good.

Furthermore, it is from Christ that we receive that

[1] Dale, *Christian Doctrine*, 110.
[2] *Oxford Lectures on Poetry*, 60.

moral dynamic and inspiration in the absence of which His message would lead us to despair. Along with the call to obedience goes the power to obey. Life's moral resources are in Him. This is an experiential truth against which the protest of this or that man that he does not have any such experience has no cogency. Men do pass out of themselves to make the will of Christ theirs and their will His; having died with Him they also live with Him. In Him they share the relationship of sons of God, and are supported in the struggle with self and evil by His sympathy and communion. They share, they really share, His conflict and His triumph.

As I have said, these are plain facts calling for explanation and synthesis. We are faced by One whose moral authority is infinite as God's is infinite; yet it is a completely human person whom we see. No view of Christ, it follows, will be adequate which is blind to this complete manhood as mediating a more than human transcendence. By this handle, indeed, the modern mind in most cases first lays hold of the Godhead of Christ. His assertion—the more deliberate because often it is unuttered—of His own complete fulfilment of the Father's will, and of His consequent authority over men, is either the acme of self-righteousness, or it is the self-revealing speech of the Son of God. But to say this is to interpret Jesus' person by His work.

(2) The atoning work performed by Christ is also a decisive index of His person. Of this principle Dr. Denney has given a brief elucidation in his *Death of Christ*,[1] arguing that the doctrine of atonement is the proper evangelical foundation of Christology. "To put it in the shortest form possible," he writes, "Christ is the Person who can do this work for us. This is the deepest and most decisive thing we can know about Him, and in answering the questions which it prompts we are starting from a basis in experience. There is a sense in which

[1] 317 ff.

Christ as the Reconciler confronts us. He is doing the will of God on our behalf, and we can only look on. It is the mercy of God in relation to our sins which we see in Him, and His presence and work on earth are a Divine gift, a Divine visitation. He is the gift of God to men, not the offering of men to God, and God gives Himself to us in and with Him. We owe to Him all that we call Divine life. On the other hand, this Divine visitation is made, and this Divine life is imparted, through a life and work which are truly human. The presence and work of Jesus in the world, even the work of bearing sin, does not prompt us to define human and Divine by contrast with each other: there is no suggestion of incongruity between them. Nevertheless, they are both there, and the fact that they are both there justifies us in raising the question as to Jesus' relation to God on the one hand, and to men on the other. . . . It is the doctrine of the Atonement which secures for Christ His place in the gospel, and which makes it inevitable that we should have a Christology or a doctrine of His Person. . . . The Atonement always says to us again, Consider how great this Man was! As long as it holds its place in the preaching of the gospel, and asserts itself in the Church, as it does in the New Testament, as the supreme inspiration to praise, so long will Christians find in the Person of their Lord a subject of high and reverent thought."

To this nothing can be added in point of cogency, but it may reward us to dwell for a moment on certain of its implications. Thus, the Christian is intuitively aware that the vicarious love revealed in Jesus' cross is the love *of God*.[1] It is He that in Christ gives us "rest by His sorrow and life by His death." It is He that stands beside us and receives our trespass, in its awful gravity for His mind and ours, upon Himself. Unless this were so, unless the passion to which we lift our eyes at Calvary were a Divine passion, through which we have sight of a

[1] Cf. for a speculative but deeply impressive statement of this, Nettleship, *Philosophical Remains*, 40–42.

grief that troubles even the Eternal Blessedness, it would simply mean nothing for religion. It could not affect the relation of man to God. On the other hand, just because as we confront Jesus, living and dying, we become conscious of the Divine sacrifice poured forth in Him, we are irresistibly impelled to form one view of His person rather than another. Something of the pathos and sublimity of that word stirs and subdues the mind: "He that spared not His own Son, but delivered Him up for us all." Narrow and poor as human terms are, we must needs employ them to formulate the certainty of faith that in the sufferings of Christ for our sake God suffered; that for us the Father hid His face from the Son, withdrew His hand, permitted the desolation, left Him to His foes. The impression we receive at the cross is unintelligible save as in Jesus we behold very God "in loving communion with our misery."

Again, the condemnation of sin visible in the life and death of Jesus is a condemnation uttered by God Himself. Not by a divinely commissioned prophet only, or other inspired deputy, but by God. We have a living sense of this as we are face to face with Jesus. There looks on us from His eyes the holiness with which evil cannot dwell. Never was sin so exposed, and, by exposure, reprobated, doomed, and sentenced as by our Lord's demeanour. In His dealings with the sinful, and with the consequences of sin, this Man is one with God; and what awes the beholder in the cross is not the meeting of sin and a good man, but the meeting of sin with the Eternal. If as true man Christ felt the horror and curse of moral evil, He also in unity with God felt and judged its guilt. And if, in spite of that judgment and condemnation, He goes to death for sinners, He thereby exemplifies in a supreme measure the moral truth that only He can forgive sin who expiates it. This judgment, then, of which Jesus is the personal manifestation, is a *Divine* judgment; at the same time, it is pronounced through the medium of perfect manhood. It comes from the lips of one who

Himself had battled with temptation and had conquered in the power of God.

Once more, the atonement raises great Christological questions by forcing us to ask how the obedience of Jesus avails for us, the guilty. It has always been a baffling problem: How can the suffering of one person benefit, or savingly embrace and comprehend, any other? In the words of Moberly: "How is it conceivable (the mind asks) that any Redeemer's work, or endurance, or goodness, be it what it may, seeing that it is outside the personalities of men, should touch the point of pressing necessity?"[1] To deal with this question fully we should have to anticipate the argument summarised under (3), but here it may at least be said that if Jesus Christ were one more human individual merely, as separate from men as we are from our fellows, the difficulty just noted would be insoluble, alike in logic and in morality. But if with St. Paul and St. John we decline to conceive Christ as one isolated person, and the Christian as another, then the representative act of sacrifice on His part is quite another thing, and the death that He died for all may have the significance which the death of all would itself have. Union between Christ and men, that is, just because it is a union, has two sides. His self-identification with us implies consequences both for Him and us. As the representative or central person—none the less truly individual, as we shall see—He stands in a momentous kinship to men; and this universality of relation forms one vital condition of His power to make atonement. It is surely the false step in many theories of atonement that they first abstract the Christian from Christ—severing them as two mutually impervious personalities—and then find it hard, naturally, to put them back into such a oneness that what Christ did and is fundamentally modifies our relation to God. But if by its very nature all Christian theology is an interpretation of believing experience from within, this oneness with Christ, of which

[1] *Atonement and Personality*, 74.

we are conscious, is our *punctum stans*; and the attempt to put it even temporarily in abeyance must be ruled out as illegitimate. We do not have to prove it, or make a doctrine of atonement apart from it; we assume it, rather, and seek to elucidate its deepest implications. And for our present purpose the relevant inference is that this absolute capacity whereby Christ gathers men into Himself and in their name, and for them, makes response to the Divine righteousness condemning sin, is something which, if we regard it closely, makes humanitarian conceptions of His being totally inadequate.

Not only so; it is precisely as we recognise the true Godhead of Christ that we are able to repel successfully one of the gravest moral difficulties which the doctrine of atonement has created. This is the difficulty men feel when they point to the impossible ideas of "an enraged Father, a victimised Son, the unrighteous punishment of the innocent, the unrighteous reward of the guilty." As against certain forms of theory we need not question the justice of the charge. But it is at least obvious that the mistake of suggesting a kind of antagonism between the Father and the Son attaches more naturally to a view of Christ which denies, than to one which asserts, His deity. If Christ were but one more good man, there might be reason in the argument that redeeming love originated in man, not in God, and that by the urgency and passion of His sacrifice Christ had induced an otherwise implacable God to show mercy. But this antagonism we cannot suspect if we are sure that in Christ God Himself has bowed down to bless us. If the required atonement has been *provided* by God, out of His own life, it is meaningless to speak any more of His implacability.

(3) Light is cast on our Lord's person, thirdly, by the Christian experience of vital union with Christ.[1] This *unio mystica*, I need hardly say, is not meant here as

[1] On what follows cf. the present writer's article, "The Unio Mystica as a Theological Conception," *Expositor*, February 1909.

implying what older writers were accustomed to describe as a union of the "substance" of Christ and the "substance" of believers. Men of to-day rightly reject any such view. But in agreeing with them, we do well to remind ourselves that substance was simply the category by which earlier thinkers strove to affirm the highest conceivable degree of reality; it was indeed their loftiest notion of God Himself. Nothing so exalted or so adequate could be said of Him as that He is the ultimate or universal Substance. Hence it is not surprising that they should have spoken freely of a substantial union with the Lord. Such a union was for their minds the most real imaginable, and was regarded as being laden with a secret and ineffable significance far transcending all conscious ethical relationships. We may so far sympathise with this as to hold that our ethical relations to Christ are in point of fact more profoundly intimate than any which obtain between one man and another, and also that they may be suitably described as "mystic." But we have to put aside the category "substance" and construe the facts freshly in terms of personality. On the accepted principle of modern philosophy that there are degrees of reality, a personal union ought to be regarded as infinitely more real than a "substantial" one.

Now in this sense it is not putting it too strongly to say that union with Christ is a brief name for all that the apostles mean by salvation. For St. Paul and St. John oneness with Christ is to be redeemed, and to be redeemed is oneness with Christ. Illustrations readily occur. For example, in a phrase, which, if we read it for the first time, would startle and confound us, St. Paul writes (1 Co 6^{17}): "He who cleaves to the Lord is one spirit." As it is said elsewhere of man and wife that they two are one flesh, so, the apostle's words imply —and they set forth, be it remembered, the classical Christian experience, not a peripheral eccentricity—a spiritual unity no less real and close in its far higher sphere is established by saving faith between a man and his Redeemer. It is a union that lasts as the other does not, and has effects the other can never have. Another remarkable metaphor occurs in Gal 4^{19}, where he speaks of Christ being formed as an embryo within the soul.[1] And there is the ever-recurrent form "in Christ," with its converse "Christ in you." But Gal 2^{20} is the *locus classicus*: "I have been crucified with Christ, and it is no longer I who live, Christ lives in me." The writer feels as if he had lost his old self and all but changed his identity. There has been the importation of another's personality into him; what he was had ceased to be, and what remained had a better right to Christ's name than his own. No doubt the verse was written at a white heat, and the apostle, had he been cross-examined, would have admitted that he did not after all mean that Christ and Paul were so utterly identical as to be indistinguishable; but this only indicates that language has broken down under an intolerable strain, and that words which at their best must always be general are unequal to expressing a fact that is totally unparalleled. What St. Paul asserts is at least infinitely nearer to truth than its negation would be. He stands for a truly spiritual union; a reciprocal appropriation and interpenetration of spirit by spirit. The bond between them is sufficiently powerful to support the assignation of the same predicates to both. Our solidarity with Christ is such that in His death we also die; in His grave we are buried; with the Risen Lord, and in Him, we too rise to newness of life. Nor can an attentive reader fail to notice that St. Paul's greatest words on the subject of atonement occur in this connection. Ro 8^{1} is typical: "There is now no condemnation to them that are in Christ Jesus"; and still more emphatic is 2 Co 5^{14}: "We thus judge, that one died for all, therefore all died." There is a sense in which Christ's death is, or becomes, ours. The sentence of death, executed on the Head, takes effect *eo ipso* on the members, not by a fictitious legal transference of rôle, but

[1] Cf. Sanday, *Christologies Ancient and Modern*, 122.

in virtue of personal incorporation. The believer, in familiar phrase, has "an interest" in Christ's death because he has an interest in Christ Himself, and has so lived himself by faith into Christ's personal being that old things have passed away, and all things—including and centring in his old self—have become new.[1]

St. John, who speaks the last word on the great Christian certainties, repeats still more convincingly the assertion that union with Christ is the secret of redemption. "This doctrine of a mystical union," says Professor Ernest Scott, "in which the higher life flows uninterruptedly from Christ to the believer, contains the central and characteristic thought of the Fourth Gospel."[2] It is true that Professor Scott goes on to argue that a totally unethical and realistic factor enters into the Johannine conception. Metaphysical categories, in his opinion, have ousted the moral and religious categories of earlier Christian thought, or at all events relegated them to a secondary place, all possibility of man's participating in the Divine life being foreclosed until the very constitution of his nature has been radically changed by the infusion of the higher quasi-physical essence present in Christ. But it is very difficult, if not quite impossible, to reconcile this view with the emphasis which the evangelist uniformly lays on faith. Union with Christ, alike in the Gospel and in the First Epistle, is the intelligible outcome, as well as the foundation and source, of ethical and spiritual experiences. At every point it is relative to personal apprehension of the word of life: "If that which ye heard from the beginning abide in you, ye also shall abide in the Son and in the Father" (1 Jn 2^{24}). So too in the Gospel it is through "belief" in the sense of personal cognizance and self-committal that the impartation of the life which resides in Christ is mediated to His people. But the crowning proof that it is mistaken to interpret

[1] For a striking argument that the Epistle to the Hebrews takes the same line, cf. E. A. Abbott, *The Message of the Son of Man*, 83.

[2] *The Fourth Gospel*, 289.

St. John's symbolic phrases in a literal or realistic sense is the fact that these very phrases, or their equivalents, are used freely by every powerful religious writer to this day, not least by those to whom the realistic view is abhorrent.

This preliminary objection disposed of, we may note the images by which St. John expresses union with Christ. They are familiar to every one. Christ is the Vine, in which believers are grafted as living branches. He is the Bread of Life, by eating which they live for ever. Exactly as in St. Paul, the mystic union is capable of being contemplated alternately from either side, and can be described equally by the phrases "ye in Me" and "I in you." The first appears to mean that the Christian's life is rooted in Christ and has in Him its encompassing vital element and medium; the second that He Himself is present in His people as the living centre, the animating principle, of their inmost being. Now in all such passages we feel that the distinction between Christology and soteriology, never more than provisional anyhow, has simply disappeared. And the point to be emphasised is this, that the experienced influence of Christ on men—still the same for us as for St. John—leads perforce to a certain definite view of His nature. He is definable as the Person who can thus be our inward Life, while on the other hand it is because He is this universal Person that His relation to us can be of this interior kind. Personality and possession mutually condition each other. To sustain this unparalleled relation to men, to impart Himself to them so that they have Him within and can hold fellowship with Him as with their own souls—this is a capacity or act which we can only interpret as specifically Divine.[1] Not only so; the fellowship thus

[1] Principal Fairbairn puts this well from the other side: "The nature that is in all men akin to Deity becomes in Christ a nature in personal union with the Deity, and the *unio personalis*, which is peculiar to Him, is the basis of the *unio mystica*, which is possible to all" (*Christ in Modern Theology*, 475).

established with Christ is set forth in the New Testament, and is still felt by all believers as being intrinsically and purely in itself fellowship with God. To have the Son is to have the Father also. Union with Christ is in no sense a preliminary step to union with God, or a preparation for it which may be ignored subsequently to the attainment of the real goal; it is union with God *per se*. Or, to put it otherwise, the one is the method of the other, the form in which it is held forth to sinful men. Now this complex yet so luminous fact, that Christ is felt to sustain a relation of indwelling in unnumbered souls, to which their indwelling in Him corresponds—and that in this relation they know themselves one with God—points to the real argument for the higher being of Jesus Christ which we feel to be implicit in the apostolic testimony as a whole.

Nothing can indeed be said as to the experimentally verified coalescence of life between the Redeemer and the redeemed which is too emphatic for the New Testament. At every point it is fundamental, for it interprets both the forgiveness of sins and the sanctification of the sinner. And if to-day many people still prefer the word "mystic" to "moral" as an adequate description of the believer's relation to Christ, this is in part because they feel that the union in which they are personally identified with Christ is far and beyond anything they have experienced in their relations to fellow-men, in part because the word "moral" makes no provision, or an insufficient one at best, for the fundamental truth that this unity is initiated on His side and sustained at every point by His power.

It may be, of course, that our conception of personality must be revised before we can make much in a philosophical way of a fact like the mystic union, but something of that kind is plainly needed and as plainly is coming. We are far away now from the point of view at which Strauss wrote that "Personality is that self-hood which shuts itself up against everything else, excluding it thereby from itself."[1] This may be described as the adamantine theory of personality; the world of persons, it implies, is best illustrated by a number of marbles in a box, as to which the last word we can say is that each of them is utterly outside its neighbour. Is that the whole truth? Is it even the best part of the truth? Surely those who have tasted the sacred joys of that human love which is our best analogue to religious communion will feel that impenetrable solitude of spirit is not the deepest thing in us. On the contrary, it is possible, in some real degree, to escape from ourselves, and mingle in love and thought and will in the lives of others. "We are persons," as it has been put, "not by our power of self-isolation, but by our power of transcending that isolation and linking ourselves to others, and others to ourselves."[2] The bearing of this on our present subject is obviously to suggest that it is only an extension of principles already implicit in our social existence as human beings when we speak of a true solidarity of life, a spiritual coalescence, between Christ and His people. And if, as Lotze has argued so impressively, personality in us is incomplete, and exists perfectly in God only, we may well conclude that this self-communicating power which we possess only in part will have its perfection and fulness in Him, and therefore also in Christ who is God apprehensible by us.[3]

Christian experience, then, as summarily described

[1] *Die christliche Glaubenslehre*, i. 504.

[2] Lofthouse, *Ethics and Atonement*, 117.

[3] Browning touches this point and resumes our whole argument in the well-known lines which conclude his *Death in the Desert*:—

> "See if, for every finger of thy hands,
> There be not found, that day the world shall end,
> Hundreds of souls, each holding by Christ's word
> That He will grow incorporate with all,
> With me as Pamphylax, with him as John,
> Groom for each bride! Can a mere man do this?
> Yet Christ saith, this He lived and died to do.
> Call Christ, then, the illimitable God."

by the term mystic union, implies a Saviour at once Divine and human.[1]

(4) We need not labour the point that Christ has given to men the perfect revelation of the Father. To redeem by authority, by atonement, by the gift of life—this *is* revelation. The words of Jesus are the voice of God. The tears of Jesus are the pity of God. The wrath of Jesus is the judgment of God. All believers confess, with adoring praise, that in their most sacred hours God and Christ merge in each other with morally indistinguishable identity. When in secret we look into God's face, still it is the face of Christ that rises up before us. To do Christ's will and God's is one thing. When we inquire as to the precise content of the term "God" for our minds, and ask how it has been authenticated, we discover, it may be with some surprise, that without reasoning we have transferred to God the features of Christ—holy and almighty love. We are really thinking of Jesus, with His essential features exalted to infinity. Indeed, the late Dr. Martineau could go so far as to maintain that Unitarians, worshipping as they thought God the Father, have all the while paid their worship to the Son.[2] In regard to the fact, then, there can be no dispute. Christ is the revealer of God. Than His revelation none more perfect can be conceived. In Him the Divine character appears in terms of manhood. It is

[1] Principal James Drummond's fine *Studies in Christian Doctrine* (1908) is written from an avowedly Unitarian standpoint, but it is difficult not to feel that it is inspired by a view of Christ for which logical Unitarianism can make no room. Thus at one point he speaks of Christianity as being "Christ in the heart, the heart resting in Christ, so full of faith and life as to find itself at home in God" (275); and he writes later: "Jesus is, to the heart that loves him, 'a quickening spirit,' one who forms the interior life, and fills it with an abounding energy" (291); "Jesus continues daily to dwell in the heart by faith, and to print there the impress of his spirit" (301). Nor is there any attempt in his pages to separate what has been fancifully called the Christ-idea from the Christ of history.

[2] *A Way out of the Trinitarian Controversy.*

set before us; we are not told about it, but we are bidden to behold it. How then does this aspect of His work—of all aspects the most comprehensive and far-reaching—give light on His person? Can we say that the experience of Christ's revealership holds a Christology in solution?

The answer may be put briefly by saying that only He can reveal perfectly who *is* what He reveals. If He be less than quite identical with that which is made manifest, the manifestation is so far religiously insufficient. If He be but a replica of God in creaturely or angelic form—more than man, perhaps, but only in some semi-divine or Arian sense—the fulness of the Godhead could not be in Him for us. For recollect what the Christian mind does. It does not place Christ alongside of God, and *argue* from one to the other; instead, it finds God personally present in Christ and responds to Him so, immediately. As the result of His being in the world, men possess and hold God in quite a new way—a possession which is unintelligible save as mediated by a Divine reality. One less than God, moreover, would in conscience have been obliged to point men quite beyond Himself, to utter a protest against the idolising love of His disciples, to warn against a too close association of the gospel with His person. This Jesus never does. Rather He lived out the transcendent life which constituted His personality, confronting men as His Divine self, and letting the fact of His being tell on their minds as a revelation. He has put the Father within our reach, as faithfully and unchangeably Redeemer, but He could do so only because He was one with that which He conveyed.

Once more, therefore, the actual work or influence of Jesus leads the mind spontaneously in the direction of a certain interpretation of His person.

In conclusion, it may be noted that if the work of Christ illuminates His person, the converse proposition also holds good.[1] The work is made luminous by the person.

[1] Cf. Edgehill, *The Revelation of the Son of God*, 141–47.

We are not getting out of touch with the New Testament when we insist on this; we are only receiving on our mind something of its richness and variety. To St. Paul, for example, the fundamental truth about Christ was not something He had done, but something that He was. His action revealed His being. "What Christ did for men is accounted for by what He is to God. The relationship of Christ to God gave supreme worth in St. Paul's eyes to His sacrifice, and turned the shameful cross into the glorious revelation of God's love to mankind."[1] The Fourth Gospel pursues this line. It seeks to understand the acts and history of Christ in the light of the assured truth that by original nature He was the Son of God. Whereas the Synoptic writers move rather from the historic facts to the person they express. But the legitimacy of both methods is indisputable. If, as we have seen, the work is the *ratio cognoscendi* of the nature, not less true is it that the nature is the *ratio essendi* of the work, and that we can see this to be the case. Hence the positivism which insists only on the facts of Jesus' recorded life, but will tolerate no Christology, does not even apprehend the facts in their proper fulness and significance. Just as in music the import of a chord depends largely on the antecedent phrases, quality as perceived being thus conditioned by its context, so in Christian religion it is of immense significance for our appreciation of the cross whether we do or do not understand that He who suffered there had come forth in grace from the eternal life of God. There are difficulties moreover in the doctrine of atonement—as our study of the mystic union has clearly shown—which we can elucidate only by taking the subject, in McLeod Campbell's phrase, "to the light of the Incarnation."

It is indeed an error alike in method and interpretation when the Atonement and the Incarnation are viewed as rival or competing interests, either of which gains at the other's cost. By some writers it has been contended that the Atonement exclusively is the proper foundation of

[1] G. G. Findlay, Hastings' *DB*. iii. 722.

theology, the Incarnation being excluded from the sphere of doctrinal inquiry, on the ground that it is either mysterious or subordinate; by others, that the Incarnation alone is what really counts, and that it mainly counts in virtue of its significance for purely speculative problems. But the contrast is false. There is no rivalry between a tree-stem and its fruit, for each *is* only as related to and determined by the other; so the Incarnation and the Atonement, the person and the work of Christ, have concrete and intelligible reality only as they constitute and define each other in the unity of a single experience. Life exhibits no break or cleft dissevering the two; in Jesus Christ supremely being and doing are one. This is true for us, who contemplate all that He was and did from the outside, but it may be true also for His own mind. It is possible that Jesus came to full self-consciousness, to the complete apprehension of His own nature in its eternity before and after, through the accomplishment on the cross of the work given Him to do.

We have now completed the discussion of certain preliminary topics which lie on the threshold of Christological inquiry. First, the need of Christology as such was canvassed, and it became clear that this perennial requirement of the Church cannot be secured either by a verbal acceptance of tradition or by the positivism which insists on bare facts and will hear nothing of interpretation. Next, we sought to define the correspondence which must obtain between Christological construction and the classical delineation of Jesus contained in the New Testament. Finally, it was shown that our view of Christ's person is invariably determined by our conception of His saving work.

The following argument will contain two main parts. In the first we shall examine the immediate utterances of faith regarding Christ as it grasps Him in the experience of redemption. In the second will be discussed the transcendent presuppositions or implicates which appear to be latent in these naive religious certainties. These remoter principles are implicit in faith, and constitute therefore a true element in the doctrine; on the other hand they are *only* implicit, not actual ingredients in that of which faith is directly conscious. It is an advantage of this division that we are enabled to do some real justice to the unanimity of believers as regards their personal and instinctive view of Christ, without being unduly perturbed in advance by subsequent problems of a more recondite nature on which opinions are certain to diverge. As we have already seen, however, these transcendent questions cannot be ignored on the ground that metaphysic has no place in theology. "The power of the Church to propagate her faith," it has been said, "is largely dependent on her power to commend the great truths of the Gospel to the understanding as well as the hearts of men."[1] It is vain to suppose that the interest in truth which is native to the religious consciousness can be suppressed by the ukase of any philosopher or theologian, or that people can be kept from asking questions about Christ, His antecedents, the constitution of His person, and His present relation to believers. When these problems are once ventilated, theology must even do her best to solve them, or—which is certainly not less important—prove convincingly why they can never be solved.

[1] Tymms, *Christian Idea of Atonement*, 4.

PART II.

THE IMMEDIATE UTTERANCES OF FAITH.

CHAPTER IV.

CHRIST THE OBJECT OF FAITH.

It is desirable, as a recent suggestive writer has urged,[1] that in Christology we should set out from some one truth or principle, simple in character, as to which a wide measure of consent may be assumed. Theologians have always tended to mark diversities of opinion more than agreement; they have weakened their case by over-indulgence in this habit; and the failure to strike the note of harmony at the outset may—in view of the immense variety of historic solutions—fill the student with a sense of despair or revulsion, leading him to throw up the problem as impenetrable. In view of this, we shall do wisely to fix our starting-point in a conviction shared by all Christian minds.

This conviction we find in the belief that Jesus is the object of religious faith. We are called not to believe like Him merely, but to believe in Him. Faith in God as

Literature—Denney, *Jesus and the Gospel*, 1908; Herrmann, *Communion with God*, 1906; Hogg, *Christ's Message of the Kingdom*, 1911; van Dyke, *The Gospel for an Age of Doubt*, 1896; Kähler, *Angewandte Dogmen*, 1908; Harnack, *What is Christianity?* 1901; Adams Brown, *Christian Theology in Outline*, 1906; Bousset, *Jesus*, 1906; Forrest, *The Authority of Christ*, 1906; Orr, *Christian View of God and the World*, 1893; Seeberg, *Grundwahrheiten der christlichen Religion*, 1903.

[1] Haering, *op. cit.* 370 ff.

Father is indissociably connected with faith in Christ as Son. It is true that a certain faith in God may exist independently of Christ, but in such a case both "faith" and "God," which are always correlates, mean less than they do within the Christian society. The first is something less than childlike confidence; the second is less than the God and Father of our Lord. From the very outset, believers were aware that a new apprehension of God had been mediated to them by Jesus. One of the first efforts at definition of a Christian is that implied in St. Peter's words: "Ye who through Him do believe in God." The faith conveyed by Jesus is no mere abstract truth separable from Himself, as the truth of the law of gravitation is separable from Newton. We are able to understand and use the laws of nature while totally ignorant of those to whose research and genius our knowledge of them is due, but the highest and purest faith in God can be attained in no way but one; it comes through a believing response to the person of Jesus Christ. It is what we see in Jesus that inspires a triumphant certainty of God. All great saints in the past, all who at this hour enjoy the peace of reconcilation and are labouring with buoyant energy at the tasks of the Divine kingdom, are evidences and illustrations of this. The apostle's two-edged word is only a transcript of experience: "Whosoever denieth the Son, the same hath not the Father: he that confesseth the Son hath the Father also." Apart from Jesus men may know much of God—of His wisdom, His power, His sublimity, even His benevolence; but of His Fatherhood, with all the loving-kindness to the sinful embraced in that great name, they can know nothing. Nowadays we speak with easy assurance of the love of God. It appears as something obvious, simple, self-explanatory. In fact, as the very familiarity of the Gospel may have concealed from us, it is in Jesus alone, and supremely in His cross, that assurance can be found that God's mind to us is the mind of a true Father. Hence it is literally accurate to say that the displacement of Christ from a central position within the object of religious belief would so change and impoverish faith as a mental attitude as to destroy its specifically Christian quality. Its unique tone of finality, joy, and unreserve would vanish, and its place would be taken by thoughts and feelings not indeed quite meagre or unworthy, yet incontestably sub-Christian in religious power and moral inspiration.

Full trust in God the Father, then, is uniformly associated with trust in Jesus.[1] It is this faith in Jesus which gives unity to the New Testament, inspires all preaching worthy of the name, and forms the vital continuity of the Christian ages. Yet somehow it is independent of, or at least distinct from, elaborated theories of Jesus' person. The striking fact that so many modern thinkers, though not unwilling to admire Jesus and applaud His social programme, should resolutely decline to acknowledge His supreme authority and Mediatorship or to be indebted to Him for everything worth calling life, and in this declinature should be perfectly conscious that they are at war with His own expressed conviction, is not without its lesson. It proves that at this point we touch the very essence of the Christian religion. Men are instinctively aware that the Gospel summons them to an infinite resolve when it bids them bow in self-abandoning trust at the feet of Christ. This is not something we can do by making a great effort, or putting a strain upon ourselves; it is something which, unaided, we cannot do at all. No man can say "Jesus is Lord" but by the Holy Spirit. It takes the very power of God to evoke such a confession as that. When we look to Jesus, and, realising the significance of the act, cast ourselves upon Him with adoring faith, giving to Him with a solemn exultation "all that the soul

[1] Harnack declares that "the Gospel, as Jesus proclaimed it, has to do with the Father only, and not with the Son" (*What is Christianity?* 147). But he is equally emphatic on the other side. Thus we are told (*DG.*[3] iii. 69 f.) that "the Gospel can only be grasped and held firm by a believing self-surrender to the Person of Christ. Every relation to God is at the same time a relation to Jesus Christ." Whether the two positions are compatible is another matter.

can ever give to God," we have done what is supernatural. It is specifically the work of God within us.

In faith of this type, be it noted clearly, God and Christ are not held apart, or connected merely by inferential reasoning; they are apprehended together in a single movement. In laying hold of Christ we lay hold of God personally present in Him, but nowhere else offered to us in this personal fashion, nowhere else certified and conveyed to us as Redeemer. Apart from Jesus, our ideas of God are imperfect and misleading. He makes a revelation of the Father which is new and "legible only by the light it gives." Of this complete faith in God, therefore, Jesus is not merely the historic origin; He is its abiding ground or medium. Trust in God and trust in Christ are vitally correlative; neither is definable in abstraction from the other. We do not believe in God irrespectively of Jesus, much less in Jesus apart from God or as worshipped independently for His own sake; we believe in God the Father as He is made near and sure to us in the Son. Only in the medium or Mediator is the great reality ours. Hence faith never transcends Christ, never, as in pseudo-mysticism, pretends to be superior to His recorded life as a source of knowledge long since antiquated, never tries to be wiser than historic fact. Jesus' word is final in its precise truth to experience: "He that hath seen Me hath seen the Father."

The classic exposition of faith in this sense is the New Testament. In its pages Jesus stands in the focus of religion; from first to last He is the object of that mingled trust, awe, and love which we call worship. It does not occur to any of the apostolic writers that this is a fact requiring either explanation or apology. We see not a trace of embarrassment; at each point they are speaking directly out of experience and striving to convey the same new sense of Christ to others. It is obvious that the spirit of Jesus dominates their spirits, modifying belief, re-shaping ideals and enthusiasms, making new the soul's environment, transmuting the flow of conscious thought, laying on the will an unseen constraint to that service which is perfect freedom. To this more than human influence they respond with an intensity which has no reserves. They rest on Jesus only for all that can be called salvation. Their monotheism is a passion which repels idolatry as the one unpardonable sin; yet in face of this they put their whole faith in Jesus Christ. Someone has observed that a high Christology has often been accompanied by a weak sense of God, but the implicit censure, however, relevant to certain historic sentimentalisms, is inapposite to the New Testament.[1] Religion, as religion, is theocentric to the core; and the irresistible impulse of which the apostles were conscious to give Jesus the central place in religion was for them the final ethical proof that He could not be lower than the highest Godhead. As source of pardon, as giver of new life, as medium and vehicle of a presence of God beyond which the mind can never go, He conveyed to them the powers of the higher world; and if the traditional concept of the Divine was incapable of making room for the creative and unparalleled content of His person, it must perforce be deepened and widened. It was at least certain that He who made the Father known must have come forth from the Father's life.

The primary documents of our religion, then, exhibit it as a distinctively Christian thing to believe in Jesus as we believe in God Himself. Not only so, but we should not miss the significance of the fact that the writers of the New Testament lay on this faith-attitude an almost exclusive stress. On this subject there is a finely toned

[1] In the New Testament there is no duplication of the object of faith. The idea that Jesus was a rival of the Father, or a surrogate, would of course have proved fatal alike to the inward coherence of the new religion and to its conflict with polytheism. But by the middle of the second century popular and unguarded language had been used which placed Jesus alongside of the Father as a second God, and in Gnosticism a kindred tendency took unbridled forms. The contrast with the New Testament is instructive.

passage in Ritschl, which is not merely interesting on other grounds, but incidentally does something to relieve a familiar difficulty. He observes that in the New Testament, in spite of our Lord's new commandment of love, only the most sparing use is made of the conception of love to Christ. But for this restraint, he urges, there are good reasons. "As a generic idea love to Christ is more indefinite than faith in Him. The former term leaves it undecided whether we put ourselves on a level with Christ or subordinate ourselves to Him. But faith in Christ includes the confession of His Godhead and His dominion over us, and thus shuts out the possibility of equality with Him." "This," he adds, "is the evident purpose which leads the Reformers to elaborate the idea of faith in Christ. If Christ takes the place of God, faith in Him is necessarily a kind of obedience."[1] The apostolic point of view — religious, experimental, immediate — could scarcely be better expressed than in the words: "Faith in Christ includes the confession of His Godhead." This is the implicit but inexorable note which runs through the Christian message as a whole. Our souls bow down instinctively before Jesus, who has saved us; and in that act of homage His deity comes home to us. It is not a matter of reasoning but of intuition. There is no process of logical conclusion; our eyes are opened, and we have a view of Christ which cannot be otherwise expressed than by the confession of His Godhead. The New Testament proves abundantly that such an experience is exactly parallel to the normative experience of the first disciples. We can see that in Christ's influence upon them they perceived the act of God, drawing near in grace. It was not that they placed Jesus alongside of God, argued next that God must be like Jesus, and moved thus by syllogism from the human appearance to the Divine reality. The matter was much more direct, vital, and personal. His power told upon them overmasteringly, raising them to communion with the Highest, and breaking all the bands

[1] *Justification and Reconciliation* (Eng. tr.), 593–94.

of sin; they had accordingly no option but to give Christ the loftiest place in faith, taking Him there and then as the pledge and equivalent of the presence of God Himself. Everything grew up out of the living contact of Jesus with their souls; all doctrine was but the confession that in that human life God Himself was turning to sinners and opening His heart to them. Of course the truth was reached by slow degrees. "To the disciples," writes Professor Cairns, "Jesus was at first, perhaps, simply man. But as their knowledge of Him widened, and deepened, and cleared, the very endeavour to understand Him, to make a unity of their thoughts about Him, led them on to conclusions about Him that caused the spirit to thrill with awe and wonder, and yet with joy. They became aware of something mysterious and transcendent in Him, something which was to the human lineaments of the Character what the Thought is to the Word. Behind and through Jesus they discerned—*God*, and that Vision it is which causes the strange thrill and glow of their later writings."[1]

In this experience of slowly dawning recognition, the first disciples are surely the forerunners and exemplars of many in our time. Indeed the situation of the modern inquirer is in some ways curiously like theirs. They were of course confronted with no august tradition on the subject of Jesus' person; as yet doctrine was all to make: the Subject of it had to win His way into the sanctuary of faith by the sheer power of a spiritual impression. That impression could operate only by degrees, and while the faith created by it involved a theology, it was so far a theology in solution, not yet precipitated in formulated doctrine. And once again to-day, for many the tradition regarding Christ may be said to be non-existent. It has at least no existence their minds can receive and grasp when presented point-blank for their acceptance; reverence, equally with candour, bids them refuse assent to theorems which they have no convincing grounds for acknowledging

[1] *Christianity in the Modern World*, 155–56.

as true. Hence they come into the presence of Jesus with a fresh, unbiassed soul. They have as it were regained "the innocence of the eye"; they can take vivid and original impressions. For them at all events—whatever may be the case for the Church—truth about Jesus has all to be built up from the foundations. And the spectacle of Jesus mastering these men, bending them before Him in homage, admiration, obedience, and finally lowly trust and worship, is the ever-renewed proof, such as doctrine needs and will always find, that in giving Jesus the supreme place our faith is based on irrefragable reality.[1]

It will no doubt be rejoined that faith has many varying stages of maturity, and that this ought not to be forgotten in a full discussion of the position attributed to Jesus in the Christian consciousness. We may accept the admonition. The place a man gives to Christ is naturally determined by the personal ascendancy Christ has gained over him and the obligations under which he feels Christ has laid him as a sinner; and in such a region, plainly, there will always be manifold and delicate gradations. In some minds there may be no more than a dim feeling that in Jesus' presence life is nobler, clearer, more profound; in others, the sense that He is rightful Lord of thought and conduct, or that He makes the Fatherhood of God more real and sure, or at a later point, perhaps, that

[1] Constantly we have need to remind ourselves that faith, in the Christian sense, is no mere otiose acknowledgment of worth, or appreciative recognition, given by us lightly or as from above; on the contrary, it is irresistibly wrung from us by One in whom all power dwells. The person of Jesus wins complete dominion over us in an experience which transforms our lives. We feel ourselves in the hands of immeasurable spiritual might. In other words, faith is submission, capitulation, obedience; looked at as an attitude lasting on in time, it is loyalty. And it is a striking and significant circumstance that the faith thus given to Christ is given in opposition to natural inclination. Our first impulse is not to submit but to resent keenly the condemnation passed on our sinfulness by Christ's mere presence, and to reject with a grudging envy the thought that He is higher than we. Withal, faith is ethical; for though "it is the gift of God," it comes through the overmastering influence of a person and the instrumentality of the truth He brings. On the whole subject, see Herrmann's priceless book, *Communion with God*.

life in a universe which definitely negated Christ would be unendurable. These are incipient forms of faith, not to be ignored by one who desires to know how the Christian mind becomes Christian. But they are something less than faith in its typical and characteristic form. They are not equivalent to that attitude which in utter self-committal gives to Christ solemnly the predicates of Best and Highest, and knows Him as living, present, and divinely strong to save. Now, in analysing faith, as the fruitful soil of doctrine, we are obviously bound to choose its most distinctive form, in which its constituent qualities and content attain most salient expression. We have to ask what Christ is, not for cool intellectual criticism, or for the historian's imaginative sympathy, or even for the movements of a sincere and eager aspiration, but for the complete faith which casts itself down into the depths of His grace as the embodied Holiness and Love of God.

The mistake of interrogating faith at one of its lower stages, rather than at the highest, appears to be mainly responsible for the obstinate contention that Jesus is but the Subject and Example of faith, not in strictness its proper object. It is a view which has never been wholly unrepresented in the Church, and it is powerfully and widely advocated now. Jesus, it is held, showed us what faith is; He did not personally claim to be "believed in." He was the prophet of an ideal higher than Himself. To think otherwise is to indulge a venial but misleading tenderness for tradition. The error of ascribing to Christ an absolute religious significance is indeed no recent one; already in New Testament days the first wrong step was taken. "The disciples," says Albert Réville, "forgot the distinction maintained by the Master, between the pure religion which He taught and exemplified, and faith in His person. Jesus Himself, and not the religious realities which Jesus had revealed to the consciousness, became the object, properly speaking, of the religious belief." The blame for a change so radical and so unfortunate rests chiefly with St. Paul. "He gave to the person of Jesus, as the object of faith, an importance so absolute, so exclusive, that Christianity, instead of remaining the faith *of* Jesus Christ became with him decidedly faith *in* Jesus Christ."[1] Ever since the Church has perpetuated his error. In recent years this general view has become more self-confident, with the result that in certain quarters the Church is earnestly exhorted to return, even thus late, from the "Gospel of Christ" to the more pure and primitive "Religion of Jesus," from faith in the Son of God, as a transcendent Saviour, to the religious beliefs which Jesus held.[2] Is this an appeal to which we can respond?

It betokens a mental attitude, clearly, which has much affinity with the ideals of the eighteenth century. The rationalism of that earlier day attached only minor importance to fellowship with God, and the cardinal truth that salvation has reality only as God takes the first step was not so much denied as urbanely relegated to obscurity. A high place was given to the dignity of man. It was felt that he possessed an inherent capacity to raise himself toward God and pursue the tasks of harmonious self-culture. To inspire him for such an enterprise there was needed less a Redeemer than a not too pre-eminent Example and Pioneer. Of course in a religious atmosphere of this kind, in which the thought of man predominates over that of God, the question of Jesus as object of faith has lost its interest. The sense of debt to Him is undermined; He is but *primus inter pares.* In wide circles the same presuppositions have now regained currency; and the comparative study of religions, or at least the principles of research deemed necessary for its pursuit, have been

[1] *History of the Dogma of the Deity of Jesus Christ*, 29, 40.

[2] A recent frank expression of this view is Heitmüller's article, "Jesus Christus," in *Die Religion in Geschichte und Gegenwart* (1911), Bd. iii. 375 ff. It takes an extreme form in P. W. Schmiedel's inexplicable assertion (*Die Person Jesu im Streit der Meinungen der Gegenwart*, 1906) that his religious life would suffer no vital loss though it were proved that Jesus never existed.

regarded as justifying a certain partial displacement of Jesus from the centre of the Christian consciousness.

History, it is argued, has no place for absolute personalities, yet such a personality Jesus must be if men are to believe on Him in the religious sense. Past phenomena are only relative at the best; each fact or process has its exactly fixed place in the uniform sequence of effects and causes. Its place in the sequence makes it what it is. When this philosophy is confronted with Jesus Christ, it will evidently be under a strong temptation to disparage His uniqueness, not arbitrarily but on principle. It will regard itself as obliged to show Him to His place in the normal progress of events, and in doing so to frown down excited talk respecting an impassable difference between Him and all other children of men. Each single fact is the creature of its conditions; as conditioned, it is and can only be relative. Hence the fact of Christ also is relative, possessing no unique or indispensable significance for the religious mind. The spiritual content of His life, the impression stamped on the apostolic faith, cannot be of final importance for the world. Doubtless its value is great as an index of the Power on which all things depend; it may even be supreme among the infinitely varied phenomena by which the great Noumenon is revealed. But only in unguarded moments can we designate it as absolute. For absolute facts there exists no room in a universe like this. Even Ritschl overstepped the mark in his effort to exhibit the apostolic view of Christ as permanently normative. What the modern mind insists upon, and needs, is not the religion of the apostles but the personal religion of the apostles' Master. He was in reality the first Christian, and we are Christians likewise in so far as we follow where He led the way.

To this we may reply, first of all, that the argument as a whole rests on a conception of the historic process as mechanically uniform which is silently assumed, but nowhere substantiated by convincing proof. This means that the emergence of a transcendent Personality, claiming faith and worthy to receive it, is discounted from the outset, as incompatible with the "laws" of history. Into the complexities of this theme we cannot enter here. But it may at least be remarked that the policy advocated by the radical theologians is one rather of prescribing conclusions to life and experience than of accepting whatever fresh revelations may be conveyed through the medium of fact. After all, if a transcendent Person should emerge, it is essential that He be acknowledged. It betrays a disabling bondage to *à priori* dogma, therefore, none the less hurtful that it is unorthodox, when men approach a stupendous problem with the tacit understanding that no results can be accepted which fail to conform to a fixed standard. To be told in advance how much you may believe is always depressing, and the implied attitude is moreover not one which encourages the hope that the greatest things in Christianity will be handled with the requisite sympathy and understanding. Yet the historic faith in Christ, as the only-begotten Son, has achieved results in the consolation and renewal of human lives which justify it, if we may put it so, in asking a reverential treatment at the hands of theories which have no such agelong record behind them.

Again, it is noticeable that while the advocates of the so-called "Jesus religion" employ the fundamental principles of Uniformity and Relativity to veto His unique transcendence, they yet affirm other cardinal truths with which these principles are equally incompatible. An instance will make this clear. Religion is definable as fellowship with God, and this fellowship has no reality apart from prayer. Now to the writers under review Jesus is no longer supernatural. The supernatural as such has been discarded once for all. Yet it is surely obvious that prayer—the vital breath of religion, as they truly hold—is itself a completely supernatural thing which shatters the monistic conception of the world as an inviolable system of mechanical causation. Prayer, in other words, has no meaning if the world is a complex of rigidly determined forces, acting and reacting in preordained ways. When we pray, we implicitly declare our faith that the meshwork of cosmic energies is the instrument of a loving Will not confined by their limits or exhausted in their effects, but capable of utilising them for sovereign and gracious ends. The devout heart, that is, assumes that reality contains transcendent factors; when we pray, God is freely communing with us, and leading us to commune with Him. The world is built on such lines as to admit thus of creative and original events.[1] Hence, in the light of prayer as an experience, it is vain to speak of an unchanging and inviolable world-process, reducing all things to one undistinguished level of uniform relativity, and excluding *inter alia* the gift of a new, infinite, unprecedented Personality, in whom sinners may believe. That is a false pre-conception with which personal religion can hold no terms. But a universe in which real prayer is possible has abundant room for a transcendent Saviour.

Once more, in the creed of this group of thinkers the forgiveness of sin retains a central place. They are sure that God receives sinners; on no subject do they speak with a more passionate or infectious thrill. "We must not hesitate," says Bousset, "to acknowlege that this is the highest and final point in our faith in God when we can accept and conceive God as the God who forgives sins."[2] As regards this element in the radical view of the Gospel two observations may be made.

In the first place, forgiveness also is a transcendent supernatural reality. It is accomplished by a transcendent God; it is something to which neither nature nor humanity is equal. In the soul of a pardoned man, as he well knows, a change has happened which is inexplicable by the mere action of immanent psychological forces. What has happened is that the burden of sin—of sin that is ours

[1] Cf. Wendland, *Miracles and Christianity*, ch. vii.
[2] *Faith of a Protestant*, 101.

and that cleaves to us with the warning that it will be ours for ever—is lifted off, and we are drawn back in love to the Father's heart. The gates of righteousness, which seemed closed against us eternally, are set open once again. God forgives; none but God *can* forgive; and when in this creative fashion He removes the power of sin to expel us from His presence, the act is one to which the normal processes of phenomenal reality are instrumental, but no more. As such an act it involves infinitely more than cosmic relations of invariable sequence. It brings God Himself into a man's life in an immediate (yet not unmediated) way and establishes a new connection in which He and that life shall henceforth stand to one another. The forgiveness of God, imparted to us in His sovereign love, is a deliverance from the necessities and fatalities of evil in which science and history seem to involve us. It is the experience in which we really become persons—not things, nor links in a chain, but free men. Doubtless the men of to-day are gravely tempted to doubt the possibility of pardon, especially if they have felt the influence of that sombre naturalistic pessimism which haunts the modern mind, bidding the guilty endure their fate, as best they may, with dumb brave stoicism. But in unnumbered lives all these misgivings have vanished in the presence of Jesus Christ. Fact has proved too strong for necessitarian logic. The man to whom pardon has become real knows once for all that within and above cosmic law there is a Father, that he is faced by no mere silent impersonal tendencies but by the living God Himself, who puts forth His hand to meet and grasp ours, ushering us through forgiveness into a new and blessed world of good. Here, then, once more the deepest things of experience compel us to break with the conception of a mechanically determined system of law (except, as it has been put, as "a scientifically useful fiction"). In forgiveness, as formerly in the case of prayer, we find ourselves in contact with a universe not really interpretable as a closed circle of forces, all the changes in which can be computed in advance by a mind sufficiently powerful. It is a universe rather whose apparent iron uniformity is but a fragment of the whole. God is a free spirit, able to bring events to pass which transcend all finite forces acting with mechanical rigour, able to release into the phenomenal order the pent-up fulness of His own Divine activity. Reality is rich, plastic, full of unimaginable potentialities. It is susceptible of new departures, and the preferential action of God affects its movement by way of real initiation. What this implies for our argument is tolerably clear. It implies that no *à priori* ground exists for asserting it to be impossible that history—the scene of the original and unparalleled—may exhibit the figure of a supernatural Redeemer as far superior to normal manhood as man is to the animals. Whether such a Person actually exists is of course a question to be decided ultimately by spiritual conviction, not by considerations of philosophic theory. But if He is real, if we are aware that in Him God is touching us and bringing us to communion with Himself, He is thereby constituted the object of religious faith in the proper sense. For to "believe" in Christ is simply to confess that in Him we find God.

Not only so. The "Jesus religion," in the sense under review, is a religion of unclouded fellowship with the Father; but if the presupposition that this relation of fellowship is mediated by Jesus be withdrawn,[1] it becomes a problem of the utmost gravity how sinful men can attain to it. To speak as if without more ado we could adopt Jesus' undimmed filial consciousness is to play with words. How shall we copy on our own account His felt union with God? How shall we venture to say with Him: "All things are delivered unto Me of the Father"? It is not

[1] According to Weinel (*Jesus im neunzehnten Jahrhundert*, 284 ff.), Jesus never regarded Himself as fulfilling a mediatorial function, for He knew that no mediator was required. For a brief interesting account of Troeltsch's similar view of Christ, see the *Report of the Fifth International Congress of Free Christianity*, 237 ff.

possible. The confusion at this point is probably owing to a misinterpretation of the fact that the religious man *longs* for union with God. His deepest yearning is for the life of unclouded sonship. But longing manifestly is not possession; desire comes short of perfect and secure fulfilment. In fidelity to the facts we are obliged to recognise a difference of type between the filial consciousness of Jesus and our own.

If then we are summoned not to have faith in Jesus but to share the faith He had, our reply is that the demand is one which of ourselves we cannot satisfy. Its point of view is sentimental rather than religious; for sentimentalism is the mood whose eyes are closed persistently to vital facts. And here the vital facts are incontestable. For one thing, Jesus' communion with God was a secret of His own soul; but so far as He revealed it openly, we can see it to be quite inimitable by us. His relation to the Father was immediate; ours, as He taught, is only in and through Him. Moreover, the consciousness of sin leads us to crave a ground of confidence external to self in our approach to God. Had we been sinless, some reason there might be in the modern invitation bidding us believe like Jesus rather than in Him, but, irrespective of other considerations, the single quality of guilt is enough to debar us from the assumption of religious independence on a par with His. The obstacle is insuperable from our side, and it is final. If we are to reach that inner sanctuary, we must be led thither by One who is Himself in perfect and uninterrupted union with the Father, and who in love manifests and seals the Father's purpose to a world of sin. A convincing and intelligible presentation of God is required which will turn our fear into glad confidence. We have need of such a revealing fact—which can only be a personal Life—as will exert upon us an inward compulsion, and give us in a moral experience the certainty of God's redeeming nearness. It is because men in every age have found this in Jesus that they have put faith in Him as God apprehensible by man.

The suggestion that the "religion of Jesus" represents the essence of Christianity may be dismissed as an impressionist and superficial error. It rests at bottom on a quite inadequate conception of what is required in a faith which shall not only admonish but redeem. Historically it is without foundation. Christianity emerges in history as faith in Jesus the Christ—a fact now admitted by all scholars, of whatever type. What we call Christian piety appeared first in the world not as a characteristic of the mind of Jesus, but as the distinctive religious attitude of His disciples. He had indeed a vital and indispensable connection with faith, but as regards the precise nature of that connection there can be no dispute. He was faith's creator, not its mere illustration. He evoked it, but He did not exemplify its specific quality of penitent self-renunciation. He made no effort to propagate in the souls of His disciples an exact reproduction of His own filial consciousness; they were not and could not be sons in the precise sense of His peculiar Sonship. Only once were the words uttered, "No man knoweth the Father save the Son, and he to whomsoever the Son willeth to reveal Him," and they can never be repeated. No prophet or apostle has dared to take them on his lips. And if it stands condemned by history, the modern hypothesis is still less convincing for religion. It is an impossible Gospel for the sinful. To approach God as Jesus did, with all His directness and serenity of feeling, but without His mediation, is an enterprise totally beyond our powers. If the Gospel becomes a demand for a faith like that of Jesus, how does it differ from a new Judaism? It is no more a great Divine gift, but an additional load for men whose hands already sink in weakness and despair. To invite us to the task is to plunge in darkness all whose conscience is alive, and who refuse to ignore the self-estimate they are irresistibly impelled to form in Jesus' presence. From this hopeless situation we escape only as our eyes are opened to behold in Jesus one whom we receive and rest upon for salvation. He is the revelation, as Herrmann puts it, "that conquers every doubt. Our yearning to meet a personal life that shall resolve every element of separation between us and it into pure trust, and thus give our spirits a home, is the longing for the living God. But we find it satisfied in Jesus in every moment when the recollection of Him takes away our fear of the abyss, and delivers us from the confusion and perplexity of the evil conscience."[1]

[1] *Communion with God*, 141–42.

CHAPTER V.

THE EXALTED LORD.

In the previous chapter we embarked upon a detailed scrutiny of the immediate utterances of faith regarding Christ, and there emerged the fundamental conviction that He is Himself the object of saving trust. Faith in God as Father is rooted firmly in the faith which apprehends Christ as Son. This result must now be defined with more exactness. The Christ thus apprehended is in fact the transcendent or exalted Lord.

At various points the conclusion has been forced upon us, that within the New Testament the proper object of faith is not the historic Jesus, but the Lord who lives to bless and rule.[1] True, this full-grown belief could not be reached at a single bound; preparatory stages led to it; yet they were after all merely provisional and introductory. The faith of the disciples differs by a wide remove from that of the apostles. The attitude of His followers to Jesus prior to the crucifixion, notwithstanding its revolutionary significance, is not so far the distinctive attitude of Christians to their Lord. A new era opens with the resurrection. Certainly the risen Christ is the same person as formerly, otherwise the apostolic gospel,

Literature—Swete, *The Apostles' Creed*, 1894; Kaftan, *Dogmatik*[6], 1909; Milligan, *Ascension and Heavenly Priesthood of our Lord*, 1892; von Dobschütz, *Ostern und Pfingsten*, 1903; Meyer, *Die Auferstehung Christi*, 1905; *Zeitschrift für Theologie und Kirche*, 1897–98; Wendt, *System der christlichen Lehre*, 1907; Schlatter, *Das christliche Dogma*, 1911; Garvie, *Studies in the Inner Life of Jesus*, 1907; J. Weiss, *Die Nachfolge Christi*, 1895.

[1] Cf. Lobstein's finely toned article, "Der evangelische Heilsglaube an die Auferstehung Christi," *ZTK*, 1892, 342 ff.

devoid of a *point d'appui* in history, would have become inept, since no one can preach a great Unknown, or ask for loyalty to a formula. At the same time Christ is now regarded in a light so new and all-transmuting that old terms of description become inadequate. The Man of Sorrows bears the Name which is above every name; He is the First and the Last; in Him dwells the fulness of the Godhead. It is not survival merely in a figurative sense whereby He persists "in lives made better by His presence," with the posthumous influence of the saint; the power of His resurrection reveals itself as a present and universal activity, a reality on which men lean, and to which they appeal in prayer. He gives a Divine life within the soul, and He sustains it. Union with Him, not assent to doctrine, is redemption. This is the distinctively Christian attitude to Christ, as it appears in the New Testament; and unless the records are of no value, it represents an estimate and a mode of behaviour evoked in believers by the appearances of the risen Lord and the subsequent manifestation of the Spirit.

It is an attitude, moreover, which has been perpetuated in the Church. Wendt, who holds no brief for orthodoxy, has said truly that faith in Christ as risen involves these four definite propositions: first, He lives really, not in the memory of disciples only; second, He lives personally, not as an entity now resolved into its ultimate constituents; third, He lives in heaven, not in the region of the dead; finally, He lives in the fullest possession of blessedness and power.[1] An impressive type of religion may no doubt subsist on less than this, but the typically Christian mind has always felt that for the triumphant discharge of her mission to humanity the Church depends on the real presence of her Lord, gracious, omnipotent, eternal. Faith's object must be now and here. Past incidents may have been crammed with meaning for onlookers, but unless they point to a reality which does not pass, and with which we can have

[1] *System*, 399.

immediate (though by no means unmediated) relations, they have no more importance for the modern mind than the notes of a bank long since extinct. Belief in the continued presence of Christ, therefore, is in no way the result of argument, though it may be argumentatively defended; it is an instinct of the Christian soul, comparable in depth and clearness, in many instances, to belief in the reality of an external world. Further, that it is no hallucination may be gathered not only from its ministration to the noblest type of character, but from its harmony with Jesus' mind and promise. On the eve of death, He bade the disciples anticipate a future which should be marked not by decay and impoverishment but by fuller victory, because inspired by His unseen guidance, and in which therefore greater achievements were possible than even during His own life. One can perceive, indeed, that much of the composure with which the evangelists record the limitations of knowledge or power observable in the historic Jesus is owing to their profound realisation of the fact that the earthly ministry was but the first chapter of a career which merged at last in universal glory and dominion. In view of the *dénouement*, they could afford to be entirely candid.

The conception of union with Christ gathers these impressions into one and articulates their meaning. It represents all believers as joined to the Lord in a spiritual fellowship of life, in a union not mediated outwardly by rite or ceremony, but produced and sustained by self-abandoning trust in a living Person. All this, which is not theology but religion, has obviously no meaning whatsoever save as implying the reality of a Saviour raised above limits of time and space. Men could not be thus intimately one with a Life that was, but is not. No fact which has ceased to be can form their link with God. Hence we may supplement the results of the last chapter by asserting that if Christology is to reproduce the Christian certainty, it must define faith in Jesus as faith in Him as the living and transcendent Lord.

To certain minds this may well appear a reactionary and perverse appeal to orthodox tradition. Tradition, however, has comparatively little to do with it. In great measure orthodoxy is a question solely for expert theologians, no one else knowing precisely what orthodoxy is. But the layman too has fixed beliefs, of which a brief and lucid compendium may be found in the best Christian hymns. And any one who is at pains to analyse the doctrinal implications of an ancient hymn like the *Te Deum*, or a modern hymn like "Jesu, Lover of my soul," may satisfy himself as to the futility of supposing that bare reverence for tradition inspires the Church's affirmation of Christ's perpetual presence. What faith longs for, and is assured of possessing, is the enlightenment, direction, power, and consolation ministered by One who Himself passed by the ways of human life, and in the veiled place where He dwells on high is not unmindful of His followers' need. The men and women who made Christian history have been animated by the faith that the exalted Lord can make the limitless resources of His transcendence available for the humblest of the saints. If by sympathy He shares their pain, they also share in the blessedness of His life with God.

Of this conviction the most natural and explicit sign is the offering of prayer directly to Christ. From the very outset a synonym for "believers" was "all that call upon the name of our Lord Jesus Christ."[1] The practice is one from which many recoil, on the ground that prayer to God in Jesus' name, and this only, is normally Christian. But the New Testament, while corroborating their main principle, does not appear to justify the inference they have drawn. The self-restraint and what may be called the spiritual tact of the apostles in this domain are manifest, yet we can perceive both that they prayed to Christ and that when they did so it was not because they regarded Him as nearer to themselves and of a more compassionate sympathy than God

[1] 1 Co 1².

the Father, but because God and Christ are utterly and wholly one. Thus every petition after all is "to the glory of God the Father." How vital this undertone is, Herrmann has shown. "Prayer to Christ," he writes, "is a very delicate matter. It may very easily be misused. Hence its use is by no means a sign of special maturity and clearness of belief. It is in general true prayer only when for the Christian at the moment of prayer every difference between the Person of Jesus and the One personal God is done away. He who truly prays must be conscious that he is raised inwardly to the One personal Spirit apart from whom there is no God. If prayer to Christ be not elevation to this God, it is no Christian prayer."[1] Christ, that is, represents to faith simply God Himself come forth for our salvation, and to speak to Him in prayer is to commune in adoring trust with One made known to us in a love and power that passes knowledge. It is the nature of faith as such to be in contact with ultimate reality, and since for faith Jesus and God are inseparably one, prayer, which is faith's vital expression, must apprehend both in a single indivisible act and movement of adoration.

Every one familiar with modern literature about Jesus is aware that much of it presents a conception opposed to this in most cardinal features. It is not denied that in a real sense our relation to God is mediated by Christ, yet it is a Christ whose direct influence on men ceased at death. On a few minds He left an impression so profound that we can still touch Him through tradition and institution, and in multitudes of souls His image is even now engraved. He lives, as others do, in the work He accomplished; He conveyed to men the content of His own spiritual life. But He does not act on us from

[1] *Worum handelt es sich in dem Streit um das Apostolikum*, 12 (quoted by Mozley, *Ritschlianism*, 190); cf. J. Weiss, *Die Nachfolge Christi*, 156–58, and a very full and balanced statement in Thieme, *Von der Gottheit Christi*, 52–65.

the unseen. In the natural poetry of faith we may speak as though He did, but it is poetry, not fact. His presence is departed, though we can drink in the spirit of His words and thus indirectly have communion with His mind. Does this afford a sufficient basis for specifically Christian life?

Take the assertion that the direct influence of Jesus terminated at the crucifixion—what does it imply? This at least, surely, that His earthly disciples received an impression of His significance more deeply and intensely personal than any now available. At death His influence was reduced in ways never to be compensated. Doubtless to His own mind it might seem expedient that He should go away and come again as an immediate personal activity, in the Spirit which should touch men with a quickening power and transform their souls; but His recorded expressions on this subject, we are told, are the ardent but unauthorised offspring of religious fancy. Now to such a plea it may surely be replied that life can only be imparted by a living Person. Even Christ's words, apart from Christ Himself, are powerless to change men. Moreover, it gravely modifies our impression of Jesus' incomparable greatness if it be ascertained that He passed out of contact with His people. If like all others He was forced to acknowledge death's separating power, and to commit the future of His cause to the influence of evaporating reminiscence, how dubious and partial His victory! Is this, in sober truth, a supposition which will account for the felt power of Christ to regenerate and transfigure—an efficacy of moral redemption which the experience of consecrated missionaries proves to be acting on the world to-day on an unprecedented scale? The writers of the New Testament are surely more convincing when they tell us that the method of Divine revelation after Jesus' death continued to be in essence what it had been formerly. In the days of His flesh Jesus made God known through His personal humanity in such modes that thenceforth the revelation became inseparable from its human medium. The same Jesus, inhabiting now a sphere in which His influence is universalised, continues to reveal the Father and to bestow a regenerating life through the instrumentality of His own personal impression. We can still be united to Him through faith. On this view, the Divine working has been marked by continuity at each stage. Throughout, the living Person of Jesus is the ultimate force in Christianity. Its real content and power are dissipated if it be cut loose from an immediate relationship with Him, mere teaching, preserved in books or traditions, being substituted for the life-giving influence of a present Lord.

Difficult then as belief in the continued activity of Christ may be, for the Christian its negation is involved in graver difficulties still. It is not merely that God has kept Christ's memory fresh and living. It is that Christ has been exalted a Prince and Saviour. On any other view our Lord was totally in the dark concerning the future of His cause, for it is certain that He anticipated His spiritual presence with believing men until the end. The proffer of this unseen companionship invariably formed part of the Christian message. That He was mistaken in an anticipation which has been abundantly fulfilled in saintly experience, becomes more incredible as the question is considered. Error is not thus the fruitful soil of triumph. Only the Living can prevail. Those who shrink from impeaching the providential course of the world will feel that grounds more convincing than any yet put forward are required to prove that He who so taught and wrought in the power of God has withdrawn into silence and inaction, as an idle, if interested, spectator of the progress of the task He inaugurated on the earth.[1]

To the Christian consciousness, then, Jesus is exalted as ever-present and almighty, or, in the profoundly significant word of the New Testament, He is " Lord " (κύριος).

[1] Cf. Garvie, *Studies in the Inner Life of Jesus*, 459.

His interposition was no transitory episode, but has become by its transcendence an eternal and all-determining factor in the relationship of God to man. To apprehend this is in essence to know what the apostles mean by Lordship. In the declaration of St. Peter that "this Jesus whom ye crucified, God hath made Lord and Christ" (Ac 2^{36}), the phrase defines Him explicitly as sovereign in the spheres both of grace and nature. Of grace first, be it noted, of nature by way of consequence. This is the real order in which the truth is mediated to faith, and in which alone it is charged with spiritual power. We first recognise Christ as Lord within the range of individual personal life, and expand this initial assurance later to universal and absolute dimensions. It has been attempted to distinguish the power of the exalted Christ, exercised solely for redemptive ends, from the sheer metaphysical omnipotence of God;[1] but the distinction is untenable. In view of the indivisible unity of the cosmos, it is futile to represent the sway of Christ as embracing the Church but not the total universe. No partition of influence is conceivable. To exclude even a portion of reality from His dominion is to suggest such an eventual dualism as must become intolerable both to faith and reason. At the same time His sovereignty bears peculiarly upon the Church in so far as the believers who compose the Church are conscious of and responsive to His perfect will, His supreme aims thus being realised by their instrumentality. His purpose prevails not by abrupt fiat, but through the mediation of saved men.

The resurrection of Christ marks the point at which this sovereign power was first made effective. Through a vast resulting expansion of activity the Son then became indistinguishable from the Father in the sense that He is now possessed of power to realise in human lives a salvation which is union with God Himself. Traditional theology largely obliterated this aspect of the resurrection as a "crisis" in the constitution of Christ's

[1] For instance by Bovon, *Dogmatique Chrétienne*, ii. 167 f.

person—naturally enough, since it regarded His personality as something completely given from the first by the positing side by side of the Divine and human natures. We lose a distinctive element in New Testament thought, however, if we slur over the universalising transition which made resurrection the culminating stage in Christ's whole development, and conferred on Him a mode of being in harmony with His spiritual greatness. Standing off from the whole spectacle of His career, we can discern that One who had it in Him to become what we now worship could not reveal Himself fully as Lord while He dwelt on earth. Not till He rose to transcendent dominion could the secret be revealed. After the resurrection, if we are to be guided by apostolic intuition, He was somehow greater than before. He received a new place in human faith. Men now honour the Son even as they honour the Father. And thus, in our human way, we may say that the incarnation has not gone for nothing. It is one of the most treasured convictions of the Christian mind that in the Divine sympathy for the children of men there is now a depth and intimacy to which that earthly career contributed, that the Son who came forth from the Father has taken out of time an eternal gain. So the grace which flows to us has been enriched by all things which Jesus underwent. God and man are one, but the unity results not from the formal juxtaposition of abstract natures, but from spiritually costly experiences of reciprocal possession and coalescence. There is now a Person in whom the focus of a human life is become indissolubly one with the last reality of being, so that the heart of man and the heart of God beat in the risen Lord with one pulsing movement, one indistinguishable passion to save and bless.

It is important to observe that the glorifying of Christ by resurrection is no mere spectacular epilogue to His earthly mission. On the contrary, it is part of the full glorifying of the Father. Not otherwise could it have been clear that the revelation mediated by Christ is

God's last word of grace, beyond which not even infinite love can go. The meaning of Christ was the disclosure of the Father as perfect love, but it is frequently overlooked that this love could not be recognised as perfect save as exhibited in prevailing absolute *power* as well as appealing moral beauty. Apart from the manifestation of an *almighty* love in the experience of the Revealer, the content of the revelation must needs have been fragmentary and ambiguous. Resurrection, therefore, crowned the demonstration of God's love as the absolute power to which all reality is subservient, and which no sin of man or independent ordinance of nature can ever defeat. But this display was protected from the danger of misconstruction in semi-pagan ways by the fact of the Cross, in which the same Divine love suffered for the guilty. When Jesus passed into the heavens, it was as bearing within Him the fruit and issue of that suffering. His glory always is the glory of the Crucified. The pain of the Righteous One is become the day-star of the world.

All that we have said is implicit in the language of the first Christian creed—Jesus is Lord.[1] These great words, to be read rightly, should be read twice, the stress falling alternately on predicate and subject. Jesus is *Lord*—He lives now in the Divine glory, omnipresent and almighty in His redeeming love. But also this Lord is *Jesus*—the Son of Man who was made in all things like His brethren, and at last bowed Himself down in shame and agony and death. Self-renouncing love on the world's throne, Christ sovereign through His passion—this, in its pure essence, is the apostolic faith; and is it wonderful that those who possessed it, or rather were possessed by it, should have made the New Testament unequalled in the world's literature for glad hopefulness and serenity?

This revolutionising faith also implies that if even now the Church recognises the sovereignty of Christ, it will one day be recognised by all. He shall yet be

[1] 1 Co 12[3], Ph 2[11].

manifested in modes not less wonderful than those of His first appearing. The instinctive conviction that His work must reach consummation and perfected fruition has always been a chief influence stimulating the Church to formulate worthy conceptions of her Lord. When the writers of the New Testament looked into the stretching future, they beheld Jesus Christ occupying a central position in the last decisive scene of history, and the felt greatness of His person, far from crushing them in dumb awe, thrilled their imagination, dilated their reason, and lifted up their kindled minds to new, undreamt-of thoughts concerning His relation to God and man. A creative religious experience will always provide the terms in which it may be fitly stated.

The relation of the exalted Christ to His followers is described by apostolic writers in two conceptions, which have been felt as representing two cardinal interests of faith. These are the conceptions of Christ as Giver of the Spirit and Intercessor with the Father.

At present, as I think, justice is done to the conception of the Spirit neither by the severer forms of traditional orthodoxy nor by modern Liberal Protestantism. If our faith on one side is solicited for a certain *corpus* of doctrinal theory, on the other we are pointed to the Carpenter of Nazareth, the heroic Man of the first century. In neither case is fellowship with a present Lord made central. This must deepen profoundly our sense of value in the New Testament conception of the Spirit. For it is only as the Spirit—one with Christ Himself—comes to perpetuate the spiritual presence of the Lord, and to cast light on the unending significance of His work, that we are quite liberated from the impersonal and external, whether it be lifeless doctrine or the historically verified events of an ever-receding past. Only through the Spirit have we contact with the living Christ. It is particularly in the pages of the Fourth Gospel that this large and fruitful idea is presented.

The coming of the Spirit, however, is not to be conceived as forming a compensation or substitute for the absent Christ; it is the higher mode in which Christ Himself is present. "I will come to you" and "when the Comforter is come" occur interchangeably, and any doctrine of the Trinity which finds this an insuperable obstacle stands so far convicted of tritheism. Between the Spirit and Christ in the heart no experimental distinction can be made. The one is the method of the other. That the Spirit should have overshadowed the historic Christ by opening a new and loftier stage of revelation is a notion which the apostolic mind could not have formed. As it has been expressed, "the office of the Spirit consists in declaring the mind of Jesus and perpetuating the work He had accomplished in His earthly life. . . . The Spirit is the perennial source of new revelation, and yet this new revelation is only the unfolding, ever more largely and clearly, of what has already been imparted in the life of Jesus. All our knowledge of God and His truth is ultimately derived from the historical manifestation, which conveys a different message to each succeeding time, but can never be superseded."[1] The glorified Saviour is identical with the Jesus who sojourned on earth, and the work resumed under larger conditions, with an access of Divine power, is but the continuation of His earthly task, in the light of which it must be interpreted. It may help our apprehension of Christ's exaltation if we inquire, very briefly, why the earthly life of Jesus should have had to close before the Spirit was poured forth.

(*a*) It is through the Spirit that men become persuaded of Jesus as Redeemer, but prior to the crucifixion His Redeemership had not been fully manifested. Apart from His death in behalf of sinners, Christ is not completely known as Saviour, for salvation consists in being reconciled to God in view of Jesus, while on the other hand before Calvary the holy love constitutive of His inmost being was incompletely revealed. To bear fruit, the

[1] Scott, *The Fourth Gospel*, 351.

corn must fall into the ground and die. Thus, until in the accomplishment of His vocation Christ had tasted death for every man, the full object which should evoke the whole-hearted faith He desired still awaited realisation. The mind of the disciples was still unready for the great gift. "Even before the ratification of the new covenant in His blood, the Messianic gift of the Spirit was ready to be bestowed upon all who by faith would appropriate this privilege, yet not till after our Lord had 'finished' His work were the conditions of receptivity present which permitted of the full outpouring."[1]

(*b*) But the resurrection of Christ equally with His death is vital to the Gospel message; hence only after He had risen could that message be proclaimed in its entirety. Apart from the resurrection the revelation of God's love in Christ is obviously faint and indecisive. Haering points out admirably that if that love is to evoke joyous and unreserved faith, it must reveal itself as not merely patient of death but triumphant over it. And triumphant in the fullest sense—*i.e.*, not only sustaining Jesus in the last agony and inspiring Him to the end with trust unconquerable, but charged with sovereign power to deliver by abolishing death and inaugurating for Him a new career of redemptive activity. Looking at Calvary we say, This love deserved to conquer; looking to the risen Lord we add, And in fact it *has* conquered. It has proved itself not merely the noblest but the most potent force of which we have any knowledge—supreme in reality as in idea. *Amor vincit omnia*—till Christ had risen the ultimate truth of this saying might be doubted; since then, none in whom He dwells can question it. The Spirit came, therefore, in connection with a completely unveiled Gospel which now proclaims a Divine grace as almighty as it is compassionate.

(*c*) The coming of the Spirit is equivalent to the return of Christ as an unseen and abiding presence, yet while Jesus lived on earth this more intimate fellowship

[1] Hogg, *Christ's Message of the Kingdom*, 213.

could not be realised. On earth He had been manifested as a human individual, hedged about by physical necessities, absent from these followers that He might be with those. And before "I am glad for your sakes that I was not there" could pass into "Lo, I am with you alway," a vast transformation in His mode of existence must occur. It was death and resurrection which formed the transition-point and installed Him in a new order of conditions, through which He became the indwelling life of His Church. "This universality of operation, both intensive and extensive," writes Dr. Forrest, "cannot belong to the Divine while clothed and localised in 'flesh and blood'; it must be liberated from these bonds before it can attain it. The external factor must disappear ere the Incarnate can enter into His glory."[1] Thus only after the resurrection could the Spirit of Christ—or Christ as Spirit—be shed forth as a widespread, actual experience.

The second mode in which the risen Lord is presented in the New Testament as sustaining active relations to believers is that of Intercession. One is occasionally tempted to ask whether this conception is not one of which we moderns have lost the key. Nor need we have any scruple in conceding to the full that the representation of Christ's heavenly intercession partakes largely of symbolism. Yet symbols may have a definite and even an inexpressibly precious significance. It was so with the Intercession of Christ. "The apostles," it has been said, "mention this sacred function with a kind of adoring awe which is quite peculiar even in the New Testament. It seems to have impressed them as one of the unimaginable wonders of redemption—something which in love went far beyond all that we could ask or think. When inspired thought touches it, it rests on it as an unsurpassable height."[2]

Admittedly the limits of human faculty interpose a veto when we attempt to explain specific acts in which

[1] *Authority of Christ*, 350. [2] Denney, *Studies in Theology*, 162.

our Lord's intercession may consist. It would be meaningless, for example, to conceive of it as taking place in words or spoken entreaty. Words imply distance and duality of a kind incongruous with the identity of life subsisting between Christ and the Father. Theirs is a unity that needs no language. On the other hand, it would be not less erroneous to empty that intercession of all personal significance. Apparently we do right to image it as involving at least His mediatorial presence before God, with knowledge of each of us and with pity for each—His glorified person being, as it were, a ceaselessly prevailing appeal to the reconciling work accomplished on the earth, and also a fact which recalls intensely the perpetual needs of men still tried and tempted as Christ had been. Thus our Lord's intercession implies at the least that He is concerned with real participating sympathy in the experiences of His Church, this sympathy being projected into His fellowship with the Father, as a true and living element in its content. In that Divine communion, those who once were purchased at so dear a price are never forgotten. "With love and longing infinite" He who made Himself utterly one with men in life and death is still consciously identified with His brethren; and the spirit and aims of the great Advocate we may gather from His parting petitions in the Fourth Gospel. "The faith of the Church, and the prayers which it utters—the responsibilities which it exercises—in virtue of its faith, will still have that support from the great soul of Christ which during His visible ministry had been the stay of the disciples in their first steps in the new life of the Kingdom."[1]

These are vast religious conceptions. They are conceptions which have imparted tone and substance to Christian preaching at its best; they have also supplied strong motives for consistent and impressive Christian life. For the soldier of righteousness it is a very fount of power to reckon on the interest and companionship of the Captain

[1] Hogg, *ut supra*, 218.

of salvation; to the humblest believer it is everything to rest in the love of that unseen Friend whose faithful care is unaffected by change of time or dignity. It is part therefore of the best Christian conviction that as our Lord now lives in God, and God in Him, His thought and power are constantly directed to all believers, and that in these most real relations with men He acts, as it were, from within the very being of God Himself. His right and ability to act, moreover, are grounded morally in the abiding value of His sacrifice, in which our interests were completely and finally identified with His. The succouring love our prayers draw forth is not created by our prayers. Rather its validity is the steadfast background and potency of all we now receive.

The danger which has long shadowed faith in the exalted Christ is that of an unbridled and capricious mysticism. Ideas gained currency respecting His interposition in human lives which have no relation to His known character. The glorified Redeemer has been isolated from the historic Jesus, while the individual soul has in turn been isolated from the vital organic brotherhood of the Church. Ritschl poured a heavy fire upon the religious *illuminati* in every age who, arrogating the right to unmediated fellowship with Christ, have shown a marked disposition to regard the historic narrative of His life as but "milk for babes."[1] It is well known to what fanatical excess such an attitude has led. A shallow and unwholesome fancy, often combined with morbid erotic passion, produced a type of sentiment and belief totally dissimilar from the religion of the New Testament. Speculation, from an opposed yet kindred point of view, has endeavoured to supersede the facts of history by the idea of a noumenal Christ or Christ-principle, which should expand the narrow faith of the Church into a religion for humanity. The circumstance that the earthly Jesus was trammelled by restrictions of space and time, and only

[1] *Theologie und Metaphysik*, 25 ff.

through death passed into a higher and boundless life, is transformed into the position that the truth present in Christianity is *per se* absolute and eternal, with a content grounded in reason not on fact, and wholly independent of the fugitive and alogical elements of the time-series. For the larger meanings of Jesus' work, accordingly, we must look not to the Spirit unfolding truth in the Christian mind of successive generations, but to "the speculative fancy, wandering at its own pleasure and arriving from time to time at new beliefs." Thus the exalted Christ vanishes in a mist of sentimentalism or dialectic. The living Person is discarded, and instead we are offered a dream of passion or a lifeless philosophic principle. In exposing the untenability of such conceptions and their claim to rank as authentically Christian, Ritschl has done a peculiarly important service. He has effectually refuted the attempt to dissolve the person of Jesus in sub-personal factors—mystical or speculative—by pointing out that validly Christian views of Christ are distinguished by two marks: they predicate of the risen Lord those personal features which are present in the historic Saviour, and they insist on the fundamental obligation to obey His commandments. No conception of His glory can be true which fails in either of these two ways.

In one respect, however, the interpretation which Ritschl places upon Christ's present sovereignty is inadequate. He contends that if this sovereignty is to possess a verifiable sense for our minds, we must find *all* its characteristics in Jesus' earthly career.[1] Now the historic Jesus displayed His Kingship by exerting a unique *moral* power upon things — by control of circumstance, by ascendancy over human souls, by triumph over obstacles, by patience in suffering, by faithfulness unto death. These alone, Ritschl argues, are the tokens of sovereignty; and the Christian message is to the effect that just by enduring the world's hatred, even in its direst consequences, Jesus overcame the world and broke its power for ever. We

[1] *Justification and Reconciliation*, 454 ff.

shall all concede that such a view contains an immense percentage of truth. Too often the majesty of Christ has been depicted in purely secular and unethical forms, more resembling the displays by which savage chieftains have sought to overawe the explorer than the holy and redeeming Love we are familiar with in the New Testament. No conception, assuredly, can be right which does not start from and revolve round the ethical forces through which Jesus overcame evil with good. But is this the whole truth?

Not, it appears, if we read the utterances of the believing consciousness in a plain natural sense. When faith calls Jesus *Lord,* simply and without qualification, it certainly implies not only that He overcame the world by invincible goodness but that all power is His in heaven and earth. He is omnipotent with the omnipotence of God; to Him belongs absolute might to continue and consummate the work begun by His life, death, and victory. Short of this the Christian mind is not expressed. When we analyse this conviction, moreover, making explicit its unconscious logic, we discover its latent reasoning to run in something of this form: Not only is Christ all-good, but there is a mode of being which answers to perfect goodness and brings it completely to effectual manifestation. Or, to put it otherwise, unity with God means for Jesus a real participation in that transcendent power to make the good prevail which constitutes deity in (so to speak) its external aspect.

Yet though the interpretation set forth by Ritschl may be thus deficient, as a transcript of full Christian faith, he insists on the much-needed lesson that our relationship to Christ, though immediate, is not unmediated. In this there is no inconsistency. I have immediate communion with my friend; yet all I know of him—all our bygone talk, meetings, mutual service—are present in that communion to make it what it is: its present is mediated through its past. So too the relation of the Christian to Christ because personal is direct; none the less, however, is it dependent on the facts of history. Save on the basis of His recorded life, fellowship with Him is meaningless. Nothing else will keep the Christian religion true to type. But this is not the equivalent of saying that in this fellowship we must at every point go round consciously by the historic Jesus. Certainly we do not make this *détour* by the past in our intercourse with friends. Resort to memory in this deliberate and habitual fashion would be evidence that genuine intimacy did not as yet exist.

Faith in the glorified Lord who is also present admittedly forms a vital factor in New Testament religion. It is, besides, the great evangelical reality which Roman theology has perverted into the Bodily Presence of Christ in the transubstantiated elements of the Eucharist. That doctrine we cannot pause to examine now. It is an attempt to translate into material and therefore misleading terms a fact which is intensely and objectively spiritual. Nevertheless it is a positive doctrine; it answers to a real craving; and it is certain that it can never be displaced by mere negations. In the Christian mind there exists an imperious longing for actual union with the Redeemer, for immediate fellowship with One who forgives sin and aids the struggling soul in its passionate pursuit of holiness. And the real strength of the theory of Transubstantiation and the Bodily Presence, it has been said truly, "lies in the impression of multitudes of men, that if they surrender their faith in the awful mystery of the Eucharist, Christ will seem no longer near to them. If He is not present in a supernatural way upon the altar, they think that they must lose Him altogether; and they are accustomed to speak about our own service as a mere 'commemoration of an absent Lord.'"[1] If we are to meet the exigencies of the soul in an age when the exclusive claims of Rome are felt as more than ever alluring by minds which historic criticism has perturbed, it is not enough to proclaim the greatness of a long-departed Hero. The world requires a living Person, in whose present grace sinners may find rest.

[1] Dale, *Essays and Addresses*, 24.

It need scarcely be added that many aspects of the doctrine under review must always remain in shadow. The conditions of the world invisible lie beyond our ken, embracing numerous subtle and elusive problems which it is vain to treat of. How Christ can be a person, yet ubiquitous; where His throne is situated; what are the nature and qualities of His ascended body—in regard to such matters a certain type of mind (like most children) is often curious. But why should we pretend to know where all is unknowable? To such inquiries we must answer that the longing for personal knowledge of Christ the Lord is satisfied not by apocalyptic vision or the pathetic efforts of mistimed logic, but from the Gospel story of His words and deeds. "The secret things belong unto the Lord our God; but the things that are revealed belong unto us and to our children for ever."[1] Christ, as depicted by apostolic men, is present with us still, present to save to the uttermost; His person, thus qualified and conditioned, is the great object held forth in the Gospel; and what is requisite for its apprehension is in no sense a vivid historical imagination, still less the trained faculty of dialectic, but a sincere, lowly, and obedient trust.

[1] Dt 29[29].

CHAPTER VI.

THE PERFECT MANHOOD OF CHRIST.

In our analysis of the believing consciousness we now come upon the clear and uncontested fact that, when faith looks at Jesus Christ, whose present glory is continuous with His earthly life, it discerns in Him uniquely perfect manhood. Jesus is the Man *par excellence.* In this treatise, however, we are concerned with His manhood less as apologists than as students of His person. Or, to put it otherwise, we wish not so much to prove it as to elicit those features in virtue of which it can be described as solitary and incomparable, and, in addition, as vitally significant for redemption.

The New Testament no more attempts to demonstrate the manhood of Jesus than the Old Testament to prove the being of God. To the apostles Jesus is human throughout in temperament, emotion, and attitude. It might therefore have been supposed that whatever the mysteries of His person, at all events the truth of His humanity was too plain ever to be in doubt. But history undeceives us. Docetism, rife in many quarters even now, was the first Christological heresy. Even in the apostolic age its influence may be detected. In the First Epistle of John the Docetæ seem to be alluded to indirectly, and the writer in a strongly controversial passage takes occasion to

Literature—J. R. Seeley, *Ecce Homo,* 1865; Sanday, *Outlines of the Life of Christ*[2], 1906; von Soden, *Die wichtigsten Fragen im Leben Jesu,* 1904; Ullmann, *Sinlessness of Jesus,* 1858; Bousset, *Jesus,* 1906; Mason, *The Conditions of our Lord's Life on Earth,* 1896; Fairbairn, *Studies in the Life of Christ,* 1880; Glover, *The Jesus of History,* 1917; Illingworth, *Personality, Human and Divine,* 1894; Du Bose, *The Gospel in the Gospels,* 1906; Drummond, *Studies in Christian Doctrine,* 1908.

reassert the truth of a veritable and indissoluble incarnation, as contrasted with the phantasmal theory of a Divine Christ walking the earth as a protracted but none the less unsubstantial theophany.[1] Thus, while one of the first disciples still lived, professing Christians were known to whom it appeared incredible that Christ had been man, and who held explicitly that His body was mere semblance. Similarly it was a tenet of second-century Gnosticism that our Lord had no real share in the material side of human life. It was said that He took on a different guise to different onlookers, and at different times. And in later ages it is common to find Jesus' identity with us in manhood either denied or in various ways curtailed, under the erroneous impression that a deeper reverence is thereby paid to His higher being. Thus a persistent tendency is observable, even in common speech, to describe His manhood in non-personal terms: it is a body, a temple, metal fused with fire, a bush in which dwells the flame of deity without consuming it.

It is not, of course, for us to censure these errors harshly, at least in their more primitive manifestations. In antiquity the belief prevailed widely that the body is itself evil, radically and incurably; not the seat or *nidus* of sin merely, but its producing cause. Men who carried this notion into the Church may well have found it hard to concur in the assertion that Jesus' body was essentially identical with ours. Again, if some questioned the reality of His body, surmising that men saw and touched Him as one may a figure in a dream,[2] others, for whom His body was quite real, were unable to believe that God incarnate possessed a completely human soul. In such a case it is doubtless open to us to say that they were dimly feeling after the idea of Christ mystical—of a personal redeeming

[1] 5^{6-8}; cf. 2^{21-23} 4^{1-3} 4^{15}. It is a remark of Professor Burkitt's that "the Gospels we have would never have become the official charters of the Church but for the theological necessity of insisting upon the true human nature of our Lord" (*Gospel History and its Transmission*, 263).

[2] This may have sprung from the narrative of Jesus' walking on the sea.

Life, that is, which is unconfined within the bounds of separate or particular individuality but rather pervades unnumbered souls with its own vitality and power. However that may be, the Church has uniformly rejected an outspoken Docetism; this we may say unreservedly in spite of the fact that arguments of an unconsciously docetic order have frequently been employed in the long debate, ancient or modern, as to the limitations of our Lord's knowledge, or the possibility in His case of painful, acute temptation. Christians have always felt that to regard the Jesus of the Gospels as no more than an abstract phantom is to take all meaning out of salvation. To the pure Docetist, the Saviour has no history.

We cannot indeed overestimate the importance of the fact that Jesus' redeeming influence on the world—all that has induced men to call Him Lord and Saviour—owes to His humanity at once its individual and its social power, and is complete only with the completeness of His manhood. It is as man that He takes His place in the historic context. Of course the influence of Jesus is more than historical; it is also what may be called super-historical, or, in one aspect, timeless and eternal. But yet this very quality of timelessness, whereby He becomes the contemporary of all ages, and touches sinful hearts in every land, conveying to faith the life of God, is something which only secured its foothold in the world through its actualisation as a real element in the time-series, a perfect earthly medium of grace. Had Jesus' manhood been fictitious or abridged, no fully saving power could pass forth from Him to win mankind, and God were still far away.

As our initial datum we may select the truth that Jesus, as man, was possessed of personal individuality. He was not only Man, He was *a* man. This might seem to be obviously implied in the facts of the Gospel narrative. It is not too much to say that no reader of the four evangelists could conceivably arrive at any other impression than that the central Figure was veritably a man—

not merely a man, indeed, but a Jew of the first century —unless a contrary view had been put into his mind from outside. Nevertheless, as we know, traditional orthodoxy came to a different finding. Slowly and by faint degrees, it is true; as late as Origen and Tertullian [1] it was openly taught by Church teachers that Jesus was a man; even the *homo* in Leo's Epistle to Flavian, if taken seriously, witnesses clearly enough to an individual humanity. But at least by the time of Cyril of Alexandria the sense of this individuality had become more dim in the Eastern Church; and we are not wrong, perhaps, in regarding a marked drift in the contrary direction as one of Apollinaris' least desirable legacies. The adjective ἐνυπόστατος was expressly coined by Leontius of Byzantium to convey the idea of a human nature which, not being personal independently or in itself, yet found its personality in the Divine Logos. But as time passed the more cautious distinctions of Leontius were in part forgotten, in part rejected; and later thought in both East and West betrayed a much closer affinity with the more uncompromising *anhypostasia* than with the *enhypostasia* which had been put forward by Leontius.[2] The point of view we may gather from Alcuin's well-known phrase: *accessit humanitas in unitatem personae filii dei.* Hence the unfortunate usage, still common in text-books, which definitely predicates of Christ "an impersonal humanity," a phrase on which, after using it, Dean Strong makes the justly severe comment that "it suggests a kind of abstract idea of man lying untenanted, and adopted by a Divine Person, and it is obvious that it opens the door to scholasticism of an unduly technical sort."[3] We are rightly told that the truth against which the phrase is designed to safeguard is this, that the humanity of our

[1] Cf. Athanasius, *de Inc.* c. 43.

[2] But in Catholic theology the impersonality of Christ's manhood is often ignored where the argument will not bear it: *e.g.* in the discussion of His atoning obedience. There is a real sense, in other words, in which Christ had to act for Himself before He could act for others.

[3] *Manual of Theology* (2nd edit.), 130.

Lord had no *independent* personality; in other words, it was intentionally framed as a bulwark against the recurrent menace of Nestorianism. And so far, doubtless, it has a certain historic title to be received. It is another question whether the position it marks is one in which the Christian mind can rest.

Be this as it may, this conception of a humanity which is not that of an individual man is notoriously still held by able writers. Thus, to take a recent example, Dr. Du Bose argues strongly in favour of the Virgin Birth that "the product of every natural union is an individual person," and that "in the light of all that Jesus Christ is to the Church and to humanity, His universality, sufficiency, and ubiquity," it is impossible to believe that He is only a human individual.[1] In a later work he grapples with the question still more directly, introducing an objector who states the counter-position not only with great impartiality, but, as I conceive, with unanswerable force. "One says: You lay great stress upon the view that our Lord was not a man, but man. I find this a difficult conception; does it mean that humanity has a concrete real existence apart from the individual persons who are human, and that this Universal becomes visible in Christ? If this be so, does it not lead us to a metaphysical realism, not now generally held?" To this Dr. Du Bose's answer, based on the right assumption that faith needs a Christ who is universal, is that "the universality of our Lord's humanity is only explicable upon the fact that His personality is a Divine one. . . . The concrete universal of humanity which may be found in Jesus Christ belongs to it not as humanity but as God in humanity. It is God in it which makes that particular humanity of our Lord, His holiness, His righteousness, His life, valid and available for all; so that every man may find himself in Christ and in Christ find himself."[2] The

[1] *Gospel in the Gospels*, 212.

[2] *Gospel according to St. Paul*, 297 (quoted by Sanday, *Life of Christ in Recent Research*, 310).

same position is apparently taken by Dr. Moberly, who writes: "If Christ might have been, yet He certainly was not, a man only, amongst men. His relation to the human race is not that He was another specimen, differing, by being another, from every one except Himself. His relation to the race was not a differentiating but a consummating relation. He was not generically, but inclusively, man." And his statement closes on the same note as Dr. Du Bose by affirming that the relation of Jesus Christ to mankind is "a Spiritual property, so sovereign, so transcendent, that it could only be a property of a Humanity which was not merely the Humanity of a finite creature, but the Humanity of the infinite God."[1] These instances sufficiently prove the deep conviction with which the idea has been set forth quite recently. The gist of the conception may perhaps be put briefly somewhat as follows: Because Christ as man is of universal and organic significance for mankind, it is not possible that He should be individual.

If, however, we take the problem into the light of the Gospel story, it is difficult to avoid stating what seems truth in terms precisely the reverse of this: Because Christ is universal and central, He is *also* an individual. It is His *differentia*, in short, to be the central individual. Let it be noted, however, that to regard Christ as an individual is in no sense equivalent to the position that He is "only one of the sons of men peculiarly favoured and most highly endowed." Too often the argument is vitiated by this assumption. The writers I have named constantly suppose that we must choose between saying that Christ was not a man, but humanity inclusive, and dismissing Him as but one more good man, a simple member of the race, to whom we are related exactly as one unit is to his neighbour. The alternative is quite unreal. To call Christ an individual is but another way of putting the fact that He can be distinguished clearly as man from (say) Peter or Thomas. And the special

[1] *Atonement and Personality*, 86, 89.

philosophy of His uniqueness which denies that He was *a* man is surely at war with this fact.

The truth is that the scholastic conception of the universal *humanitas* as itself real and concrete no longer satisfies the mind. In the domain of reality there is no such thing existing independently as *humanitas*, or "man in general." To say so leaves the validity of knowledge untouched, since no one can think of or mentally represent a "man in general." No one can represent a man who also *is* the nature common to all members of the class "man." Of course it is true that particular existences do in fact share a common character. Nor is this common character a figment of the mind; rather it explains why different individuals, even though different, have the same name. It indicates the common possession by such individuals of certain attributes or qualities. This, however, while no less truly an aspect or function of reality than the concrete instances in which it is exemplified, is *per se* a pure abstraction, which has not and cannot have existence independently or by itself. The real human universe, then, is made up of individual men possessing common properties or a common character. In any other light *humanitas* is a purely enigmatical entity. Applied to our question, this means that while mankind is in a true sense one, and is qualified by solidarity, while also God has mediated redemption through this oneness, we are not therefore justified in saying that Christ *is* this oneness, this solidarity incarnate. Rather it is in virtue of such oneness, such bonds of mutual involution between life and life, that we believe Jesus Christ, a real individual, to be able to exert universal saving power. The individual, in short, is not the contrary of the universal; in varied degree he is the universal in concrete form. Hence, without ceasing to be individual, Christ may be the universal, focal member of our organic race. No incongruity obtains as between these two things. On the contrary, it is matter of common knowledge that the greater a man is—the more numerous the points at which he has contact with, and affects, the human environment—the more self-possessed and concrete his individuality. We can only think of the Lord Jesus Christ as the ideal limit of this conjunction, linked to all men in His Divine outflowing love, yet always master of His self-conditioned life. As Bishop D'Arcy has expressed it: "The personality of our Lord is the most distinct and concrete of which we have any knowledge. . . . To confuse the boundaries which give the Ego its distinctness, for the sake of making an abstract doctrine appear more intelligible, is surely a dangerous error. Our Lord was very man, and His Ego had all the self-possession and self-consciousness which give to every human soul its personal distinctness."[1]

I should therefore incline to say that what mainly invites criticism in Dr. Du Bose's able statement is his view of the individual. That cannot be defined simply as the opposite of the universal.[2] We may accept without reserve his remark that "it is God in it which makes that particular humanity of our Lord, His holiness, His righteousness, His life, valid and available for all," merely pointing out that by thus using the words "that particular humanity of our Lord" he grants all we ask. After all, it appears Christ's humanity *is* particular or—the better word—individual; yet it is also universal. On the facts, then, there is no dispute; what leads to divergence of opinion is an old but outworn philosophic conception of the universal. If we are not to trust our intuitive perception that the Christ we read of in the Gospels is an individual man, it is hard to say what perception could be trusted.[3] As we follow His life, we become infinitely more sure of His human individuality than we can ever be of the fallible human logic which denies it.

[1] Hastings' *DCG.* ii. art. "Trinity."

[2] Cf. A. D. Lindsay, *Philosophy of Bergson*, 189.

[3] Dr. Mason points out that more than once in the New Testament Christ is called not ἄνθρωπος merely, but ἀνήρ, and that ἀνήρ carries the sense of distinct individuality (*Conditions of our Lord's Life on Earth*, 46–47).

Turning now to a new aspect, let us inquire whether we can impart a more than logical sense to the universality just affirmed. Can we fill it out with an ethical and spiritual significance which reveals it as human, concrete, intelligible? In part we may, I think. We rightly signalise, for example, the wondrous combination in Christ of qualities which tend in other men to be only opposed angularities, but which by their perfect harmony in Jesus fit Him to be Saviour alike of the single life and of society. Thus He was stern with an awful gravity that shook the heart, made undreamt-of claims, and shrank from no menace of judgment or unrelenting exposure of evil; yet He has given to men a new conception of love, and lives on in their souls by the memory of a tireless pity that received sinners, wept over their blindness, and at last bore death itself in a passion to redeem. Between the two—the indignation and the tenderness—there is no random vacillation, no capricious change; each rather is the support, content, and basis of the other. He lives above the power of earthly things, yet with no disdain. Never was ascetic less the captive of mere pleasure, yet life is holy for Him in all its elements; if He has not where to lay His head, He can still be partaker in the innocent joy of a wedding-feast. He ate and drank as a man with men, He bade them pray for daily bread, He set forth the uncareful happiness of children as model; yet when He calls they must leave home and goods and honour all behind, as having no value in competition with the Kingdom and its righteousness. There joined in Him the loftiest consciousness of self and the lowliest humility. He was more than Solomon or the Temple—He was the Lord of His disciples, and the very Son of God; yet He is baptized at the hands of John, He comes not to be ministered unto but to minister, He puts aside the glory men can give. In His piety the two strands of fervid ecstasy and quiet faith are so intertwined that it is hard if not impossible to tell which predominates. In His relations to others we see Him now as disposed to private friendships, now as caring for the multitude, now as the Solitary; yet always and in every case Himself. Thus, as von Soden has expressed it, "in the nature of Jesus there was no lack of contrasts. But they are always resolved in the wonderful completeness and harmony of His being. The opposites are always in equilibrium. Therefore His personality, many-sided as it is, is not complicated. In the last resort they are not indeed so many independent qualities; but, strictly speaking, under the action of His human nature and its surroundings, they are just so many prismatic rays in the diamond of His soul."[1] Now this incomparable diversity of interests or qualities, all fused obediently in a character single and distinct, like a flavour or a fragrance, is part of what we mean by the universality of Jesus' manhood. The true attributes of humanity meet in Him, yet they meet in an individual life which thus reaches out to every member of the race, and forms its proper centre and rallying-point. In virtue of this ethical universality, Jesus is more real, sure, and near to men of every time than friend to friend. Christian missions are the proof. Though set within a specific race and age, He is none the less in the plenitude of His manhood the Man of every age, the Elder Brother of us all.

This becomes still clearer when we survey the life-work He accomplished. Here also is seen a perfect harmony of the individual and the universal. For on the one hand, the vocation given Him by the Father is sharply limited and defined. The religious life is incumbent on all men; but what we cannot fail to note is that for Jesus it became a strictly exclusive and all-absorbing task. This has occasionally been slurred over in vague eulogies to the effect that He was complete, ideal man, and under cover of this general description He is represented as in possession of all the human talents. "As a philosopher," says one writer, "He would have surpassed Socrates, as an orator have eclipsed Demosthenes."

[1] *Die wichtigsten Fragen im Leben Jesu*, 88 (quoted by Sanday).

If this means that in philosophy Jesus' gifts were superior to those of Socrates, in oratory to those of Demosthenes—for consistency we are bound to add, in mathematics to Newton, in painting to Velasquez—the statement, so far as evidence is concerned, must be repelled as baseless. In the fields of science or art Jesus was not supreme, for there God has chosen to cast mankind upon their own exertions; and it is surely clear that, by engaging in any of these specialised lines of service, He would have forfeited just so much universality. For religion, concerned as it is with man's relation to God, is the most manifold and comprehensive of all interests, in contrast to which others are provincial; it was not possible therefore that Jesus should confine Himself within more special bounds except at the cost of becoming one of a class, and thus failing in centrality. His life-work was unique, not in the sense of being narrowly engrossed in a single sphere, like that of the merchant, the politician, or the divine; but in the sense that it bore on that which is deepest in all men. *Non multa sed multum* was the signature of His career; to put more into His life-programme would in fact have been to put infinitely less. As He laboured solely within the house of Israel, in order thereby to lay the corner-stone of the Church universal and catholic, so, with equal reason, He confined His life-work to the task of Mediatorship that He might fulfil God's purpose for all mankind.[1]

Yet in this life, limited to the central and the absolute, His own consciousness found no omission, no unfinished page. Of the dim regrets which torture even the best men, as they question half-sadly at the end whether all has been done that might be done, there is no trace. Jesus' life is a unity, woven without seam from

[1] The late T. H. Green has well expressed this: "It is because Jesus, under limiting conditions, lived a life which is limited to no conditions, and under special circumstances proclaimed a principle which is applicable to all circumstances, that His life and His principle are rightly called absolute" (*Works*, iii. p. xxxix).

the top to the bottom. Even in Gethsemane, His momentary doubt is not whether He must obey the Father; rather it is an implicit question as to the Father's will, an inquiry whether the cup now at His lips has been placed there with the full intent that He shall drink it. Thus at the last it is on a noticeably specific note that His mind rests: "I have finished the work that Thou gavest me to do." No vague or general vocation had been appointed Him, nor yet one so circumscribed as to fence Him off from all but a certain defined class; but the distinct, fundamentally universal task of establishing the Kingdom and reconciling man to God.

As we have seen, it is supremely in the resurrection that the universality of Jesus is illustrated and revealed. As the climax of a human life, resurrection is wholly exceptional; and He of whom it is predicable is thereby determined as both unprecedented and inimitable. True, His victory over death is prophetic of ours in Him, yet all His uniqueness is still guaranteed by His mediation to us of the last triumph. Through His rising from the dead, the universality of life, of appeal, of redeeming power which had from the first belonged to Him *de jure*, took on *de facto* the mode of being which answers to its real character. It rose above the bounds of space and time. If till that crisis it had been exerted only in special instances, though world-wide in essential import, it at last became available and effective for the whole world. If till then He had been hedged in by physical restraints —distant from Bethany when Lazarus His friend fell asleep, so that it could be said, "Lord, if Thou hadst been here"—henceforward He was known and felt, everywhere and always, as an unseen Presence. Thus the Jesus of history passed into the Christ of experience, not in virtue of any mere change in the imagination of His followers, but by the objective universalisation of His power.

This individual yet universal life, again, is marked in the fullest sense by reality and integrity. It is no mutilated manhood we see in Christ. A proof that this has been intuitively recognised is the fact that countless believers have confessed to a deep sense of Christ's perfect sympathy with their need and pain and joy. Not only so; they have been conscious of a deep sympathy with Him. As we contemplate His life, its action and passion, the aspirations which move it and the sinless infirmity by which it is encompassed; as we listen to His voice, or look upon His deeds of power and mercy, nothing in it all is alien to our mind. It takes form and shape in a medium with which we are familiar. And we can say, not of their quality, which is untainted, but of their nature, "These are our acts, our thoughts, our feelings; they are the very emotions and impulses of soul by which we too are agitated. He speaks our tongue, He endures our pain, our anguish and distress He bears with us, and as we bear it. Bone of our bone and flesh of our flesh, nothing in human nature escapes Him who names Himself Son of Man, nothing in life and nothing in death: He is our Brother even to the end."[1]

We may illustrate the integrity of Christ's manhood, then; what we cannot do is to prove it by logic. It is impossible to strengthen by demonstration what is self-evident from the first. To all who read the Gospels with an open mind it is plain that Jesus was completely man. Were it conceivable indeed that we were forced to choose —as we are not—between the conviction that Jesus possessed true manhood in all its parts, and the assurance that He was the Son of God come in flesh for our salvation, our plain duty would be to affirm His humanity and renounce His deity. Doubtless in point of fact both things are sure to faith; but none the less it is from the primary and fundamental certitude of His unity with us in manhood that we rise up to the truth of His higher nature. He is at all events complete man, whatever more.

Let us briefly exemplify this by the various aspects or elements of human life — corporeal, moral, social,

[1] Gaston Frommel, *Études morales et religieuses*, 59 f.

emotional, intellectual, religious. Everywhere the integrity of Jesus' life as man is clear. His body was flesh and blood like ours. Its capacity of pain, of privation, of fatigue; its tears and agony and cries; its shrinking from the hour of death; its sensitiveness to the contact of other men; its susceptibility to the influence of nature, felt in the thrill of gladness begotten by the sunlight and the flowers—all this is authentically human. Always the body of Jesus, through its vital and mobile relations to the world, served and nourished the growth of His self-consciousness. His moral experience too was human. Duty was to Him a vast, solemn fact, presenting itself uniformly as the Father's will; as we read on we can discern that even for this "Son" there was assigned a piece-by-piece discovery of the right way, a gradual acceptance of unforeseen responsibilities disclosed by the progress of life. He must choose out His own path, develop His purpose, do justice to His own nature. His career was no irresponsible adventure. Each step had moral value, and called for insight, courage, fidelity, patience. Once more, His emotional life reveals the shifting play of joy and pain and wonder. The story of His soul is no surface uniformly blank and regular, but a varied landscape, a country with an atmosphere. The light and shade of feeling move across it—love, anger, grief, compassion; to all He is humanly sensitive, not staying coldly on the outmost rim of the capacity of emotion but entering it with a natural immediacy; yet never seeking joy or sorrow for its own sake only or permitting it to overmaster the focus of consciousness. How He is altogether one with His brethren in that piercing question, "Could ye not watch with Me one hour?" or in the tears at Lazarus' grave preceded by that strange brief gust of "indignation," in which, as it would seem, His spirit revolted against the miseries of the world and the broken hearts of those that loved Him.[1] That dying care for His mother; that peculiar affection for one disciple; that look cast on the

[1] Jn 11[33].

young ruler, or on the follower who a moment earlier had forsworn Him: such traits of nature appear with simple and vivid power, and they come not as exterior and official evidences of a humanity which needs attestation but as the spontaneous outflow of a human life that can be nothing but itself.

Time was when debate gathered keenly round the intellectual experience of Jesus. It was felt to be perilous and revolutionary to hold that the normal limitations of knowledge in His age and country must in some true sense be predicated of Himself. The difficulty was rendered none the less acute by the fact that the Gospels quite plainly ascribe to Jesus a certain range of supernormal discernment both of human thought and of future events. Still, preternatural knowledge, such as may be more or less paralleled from the life of Isaiah, Jeremiah, or St. Paul, cannot be regarded as the equivalent of omniscience; and omniscience is, after all, the only possible alternative to a knowledge qualified by limitation. The question can be decided solely by loyalty to facts; and these, it is not too much to say, are peremptory. Not only is it related that Jesus asked questions to elicit information—regarding the site of Lazarus' tomb, for example, or the number of the loaves, or the name of the demented Gadarene—but at one point there is a clear acknowledgment of ignorance. "Of that day or that hour," He said, respecting the Parousia, "knoweth no man, not even the angels in heaven, neither the Son, but the Father."[1] If He could thus be ignorant of a detail connected in some measure with His redemptive work, the conclusion is unavoidable that in secular affairs His knowledge was but the knowledge of His time. It was possible for Him to feel surprise. The subject is one, however, on which controversy is over now. Conservative writers freely admit the obvious significance of the narrated facts. "That our Lord's knowledge," Dr. Dykes has said, "advanced from infantile ignorance, and

[1] Mk 13[32].

advanced as that of other men does by the ordinary methods by which men gain information; that what He thus came to know could not be at all times equally present to His mind and was wholly absent from His mind in the unconscious intervals of slumber;—this simply follows from His possession of a human mind at all. It is human to know in part, to retain much in memory which is not present to thought, and at each moment of consciousness to attend only to a very limited sum of impressions and ideas."[1] In a recent work, Dr. Sanday has devoted to the same topic a few pages of the highest value. "We may venture," he writes, "to picture to ourselves the working of our Lord's consciousness in some such way as this. His life on earth presented all the outward appearance of the life of any other contemporary Galilean. His bodily organism discharged the same ordinary functions and ministered to the life of the soul in the same ordinary ways. He had the same sensations of pleasure and pain, of distress and ease, of craving and satisfaction. Impressions received through the senses and emotions awakened by them were recollected and stored up for use by the same wonderful processes by which any one of us becomes the living receptacle of personal experiences. His mind played over all these accumulated memories, sifting, digesting, analysing, extracting, combining, and recombining. Out of such constituent elements, physical, rational, moral, and spiritual, character was formed in Him as in any one of ourselves, though with unwonted care and attention. Not that we need suppose that the actual process of character-forming was more self-conscious with Him than it is with us. The forming of character is the unconscious automatic effect of particular decisions of judgment and acts of will. Conscience discriminates between right and wrong; in His case it invariably chose the right and eschewed the wrong. But out of the midst of all these moral decisions and actions, out of the

[1] *Expos. Times*, Jan. 1906, 152–53.

interplay of social relations, under the guidance of observation and reflection, there gradually grew up a sense of deliberate purpose, a consciousness of mission."[1]

Attention has recently been drawn, in a special manner, to the perfectly human quality of our Lord's religious life. The vivid simplicity of New Testament representations has been felt anew, and, like the writer to the Hebrews, men have dwelt on the piety of Jesus. For long it had been half-forgotten how this colours His whole experience. Take His most absorbing affection, from which all others drew their strength and purity—His love for the Father. It is easy to read the Gospels over and over again and yet miss the greatness of this love as a simple consciousness, an atmosphere in which all action is done and all feeling felt, the perpetual bright flower of the absolute unity of will between the Father and the Son. Or take His habit of prayer and faith, of asking and receiving. No Christology is true which makes a Christ for whom prayer is either unnatural or impossible.[2] It is striking that the Fourth Gospel, which dwells with such steady emphasis on His higher being, should exhibit Him even more constantly than the Synoptics in the posture and mood of prayer. He needs God, even though sharer of His life. In Hebrews, too, there are daring words as to the awful struggle in Gethsemane, and the "strong crying and tears unto Him that was able to save Him from death." This is in no sense incongruous with the power that dwelt in Him; for prayer is the one source of power. He is so great amongst men because of that secret communion. Apart from God, He has no thoughts, no desires, no will. Along with this is combined a faith and receptivity which is not that of a frail sinner, but of a sinless Son. The recurrence of the sweet and deep name Father unveils the secret of His being. His

[1] *Christologies Ancient and Modern*, 179 ff.

[2] In his *Von der Gottheit Christi*, 41 ff., Thieme argues at length that Jesus' habit of prayer compels us to reject His *essential* unity with God and assert rather a *representative* unity.

heart is at rest in God. There is a trust born of communion with the Father which in the narrative is not so much heard as overheard—a confidence so deep-set and immovable that even when in the last hour it could find in the words of an ancient Psalmist the truest symbol and expression of inward darkness, it yet clung passionately to the unseen God and Father. Here also the Fourth Gospel is richest in memories. It is our most faithful record of this filial dependence. "The Son can do nothing of Himself, but what He seeth the Father doing"; "He that hath sent Me is with Me, He hath not left Me alone"; "the Father abiding in Me doeth His works"[1]—these are typical words out of many, and through them, as through a transparent medium, we perceive that the focus of His life and consciousness was not in Himself merely, but in His unity with God. Only so could He make the Father known. Revelation, if it be more than a theoretic verbal declaration, must come through an absolute reflection of the Father caught by and flung out from a perfect human soul, in whose depths men should read and love it.

The manhood of Jesus, then, is a manhood essentially one with ours. His life is a distinctively human phenomenon, moving always within the lines of an authentically human mind and will, and constituting thus a revelation of God in humanity, "not partly in it and partly out of it." Yet it is just when this has been made clear that we adequately realise the wholly exceptional quality of this human life. Jesus may be described as ideal or normal man; but these just epithets produce a totally wrong impression if we do not add immediately that manhood of this ideal type has existed but once in history.[2] He is unique in virtue of His sinlessness—the one quite unspotted life that has been

[1] Jn 5^{19} 8^{29} 14^{10}.

[2] A character at once perfectly ideal and completely human is not inconceivable, as has been maintained; but how difficult the conception is may be seen from the fact that it has never been represented with success in

lived within our sinful race. The deep and ineffaceable impression made by Jesus on those around Him cannot be dismissed as illusory. It is clear that His own consciousness of sin, had it existed, however faintly, must have affected His demeanour; that His followers must have observed the tokens of a bad conscience; and that such tokens, had they been present, must have profoundly modified their view of Jesus. No one doubts, then, that the disciples represented Jesus as without sin, and it is morally inconceivable that they should have held to this belief in defiance of better knowledge. Once the fact of His sinlessness has been apprehended, however, we can put forward strong antecedent grounds for accepting it. Only a sinless person can guarantee the Divine pardon of sin. If redemption is to be achieved, the Redeemer must stand free of moral evil. As the source of victorious spiritual energy He must Himself be in utter oneness with the will of God. The perfect moral health, the unstained conscience, to which He is slowly raising others, must be present absolutely in His own life. If He shed His blood for the remission of sins, it is because He is without spot or blemish. Like to His brethren in all else, He is unlike them here. Yet it is no paradox to say that such unlikeness makes His kinship perfect; for sin had made Him not more a man, but less. Sin dehumanises, and by its entrance the perfection of His vital sympathy would have been irrecoverably lost.

Just here is our problem. As the record proves, Jesus underwent repeated and acute temptation; tempted, we feel, He must have been, if we are right in counting on His sympathy in the struggle. Yet are the temptations of the sinless real? In such a nature, what door can open and let in the base allurement? How can evil find resonance where there is neither inherited bias to evil nor weakness due to previous transgression?

imaginative literature. Tennyson's Arthur and George Eliot's Daniel Deronda are the best-known modern failures. Of Jesus only can it be said, *Das Unzulängliche, hier wird's Ereigniss.*

Now we must distinguish clearly between temptation and sin. Temptation has become actual when the lower aim is felt as in collision with the higher; and if the lower aim be justifiable in its own time and place, as an appeal to inborn instinct, the felt shock of both within the moral consciousness is not yet sin. Not even the struggle that may ensue is sin. But sin is present when the decision for the higher fails, or comes too slowly. Now Jesus' nature, being integrally human, formed a medium through which the solicitation alike of higher and lower ends came knocking at His heart. It may well be that certain species of temptation—to forms of evil we name carnal—had virtually no existence for His mind. If it was so, His redeeming power over the slaves of sensuality is not thereby limited; for to the completeness of the Redeemer it is not essential that He should undergo each individual temptation by which men may be assailed. What is essential is that He should be "schooled" in temptation, should taste and see what it is to repel the approach of evil through a lowly trust in God. But however this may be, at least He was vulnerable in all His normal instincts, emotions, desires. The longing for triumph; the impulse to take the shortest path to power; a fear of death which is something almost wholly physical; a shrinking from close contact with sin—these natural, innocent tendencies and the like supplied very real opportunities of rebellion. They constituted what Moberly has called "the external capacity, and as it were machinery, for selfishness"; they meant a pressure on the will against which force must be exerted in steadfast resistance and with a real pain of conflict. Thus the Holy One learned obedience. For the holiness of Jesus was no automatic necessity of being. It was possessed only by being perpetually won anew, in a dependence of self-committal which had indeed no relation to a consciousness of sin, as with us, but which rested none the less on the felt need of an uninterrupted derivation of life and power from the Father. Precisely how this reality of tempted conflict can have occurred within a sinless mind is no doubt inscrutable. For us indeed it must be so; since the only psychological analogies we can use have their origin in our own sinful experience.[1]

It may be that we speak too much of Jesus' conflict, forgetting that His was a goodness altogether radiant, victorious, full of charm. Holiness in Him revealed that ease and mastery which belong to all perfection: "He did the most wonderful things as if nothing else were conceivable." Yet, on the other hand, while temptation never made appeal in Him to frailty resulting from previous sin, He was not therefore absolved from painful effort. Sinless temptations may be the most severe. The acquired appetite of the drunkard may be resisted with benefit to himself; but the natural appetite of thirst, if persistently denied satisfaction, will prove fatal. Not only so; but the resistance of temptation may be torture to a good man, whereas a bad man yields easily. In the light of these things we can see that our Lord, sinless as He was, had no exemption from keen and cruel warfare. None was ever tempted so subtly, and triumph came through agony. Thus the great High Priest of men gained an inner view of the tempted life, and can be touched with a feeling of our infirmities.

No miracle of Christ equals the miracle of His sinless life. To be holy in all thought and feeling; never to fail in duty to others, never to transgress the law of perfect love to God or man, never to exceed or to come short—this is a condition outstripping the power of imagination and almost of belief. Here is a casement opening on a Diviner world.

But it is essential that we should not leave the sinlessness of Jesus as a bare, uninterpreted fact. Plainly it is in no sense self-explanatory. It asks for deeper elucidation and analysis. And reflection proves that the ground or reason of it must be sought in our Lord's unique

[1] Ultimately, it may be argued, the complete certainty that Jesus never sinned is given by our faith in His person; for there is no way of proving experimentally the impossibility of a fact.

relation to God. The moral transcendence of Jesus' life is unintelligible save as it originated in, and was nourished by, a vital and organic connection with the Father, who alone is holy with the holiness manifest in Jesus. It is vain to speak of Him simply as different from others in degree; the difference is one of type. When we ask why He uniformly triumphed over sin, whereas we fail, the answer, as we shall see, must lie in that element of His being in virtue of which He is one with God.[1] Or, to put it otherwise, by the side of yet suffused with those qualities in Christ which we are summoned to imitate and reproduce, and which reveal Him as the pattern of filial life, we discern a yet more august quality—inimitable, solitary, supreme. It is a new and lonely type of spiritual consciousness, an unshared relation of identity with the Father. Divinity is here the source and basis of perfect manhood.

And the bearing of all this on personal religion? Has faith a vital stake in the complete yet wholly exceptional humanity of Jesus Christ? Only a partial answer can be attempted now. The true manhood of Jesus is of cardinal significance in four ways.

(1) It guarantees a veritable incarnation. If the manhood of Christ is unreal, at any remotest point, God has not quite stooped to unity with man. He has not come so low as we require; there has been reservation and refusal; some part of our burden, after all, has been left untouched. "The unassumed is the unhealed." In that case, no matter from what height Christ came, He has not reached to *us*, but has stopped short. "The little less, and what worlds away!" But it has not been so. The centre of the catholic faith is that God in Christ came the whole way: "forasmuch as the children were sharers in flesh and blood, He also in like manner partook of the same." He drew near in person, that we might clasp Him as a kinsman in our arms, and feel the Infinite One to be our own. This has touched men most, breaking the world's

[1] Cf. *infra*, chap. vii.

hard heart. The measure of Jesus' humanity is the measure of God's love. As it has been put, "love is not in full possession until it can fully display itself"; and as Christ passed from depth to depth, entering one chamber after another of human experience, and submitting at length to death itself, He gave a proof of Divine love than which nothing greater can be conceived.[1] Any other reading of the Gospel, such as that of modern liberalism, offers a great view of God's love, but not the greatest we can imagine. *That* we find only in the Life truly incarnate. So that the reality of the manhood is cardinal. There was a day, not long past, when prophetic inspiration was thought of as submerging and all but obliterating the prophet's consciousness. Of him it might be said: the more a seer, the less a man. We have learnt that this is really unethical, and that on these lines no sort of justice can be done to moral personality. So there are ways of conceiving the advent of God in human life which frankly supersede the finitely personal, making human powers no more than selfless organs of Deity. But to redeem us God must not merely express Himself; He must express Himself in terms of an experience which is our own.

(2) It provides an essential basis of atonement. All true Christian ideas in regard to atonement may be viewed as aspects of Jesus' self-identification with the sinful. If then He who lived and died for men had Himself been man only in seeming, or in part, no expiation were after all made in our name; for only He can act with God for man who speaks from man's side. It is as Christ became our fellow, moving in a true manhood through obedience, conflict, and death, that He entered into our condition fully and availed in our behalf to receive from God's hand the suffering in which is expressed the Divine judgment upon sin. Jesus' manhood is the corner-stone of reconciliation.

(3) It secures the reality of a perfect example. Jesus is our pattern in faith and prayer; but it cannot be too clearly understood that no act can be exemplary which is

[1] Cf. Macgregor, *Jesus Christ the Son of God*, 204.

not first of all dutiful. The human Christ prayed, not in order that He might furnish a model to His disciples, but because to Him prayer was an inward need and duty. So profound and unmanning was His fear in Gethsemane that like the children of men He took refuge under God's shadow, and was heard for His reverent trust. In our temptations it is everything to know that He also was tempted. And here that *sinless* manhood, which has seemed at times to remove Him from us, and to make sympathy impossible, reveals itself as the nerve and spring of His redemptive power. It is not, one may surmise, to those who themselves once fell in drunkenness or lust that frail men and women instinctively look for aid and hope; it is rather to those who, although schooled in fellow-feeling by temptation, have kept their virtue pure. So Jesus' victory constitutes Him the source of victory for men; in Him, if we may put it so, Divine grace is humanised, and made available for sinners. Abstract ethical and religious truth may prove lacking in power to sustain the will; whereas it wins us as both vital and vitalising when embodied in a living form. In the Son of Man, the Word made flesh, perfect righteousness is put within the range of trust and love. The fruits of the Spirit are but the aspects of Jesus' character.

(4) It points to our eternal destiny. It is because Jesus the Man has risen from the grave and passed to a transcendent life with God that we too may triumph in prospect over death. As St. Paul has expressed it, with his most delicate precision in the use of our Lord's names, "if we believe that *Jesus* died and rose again, even so them also which sleep in Jesus shall God bring with Him." For the resurrection of Jesus, our human Surety and Comrade, is a test case; and as such it has fixed a principle, revealing as it does how the Father's love and power will deal with all believers. Thus once more the central significance of Christ's true humanity is manifest. On its integrity and perfect wholeness rest for us the unspeakable consolations of faith in a blessed immortality.

CHAPTER VII.

THE DIVINITY OF CHRIST.

In the foregoing chapters we have essayed to bring out in order the immediate certainties of the believing mind as it apprehends the person of Jesus. Three points have so far been ascertained. First, the distinctive attitude of believers to Jesus is that of faith. Secondly, in its most characteristic moments He is beheld as the Risen One, exalted and transcendent above all limits of space and time. Thirdly, He is recognised as perfect Man. In the last analysis each of these three points is vital—each involves and is involved in the others. In the present chapter our scrutiny of the intuitive affirmations of faith is completed, and we endeavour to signalise the truth that it spontaneously regards Christ as the personal manifestation of God in human form. Prior to all theories of the fact stands this spiritual assurance that He is Divine. It will appear that this is less a new additional result—though it may be stated with a new emphasis—than the one adequate method in which previous results can be formulated.

The question of Christ's divinity, as a doctrinal issue, may obviously be approached from more than one side. It may be approached, for example, by way of *à priori*

Literature—Réville, *History of the Dogma of the Deity of Jesus Christ*, 1878; Dale, *Christian Doctrine*, 1894; Herrmann, *Communion with God*, 1906; Gore, *Bampton Lectures*, 1891; *Contentio Veritatis*, 1907; Nitzsch, *Evangelische Dogmatik*², 1896; Kunze, *Die ewige Gottheit Jesu Christi*, 1904; Fairbairn, *Christ in Modern Theology*, 1893; Liddon, *Divinity of our Lord*, 1867; Dykes in *Expository Times*, Oct. 1905–Jan. 1906; Thieme, *Von der Gottheit Christi*, 1911.

postulate. Starting from the human need of redemption, the theologian may inquire how the Redeemer's person must be constituted in order to satisfy this need, arriving finally at the conclusion that since only God can redeem, Christ must be a God-man, in whom divinity and humanity are combined. Clearly, however, this severely logical procedure, of which the *Cur Deus Homo* of Anselm is the best-known instance, provides no independently real guarantee of truth. Like the ontological proof of God, it is a piece of purely conceptual argumentation, not indeed without utility as giving to our thought direction and expectancy, but incapable by itself of convincing modern minds. To fix our idea of Christ by logic, even if our point of departure be the infinite gravity of sin, must be described as an infidelity to the fundamental principle that Christology is always experimental, and that the relevant experience is kindled by the touch of fact. The real Christ is given in history, not constructed in the laboratory of consciousness.

The second method is the experiential. Not the need of redemption but the fact of redeemed souls is the datum. Taking a line laid down by Schleiermacher, the argument moves back from the influence of Jesus on men to the character of His person as influential cause. Of this Man who does a Divine work upon us—opening to the estranged a way into God's communion, making goodness an assured career—we have no option but to predicate personal Godhead. The Redeemer is as the redemption. We have already seen that as a mode of proceeding this is quite essential to a spiritual conception of Christ. By any other route we reach only historical information or statutory dogma. True faith in Jesus' higher nature is a personal confession. It is the result of our finding in Him "the presence and power of what declares itself to be not less than God Himself." Apart from this, there is no recognisable reality in the doctrine of His Godhead.

Yet we must not too hastily conclude that an experiential view is self-sufficient as it stands, with a cogency which requires no reference to the trans-subjective sphere of things. After all, the primal and creative source of belief concerning Jesus is recorded fact. Hence the question of His divinity has in recent times been approached chiefly from the side of His self-consciousness as unfolded in the Gospels. We are justified in assuming that in works and life and word Jesus veritably revealed His inmost being. No assertion of His loftier nature is tenable which is out of relation to His convictions about Himself; if to the end He remained personally unconscious of transcendent oneness with God, our affirmation of it will produce no impression. The final court of appeal, therefore, is Jesus' witness to Himself as echoed and apprehended by the believing mind. Faith is a response to His self-presentation. We are obliged to call Jesus what He called Himself and what the new life He inspires proves Him to have been.

As to the fact that Jesus constrains men to assert His Godhead—constrains them alike by His self-revelation and by His redeeming influence in their lives—no question is really possible. In believing Him to be God the Christian consciousness may be right or wrong, but that it does actually believe this is incontestable. It knows Him as supreme, transcendent, and only to be adored. No one will plead that a consideration of this sort covers or vindicates the countless subtle refinements of ecclesiastical Christology; none the less, however, it points with unwavering conviction to what is properly the heart and substance of Christological belief, the truth that Christ is God incarnate. To this the Church has expressly committed itself age after age. Not indeed that faith is always fully aware how much is involved in giving Christ, experimentally, the highest place. Even under strong pressure, men have frequently chosen to ignore the intellectual conclusions in which religious practice ought reasonably to terminate. Moral acceptance of Christ's divinity, combined with a refusal to acquiesce in its explicit affirmation, is no unfamiliar phenomenon. It may be due to philosophical agnosticism in part, or to a conception of God more ontological than ethical which on that account is felt to have no recognisable oneness or identity with the historic Jesus. Whatever the cause, at least it is certain that many sincere minds to-day are conscious of perplexity and reluctance when presented with credal statements that in very truth "God was in Christ." As a symbol or metaphor dimly shadowing the greatness of His redemptive powers they are eager to accept these words. But they are staggered by the doctrine, as a doctrine, that Christ is personally one with the Highest.

Nevertheless, if we may not rest in an eventual antinomy which holds religious and intellectual convictions apart for ever, it is incumbent on us to enunciate the right conclusion which follows from Jesus' felt power in life. What He is to us reveals what He is truly in Himself; and the revelation may and must be put in words. Our findings in earlier parts of the argument leave us no choice. Thus, it may be remembered, we were led to the conclusion that Christian Theology must embrace Christology as a vital and integral constituent; but Christology is only a reasoned account of how the Man Jesus has for us the value and reality of God. Christ is part of what believers mean by "Godhead"; and this fact, which merely as a fact is unquestioned, must be taken seriously in our doctrinal formulations. Again, the moral authority of Christ presents itself in the Christian conscience as invested with absolute supremacy, as infinite with the infinitude of God; also a fact which insists on doctrinal interpretation. It means that the voice of Jesus finds us at depths of our being accessible to God only. Again, we have an intuition of Divine suffering in the cross. Involuntarily we are made aware in presence of Christ's passion that it is God Himself who bears our sin and carries our sorrow; that the judgment upon evil uttered at Calvary is manifested through suffering veritably Divine, and that Christ shares the Divine life He thus pours out for sinners. Again,

Christ abides within His people, His life pervading theirs with a creative underived power; but this capacity to inhabit the inner man, kindling life by an originating impulse, is clearly something not predicable of a simply human personality. If He be the Giver of a Divine spiritual energy, how escape the assurance that He is Himself Divine? Or if He reveals the Father perfectly, must He not participate by right of nature in that which He reveals? Finally, we arrived at the clear position that specifically Christian faith in God the Father is linked indissociably to faith in Christ the Son. Without any duplication of the object grasped by faith—which would be polytheism—believers cast themselves down into the depths of Christ's compassion, and in Him find rest for their souls. Yet nothing can be more certain than that in this sense Christians can believe in God only.

How shall we describe this wondrous Person, in whom these attributes of power and supremacy are found, this Jesus who transmits a life no one else had transmitted to Him? He is highest in the highest realm we know; through Him, as first cause, our race has received the creative inflow of the Unseen pouring from fountains of the great deep. Which is the right predicate? How name the Presence that constitutes Him our Redeemer? Surely it is very God Himself. Nor in His case can we employ that supreme term seriously except as we employ it in its loftiest meaning; conscience will be put off with nothing less, for conscience is monotheistic through and through. "The supreme thing," it has been said, "is for Christ to be really God to the affections, the conscience, and the will. He whom I obey as the supreme authority over my life, He whom I trust for the pardon of my sins, He to whom I look for the power to live righteously, . . . He, by whatever name I may call Him, is my God. If I attribute the *name* to another, I attribute to Christ the reality for which the name stands: and unless, for me, Christ is one with the Eternal, He is really above the Eternal—has Diviner prerogatives and achieves Diviner works."[1] We cannot debar Him from the highest place. The hypothesis that while more than man He is less than God, has lost all interest for the human mind. That issue was fought to a finish, and will not be reopened; all agree that with the victory of Arius the Church would have sunk into polydemonistic heathenism. Faith knows its Lord as Divine equally in value and fact—not a higher angelic visitant, not a man sainted or deified, but a historic incarnation of the only God there is.

So far we have searched for the exact descriptive term apposite to One who does for us a specific service and sustains towards us a specific relation. By simple transcript of experience we predicate of Christ true deity. Nothing more high is possible, nothing lower is veracious. But this immediate utterance of faith is found on examination to harmonise with the only admissible interpretation of certain notable features of our Lord's human experience. That unique manhood asks to be explained in the sense that we are bound to seek for its dynamic ground and sufficient reason. To stand before the fact of Christ dumb and uninquiring is impossible. Nor is it enough to pronounce Him only an exception to the normal course of things, a variation, a mysterious and inscrutable Solitary who is dispensed unaccountably from our conditions. This is to restate the problem, not solve it.

I would single out three distinct aspects of Christ's unique humanity which are intelligible only if construed as based upon and vitally conditioned by His true Godhead. These are His sinlessness, His special Sonship, and His transcendent risen life.

(*a*) Jesus' complete freedom from sin is obviously more than a moral accident without parallel before or since. In the supreme point of view—that of the Divine purpose to save men—His complete victory over sin is not something merely which happened; it is something which was bound to happen. Faith cannot acquiesce in the

[1] Dale, *Christian Doctrine*, 313.

thought that conceivably the Divine redeeming plan might have been frustrated; yet frustration would have been had Jesus yielded to temptation even once. On the other hand, the realisation of a plan which is Divine is necessarily due to God; to God's presence in Christ, accordingly, we must ascribe the stainlessness of His career. It was not humanity which achieved its own salvation, using this particular member of the race as agent or medium; redemption as a whole and in every stage is something of which God properly is Doer, by whom each decisive saving act is done. And this means that all hung upon Jesus' sinless fulfilment of His vocation, while yet if that fulfilment was to issue in salvation it could never be the individual unauthorised exploit of a man, but the outcome rather of a thought and energy in which was moving the very life of God.

Not only so; but a study of what we may call the life-history of sinlessness—all that mediates it as a quality of adult consciousness—shows it to be possible only in One whose interconnection with the tissue and fibre of human life is, somehow, conditioned. For when in us the stage of infancy passes into childhood, the marks of congenital imperfection are already evident. Sin in us may be described as a thing of nature—of a nature radically social in antecedents and environment—before it is a thing of full conscious volition. Now the mature adult life of Christ was pure from all trace of sin, which means that in His case this initial derangement or sickness of soul was absent wholly; during the months and years of the soul's awakening those strong efficacious germs of evil which unfailingly develop within us later, left Him untouched. In other words, there was that in Him from the first which offered a completely effective resistance to the corrupt influence of environment, obviated the disturbance of His perfect spiritual growth, and secured the inner fount of subsequent feeling and will from all defilement. Hence, when the infant Christ woke up gradually into clear ethical experience, it was with a nature untainted, immaculate, nowise handicapped from the very outset by seeds of evil already germinating in the soil of character. In all others the earliest stirrings of self-consciousness are vitiated by a hereditary disposition to go wrong; in Christ this predisposition is non-existent, for in our human circumstances a sinless personality cannot be preceded by a sinful infancy. How shall we account for this quite exceptional life-story? If we feel dissatisfied with agnosticism or with a merely positive acknowledgment of the exceptionalness as a fact, if we wish to see it based in some real intelligible ground, this, it appears, can only lie in Jesus' possession of some inward and essential relationship with God, a living actuality which formed the conditioning *prius* of His ethical self-determination, and gave rise to such formative impulses as secured that He should pass through the immaturities of childhood with an undiminished and unimpeded capacity to accomplish His redeeming task. Not indeed that Jesus' unity with God is a natural phenomenon, manifesting itself by (as it were) purely mechanical automatisms. His original oneness with God stands here solely for the potentiality and basis of sinless manhood; but it stands for nothing less than this. The sinless preface to a sinless adult life is in itself suggestive of a vital and inherent identity with the Divine. "It is a miracle," Kähler has said, "which you cannot explain merely by an uncorrupted basis of nature. It is intelligible only if this Child entered on earthly existence with other contents of personal life given Him from the beginning than we all; if in all forms and at every stage of His soul-life there was working itself out an unconditionally independent Will, if God's grace and truth are become flesh in Him."[1] This means, in psychological terms, that from outset to end no desire, motion, conception, or resolve existed in the soul of Jesus which was not the affirmation and execution of the will of God, dwelling in Him and informing His entire life. Only one limit to God's pres-

[1] *Der sogennante historische Jesus*[2], 54.

ence in Him remained—the limit of finitude. In His every act, "in the patience and the venture and the sacrifice of self which lost life only to find it," we behold adoringly the human life of God.

(*b*) The Gospels reveal Jesus as living in a relation toward the Father of peculiar intimacy. It is a relation which He Himself designates as that of Sonship, but the Sonship is such as to be *per se* unattainable by others; "as there is only one Person who can be called the Father, so there is only one who can be called the Son."[1] The consciousness of thus belonging to God dates at all events from the Baptism. Many great sayings of Christ evidently presuppose this impassable difference between the Son and all mankind. Moreover, He at no time leaves it doubtful that this His peculiar Sonship is the medium to the world of God's redeeming life. Sonship, that is, is not something which denotes and interprets His likeness to the men around Him—His presence on their plane, His temptability, His lowliness, the limitations of His knowledge; it is something which signalises His distinction from them, His incomparable and transcendent dignity. Not because but *though* He was a Son, He learned obedience through suffering. The term certainly implies subordination; none the less it points to and emphasises an unshared position of nearness to God by which His very person was constituted. All this comes to the surface in the greatest Christological passage in the New Testament, Mt 11^{25-30}, the climax of Jesus' witness to Himself. In spite of attempts to re-write these verses, we are justified in saying that the knowledge of God professed by Jesus is conceived exclusively as given in and with His filial consciousness. He does not mean to tell us how the Son came to know the Father, any more than how the Father came to know the Son. He is speaking of a knowledge possessed by the Son, *qua* Son. As the context indicates, it is a knowledge of the Father which comprehends His formerly incompletely revealed purpose to save men, and

[1] Denney, *Jesus and the Gospel*, 268.

of the Divine will and nature of which that purpose, now realised in Jesus, is a manifestation. In communicating to sinful men what they can receive of this life-giving truth, Jesus is the Father's perfect organ, the measure of His perfectness being stated in the unqualified and quite amazing words: "No one knoweth the Son save the Father." There is that in Jesus which is so great, so worthy of His mission, so infinite, that it is comprehended by the Father only.

It is then agreed on all hands that Jesus lived in a perfect reciprocal understanding with God; it is agreed, further, that according to the documents this Sonship signified for Jesus' own mind a unique and incommunicable relation to God and man. Assuming the truth of Jesus' interpretation, how far does a relationship carry with it a theory of its own nature? Is it a simple fact not admitting of deeper scrutiny; a fact to be accepted, not explained? Is the Sonship exhausted in Jesus' mental experience of it, or is that mental experience itself the phenomenon, the symptom and manifestation, of an uncreated noumenal reality?

The point is one of difficulty. Thus by many writers the Sonship of Christ is virtually defined as the equivalent of His feeling of unity with God; He was Son because He knew God in a specific manner—that of uninterrupted filial communion. Dissatisfied with this, others have insisted that behind the will and thought of Jesus stood a Divine substance or nature, of which will and thought are but attributes, and which is somehow real apart from them. This, however, is equally unsatisfactory with the position it controverts, and indeed has no meaning except on the assumption that substance as a category is higher and more adequate than Subject, or intelligent conscious Will—a view against which the history of philosophy since Kant has been one long and convincing protest. If we have learnt anything from the modern criticism of categories, it surely is that no category can be higher than personality or self-consciousness. For us, then, the proper inference is that the essential and noumenal divinity of Christ the Son ought to be formulated in conceptions other than substance or nature and the like, which really oppose the metaphysical aspect of Sonship to the ethical. Theology has been seriously discredited in the past by neglect of the truth that our Lord's Sonship, whatever more, is ethical through and through, and that unless we could fill up the idea of Sonship with the love, trust, and obedience which make life filial, it would mean nothing for our minds. From these misunderstandings, however, we are slowly being freed. Perhaps the modern danger is that in our new-found joy in the ethical, we should forget that the ethical is *also* the metaphysical, that it represents the key to being as such. The ultimate and central reality of things is Will. Now the will of Christ as Son is one with God's will not partially, or intermittently, or by way of metaphor; it is one identically. No doubt we speak loosely of making *our* wills one with God's; but although our wills may be harmonious with God's will, or obedient to it, or (so to speak) parallel with it, they are never really one with it. Yet such real unity is precisely what we predicate of Christ; the self-conscious active principle of the Son's life subsisted in perfect and identical union with the Father. This of course does not carry us once more beyond the moral relations of love and trust; that were to de-ethicise Sonship all over again. What is meant is that these relations must be interpreted at their full value—as significant of truth proper, not mere metaphors—and when we take them so, it appears that essentially (which means not in virtue of some ineffable substance, but in that central Will by which personality is constituted) Christ is one with God. The name Son, therefore, signifies two things: first, Christ's true subordination to the Father; secondly, His inherent and personal unity with the Father. The Divine intimacies of His relation to the Eternal are only interpretable in terms which exhibit Him not merely as the perfect saint, but as

One whose life is definitively centred within the life of God.

(*c*) The risen Life. As an additional third point, this is strictly relative to the former two. Jesus' utter sinlessness, His unique Sonship, and finally His exalted life constitute a chain of facts not properly intelligible apart from His personal divinity. They are mutually illuminative facts. The resurrection was not the only event which revealed Christ's greatness, but it did reveal it. By it He was declared Son of God with power, and its significance, for the first witnesses, was due to the fact that it arrived as the climax and interpretation of the incomparable life by which it was preceded. Jesus' freedom from all sin and His unprecedented experience of filial communion had stirred deep questionings which the resurrection answered. Hitherto the disciples had perceived the transcendent quality of His being only by faintest intuition; now at length all things fell into place as His inherent oneness with God was realised. They beheld Him thenceforward in "glory"—entered, that is, on a career of redeeming efficacy which embraces the whole world and pervades the secret chambers of the soul. That faith we share; their argument, accordingly, we repeat (though it may be in other forms), that this exaltation to the exercise of an omnipotent and universal love indicates a more than creaturely being which needs for its true and precise explication the categories of the Divine. Obviously this argument would be worthless if, for Jesus, resurrection were no more than re-animation. But the resurrection of Jesus is really differentiated from all imaginable parallels by its sequel, by all to which it formed the porch and gateway. The sovereign power of His risen life is something in which *ex hypothesi* He can have no successor. Thus the transcendent activities briefly described in the word "exaltation" not only point in the same direction as Jesus' sinlessness and special Sonship; it is harmonious with them: there is an interior correlation between the perfect filial life and the universal glory in which at last it merged. In each case an unshared experience proclaims an unshared identity with the Divine. It is part then of the final truth of things that only He to whom belongs the free independence of the Infinite over against the finite can fill the place in which Christian faith now beholds its Lord.

And yet the question may be asked, asked by faith not unbelief, whether "Godhead" is the perfectly right word. Haering's exposition of the Christian view of Jesus is so admirably clear and loyal that a peculiar interest attaches to his suggestion of a doubt.[1] Not that he questions the historic claims of the word "Godhead." To think of Christ as of God has, he points out, been the hall-mark of Christian life and Christian theology throughout the centuries, except in Rationalistic circles of the eighteenth century. Further, although the designation of Christ as "God" seldom occurs in the writings of the New Testament, as fair exegesis will admit, yet to infer that the early Church felt the designation a too lofty one would be erroneous. Various other expressions are equivalent. Christ is bracketed with God the Father; titles reserved for Jehovah in the Old Testament are ascribed to Him with unembarrassed simplicity. What the Christians meant, indeed, is shown by the impression made on the non-Christian world, which had not the least objection to a new additional deity being included in the pantheon, but instantly recognised that to worship Jesus Christ was a wholly different matter, implying as it did a revolutionising change in moral attitude. It is not going too far to say that the Church, aware of the loose usage of "God" in heathen quarters, must have been peculiarly sensitive to the perils of misconception within the Christian community itself, and must therefore have been at especial pains to ensure that the term was attributed

[1] *Dogmatik*, 425–26. Cf. also a deeply interesting passage in Harnack, *Aus Wissenschaft und Leben*, ii. 70–71, where it is suggested that "Godmanhood" alone is the correct term.

to Jesus' person with a quite new significance. Haering inclines on this ground to believe that the infrequency of the word in the New Testament is due really to its defect in clarity, its liability to misconstruction, and the fatal ease with which it could be made to yield the polytheistic suggestion of "a second God." Pursuing this line, he contends that everything faith longs to say about Christ can be said, adequately and lucidly, without employing the term "Godhead," *e.g.* by the phrases Son of God, Lord, or simply Jesus Christ. All believers are united in the confession of Jesus Christ; but under the conditions in which we moderns live the assertion of His "Godhead" is certain to divide. It will prove a burden and perplexity to many who nevertheless adore Jesus as their Lord and Saviour.

A second typical statement on the same side is that of Faut.[1] Granting the absolute character of the redemption which Jesus mediates and in consequence the absolute character of the Mediator's person, he yet holds that the difficulties of predicating real deity are insurmountable. He insists that Godhead was first ascribed to the exalted Lord. But if we go so far, in logic we must go still further and attribute Godhead also to Jesus of Nazareth—which gives us pause. It is unfitting to speak of the historic Christ as God, medium of the final revelation though He be. For it blurs the interpretation of His earthly life; also it conflicts gravely with Jesus' monotheism. The one thing we dare not do is to create antagonism between faith in Jesus and His own creed. It is simply unevangelical to dim the clear shining of the Gospel by dogmatic assertions which collide with trust in one only God, the Father Almighty.

In reply, it is to be observed in the first place that the presence of difficulties cannot be final as an objection to a given view. On any view the difficulties are immense, the facts are full of them. Excessive simplification of the data is often the bane of scientific inquiry; and in the

[1] *Die Christologie seit Schleiermacher*, 97–98.

present instance the data may be so complex or many-sided that—provided we have made up our mind to interpret them doctrinally—nothing but a complex interpretation will serve. It is also questionable whether the feeling that Godhead is an unfitting predicate, as blurring the outline of the human Jesus, may not be due to the abstractness of the conception, and a too purely logical view of the attributes it implies. Of course the notion of deity may be construed in ways which render Christ's true manhood indistinct or actually dubious; but these ways are wrong. Thus, confusing, as logicians say, the *dictum simpliciter* with the *dictum secundum quid*, we may argue that since Godhead as such is omniscient and omnipresent, the Divine Christ must have been so; whereas the question can only be decided by the recorded evidence of the Gospels, from which alone we can learn what Godhead signifies in an Incarnate experience. Or again, placing the reality of God not in His will and character but in an inscrutable and unethical substance, we may conclude that deity could be present in Christ only by being laid alongside of His manhood, not in qualitative identity but in quantitative juxtaposition; and this also will prevent our seeing the individual Jesus as intelligibly Divine. It will mislead us, in Moberly's phrase, into keeping open a non-human sphere of the Incarnation. It was precisely the wish to read the divinity of Christ through His true humanity which inspired the Kenotic theories of His person; and whatever may be thought of certain speculative details in which they became entangled, it is still conceivable that the principle they represent, not necessarily in the older form, may succeed in mitigating the difficulties of the problem.

Even if difficulties remain, still the facts which the name "God" indicates may be so organic to Christian experience as to force us, even against our will, to insist upon its truth. We may not be able (as it were) to get our hand round the reality to which it points, but we perceive or feel its presence. For after all, Christianity lives not in a vacuum but in the world of real men. It is preached to keen and independent minds, who ask questions they wish to be answered. Is it possible to proclaim Christ in such an audience as Lord of all, who shares the throne of God, on whom faith and love and hope depend, the transcendent source of new life, the unseen Presence that arraigns the conscience and sustains the fainting heart, without evoking the simple interpellation: This Christ of whom you speak, is He, or is He not, one with the Ultimate Reality whom we name God? If Christianity is a religion, not a contribution to moral philosophy, where do we place Him in the sphere of things, on God's side, or merely on ours? When once these questions rise, they cannot long be evaded; no well-intentioned conspiracy of silence, no combination of ultra-cautious propositions, will avail to suppress the interrogator whose Christology in reality is part of his spiritual life. Had the Church passed by the question in the creeds, the outsider would have raised it. We have seen that writers like Haering are themselves clear that to speak of Christ's "Godhead" is justifiable if we thereby mean simply to express an authentically religious faith; and certainly we mean no more. It is only as a brief statement of the Gospel that the term has any value. But what is here contended is that the Gospel cannot be expressed completely apart from this word, because the word "God" has no synonyms. What the believer wishes to assert is not that Christ is manifestly superhuman and so far partially Divine, but that His will, the personal energy which moved in Him, is identically the will of God. Now *that*, in the last resort, can only be affirmed in one way. "In the work Christ does upon us," writes Herrmann, "we get a view of His Person which can only be rightly indicated in the confession of His Deity."[1] Give faith its own way, not curbing or tutoring or sophisticating it, and this is the predicate for which it asks.

If it be said that deity, though possibly implied in the believing view of Christ, is at all events not necessarily

[1] *Communion with God*, 142.

a *conscious* implication, this may be readily conceded. At the same time, it is the very business of theology to bring faith's content to complete consciousness, and to articulate in explicit and coherent terms what may lie enfolded in unreflective experience. So by a wide circuit we return to our starting-point; to the conviction, namely, that Christology as such is meaningless save on the presupposition of Christ's Godhead, while on the other hand His Godhead is no random or arbitrary postulate, but the reverse side of the assurance that He is the proper object of saving faith. "Worship *God* through Christ, and Christ only as God," is an axiom inviolable and sacrosanct.

Is there the promise of light in the suggestion that Christ's Godhead, though real, has been acquired? The idea sounds mythological, certainly; yet it is not wholly without advocates in recent literature. Thus, in his well-known book on the *Gottheit Christi*, Schultz can speak of Jesus at one point as a man "who became God in becoming the Christ."[1] Beyschlag has put forward a similar view. A few Ritschlians also may possibly have covered an opinion rather like this with the phrase that Christ has for us the religious value of God—in forgetfulness of the maxim that *usus sine re est figmentum*. Now to find in the New Testament the conception of a deity which *became*, is simply a forlorn hope; since the Jewish mind was by its very constitution incapable of applying to God the category of creation.[2] It belongs to deity, not indeed to be immutable but to be eternal—not born out of nothing or moving from zero to an actual positive magnitude. So faith views Jesus not merely as One who through grace rose to a union with the Highest comparable to that achieved by saints, though far more intimate, but as One whose development in Divine-human personality took place

[1] 725–26.

[2] I cannot follow Titius in his plea that the name "God" is employed in the New Testament with a certain fluidity and indecision which would admit of its being seriously applied to a creature. He cites 1 Co 8^{5}, 2 Co 4^{4}, Jn $10^{34f.}$ (*Theologische Rundschau*, 1905, p. 365).

within His own native sphere of transcendence. Real gains there were which accrued from His ethically conditioned triumph—a new, universal place in the faith and adoration of mankind; but the quality of being which made this place befitting, and which empowered Him for its functions, reveals itself as no creation of time but an eternal fact. Further, on the hypothesis according to which the Godhead of Christ represents an extraneous acquisition, we surrender the vast New Testament conviction (implying a new thought of God) that the first step into the human sphere taken by God in Christ was one of self-abnegation. Love, the spirit which gives its own life to others, is the inmost reality of Christ and of God, and it was manifested transcendently in His historical advent. It was because deity was His from before all time that He possessed the unspeakable gift to lay on love's altar. On the other hand, the conception of an acquired divinity stands on a lower ethical plane; it has parted with the aspect of sublimity.[1]

Thus a point emerges which in such debates it is only too easy to ignore—the commanding place of the incarnation in the Christian message. If the Church's mind is to retain a luminous and defensible faith in our Lord's divinity, that faith must present itself as so wonderful in intensity and range, in triumphant redeeming power, as to admit of no rival or surrogate. Let men perceive that in Christ there stands before them One who in spiritual being—that is, in will and character—is *identical* with God Himself, that in Him we have to do with nothing less than the Eternal, and at once it becomes plain that revelation can go no further. In other words, the *dimensions* of this revelation form the differential

[1] Thieme has recently contended that we should drop the adjectives "Divine" and even "Divine-human," and proposes instead that Jesus should be characterised as "the Human Representative of God in ruling the world" (*Von der Gottheit Christi*, 65). Does this make things easier? Curiously, it is the revival of an old Judaistic conception of the Messiah (Renan, *Vie de Jésus*, 258).

feature of Christianity. It is not that Jesus Christ, even if viewed as a historic personality with such a limited and derived resemblance to God as is possible to other men, may not convey a real manifestation of the Father—His judgment and His mercy, His irreconcilable antagonism to sin, His unwearied passion to reach and win the sinful. "In what Jesus does to us," says Herrmann, "we grasp the expression God gives us of His feeling towards us, or God Himself as a Personal Spirit working upon us. This is the form in which every man who has been reconciled to God through Christ necessarily confesses His Deity, even although he may decline to adopt the formula."[1] Now by "declining the formula" is meant occasionally that the restricted and humanitarian Christ is sufficient for human need, and to this the answer is simply that we can conceive a far more glorious Gospel. We can conceive the thought that God Himself should be present to heal and save. And we judge that the most glorious thought of God, always, is truest. Love in essence is desire and will to suffer for the sake of the beloved: to enter his condition, to take his load, to renounce every privilege. Not to send a sympathetic message simply, or appear by deputy, but to come in person, obstacles and counter-reasons notwithstanding. Otherwise love is not known as love. Even of God it is true that he who would save his life must lose it.[2]

Humanity in every age has put its final misgiving into the question whether God, if there be a God, is near to us actively in love. It is a question audible in the deeper undertones of the world's literature as well as in those desperate experiments of supplication of which the lower religions are full. Only in the message of Christ's identity with God does it obtain an answer. Certainly we are not justified in using such ideas in *à priori* modes, so dictating beforehand how a Redeemer must be fashioned. Yet if our thought has been educated and expanded by

[1] *Communion with God*, 143.

[2] Cf. Macgregor, *Jesus Christ the Son of God*, 198 ff.

our discoveries in Jesus we shall have courage to believe that the Love manifest in Him would shrink from no moral possibility essential to the accomplishment of its aim. This, so far from being a romantic modern notion, was from the very outset the living core of apostolic preaching. The discovery of Jesus' real identity had created a quite new conception of Divine grace. "Herein is love," writes St. John, "not that we loved God, but that He loved us, and sent His Son." And the message broke the world's hard heart. Our former insistence on Christ's true manhood is in no sense incongruous with this, much less its refutation; for the acceptance of the authentic human experience seals the eternal love as infinite. Thus it is religion, not theology, which has the deepest stake in the divinity of Christ. Let men be persuaded that it is after all a metaphor only, an over-wrought symbol, the adoring hyperbole of which must be quietly confessed in the sane mood of reflection, and the high appeal which has so long moved them will be impoverished past remedy. The glory of God's love will fade into dimmer hues. There will remain problems no word but this can solve, and needs which no lesser gift can satisfy.

PART III.

THE TRANSCENDENT IMPLICATES OF FAITH.

CHAPTER VIII.

THE CHRISTIAN IDEA OF INCARNATION.

AT an earlier point, in a brief forecast of the argument, we proposed to deal first with the immediate utterances of faith regarding Christ, in the second place with such remoter implicates or presuppositions as faith may involve. The first part of our task now lies behind us. We have sought to analyse and vindicate the instinctive or naive content of faith. It has been made clear that for the believing consciousness Christ has a central and incommunicable place in the religious sphere, that He reigns for ever in the sovereign glory of His resurrection, that He is perfect Man, and that He is inherently Divine. Of these positions the Church is well assured; when it looks into its own mind, it finds them there.

We now turn to consider the transcendent problems which the person of our Lord, thus believed in, offers to intelligence in its work of constructive synthesis and inter-

LITERATURE—Illingworth, *Divine Immanence*, 1903; Reischle, *Theologie und Religionsgeschichte*, 1904; Troeltsch, *Die Absolutheit des Christentums und die Religionsgeschichte*, 1902; Fairbairn, *Philosophy of the Christian Religion*, 1903; Walker, *The Spirit and the Incarnation*, 1901; D'Arcy, *Idealism and Theology*, 1899; Caird, *Fundamental Ideas of Christianity*, 1899; Dorner, *System of Christian Doctrine*, 1890; Biedermann, *Christliche Dogmatik*, 1869; Gess, *Christi Person und Werk*, 1870–87.

pretation.[1] Mysteries of faith can never be secluded from the activities of reason; for the mind must strive to discover its own unity even in its supreme object. If Christianity proclaims Jesus as the keystone of the arch of history, the redeeming presence of God in time, it must not shrink from the attempt to think out and think through the implied questions as to His ultimate relation to God and man, and the union of Godhead and manhood in His person. Among these questions one of the foremost and most baffling is the idea of incarnation. By asserting the divinity of Christ we have bound ourselves to the doctrine that He is in some real sense God incarnate, and we must now inquire as to the general significance and credibility of this conception.

It has often been suggested that incarnation in the case of Christ is rendered improbable by the fact that allied beliefs occur in various ethnic religions. The conviction that deity may take embodied form in this or that great man was widely spread, for example, in Greece and India. Out of this ineradicable mental tendency have sprung a multitude of myths resembling the Christian story. And this, it is held, discredits our doctrine from the first. Jesus was deemed to be God incarnate only because in that age the thought-form of incarnation was commonly applied to impressive personalities. Men stood ready with the conception, and no grave sense of intellectual difficulty restrained their use of it.

But it may be pointed out that in a moral world it is no argument against the reality of a particular event that its occurrence was expected. To those who believe in a loving God it must always appear antecedently credible that He will make answer in person to the religious yearnings, the mysterious hopes, the infinite premonitory

[1] They are real problems, and theology will always strive to solve them by reasoned thought, but we are much more sure of our facts than of our theories. While the fact of Christ's oneness with God is certain for faith, interpretations of this oneness will vary to the end. But every form of interpretation presupposes the initial impression of His transcendence.

gleams with which devout minds have been filled. These considerations do not entitle us to disparage concrete evidence. But if in the record of the past we encounter One whose self-consciousness was undeniably unique, and who has been able to communicate to men a new Divine life, we need not refrain from acknowledging Him as God manifest in the flesh merely on the ground that there have been many "pagan Christs." The wants and longings which led men to worship these redeemers of heathenism were inspired of God, and into the empty pathetic hands thus stretched to the skies He was in due time to put the perfect fulfilment of the world's desire. Such experiences formed the *preparatio evangelica* of ethnic man. They constitute no proof that a real incarnation did not come at last; at least they do so only if we illegitimately assume that incarnation is *per se* impossible. Indeed they corroborate our faith, for it is in keeping with what we know of the Divine providential action that the final redemption should not have been given abruptly, but in relation to a rudimentary apparatus of ideas by which it might be apprehended. As it has been admirably put: "If we are so made that a Son of God must deliver us, is it odd that Patagonians (and others) should dream of a Son of God?"[1] These immemorial premonitions were not the cause of the Gospel, but they enabled men to appreciate it when it came.

Furthermore, it may be taken as certain that the first believers did not borrow their greatest thoughts of Christ. The source of their vocabulary—of such terms as "Lord" and "Redeemer"—is comparatively unimportant; in any case, older associations could not have dictated the apostolic use of words. Echoes of pagan terminology may doubtless occur in the New Testament, since there is no copyright in phrases; but the resemblance is in expression only, not in meaning. We must not be imposed upon by what is but a specious verbal coincidence. Current ideas of incarnation or apotheosis, far from impressing men of

[1] Chesterton, *Religious Doubts of Democracy*, 18.

St. Paul's stamp, were dismissed as abhorrently blasphemous. No pagan tales of theophany can have helped out a Jewish apostle with his Christology, whatever may have been the case with his Gentile hearers. It was his unique experience of Christ, not the common habit of naming the Emperor "Son of God," that led St. Paul up to the loftiest summits of doctrine. He felt that in Jesus the Lord there had been given him One of whom other "lords" were false and usurping shadows.

And yet again, the Christian idea of incarnation is sharply differentiated from all others by its purely ethical quality. To the most cursory reader of the Greek myths, on the other hand, it is plain that the Divine life is conceived as moving on the lines of the physical world. To quote Sir W. M. Ramsay: "The Divine nature, which is the model and prototype of all the activity of man, was seen living and dying in the life of trees and plants, of grass and corn. . . . The life of nature never ends; it dies only to be born, different and yet the same. Men mourn for the dead god, and immediately their mourning is turned into joy, for the god is reborn."[1] The fundamental conception of deity is imperfectly moralised. Apollo could be pictured as the son of a wolf-mother. The *avataras* of the god Vishnu, as narrated in Hindu legend, betray in a variety of features the lowering influence of a strongly pantheistic view of the world. The Hindu mind is also lacking in a sense for history; and when we meet with the idea of incarnation in "the encyclopædic aggregation of cults and customs we know as Hinduism," we must carefully guard ourselves against supposing that supreme significance is thereby attributed to some real personality, with a distinct place in the time-series. The single fact that for Hinduism history belongs to the realm of the illusory, while for Greek thought its reality, in comparison with the unchanging forms of being, is at most second-rate, is enough to prove how far in each case the underlying philosophy differs from the Christian.

[1] Hastings' *DB.* (Extra Volume), 123–24.

It is significant that both in Greek and Indian myth the notion of a god becoming man appears in the most varied circumstances and with the most diverse colours. The metamorphosis takes place often, in many ages and many lands. Incarnation and apotheosis melt into each other; for if the conception of Godhead is such that a whole pantheon can be formed by the successive promotion of princes and heroes, a plurality of Divine advents may be easily conceded.

In Christianity, on the other hand, the idea of incarnation, controlled as it is by a perfectly ethical idea of God, is once for all lifted to a higher plane. It is ethically conditioned, sustained by ethical motives, directed to an ethical goal or final end. Jesus comes to achieve a spiritual redemption, in modes appealing to mind and conscience; and the qualities which bring men to recognise Him are love, holiness, and redeeming power. Only those who owe Him salvation can realise His higher nature, and it is moral regeneration which gives the vision of His glory. This is frequently ignored even in modern statements, which confuse the ethical quality of Christ with what is physical or natural in man as such, and, misled by the erroneous premise, talk loosely of the Christ in every man. But for all religion controlled by the New Testament our Lord is not merely *an* incarnation of God, as others may be in their own place; He is the unique and essential appearance of God in history. No duplication is conceivable. Thus whatever dim foreshadowings of truth may have visited the ethnic mind, they fail utterly to explain the full and spiritual Christian faith. They are shifting expressions of man's thought of God, not God's self-expression to man.

No conception has seized the modern mind more powerfully than that of Divine immanence, and we must now inquire how it is related to the higher thought of incarnation? Let us first clear up our minds as to the kind of immanence Christian men are free to assert. It must be in harmony with that ethical monotheism which the Old Testament transmitted to the New. Immanence as expounded, for example, by Spinoza, who, though no materialist, yet declares that God is a being neither mind nor matter, but revealing Himself in both, and not apparently more in one than in the other, has always failed to meet the requirements of conscience. Nor will any view suffice which—often no doubt unconsciously—represents God as an extremely attenuated kind of matter diffused throughout space. It is also necessary that we should avoid confusing immanence with identity. God inhabits, pervades, moves, inspires the world; in this sense He is immanent as the soul is immanent in the body, with a dynamic ubiquity involving a directly active relation to each part. Yet soul and body are not identical, nor by analogy is God identical with the world. In order that the will of God may be the energy of the universe, it must be transcendent to that which it indwells. No one can be so keenly aware of the limits of the Divine immanence as the sinner, to whom repentance has brought home the divergence of self and God with a vivid realisation which is sharpened and registered by the sense of guilt. In short, we cannot operate with any conception of immanence that blots out, or shows indifference to, ethical distinctions. But this all views eventually do which have been formed on the analogy of space in relation to its contents.

Fidelity to moral fact, then, obliges us to emphasise, as a fundamental principle, the truth that Divine immanence is essentially a matter of *degree*, and that the degrees of it are morally conditioned. This means that in adjusting the idea of incarnation to it we obtain much less light or help than might have been supposed from the conception of Divine immanence in nature—the progressive manifestation of God in matter, as it has been called; primarily for the reason that matter is incapable of assimilating or reflecting the characteristic qualities of God, holiness and love. It must always be for us an opaque and inscrutable problem how the impersonal, the unconscious or merely sentient, can be the organ or abode of Supreme Mind. So inadequate is form to content that they seem for ever incommensurable. More light is derivable from the Divine indwelling in man, as revealed by the voice of conscience. But we rise still higher when we consider the inestimable privilege of Divine sonship conferred on all those who are united to God by faith; for in them, and their renovated being, there is seen a free realisation by man of the righteousness, the blessedness, and the glory of the Divine life. Christian experience then proves the reality of union with God; only, the union so proved is no mere nature-fact, but the object of aspiration, faith, and effort. Now of this Divine inhabitation we are entitled to regard Christ as the transcendent climax, shedding the light of interpretation on each preceding stage. All that can be named Divine immanence comes to itself in Him and is consummated, for in Him alone there exist ethical conditions which make form and content equal to each other. And on the valid principle that lower modes of being are explicable by the higher, it is clear that the conception of immanence is more significant and luminous if we start from the person of Christ, and the absolute presence of God in Him, than if our point of departure be the Divine permeation of the universe as a whole. To move down from God in Christ is more convincing than to move up from God in nature. It is in Jesus, not elsewhere, that the true light shines by which we may read the wider problem. Creation finds its key in redemptive incarnation. "In short," as it has been put, "there is no problem raised by the idea of God manifest in the flesh as to the relation of the Divine nature to the human in the unity of one person, or as to the historical origin of such a relation, *i.e.* its beginning in time; or as to the action of the limited manhood on the illimitable Godhood, which is not equally raised by the inter-relations of God and nature. For in a perfectly real sense creation is incarnation; nature is the body of the infinite Spirit, the organism which the Divine thought has articulated and filled with the breath of life.

But while the problems are analogous, the factors which promise solution are more potent in the case of the incarnation than of creation. For in nature the idea of God demands for its expression no more than physical and logical categories, but in Christ the categories become rational, ethical, emotional, *i.e.* they involve personal qualities and relations rather than mere cosmical modes and energies. And so, by investing God with a higher degree of reality and higher qualities of being, it makes all His attributes and relations more actual, all His actions and ways more intelligible and real." [1]

One true mode of describing Christ, accordingly, is to speak of His person as representing the *absolute immanence* of God.[2] For the Divine indwelling must vary in quality and intensity with the receptiveness of man; hence as it deepens it must from time to time involve new departures, turning-points, crises of an epoch-making character. Of these the life of Christ is the last and highest. He opens a new order; we may certainly put it so if we add that in this new order He is unique. And by using the term "immanence" we mark the fact that even in Christ the influx of Godhead is not unrelated to the past. For God has been coming to man from the beginning. Very specially the Divine Spirit dwelt in the prophets, enduing them with power and insight; yet His presence there was after all only intermittent and partial: a broken, fitful, imperfect thing, with a vast discrepancy between the earthen vessel and the higher gift. From the very outset the tendency or movement of Divine love has been toward such a self-expression within finite consciousness as must evoke faith and hope and love in their fulness; with Luther we may say that God has always longed for humanity as His own form of existence. At each point our thought is of course hampered by the mystery of time in relation to eternity. None the less, we see God as it were ever on His way to incarnation, moving on by new

[1] Fairbairn, *Philosophy of the Christian Religion*, 479.

[2] Kirn, *Dogmatik*, 106; cf. Illingworth, *Divine Immanence*, 77.

accesses of self-communication, approaching always nearer to complete personal union, in creation and prophecy and redemption. It is in this direction that our minds are led by the great Johannine conception of the Logos or Eternal Son; for the Logos, now manifest in Jesus, is but a name for the one God as He ever goes forth to the world in self-revealing act.[1]

To meet this Divine self-impartation, on the other hand, there comes the true receptivity of man; a receptivity deeply grounded in his ethical constitution, and capable of endless expansion under the purifying and enlightening influence of God. The Divine bends towards the human, and in Jesus is realised the ideal limit of their confluence. A humanity which is never self-sufficient requires the Divine as its very life, while to this need there answers a boundless love energising in holy power. No wholly mean or mechanical theory of manhood and its conditions has room for the thought of incarnation. That goes only with an ennobling thought of man. Thus the characteristic of Godhead, to give self and appropriate

[1] It is perhaps from this point of view that the speculative mind will always tend to approach the cosmical Christology of the New Testament, as expressed, *e.g.*, in Colossians and the prologue to the Fourth Gospel. The process of the world, culminating in redeemed man, is interpretable as the gradual reproduction in time of a Divine sonship, a filial life, grounded in and modelled on the eternal Sonship characteristic of the inner life of God. In sonship we find the ideal principle which unifies and renders intelligible the phenomena of finitude. It enables us to see all creation and history in the light of a single spiritual conception, which is, however, not merely an imperfect human symbol but represents the intra-mundane self-fulfilment of a personal originative principle interior to the being of God Himself. In the words of Dr. Forrest: "As all creation is in its final purpose but the self-projection of the divine, or the realisation *without* the Godhead of that sonship which eternally exists *within*, it can only find its goal in a rational and spiritual being, who not merely receives but returns love in a conscious fellowship. The filial will in us is not simply our human response to the divine; it has its root in the divine nature" (*Christ of History*, 183). The past and future of mankind, nay, all reality of whatever kind, is to be construed through the fulness of grace which has come to us in Jesus Christ and has its source within the Divine life. What we receive from such intimations as those of Colossians is something more than a Christian view of the universe: it is an ultimate view of God.

the personal life to which self is given, and the characteristic of manhood, to need and be susceptible of such infinite bestowal, are finally correlative; and although, considered in themselves, they entitle us to assert only the possibility of incarnation, not the fact itself, yet they prepare the way for intelligence in its effort to construe the one Divine-human person of Christ.

But we have spoken of *absolute* immanence; and the emphatic adjective is witness to the fact that in Christ immanence reaches its climax. It is a climax which crowns the series by its likeness to the past and transcends it by singularity and difference. The self-giving God is wholly present in Jesus. So new, so decisive is the act that it can be compared to nothing but creation. If prophets were inspired by the Spirit for their vocation, the same Divine life fills Jesus with an organic unity and totality which constitute Him the final self-presentation of God in the human sphere. Bestowal and apprehension can go no further. Without bestowal there is no salvation from above, no amazing sacrifice on the part of God; without apprehension as a moral act or process we are still on the plane of nature. And in both these ways the fact of Jesus is incomparable. What has been realised in Him is not simply more than the past, measured backward from His advent; it is likewise more than all the future: for through Him is mediated now and for ever that union with God which is salvation and blessedness.

At this standpoint it becomes clear that the loose and confused notion of "incarnation in the race," which has been offered as a profounder substitute for the Christian view, is out of harmony with concrete fact. Any attractiveness it may seem to possess is in reality owing to a crude obliteration of moral distinctions, resting on the mistaken assumption that the relations of God and man are completely interpretable in physical and logical categories. But reality as it is when moral conditions have been withdrawn is not the reality in which we live. Our deepest ground for predicating divinity of Jesus is the presence in His life of that love, holiness, and redeeming power which constitute the essential definition of Godhead; but when we survey humanity as a whole, or in its individual members, this ground of predication is plainly lacking. Whatever be the truth as to the latent moral potencies of man, the actuality is notoriously imperfect. It is futile, therefore, to employ terms at this point which suggest that God was as really though less completely incarnate in Judas as in Christ. It is not even true that in due time we *shall be* as Divine as Christ. We are not called upon to be for God that which Christ was; hence it cannot be our ideal, or anything we can aspire to, that we should become Sons of God in the same sense. To the end, be the acquired likeness what it may, the difference of person and vocation must remain. To the end our life will be derived, mediated through His unique life; and the colloquial use of the same term—Sonship—to denote our differing relations ought not to cajole us into a superficial identification of the two. In respect of immanence, accordingly, the last word lies with conscience. The final objection to saying that all minds are parts of God is not merely that thoroughly wicked persons exist, but that we are all wicked in our measure. If man is part of God simply *qua* man, so that my experience of sinning is positively and in something of the same sense God's experience, deity has ceased to be moral. Thus we are justified in asserting not merely that immanence is a thing of degree, but that the degrees of it are ethically qualified. "Universal incarnation" ignores this patent fact. It is true that the work done for God by a creative personality is the measure of the Divine presence or the Divine energy immanent within him; but it is only because the work he does *is* God's, resembling the Divine in quality and purpose, that the higher presence is discernible.

Evolution—or immanence stated in dynamic terms—is the unfolding within the world of the Divine principle of life. One mode of conceiving Christ, therefore, though it may not be the most significant mode, is to regard Him as the transcendent crown of Evolution. It has been objected that the principle of Evolution must needs veto the reality of a Person who is the final revelation of God because His personal advent in time, and attachment to whom constitutes the absolute religion. Now it is true that certain forms of evolutionary metaphysic are incompatible with the finality of Christ, as they are incompatible with unconditional values of every kind. But they are modes of thought which reject the divinity of Christ because they may be said to have first rejected the divinity of God Himself—His eternal personality, His absolute holy love, His power to enter human life. This is not the place for a detailed scrutiny of their philosophic claims. But at least it may be said that they offend either by applying to self-conscious life the too meagre conceptions of natural science, or by a culpable neglect of the maxim that whatever is evolved must be conceived as having first existed in an involved or potential form. Apart from this, however, the ethical principles underlying most of the objections urged at this point of view are dubious in the extreme. Thus the doctrine of the incarnation, of the Divine life as present in a single finite spirit, has been impugned as essentially "unjust." "The Idea," according to Strauss, "loves not to pour all its fulness into one example, in jealousy towards all the rest." Some colour might be lent to this strange misconception were the forth-streaming Divine life represented as having been totally confined to Jesus, His so exclusively as to be available for no one else. But in truth the love of God is concentrated in Jesus only that it may fill the world. "Out of His fulness have all we received, and grace upon grace."

Finally, it may be pointed out that one familiar assumption is an assumption and no more. Frequently it has been taken for granted that the absolute union of the human and Divine is only at best a dim forecast or far-off prevision, and that the consummation of the evolutionary process, by the nature of the case, must arrive only at its close. As an *ex parte* impression this may have an interest, but its claim to rank as a dictum of reason must be disallowed. History can show examples, such as the faultless art of Greece, of spiritual movements culminating in a perfection never repeated in later times. Hellas has not reproduced Phidias, or Sophocles, or Plato. It is vain to lay down *à priori* rules for the movement of the world. The cosmic process, as it has been put, "may be like a symphony in which at definite points new instruments appear even in moments of absolute stillness. To say, moreover, that the most perfect instrument, most significant for the whole symphony, must appear at the end, is an arbitrary assumption."[1] One who is not only the goal but the means of human perfection must appear within the course of history.

It is clear then that Divine immanence, construed in a Christian sense, and regarded as having attained in Christ a culmination which is *sui generis*, is interpretable only in the light of a great implication. It implies not the contrast, but the mutual affinity, of the human and the Divine. It implies that God is deeply kin to man, who is made in His image, while man in turn is susceptible of God. To assume an ultimate dualism in this sphere is to condemn the Christologian to failure from the start. "If our notions of divinity and humanity contain heterogeneous or contradictory elements, it is a truism to say that we can no more combine them in the conception of one and the same personality than we can think of a square circle, or a quadrilateral triangle, or a straight curve."[2] But in the view of Scripture there is no such inherent disparity between the Divine and human as to make their union inconceivable. The likeness to Christ which St. John holds forth as the future heritage of saints must have its root and ground in the essential constitution of humanity. Man is the son of God, even if a lost son; and it is his proper destiny to be partaker of the Divine life.

[1] G. B. Foster, *Finality of the Christian Religion.*
[2] J. Caird, *Fundamental Ideas*, ii. 105.

If, as we know him, he appears incapable of personal oneness with the Eternal, it is to be remembered that his nature has been completely manifested in Christ alone, and that the potentialities thus disclosed are not the less human because they have emerged once, and only once, in history. Infinite and finite spirit alike share in ethical self-consciousness. To each we ascribe mind, will, and feeling. None but the personal God could be incarnate in such a being as man; none but a personal humanity could be the medium of Divine life in time.

Thus far it has been assumed that the incarnation of God in Christ is remedial in aim. It was an act of love for the salvation of the world. Whatever our theoretical conception of the doctrine of atonement, it is assumed in the preceding pages that the Cross reveals to us the impelling motive which led to the personal advent of God. It is only in the light of the Cross that we see Christ, who is an abstraction apart from it; and it is to the Cross we owe that profound and poignant interest which alone makes it worth while to have a Christology at all. But we must now glance briefly at the theory which denies this, or which at least contends that it is a limited and narrow reading of the facts. According to this view, the incarnation would have taken place quite apart from sin. Even a sinless race must have required, and would have received, just such a manifestation of God as was contained in Jesus, enabling it to reach the full height of its development. The very make of the universe implies Christ, and while in the absence of sin His career would have been differently conditioned, and in particular would have been crowned with a different issue, yet He must still have come forth in pursuance of an original and unchangeable Divine purpose. What shall we say of this view, which is covered by great names?[1]

[1] It is strongly maintained by Dorner, *System of Christian Doctrine*, ii. 218. See also Westcott's essay on the "Gospel of Creation" in his Commentary on 1 John.

No one will claim to prove it by the explicit teaching of the New Testament. While there are many texts in which the mission of Christ is directly associated with the conquest of sin, no instance can be quoted on the other side. "God was in Christ reconciling the world unto Himself"; "He loved us and sent His Son to be the propitiation for our sins"; "Since then the children are sharers in flesh and blood, He also Himself in like manner partook of the same, that through death He might bring to nought him that had the power of death, that is, the devil"[1]—these passages from St. Paul, St. John, and the writer of the Epistle to the Hebrews, are typical of many more. It is possible, no doubt, to go behind these plain words and construct for the apostolic mind a wider view, in which the reference to sin is incidental, and which puts the incarnation in its place as an unconditioned element in the Divine world-plan. But against this it may be urged that it would involve the complete readjustment of the New Testament perspective. It attributes to the apostles a willingness to abstract from the problem of sin, in what is ultimately a speculative interest, of which they have given no sign. We cannot think of them as prepared to define the relation of God and man apart from the experience of redemption.

Nor is this all. The theory has the weakness of every purely hypothetical assertion; for it must be admitted tha the only universe known to us is one in which sin is real. Not so real, certainly, as God Himself; this much of truth is suggested by speculative attempts to interpret sin as mere negation, not to say an imperfect or undeveloped form of goodness: but possessed of such a degree of positive reality that in the absence of Divine counteraction it will destroy us. In that case, the wise will regard with suspicion problems so hypothetical as barely to be capable of intelligible formulation. The question: "What would have occurred if Christian experience had been completely different from what it

[1] 2 Co 5^{19}, 1 Jn 4^{10}, He 2^{14}.

is?" is ultimately devoid of meaning. Our conception of Christ, as we have seen, is relative to His redeeming work; strike out the redeeming work, even by supposition, and the materials for a judgment disappear. The content of the term "Christ" becomes uncontrollably obscure. Experimental theology can have no concern with those imaginary situations which the mediæval dialectic sought to cover by the *scientia media* of God, but which, as the use of that indomitable scholastic device admits implicitly, have no relation to our knowledge.

It will not do to reply that a central fact like the incarnation cannot ultimately have depended for realisation on the "contingency" of human sin. From the human angle, of course, sin may be described as a contingent element, in so far as it has no necessary or absolute existence, and we are able to conceive its abolition. But we cannot transfer this to the Divine side. We cannot argue that because sin is an intrusion it is also a surprise for God, an unforeseen and disturbing emergency for which secondary provision had to be made. We cannot conceive of Him awaiting the issue of man's first contact with temptation with a feeling similar to what we know as suspense. His prescience of the world was a prescience also of moral evil. Sin was before His mind from the first; His redemptive thought is as eternal as His creative. In point of fact, redemption and creation are presented to us as an organic unity, forming a single historic process; and it is idle to attempt a disintegration of this unity or to draw out by logic the consequences of a radical change in our conception of what the process is. Nothing, indeed, can be more deeply characteristic of the Christian consciousness than the assurance that the redemptive love of God had no beginning, but forms the essential core of His thought of man.

For it must be again said firmly that from the outset Christology has been controlled and inspired exclusively by a soteriological interest. And redemption must still be the light of all our seeing. If the idea of incarnation is to retain a secure hold of our minds, we must find its great *raison d'être* in the dread problem created both for God and man by the reality of sin. Because sin had desolated humanity and man must have forgiveness if he is to live in God's sight, therefore God became man. But this means an insuperable difficulty for the theory before us. If earnest men who are conscious of pardon and its untold blessedness, yet awake to the difficulties of belief, have to choose between saying that the incarnation is credible because it is *per se* implied in the nature of God and man, and saying that it is credible because a stupendous work had to be accomplished in rescuing the guilty, their choice is simple. Assert that the incarnation was *for* the atonement, and a view of its purpose so vivid, so ethical, and so profound enables us in some real measure to apprehend the fact, however unique and wonderful. Remove this vital reference to sin, and Christ as we know Him appears in a purely philosophic relation to the most vital things in Christian experience. Thus one result of construing the personal presence of God in Jesus as a corollary from the intrinsic nature of Infinite and finite is to reduce the question from the level of historic and ethical truth to that of speculation, to minimise the gravity of sin, as a fact so vast and awful as to require nothing less than *this* for its annihilation, and to impair the sense of adoring wonder with which forgiven men contemplate the miracle of Divine love.[1]

[1] It is convenient to touch here on the objection which employs what I may call "astronomical intimidation." Can we believe, it is asked, that a tiny planet known to be but a speck in the stellar immensities was chosen as the scene of the astounding miracle of incarnation? Why this special favour to one world out of myriads? Does not our cosmical insignificance veto the notion as a preposterous incredibility? But this, as has been said, "is simply an attempt to terrorise the imagination" (Simpson, *Fact of Christ*, 116). Its plausibility vanishes when we recall the love of God and the greatness of the soul. To find difficulty in the thought that our sphere was "selected" for the incarnation is in the first place to assume—what we cannot know—that other worlds are inhabited; and secondly, to forget that man is not less man though there may be beings like him in other worlds, while it is only if the power of God were limited that the probability of His

visiting us redemptively would be lessened by their existence. The real point, however, is that considerations of quantity, in space or time, are totally irrelevant in a discussion of infinite spiritual issues. If God is the Father revealed in Jesus, the presumption lies not in anticipating too much, but too little. The notion that incarnation is unworthy of God's dignity ignores the superiority of the moral to the physical, and, though it may appeal to minds in unconscious sympathy with Nietzsche, erects material magnitude into the supreme criterion of value. It was derogatory to God to become man only if the end contemplated were less than the highest good. No one who believes in the incarnation would of course deny that it is opposed to "common sense"; but common sense is after all only a rough deposit of common events; while the incarnation, on any theory of it, is wholly unique. These considerations are not obsolete because in the main they are very old, but their cogency obviously rests on a conception of incarnation determined by its remedial purpose.

CHAPTER IX.

THE PRE-EXISTENCE OF THE SON.

It may safely be asserted that the idea of Christ's pre-existence, when it becomes explicit in the Christian mind, does so distinctly by way of inferential interpretation. It is less a conscious element in the faith which apprehends salvation in Jesus than a conception of reflective thought; or to put it otherwise, we predicate it of our Lord only in virtue of what we already know regarding Him, as sole Mediator and our indwelling Life. Were He but one more man in the world, not uniquely and incomparably Redeemer, it would not have occurred to the writers of the New Testament—it would not occur to any one now—to affirm that prior to His earthly life He had lived elsewhere. His career would then be dated from His birth, and the attempt to refer His existence to eternity would lapse as mere fantasy. If, however, we instinctively place Him on the Divine side of reality, as One not destined to be judged but Himself the Judge of quick and dead, with a Sonship not simply charismatic but essential, the thought of His eternal being will be apt to follow of itself. It will rise unbidden in our minds. His uniqueness, we shall say, has its ground and explanation in uncreated being.

We have alread seen that no convincing reasons can

Literature—Lobstein, *La Notion de la préexistence du Fils de Dieu*, 1883; Bornemann, *Unterricht im Christentum*[2], 1891; Denney, *Studies in Theology*, 1894; Grétillat, *Exposé de Théologie Systematique*, 1888–90; Schaeder, *Theozentrische Theologie*, 1909; Beyschlag, *New Testament Theology*, 1895; Moberly, *Atonement and Personality*, 1901; Mozley, *Ritschlianism*, 1909.

be given for denying that Jesus Himself spoke expressly of His pre-temporal life.[1] But only the Fourth Gospel alludes definitely to the subject, and, if we may assume that its representations are founded in historic fact, there is much attractiveness in the suggestion that Christ's consciousness of eternal being is not so much reminiscence as knowledge formed slowly in His mature mind. "We must maintain," writes Dr. Garvie, "that the contents of the consciousness of the child Jesus growing in wisdom and in favour with God and man were not identical with the consciousness of the Eternal Word and Son, that Jesus did not in His temporal existence remember the circumstances and conditions of His pre-temporal state. . . . It is simply impossible to imagine or conceive a continuity of self-consciousness from Word or Son in pre-incarnate state through the moment of incarnation, the developing and expanding mind of the boy and youth to the maturity of the man Jesus. We must maintain that the consciousness of eternal relation as Son to the Father, as Word to the world, emerged in the consciousness of Jesus in the course of His history, and in His temporal condition its eternal presented itself as a pre-temporal form. Independent of history it is represented as prior to history."[2] This has the advantage of enabling us to regard pre-existence as a profoundly religious thought for Jesus' own mind—an aspect or expression of His awareness that He was connected with the Father by bonds to which time was irrelevant. The absoluteness of the relation involved its eternity. As He grew and strengthened, the consciousness of God as Father also grew and filled His whole mind; and we may believe that a time came at last when the sense of this indefinably profound connection became explicitly what it had always been potentially—a clear perception of the union of Son with Father as increate and unbeginning. This is still irrespective of the further question whether the distinct consciousness of His eternity was vouchsafed only in

[1] Cf. *supra*, pp. 29, 106.

[2] *Studies, etc.*, 85–86.

certain high hours, or formed from the time of its emergence a permanent background in His mind. If as He looked forward, gradually His eyes were opened to the destiny awaiting Him, He also looked backward and realised that behind or above Him lay a timeless unity with God in which earthly life formed an infinitely momentous episode. When such knowledge was attained, and through what media, we cannot tell. But it is natural to suppose that it came to Him in the fulness of manhood, as something enfolded in the complete significance of His filial relation and now drawn into clearer light by brooding thought on His redemptive mission. As with His certainty of triumph over death, it flowed from an inward spring.

The conception of pre-existence was also employed by the apostles in setting forth to the imagination the absolute significance of their Master. Allusions to the pre-incarnate life of Christ never occur in the Epistles by way of dialectic flourish or random ornament; the belief is put forward, rather, as a fundamental certainty, and it is assumed that every Christian will appreciate the vast truth for which it stands. It has a prominent place in the religious conviction of St. Paul, St. John, and the writer of the Epistle to the Hebrews. Nothing at all is specified in that life "ere the worlds began to be," save the agency of the Son in creation; no curious speculative or mythological details are offered regarding the relationship of Father and Son "in the counsels of eternity."[1] Further, the only pre-existence in which apostolic writers are interested is not ideal but real and personal. The love which entered history in Jesus could come only through a personal channel.

Now the element in this apostolic belief from which the modern mind revolts most emphatically is of course its cosmic reference—the suggestion, in other words, that

[1] But the idea had a genuinely religious bearing on their sense of the continuity of the Christian movement with the history of salvation in Israel, and this St. Paul expresses in his own way, 1 Co 10^4.

Christ is both the Divine Agent in creation and the unifying principle of finite being. On a certain view of Christ, this is no doubt mere madness. If He is but one of the innumerable waves on the sea of human life, sinking as it rose, a voice which sounded forth its message and fell to silence, to speak of His cosmic function and significance may well seem no more than the devout symbolism of an uninstructed fancy. On the other hand, if we hold Him to be the organising centre of that world of values by which faith lives, and in which it has its being, then, we may argue, not merely is it conceivable that He should be central also in the world of facts, but the two things—if there is ultimately a single universe—are inherently and indissociably linked together. Redemption and creation constitute a spiritual unity. Creation is consummated in redemption, which at long last discloses the principle which has been operative and controlling in each successive period of cosmic development. If perfect love, moreover, demands a true mutuality of giving and receiving, a reciprocal personal immanence of life, it may reasonably be held that Father-Sonship is the ultimate Divine reality, of which and through which and to which are all things; and that the universe of created being, whether physical or spiritual—the sphere, that is, of the recipient and the responsive—has Sonship for its deepest ground and motive-power, sonship in man thus forming the finite reflex and product of Eternal Sonship in God. Many have felt that the cosmic Christology of the apostles, interpreted on these lines, tends to lose its alien aspect and gains a secure hold on intelligence. It is interpretable as suggesting not simply that Christ, now revealed as Divine by His exaltation, must have been Divine from before all worlds, but also that God has progressively stamped His own essential character on His workmanship, moving upward in His work to find at length in man an adequate image and true child, who in free obedience can apprehend, answer, and reproduce the Eternal Love which seeks him. So we catch sight of two great things: first, a potential basis for incarnation, since human nature is thus filial in its formative idea and therefore capable of receiving the Son *in sensu eminenti*; secondly, the intrinsic nobleness of humanity. For what must be the kinship and likeness between Godhead and manhood when into the frail vehicle of our life that wondrous treasure could be poured!

Criticism unfavourable to the idea of Christ's pre-existence has moved, broadly speaking, on two main lines —the historical and the conceptual..

(*a*) During the last two decades, scholars have laboured zealously at the investigation of points in the contemporary religious thought of Palestine and Alexandria to which belief in the eternity of Christ might be fastened, and it is assumed that very moderate success in this search entitles us to discount the apostolic thought as the natural but obsolete result of religious syncretism. Harnack[1] pleads that certain Jewish apocalypse-writers had come to assert pre-existence of the Messiah. In that age it was customary to express the peculiar value of a person or thing by distinguishing within it essence and appearance, hypostatising the first, and then lifting it into sheer transcendence above the limits of space and time. Not only were great men credited with pre-existence, such as Adam, Enoch, or Moses, but even the tabernacle, the temple, and the tables of the Divine law. The idea, in short, was one which primitive Christianity found ready-made, and which naturally it utilised to set forth the enduring value and felt mystery of Jesus' person; other conceptions such as supernatural birth and the incarnation of the Word being employed for the same purpose.

That its similarity to a prior idea must discredit the Christian belief could only be conceded on the obviously untenable assumption that no true idea is ever providentially prepared for. It may well be that certain current

[1] *Dogmengeschichte*[4], i. 115–19.

Jewish theologoumena operated by suggestion, just as Greek ideas of incarnation made way for sublimer thoughts connected with Jesus. But such possibilities, which are not to be denied, no more explain St. Paul's characteristic usage of pre-existence, say in Ph 2, than *In Memoriam* is explained by the fact that every word found in the poem existed previously in the dictionary. In the Jewish conceptions, be they what they may, there is nothing corresponding to the *ethical* fact of pre-temporal Divine self-sacrifice, which alone engages the apostle's attention. Apart from this, however, we are bound to ask whether Harnack is right as to his facts. Dalman, an unrivalled authority, has denied emphatically that a general belief in pre-existence was a Jewish characteristic; Bousset and he, indeed, leave it very questionable whether the older Rabbinism asserted anything more than the pre-existence of the Messiah's *name*. But in any case the Christian and the Jewish conceptions have properly no resemblance. In Rabbinism the celestial archetype is only a double of the earthly object; in the New Testament, the very signature of Christology is the faith that the Divine Son passed from glory to humiliation; and it is mere inaccuracy to say that these ideas are equivalent, or analogous, or that one of them suffices to explain the other. What is asserted of Jesus goes far beyond all previous assertions: the elements of the idea are new and are combined in new ways. Not only so; it is one thing to speculate freely on pre-existence in the abstract and quite another to believe in the eternal reality of a specific Person, with whom the speakers had lived in the most intimate association. This last is only explicable by an overwhelming religious impression.

(*b*) More frequently, however, objections have rested on grounds of theory. Thus Ritschl, from the standpoint of theological positivism, has insisted that the predicate of deity is applicable only to Christ's earthly life, on the principle that theology must not ask *how* the person of Christ derives from God, or has come to possess its felt supreme religious value. We want facts, not theory. "The eternal Godhead of the Son," he writes, "is perfectly intelligible only as the object of the Divine mind and will, that is, only for God Himself. But if at the same time we discount, in the case of God, the interval between purpose and accomplishment, then we get the formula that Christ exists for God eternally as that which He appears to us under the limitations of time. But only for God, since for us, as pre-existent, Christ is hidden."[1] This is put from a standpoint we have already seen reason to reject; and if we do not feel ourselves precluded on principle from the transcendental interpretation of experienced facts, we are at liberty, assuming the grounds to be sufficient, to infer the eternity of Christ from His revealed greatness. Again, it is difficult to fix precisely the meaning of the words: "Christ exists for God eternally as that which He appears to us under the limitations of time." Either this is tantamount to an assertion of ideal pre-existence, in which case we may for the moment reserve it, or it definitely means something more. If it means more, however, the particular additional element of meaning must be pronounced unintelligible or at least inadequate. On the one hand, God can only know things as they are, hence Christ's existence *in time* cannot figure in the Divine cognition as an *eternal* fact, which it is not; on the other hand, if this is not Ritschl's meaning, what he has done is to negate for the Divine mind the difference between the pre-temporal condition of the Son and that on which He entered by incarnation, thus cancelling, expressly from the highest standpoint, the personal Divine sacrifice involved in our Lord's mission. But if Christ had a pre-incarnate life in any sense, obviously it must have been otherwise conditioned than His self-manifestation on earth. And faith will refuse to annul the difference between the two—between "the form of God" and "the form of a servant"—finding as it does in this difference the very measure of God's love.

[1] *Justification and Reconciliation* (Eng. tr.), 471.

Wendt has also contended[1] that it is impossible to maintain the personal pre-existence of Christ without falling into Tritheism, at all events if with Western tradition we interpret the eternal being of the Son as involving full equality with the Father. We may choose to conserve the Divine unity by regarding the eternal Word or Son as essentially Divine, but not personal, or as personal, but not properly Divine. To combine the two is fatal. It wrecks monotheism by introducing plurality in God. Not only so; but pre-existence is incompatible with Jesus' spiritual life as man. For then we should have to conceive the personal Logos as having been united in Him with a complete human life—a dualism which makes a true ethical experience impossible. The second objection has already been dealt with. As regards the first, it is plain that Wendt's argument is valid only on the assumption that the Logos or Son, conceived as eternal, is a person in the usual acceptation. Passages may unquestionably be found in otherwise good writers on the Trinity which justify the assumption, by their naively unconscious defence of Tritheism. But it is rash to neglect the famous caution of Augustine: *Dictum est, Tres Personae, non ut diceretur, sed ne taceretur.*[2] In reality, the word "person" is forced upon us by the poverty of language. Since no better offers, we employ it to mark our belief in a real distinction within the Godhead—a differentiation of being or function; not to affirm the reality of independent conscious beings, qualified by separate "essences." The eternal principle or distinction to which the fact of Christ refers us, we designate Son or Logos. Each of these terms has advantages; each no less clearly has grave defects. "Logos" no doubt avoids the suggestion of "person" in the sense of individuality, a sense which it is quite certain *persona* did not bear till long after it had become a *terminus technicus* of Trinitarianism. "Son," however, is even more attractive, inasmuch as it keeps our

[1] *System der christlichen Lehre,* 368 ff.
[2] *De Trin.* v. 10.

mind firmly at the ethical and spiritual plane of thought, in the faith that moral relationships, of love, of trust, of obedience, are not strange to the inner life of deity, but find there both an eternal basis and a perfect realisation. Also it provides that our conception of the Eternal Son shall retain a true continuity with the Christ of history, to whom the name "Son" primarily belongs. "As far as nomenclature is concerned," Moberly observes, "the words 'Father' and 'Son' express most primarily and most unreservedly the relation between the Eternal and the Incarnate, between God as God and God as man; and analogously rather than primarily, in dim suggestion rather than directly, those eternal relations which are hardly capable of any other than an indirect and analogous expression."[1] Thus Wendt may be answered; but the answer, let it be conceded frankly, is one which from the nature of the case cannot be made really cogent or convincing; for the realm of discussion here is such that we have to resist firmly the temptation to lay an undue crudeness of emphasis on those aspects of it which we least comprehend. We may indeed (and must) throw back our minds, by postulate, from the data of redemptive history to antecedent realities of an eternal order; but this does not authorise us to mount up into that rare and high domain and expatiate at large in a transcendence which has lost touch with controlling facts.

But to this it may be replied: You urge the pre-existence of Christ, because, as you hold, nothing else or less can signalise the marvellous exhibition of redeeming love implied in His being here at all. "Ye know the grace of our Lord Jesus Christ, that though He were rich, yet for your sake He became poor"—in a verse like this, so often quoted with emphasis, there is surely little or no significance unless the pre-existent One is a "person," a "self" in the usual connotation. Is not the apostle simply proclaiming that the Jesus Christ we know stooped down in grace to save the lost? How can this be, if the

[1] *Atonement and Personality*, 213.

Eternal "Son" is not a person, *i.e.* an independent centre of self-consciousness and self-determination? Now—apart from the consideration that subtle problems of theory were not before the apostle—it may reasonably be held that when the Christian mind gratefully responds to the love exhibited in the incarnation, it is not concerned to maintain that this Divine passion of self-abnegation was felt, and expressed in act, by the pre-existent One *as a separate individuality.* Enough that the manifestation of love was a manifestation of *Divine* love, sublime and overwhelming; enough that the sacrifice undergone prior to Christ's advent took place within God's very being, and that out of the Divine life-fulness, at love's behest, He came forth whom in the fields of time we know as Jesus. Further, it must be remembered that faith no less than theology revolts from Tritheism. Hence it must see the pre-incarnate One *in* God, not alongside of God, not as an entity to be known and appreciated in abstraction from God. Thus in a purely religious interest it is equally misleading to regard the eternal "Son" as a mere impersonal law or force or principle on the one hand, and on the other as an independent Divine individuality. "Not from any wanton intrusion into mysteries but under the necessity of breaking silence," we designate Him an eternal personal mode or distinction within the one self-conscious life of God.

A refuge from these perplexities has been sought by numerous modern thinkers in the conception of *ideal* pre-existence.[1] There was no time when Christ was not in the Father's purpose. He is as old as the saving love of God; His mission, embracing life and death and triumph, formed eternally an integral and cardinal element of the

[1] The conception of ideal pre-existence has been criticised as though it simply meant that Christ pre-exists in God as theorems relating to the circle do in its definition. But this is misleading. It ignores the element of redeeming Will which is central in the Christian thought of God, and which has nothing corresponding to it in the sphere of mathematics.

Divine plan. Thus Lobstein, to whom pre-existence is distasteful because it savours of metaphysic, prefers to replace it by the idea of election. From eternity it was decreed that one day there should be born into human history a Person uniquely endowed, and possessed of the fulness of the Spirit. This being so, we are entitled, he maintains, to say that Jesus Christ, the Divine Son, had reality in God's thought from before all time, as willed and chosen by the Father. It would perhaps be a fair criticism that a theory like this transcends immediate religious experience quite as definitely as orthodoxy itself, and that to speak of the eternal contents of God's mind is even tolerably speculative. But, apart from this, it is noteworthy that the New Testament is quite familiar with the distinction of pre-existence and election, and enforces it without hesitation. When St. Paul declares that the saints were chosen of God in Christ before the foundation of the world,[1] he conceives them as having had what may be called ideal reality for the prescience of God through infinite ages, and as having been embraced in His gracious design to call them, in due time, to faith and service. But he never dreams of saying that they pre-existed. Not even of apostles does he say that. Now if this obvious Jewish category, which Rabbis had applied freely to Old Testament saints, lay simply waiting to be used, why has he not used it? Certainly not by accident. On the contrary, the predication of election in the case of Christians, and of pre-existence in the case of Christ, constitutes one of the apostle's most characteristic modes of accentuating the essential difference between them.

It is, of course, true that Christ, both in His own mind and in that of the apostles, stands in positive relations to the Divine fore-knowledge. But we do not exhaust the special connection of Christ with God by relating Him merely to the Divine *thought*. So far He is on the same plane as the creatures. The filial connection is so close that we must also think Christ as eternally related, and

[1] Eph 1[4]

related as an eternal fact, to the *will* of God—as the timeless object of His producing and sustaining love. The thought and will of God cannot be conceived save as imparting reality to Christ. Or, to put it otherwise, the Father revealed in the Son cannot be thought as fully real in abstraction from the Son in whom alone we apprehend Him.

By some recent thinkers the conception of our Lord's pre-existence has been defined as in strictness only a *Grenzbegriff*: a conception, that is, indicative of reality lying just across the border-line of our knowledge, yet looming on us indefinably, as it were, out of penumbral mists. It affirms, as Kirn has put it, "that the historic Christ has eternally a central and universal place in God's saving purpose, and that the content of His life—*i.e.* His holy redeeming love—is rooted in God and belongs to the eternal content of God's transcendent life. Hence," he proceeds, "it were better to speak of the *supra-historic* character of the revelation given in Christ than of the *pre-historic* existence of Christ with the Father."[1] This particular *Grenzbegriff*, it is contended, is an ideal conception placed on the very limits of human cognition and employed in self-defence by the believing mind as it strives to conserve to the utmost the impression of unspeakable Divine love vouchsafed to us in Christ. In other words, pre-existence is a symbol. Now, that the eternal being of Christ, if known at all, is known by faith and in faith only, will at once be conceded. On the other hand, symbols have real meaning; if faith speaks to us of Christ's pre-existence, be the language as symbolic as it may, it speaks of it as real. The object symbolically conceived lies, it is true, on the farther side of terrestrial knowledge, but in this respect it resembles all the other transcendent objects of which faith is sure, *e.g.* the present sovereignty of Christ. It therefore appears that the conception of a *Grenzbegriff*, when thoroughly elucidated, indicates that the real object dimly grasped in our neces-

[1] *Dogmatik*[3], 107.

sarily symbolic forms is in no sense emptier or poorer than the symbol, but, like all transcendent facts in Christianity, infinitely more rich and full.

In the light of these discussions, we need have no hesitation in confessing that the pre-existence of Christ outstrips our faculty of conception, and that no theoretic refinements alter this in the very least. Not merely are we faced here by the impossibility of beholding the life of God on its inward side, which means that thought is working altogether apart from experience; but in addition we encounter once more the haunting and insoluble enigma of time as ultimately related to eternity. And other not less formidable difficulties remain. We cannot think eternity crudely as equivalent to time without beginning and without end; and the chronological quality of pre-existence is therefore fatal to its adequacy as a final or coherent representation of what, *ex hypothesi*, is above time. Christ cannot after all be pre-existent in any sense except that in which God Himself is so relatively to the incarnation; and our instinctive use of "eternal" as the epithet befitting God suggests that the idea we wish to convey regarding Christ should also be expressed by the terms "eternity" or "supra-temporality." Again, when we speak of the pre-existent One, what is, as logicians say, the subject of discourse? *Who* pre-exists? Not the historic Jesus, exactly as He is known in the Gospels. The Church has never affirmed that the humanity of Christ was real prior to the birth in Bethlehem; and if, as must be admitted, certain apostolic statements, interpreted *au pied de la lettre*, have the appearance of saying quite the opposite, it must be considered that this was inevitable in the case of men using the intensely concrete language of religion, not the coldly correct phraseology of the schools. Neither can we simply equate the pretemporal One with the exalted Lord, for incarnation as such means that these two "estates" are separated by a vast redemptive act of self-humiliation, initiated on the Divine side of reality. These are a few of the perplexities by which we are met in the effort to derive from history the content of "the Pre-existent."

We have then to concede that the idea of pre-existence is an imperfect means of representing eternity in forms of time. And if problems so baffling gather round it, the pre-temporal being of the Son cannot surely be a datum for faith—part of the message, that is, which we hold forth as evangelists with the hope of creating faith where as yet it does not exist; it must rather be a corollary or implicate to which conscious faith gives rise. It is, I believe, a thought of which fully conscious Christian belief will not consent to be deprived, but at least theology cannot start from it.[1] The question, let it be noted, is one not of antagonism but of order. It should be clear that whether we can or cannot discriminate between elements united to form Christ's person, at least there is no admissible point of departure but the given realities of fact. Christ in the New Testament is nearer to our minds, as well as more fundamental for religion, than any prior potencies out of which He rose. Detailed speculations on the pre-incarnate life, like professedly minute descriptions of the Divine self-consciousness, betray in fact a culpably Gnostic tendency, and are apt to end in the suspicion that when once we have penetrated to the eternal Godhead latent in Jesus, the human and temporal facts of His career lose more than half their value. As a protest against this, we can even appreciate the famous remark of Herrmann, in a conference at Eisenach, when he bade his audience turn from speculation on the subject of pre-existence "with hearts as cold as ice."

Nevertheless in both cases—that of the Divine self-consciousness and that of Christ's pre-existence—Christian intelligence pondering on its data will always insist, I am convinced, on postulating the ineffable reality. It is essential to recollect that what the New Testament affirms

[1] Cf. Herrmann, *Die Religion im Verhältnis zum Welterkennen und Sittlichkeit*, 399, 438 ff.

is not the eternal being of this or that chance individual, but of the Lord Jesus Christ, with His arresting and unparalleled self-consciousness, His present glory, His almighty power to save. Thoughts are in place regarding Him which elsewhere must be irrelevant. Soon or late the question must rise: Are the dimensions of our conception of His person so deep and broad and high that nothing is consonant with them, or with the effort which the soul makes in apprehending them, except the faith that He lived in God before all things?

It is this belief, as a matter of history, which formed the seed-plot of all Christological and Trinitarian reflection. Where lies its religious interest? Surely in the Christian certainty that salvation is of the Lord. Faith's view of the world, be it remembered, is always and unconditionally theocentric. And the argument which this yields, though capable of being drawn out in syllogistic form, is really intuitive. Only the eternal God can save; Christ is Saviour; therefore in eternity both before and after, Christ is one with God. He who fills the soul's horizon can be no mere incident of human history, but must have His roots of being within unbeginning deity. Otherwise in the last resort it is a Man who is given, or assumes, the central place in faith's universe, with the inevitable result that theology, while remaining Christocentric, ceases to be theocentric.[1] It is only kept theocentric by the unflinching faith that the Christ in whom we believe is not merely One who lived a life of uninterrupted fellowship with God, so constituting the perfect Exemplar of religion, but One whom we are justified in referring unequivocally to the Divine side of reality, not as having attained that place progressively, nor even as having received it by privileged election, but as having emerged in love "from the bosom of the Father." When this is denied, it is frequently in obedience to a relativistic view of knowledge. Men have made up their minds that no phenomenal historic facts can disclose the Divine noumenal reality, though they may

[1] Cf. Schaeder, *Theozentrische Theologie*, 175 ff.

imperfectly symbolise it; and if Christ has the religious value of God, no one can really determine the ultimate relation of this practical religious supremacy—this quality of being morally indistinguishable from God—to the unknown and inaccessible life of God as such. In an argument of this kind, however, it is too much forgotten that—revelation and faith being vital correlates—a partial and conditioned revelation can never evoke more than a partial and conditioned faith. And this brings us to the crucial point.

It will not be seriously questioned that the chief glory of the Christian religion is its characteristic conception of the Divine love. God's love in Christ is triumphantly set forth as something infinite and measureless. But is it really so, apart from Christ's eternity? Is it the fact, His eternity once denied, that we cannot imagine a vaster exhibition of Divine mercy to the world? If in Christ we have something less than "God's presence and His very self," because He grows on the soil of human nature, as simply human, it is surely clear that the scale on which the love of the Eternal has been made manifest is now gravely altered. We have somehow to abridge our once glorious vision of self-sacrifice as the inmost core and focus of the Divine life. It is not that God cannot be known as Love apart from His incarnation in Christ. To say so would be false. But it is *not* false to say that apart from the gift of Christ out of an eternal being, God's love would not be displayed so amazingly, in a form and magnitude which inspire, awe, and overwhelm the soul. A Christ who is eternal, and a Christ of whom we cannot tell whether He is eternal or not, are positively and profoundly different, and the types of faith they respectively call forth will differ correspondingly both in spiritual horizon and in moral inspiration. Our sense of Christ's self-abnegation—His lowliness, His grace, His utter passion of sacrifice—is perceptibly expanded or reduced according as we do or do not hold that He who bore these things had entered by Divine volition into the situation of which they form a part. Something which is irreplaceable drops away when His eternity has been cancelled. The Gospel can never be the same again, and the loss is borne not by speculative dogmatic but by personal religion. Especially the preacher has parted with a certain leverage of moral appeal no more to be regained. It is harder now to persuade men that God loves us better than He loves Himself.

Considerations of this simple and familiar kind may help to dissipate the impression that the conception of pre-existence is incurably "speculative" or "metaphysical." Whatever these formidable adjectives mean, they at least mean something which it requires a strong intellectual effort to apprehend. But in this esoteric sense the conception is not speculative in the least. On the contrary, it is constantly found in hymns of childhood. It is of course intensely difficult in its remoter implications, as, for that matter, are also the conceptions of moral freedom or the Divine personality. And the proper inference to draw is that belief on this subject must follow faith in Christ Himself, not precede it. We cannot know the pre-temporal as we do the earthly life of Christ, or even as we do (in a real sense) His life of exalted glory. The stage in His career at which we meet with Him is after Bethlehem, not before it; we meet with Him supremely in His recorded words and actions; and he who has not found God in the record of these three sinless years can have no stake of a vital or intelligible kind in the question whether they stand out against an infinite and eternal background. But indeed the Church has clung to faith in Christ's pre-existence on purely religious grounds. She has clung to it as the only means open to human thought of affirming the priceless truth that He is not the perfect Saint merely, offered by humanity to God, but the beloved Son sent forth by the Father, cast in grace upon "this bank and shoal of time," that in love He might give Himself for us all. It scarcely admits of doubt which of the two views will inspire the more subduing Gospel. Men say that the conception of eternity mingling thus with time is too vast for truth; with the apostles we may answer that its vastness is its evidence, since the God made known in Jesus gives only gifts so great that none greater can be conceived. To part with the glory and wonder of this faith is in a grave measure to part with the native joy of the Christian religion, and to remove the scene of sacrifice from heaven to earth will inevitably stimulate the less worthy impulse felt at some time by all to preach about man instead of God.[1]

[1] It is significant that a modern theologian like Haering of Tübingen, in his peculiarly rich and stimulating *Dogmatik* (1906), should offer the following sympathetic rendering of our theme, though with the reminder that at this point knowledge largely passes into symbol. "The love of God," he writes, "which acts on us in Christ the Son, is so utterly God's love and the active self-disclosure of His being, that it is eternally directed upon Him as Bearer of this eternal love. And this not only in the sense of ideal pre-existence—for then He were but the temporal and historic correlate of God's eternal love—but even irrespectively of His earthly existence; God's love directed upon Him is the love of the Father to the Son in the secret of the eternal Divine life, or, to put it so (since no other terms are possible), in a real pre-existence. Also—to take the other side of the same conception—this Son, loved eternally of God, is not only sent by the Father into the world; He has come by His own loving act" (449).

CHAPTER X.

THE SELF-LIMITATION OF GOD IN CHRIST.

CERTAIN phenomena in the recent history of British dogmatics entitle one to speak of a strongly revived interest in what are known as the Kenotic theories of our Lord's person. Nor is this renascence at all surprising. For the criticism poured upon the Kenotic hypothesis on its first announcement, though frequently described as shattering, does not impress the reader of a later generation as having been particularly sympathetic or far-seeing. It was in part the hostility of the unimaginative. And some of the objections had that very bad quality in an argument, that they proved too much. They failed to allow for the distinction between a principle and the forms in which it may be applied.

A quickened sense of the real issues at stake has induced several living theologians to re-open the problem on Kenotic lines. It would be foolish to say that anything like a movement has begun. But the coincidence of result is striking when we take a series of important works published within the last fifteen years. I need not pause upon the books of Principal Fairbairn and Dr. Forrest,

LITERATURE—Gifford, *The Incarnation*, 1897 ; Thomasius, *Christi Person und Werk*, 1853 ff. ; Gess, *Christi Person und Werk*, 1870–87; Frank, *System der christlichen Wahrheit*³, 1894 ; Godet, *Commentary on St. John's Gospel*, 1877 ; Bruce, *Humiliation of Christ*², 1881 ; Bensow, *Die Lehre von der Kenose*, 1903 ; Forsyth, *Person and Place of Jesus Christ*, 1909 ; Gore, *Dissertations*, 1898 ; Weston, *The One Christ*, 1907; Mason, *Conditions of our Lord's Life on Earth*, 1896 ; Powell, *Principle of the Incarnation*, 1896 ; Forrest, *The Authority of Christ*, 1906 ; Adams Brown, *Christian Theology in Outline*, 1906.

though it is noteworthy that Dr. Forrest's attitude to the Kenotic view has become even more decisively that of championship in his *Authority of Christ* (1906) than in his *Christ of History and of Experience* (1897). In a valuable article on the Trinity, Bishop D'Arcy, after speaking of the subordinate character of the divinity of the Son as portrayed in the New Testament, adds: "It is this derivative character which helps us to realise that the limitations to which He submitted during His life on earth involved no breach of His Divine identity. . . . His Divinity is dependent from moment to moment upon the Father; and therefore there is no difficulty in accepting what seems to be a necessary inference from the facts of the Gospel history, that, during our Lord's life on earth, there took place a limitation of the Divine effluence."[1] On kindred lines Principal Garvie and Mr. W. L. Walker appear to be at one in regarding the temporal *kenosis*, if the phrase may be permitted, as the symptom and manifestation of an eternal process of self-emptying native to Godhead as such. Mr. Walker, taking the Cross as the distinctive symbol of the inmost being of deity, insists on this timeless background of the earthly drama. "The life of God," he writes, "is for ever the same life of self-denial and self-sacrifice, because it is the life of perfect Love. Out of His overflowing fulness He is constantly giving of Himself in creation in order to find Himself again in those whom He has raised to participation in the Divine life. This is that eternal *kenosis* in which 'the Son' is for ever passing out of 'the Father' and again returning to the bosom of God."[2] It is also from this point of view that Dr. Garvie finds it possible to harmonise the higher being of Christ with His searching experience of temptation, and to reach a more spiritual construction of His miracles. "The miracles," he contends, "did not lessen the self-emptying of the incarnation"; for there still existed conditions of an ethical character under which alone the derived power could be employed, namely, intense sympathy

[1] *DCG.* ii. 762. [2] *Gospel of Reconciliation*, 169.

with man and absolute trust in God.[1] Notwithstanding this, Dr. Garvie claims the right to criticise the older forms of Kenoticism, and does so with much severity; thus acknowledging the distinction just laid down between a principle and the varying methods of its application. In 1907 Bishop Weston published a work of high ability, entitled *The One Christ,* in which a reserved and circumspect yet clearly-marked form of Kenotic theory was put forward and defended at full length. He speaks, for instance, of the Christ of the Gospels as "the Son of God self-restrained in conditions of manhood." "We seem committed by the Evangelists," he writes, "to the opinion that the Incarnate did really and truly become man, following the law of human life from its very beginning; so that the law of self-restraint, self-imposed before the act of Incarnation, required of Him that He should taste of the unconsciousness or practical unconsciousness of the unborn child" and "made it both necessary and possible that in the state of His humiliation He should have no consciousness that His assumed, human soul could not mediate."[2] And, to take a final example, in 1909 there appeared Principal Forsyth's rich and living volume, *The Person and Place of Jesus Christ,* the closing chapters of which are an exposition not so much of a speculative theory of the incarnation as of certain vital religious postulates inseparable from firm belief in Christ's divinity. Taking the Kenotic idea as clue (rightly combined with the conception of a progressively realised Incarnate person), he argues that "we face in Christ a Godhead self-reduced but real, whose infinite power took effect in self-humiliation," and adduces the further consideration that "as God, the Son in His freedom would have a Kenotic power over Himself corresponding to the infinite power of self-determination which belongs to deity."[3] The difficulties of such a view impress him as more scientific than religious. And yet in spite of this Dr. Forsyth nowhere confuses the principle with specific

[1] *Studies, etc.,* 234.
[2] *The One Christ,* 190, 181, 184.
[3] Lecture XI.

examples of it, but feels free to say that there is something presumptuous in certain older Kenotic efforts to body forth just what the Son of God must have undergone in becoming man.

These typical quotations, which it would be easy to multiply, indicate that the conception they involve is once more striving for expression. It is a conception of immense *religious* significance. Somehow—to describe the method exactly may of course be beyond us—somehow God in Christ has brought His greatness down to the narrow measures of our life, becoming poor for our sake. This must be taken as seriously in dogmatic as in Christian piety, and a place must be found for the real fact which it denotes in our construction of the Incarnate life. To surround or accompany it with neutralising qualifications is inept. The difficulties of a Kenotic view are no doubt extremely grave; yet they are such as no bold construction can avoid, and in these circumstances it is natural to prefer a view which both conserves the vital religious interest in the self-abnegating descent of God (*Deus humilis*) and adheres steadfastly to the concrete details of the historic record. Obviously these details constitute our sole medium of revelation; and orthodox writers are occasionally prone to forget that it is no merit in a Christological doctrine that it claims to deal successfully with remoter problems not forced on the mind by New Testament representations of Jesus, while at the same time it makes our one trustworthy source of information, the Gospel narrative, dubious or unintelligible. Our only use for a theory is to synthesise facts definitely before us, not to do something else.

Take the central thought of the Gospel, which has captured and subdued the Christian soul, and let us ask whether it has received full justice at the hands of ecclesiastical Christology. God in Christ, we believe, came down to the plane of suffering men that He might lift them up. Descending into poverty, shame, and weakness, the Lord was stripped of all credit, despoiled of every right, humbled to the very depths of social and historical ignominy, that in this self-abasement of God there might be found the redemption of man. So that the Gospel tells of Divine sacrifice, with the cross as its unspeakable consummation; the Saviour's lot was one of poverty, suffering, and humiliation, until the triumphant death and resurrection which wrought deliverance and called mankind from its grave. Hearts have thrilled to this message that Christ came from such a height and to such a depth! He took our human frailty to be His own. So dear were human souls to God, that He travelled far and stooped low that He might thus touch and raise the needy. Now this is an unheard-of truth, casting an amazing light on God, and revolutionising the world's faint notions of what it means for Him to be Father; but traditional Christology, on the whole, has found it too much to believe. Its persistent obscuration of Jesus' real manhood proves that after all it shrank from the thought of a true "kinsman Redeemer"—one of ourselves in flesh and spirit. Christ's point of departure was Godhead, no doubt, yet in His descent He stopped half-way. The quasi-manhood He wore is so filled with Divine powers as to cease to belong to the human order.

He became poor—there a new light falls on God, who for us became subject to pain; but one may well feel that the light is not enhanced but rather diminished if with tradition we have to add that nevertheless He all the time remained rich. For in so far as He remained rich—in the same sense of riches—and gave up nothing to be near us, our need of a Divine Helper to bear our load would be still unsatisfied. What we require is the never-failing sympathy which takes shape in action, "entering," as it has been put, "into conditions that are foreign to it in order to prove its quality." Jesus' life then becomes a study in the power, not the weakness, of limitations, while yet the higher Divine content transfigures the limits that confine it. And it is just this sympathy without reserve which appears when the fact of Christ becomes for us a transparent medium through which the very grace of God is shining.

God, we now know, is love; but it was necessary that He should live beside us, in the form of one finite spirit, in order that His love and its sacrifice might be known to men and win back their love. So Browning thought of it:—

> "What lacks then of perfection fit for God,
> But just the instance which this tale supplies
> Of love without a limit? So is strength,
> So is intelligence; let love be so,
> Unlimited in its self-sacrifice,
> Then is the tale true and God shows complete."

There are obvious differences between the older Kenotic theories and the new. For the Christian thinker of to-day is more reserved and proportionally less vulnerable on points of speculation. A favourite charge against the older construction was the charge of mythology. Kenoticism, it was said, was like nothing so much as pagan stories of the gods.[1] The reproach is natural on the lips of one who totally repudiates the idea of incarnation. If a man does not feel that in Christ we stand confronted with the outcome of a vast Divine sacrifice—with what is nothing less than an ineffable fact of Divine history—for him the problem which Thomasius and the rest were trying to solve (and, as a preliminary, to state) has of course no existence. He cannot see what the discussion is about. But the more recent Kenotic statements have the advantage that they aim rather at proceeding by way of interpretative postulate, *a parte post*, so reaching after the Kenotic conception as the key by which alone it is possible to unlock the problems of the historic Life, but not venturing, as some earlier hypotheses had ventured, to expatiate in the domain of speculation *a parte ante*, or to describe the steps in which the incarnation was actualised with theosophical minuteness. We have learnt from Lotze, many of us, that it is vain to ask "how being is made." It is vain to speak as if the view-point of Deity were our own, or to ignore the peripheral character of our judgments; and any con-

[1] Some of the modern objections were anticipated by Celsus (cf. Glover, *The Conflict of Religions*, 246).

struction of Christ's person in which the modern mind is to feel an interest must start from, and proceed through, the known facts of His human life. The known facts, we say advisedly; for discussion has made it clear that Kenoticism, be it right or wrong, does not in the least depend for its cogency on two or three isolated passages in St. Paul. We have only to place side by side the two words of Jesus: "Lo, I am with you alway, even unto the end of the world," and "Of that day and that hour knoweth no man, neither the Son but the Father," to have the entire problem before us. It is present in the unchallenged facts of the New Testament, whether or not we choose to theologise upon it.

Four positions may be taken, I think, as implicit in the completely Christian view of Jesus; and it is difficult to see how Kenoticism in some form is to be avoided by one who asserts them all, and at the same time believes that a reasoned Christology is possible. They may be put as follows:—

(1) Christ is now Divine, as being the object of faith and worship, with whom believing men have immediate, though not unmediated, fellowship.

(2) In some personal sense His Divinity is eternal, not the fruit of time, since by definition Godhead cannot have come to be *ex nihilo*; His pre-mundane being therefore is real, not ideal merely.

(3) His life on earth was unequivocally human. Jesus was a man, a Jew of the first century, with a life localised in and restricted by a body organic to His self-consciousness; of limited power, which could be, and was, thwarted by persistent unbelief; of limited knowledge, which, being gradually built up by experience, made Him liable to surprise and disappointment; of a moral nature susceptible of growth, and exposed to life-long temptation; of a piety and personal religion characterised at each point by dependence on God. In short, He moved always within the lines of an experience humanly normal in

constitution, even if abnormal in its sinless quality. The life Divine in Him found expression through human faculty, with a self-consciousness and activity mediated by His human *milieu.*

(4) We cannot predicate of Him two consciousnesses or two wills; the New Testament indicates nothing of the kind, nor indeed is it congruous with an intelligible psychology. The unity of His personal life is axiomatic.

Now it is impossible to think these four positions together save as we proceed to infer that a real surrender of the glory and prerogatives of deity, "a moral act in the heavenly sphere," must have preceded the advent of God in Christ. We are faced by a Divine self-reduction which entailed obedience, temptation, and death. So that religion has a vast stake in the *kenosis* as a fact, whatever the difficulties as to its method may be. No human life of God is possible without a prior self-adjustment of deity. The Son must empty Himself in order that from within mankind He may declare the Father's name, offer the great sacrifice, triumph over death; and the reality with which, to reach this end, He laid aside the form and privilege of deity is the measure of that love which had throbbed in the Divine heart from all eternity.

It is clear that the value of this discussion, if any, will lie not in the untrammelled nature of a speculation, but in the luminous explication of historic fact. We would know the limits within which must lie the truth we are seeking, but there is no suggestion that it is given to man to watch God as He becomes incarnate. Yet once it has been made clear that Christ is God—since redemption is as typically a Divine work as creation—the possible alternatives are few. It may be said that He acquired Godhead—which is pagan. Or that He carried eternal deity unmodified into the sphere of time—which is unhistoric. Exclude these options, and it only remains to say that in Christ we are face to face with God, who in one of the distinguishable constituents of His being came amongst us by a great act of self-abnegation. But there is no possibility of forming a precise scientific conception of what took place; for that, be it reverently said, we should have to become incarnate personally. We cannot know with final intimacy any experience through which we have not passed. Everywhere in life, in nature, in history, in personality, there are, for each of us, irreducible and enigmatic facts, which we can touch and recognise and register, but of which we never become masters intellectually. Nature itself is full of new beginnings, of real increase, of novel fact not deducible from the previous phases of the cosmos; and this we are bound simply to report, admitting its inscrutability. In short, there is an alogical element in things, not to be measured by the canons of discursive mind. Over and over again it meets us in theology. There is for example the relation of an eternal God to events of time. No mystery could be deeper than the fact—accepted by all types of Christianity—that the Eternal has revealed Himself notably in a human being who lived at the beginning of the Christian era, and that the *meaning* of Jesus is at once immersed in past historic fact and perpetually present to faith. But if this difficulty, so opaque for minds like ours, is an essential implicate of belief in revelation, may it not be that such mystery as is involved in the passage of the Son from His eternal being to a life of limitation and growth is inseparable from a reasoned conviction of Christ's higher nature? Have we the right to ask that Christology should be more transparent than Theology? Whether we are dealing with the surprises of nature, the free personal entanglements of history, the antinomies of grace and freedom, or the incarnation of the living God, plainly we must follow the same path. If the facts contain a wonderful and transcendent element, the theory by which we elucidate them will reproduce this wonderfulness and transcendence. In any case, being is too rich and manifold for us to lay down *à priori* regulations to the effect that this or that, even though worthy and morally credible, is impossible for God.

It is essential, however, that the categories we employ should be genuinely moralised. Our theological calculus must rise above the physical and partially mechanical conceptions which served the Ancient Church. There will always be metaphysic in Christology, but it ought to be a metaphysic of the conscience, in which not substance but Holy Love is supreme.[1] Nothing in Dr. Forsyth's treatise is more wholesome or more inspiring than his sustained contention that we may help our age to conceive the incarnation by giving full scope to this ethicising vein. He shows that the habit of ethical construction must be carried over the whole field. A real *kenosis* is a moral as well as a theological necessity: the impulse from which it sprang was moral; it is the moral constitution of God-head which made it possible; moral forces sustained the self-reduced Life on earth and gave it spiritual value. As it has been put, the conditions under which Christ lived "were the moral result of a moral pre-mundane act, an act in virtue of which, and of its moral quality continued through His life and culminating in His death, Christ redeems and saves."[2] And yet in all this there is nothing of mere dull "moralism," draining the red life-blood out of a great Gospel; instead, the incarnation comes home to us as an ethically appealing act of God, not overwhelming us by display, but subduing, because enlightening and persuading, the conscience and the will.

This is too often ignored when the discussion comes to circle round the idea of Divine immutability. For then the subject of *kenosis* may be canvassed quite irrespectively of holy love, the changelessness of the Absolute—with its implicit denial that prayer is answered, or that there can be such a thing as a Divine saving *act*—being used to put the very idea of Divine self-limitation out of court. Sheer unchangeableness is, of course, something

[1] Cf. a suggestive article by Drown in the *Hibbert Journal* for April 1906.

[2] J. K. Mozley, reviewing Forsyth, in the *Journal of Theological Studies* for Jan. 1911, p. 300.

against which no human pleading can bear up; but it is worth asking whether it ought to figure in a Christian argument. The immutability to which certain writers appeal would really involve—given a world of changing moral agents—the gravest ethical caprice. God would be arbitrary, inasmuch as in varying moral situations He would act with mere mechanical self-consistency. Now it is not at all excessive to say that what Christ reveals in God is rather the infinite mobility of absolute grace bent on the redemption of the lost, the willingness to do and bear whatever is compatible with a moral nature. What is immutable in God is the holy love which makes His essence. We must let Infinitude be genuinely infinite in its moral expedients; we must credit God with infinite sacrifice based on His self-consciousness of omnipotence. We must believe that the love of God is "an almighty love in the sense that it is capable of limiting itself, and, while an end, becoming also a means, to an extent adequate to all love's infinite ends. This self-renouncing, self-retracting act of the Son's will, this reduction of Himself from the supreme end to be the supreme means for the soul, is no negation of His nature; it is the opposite, it is the last assertion of His nature as love."[1]

This may be put otherwise by saying that omnipotence—in this discussion a quite fundamental attribute—exists and operates in a moral universe and under moral conditions, and that if we think away this pervasive ethical quality from almightiness, it is not predicable of the God we Christians believe in. Now, while omnipotence is in one sense limited or conditioned by holy love, in another sense it is magnified. In virtue of that love, its range of possibility broadens out endlessly. God's moral freedom opens doors to Him which otherwise are shut. May it not be that only the perfectly Holy is free to transcend self and live in other lives, the sinful being so immured in self that for them it is impossible to overflow the estranging bounds, and pass into alien forms of experience? Love

[1] Forsyth, *op. cit.* 313–14.

with resource like God's has a boundless capacity of self-determination. For us men and our salvation, it may well be, He committed Himself, in one aspect of His personal being, to a grade of experience qualified by change and development, thus stooping to conquer and permitting the conditions of manhood to prevail over His own freedom. If the alternatives are an unethical conception of immutability and a pure thought of moral omnipotence, which makes room for Divine sacrifice, the Christian mind need not hesitate. Every theory which accepts a real incarnation must deny that the lowliness of our life is incongruous with Godhead, and hold that, as it has been put, our Lord became "representative of mankind not only on the sacrificial side but also on the side of human weakness."[1]

Can analogies be found which help us with the thought of Divine self-limitation? None certainly which take us the whole way. It is the very depth of nature in deity which makes the idea of self-confinement difficult; for we cannot see how infinitude could narrow its own circle. Yet it is noteworthy that always in the human world growth of moral nature brings with it a deepened power of self-abnegation. Elevation of life means more power to descend. From omnipotence let us now turn to omniscience. Here it is easy to make a commencement. We are constantly limiting our actually present knowledge without altering our personal identity. We do this when we voluntarily close our eyes, or fall asleep, or, for love's sake or duty's, withdraw our minds

[1] "For supreme Spirit subject was to clay,
And Law from its own servants learned a law,
And Light besought a lamp unto its way,
And Awe was reined in awe,
At one small house of Nazareth;
And Golgotha
Saw Breath to breathlessness resign its breath,
And Life do homage for its crown to death."
(Francis Thompson, *Selected Poems*, 28.)

from the sources of mental interest and enrichment. Dr. Forsyth has recently elaborated these analogies with special care. He selects the instances of the reduction or obscuring of self-consciousness by a drug voluntarily taken in self-sacrifice; of the musical genius, who renounces the practice of his art for social love and service until "the first brief years of artistic joy and fame might well seem to him at moments almost to belong to another life"; of the young keen philosopher, who at the call of family need abjures the life of speculative thought to merge himself in the pedestrian actualities of an existence far from "the native land of his suppressed powers." In each case the mental field is narrowed and impoverished at the behest of sympathy. Or we may urge the analogy of the man summoned by need of fatherland or city to abandon the high simplicities of refined private life, where the transparent moral situations are easily controlled, and insight is equal to duty, for the coarser and often baffling moral perplexities of war or politics, with the resulting all but incessant conflict between competing forms of right action—between the legitimate claims, say, of kindred or old friendship, and of national or civic trust. At first it may seem as if he had mutilated his moral being by a descent into the field of dubious practical compromise. Increase in a certain kind of knowledge entails a multiplication of perils for his conscience. But yet, given a true man—of Lincoln's stamp—character visibly strengthens under the strain. Just through these hardships of ethical decision, and the stern duty of temporarily averting his mind from the lucid moral rules that once sufficed, and of searching out with care, and it may be agony, the more complex principles needed to guide him in the multiform intricacies of the new life, the man's inward stature and moral reach expand. The utterances of his moral consciousness are deeper now, broader, more worthy of man at his best and highest. Some picture like this may render it less impossible to conceive the free act of God in Christ as He subdued

Himself to the conditions of human life. The analogy, I am aware, holds solely in this point, that the "Son" left a sphere above the conflict of good and evil that in love He might enter a world of pain, struggle, and dependence; yet as an analogy it has the advantage of moving always within the field of ethical experience. It was in the province of moral realities, of knowledge at its highest, that He who humbled Himself to the death of the cross gained the name above every name.

Of course no analogy is commensurate with the Divine fact. Too often we form ideals of self-sacrifice, only to discover with shame that they are partial transcripts of our character, and that we are unable to *conceive* anything more than a certain degree nobler than we *are*. And this means that we are ethically incompetent to imagine all the Divine capacity of self-renunciation. We can but believe in it as more than we could ask or think.

How then shall we speak intelligibly of the experience undergone by God the Son as He passed into the sphere of change?[1] Thomasius, as we have seen, taught the abandonment of relative attributes of deity such as omnipotence and omniscience, and the retention of essential attributes like holiness and love. But the distinction is not one which can be maintained. For one thing, it is only if creation is not eternal, if there is not always a world to be ruled and known and pervaded, that the term "relative" holds. Apart from this, and assuming that the world had a beginning in time, still it must be held that once the world is there the Divine relations of omnipotence, omniscience, and the like are as really essential as righteousness or grace. Each is a necessary determination of Godhead. "In short," as it has been put, "we cannot think away the relative attributes of God without at the same time thinking away the relation. But this holds not of God merely, but of all subjects whatsoever. Dispersion into the colours of the spectrum is not essential to sunlight as

[1] Cf. the argument of Bensow, *Die Lehre von der Kenose*, 272 ff.

such, but so soon as we use a prism this relative attribute of light cannot but appear."[1]

Thus to talk of the abandonment of this or that attribute on the part of the Eternal Son is a conception too sharp and crude, too rough in shading, for our present problem. God ceases to be God not merely when (as with Gess) there is a self-renunciation actually of the Divine self-consciousness, but even when such qualities as omnipotence are parted with. Still, though not parted with, attributes may be transposed. They may come to function in new ways, to assume new forms of activity, readjusted to the new condition of the Subject. It is possible to conceive the Son, who has entered at love's behest on the region of growth and progress, as now possessing *all*[2] the qualities of Godhead in the form of concentrated potency rather than of full actuality, δυνάμει rather than ἐνεργείᾳ. For example, in its eternal form the absolute intelligence of God acts as an intuitive and synchronous knowledge of all things; when the Eternal passes into time, however, knowledge for Him must take on a discursive and progressive character. Similarly, a man who has tested his own abilities may know that all mathematics is potentially in his grasp, although in point of fact he has mastered no more than is needful for his calling. So Christ, who in virtue of His relation to the Father had Divine knowledge within reach, took only what was essential to His vocation. Though on many subjects He shared the ignorance as well as the knowledge of His contemporaries, yet He had at command all higher truth which can be assimilated by perfect human faculty. In His unique knowledge of God He knows that relatively to which all else is but subordinate detail. This is the

[1] Bensow, *op. cit.* 125.

[2] I say all qualities equally, ethical and physical; for while no stain of sin ever touched His holiness, it is clear from Jesus' reply to the youth who called Him "good Master" that we cannot predicate of Him the changeless and untemptable perfection of God *per se*. There is a modification therefore even of the attributes which Thomasius calls immanent, but the modification is not in their essence but in their form of existence.

kind of *spiritual* omniscience that seems to be claimed for Him in the Gospels.

The same principle may be applied to omnipotence, provided we bear well in mind that there is no such thing, even in God, as an omnipotence which is not morally conditioned. God is almighty in the sense that He has power to do whatever He may will; and that He may will, for the sake of His human children, to limit His almightiness, translating it into a form compatible with our experience, is very credible to those who believe in the supremacy of Holy Love. Not only so, but in the historic Jesus there is a derived power over the souls of men, as over nature, which may be viewed as a modified form of the power of Godhead. It is not omnipotence *simpliciter*, but it is such power within the human limits as we feel to be akin to almightiness and prophetic of the hour when the Risen Lord should say: "All power is given Me in heaven and in earth." Omnipresence is more baffling; and yet perhaps only at first sight. We have to strip off the false deistic or pantheistic associations with which the idea has become encrusted, and to recognise that what faith asserts of God is not that He is everywhere present in an infinitely extended universe, with a physical ubiquity like that of ether, but that He is absolutely superior to, and independent of, the limitations of space and distance. But as the Eternal may enter time, so He may have positive relations to space and the spatial life we live. Now this transcendence of spatial limitations, combined with these positive relationships, is present or implicit in Christ's redemptive mission—in His triumphant capacity, that is, to accomplish in Palestine a universally and eternally valid work unhampered by the bounds of "here and there." As part of history, His work has a date and place, yet its power far transcends them. So the eternal form of Divine existence and the time-form are here vitally related to each other. The exchange of the one for the other is no negation of God's specific being; it is the supreme energetic act of perfect Love. Love is the link which binds the pre-temporal Word to the living and dying Jesus.

It may be said that such a conception of "potentiality" means in strictness that the human Jesus *became* God by slow degrees; but the objection cannot, I think, be made good. This is no case of a mere man rising at last to Divine honours; throughout the Person in view is One whose life is continuous with the life of God, in whom, as an infinite fountain, there exists eternally all that Jesus is to grow to. What Christ is by potency, with a potentiality based in His personal uniqueness, God is actually for ever. Moreover, the willed latency to which the properties of absolute Godhead are reduced in the life of earthly change and shadow is destined to be replaced, through moral triumph, by the fulness of life dwelling in the exalted Lord. From beginning to end there is no breach of personal continuity, nor any ascent of bare manhood to a greatness it has neither right to hold nor power to wield.

The Gospel facts reveal the outcome of this Divine act of self-abnegation. It is a life wholly restrained within the bounds of manhood. Outside the conditions imposed by the choice of life as man the Son has no activity or knowledge. At each point His experience is mediated through the authentic powers of manhood: thought, feeling, volition, speech are qualified by the supreme fact that now He lives in finitude and must make His own finite and successive adjustment of the relationships which obtain between perfect man and the Father, between the true Brother and His brethren. The primary act of will by which He came here has made it impossible that He should arbitrarily pass into the non-human sphere, for its moral quality and content persist in all His experience on earth. It was vital to His human goodness, as to His piety, that He should dwell within the self-chosen limits, evoking from mundane conditions the utmost they are capable of yielding to a sinless nature. Abnormal power and knowledge, it is true, are His intermittently; but at each juncture they were such as His work demanded, and faint analogies even to His possession of the Spirit may be found in the life of prophet and apostle. He was simply bound to be what He *seemed* to be. Prayer and death are the seals of His oneness with us. He needs God, even when He shares His life; and in prayer He finds Him day by day. And as death is the most real thing we do, so Jesus died when His hour had come, accepting this destiny as one in whom there dwelt no power which a perfect manhood could not mediate. "In His human life on earth, as Incarnate," writes Moberly, "He is not sometimes, but consistently, always, in every act and every detail, human. The Incarnate never leaves His Incarnation. . . . Whatever the reverence of their motive may be, men do harm to consistency and truth by keeping open as it were a non-human sphere or aspect of the Incarnation. This opening we should unreservedly desire to close. There were not two existences of, or within, the Incarnate, side by side with one another. If it is all Divine, it is all human too. By looking for the Divine side by side with the human, instead of discerning the Divine within the human, we miss the significance of them both."[1] It is fatal to tamper with the Gospel stories by checking our first instinct to understand them humanly; by applying an unknown standard of divinity we shall but lose the man, and be no nearer God.

This, however, brings up the question whether the Son Incarnate can ever have known Himself to be Divine. Was the *kenosis* such that it annulled even the consciousness of a higher relationship? Some writers have contended that to the end Christ remained unaware of His being God in flesh, urging that on no other terms can we assert the genuinely human character of His experience. In particular, it has been held that while sin was an impossibility for Jesus, we may conceive this impossibility as having been

[1] *Atonement and Personality*, 97.

hidden from Himself, so that He faced each new conflict with that reality of effort, that refusal to count the issue a foregone conclusion which is vitally characteristic of moral life. And from this it might seem to follow that His primary descent into the sphere of finitude had veiled in nescience His eternal relationship to the Father. Yet we need not entangle the two positions with each other. It can only have been in mature manhood and perhaps intermittently that Christ became aware of His divinity—which must have remained for Him an object of *faith* to the very end. Now, if incarnation means Divine self-subjection to the conditions of our life, it does not appear that even such a discovery on Christ's part of His own essential Sonship must inevitably suggest to Him the total impossibility of moral failure. But while His assurance of victory can never have been mechanical, or such as to dispense Him from vigilance, or effort, or seasons of depression, it was none the less real and commanding. There is no reason why His consciousness of unique intimacy with the Father, and of the crucial importance of His mission, should not have imparted to Jesus, in each temptation, a firmly-based confidence of victory, though He knew not in advance how or how soon the final triumph would be vouchsafed.

In any case, it is only by degrees that the full meaning of His relationship to the Father, with its eternal implicates, can have broken on Jesus' mind. The self-sacrifice in which His earthly life originated drew a veil over these ultimate realities. But if He lives in glory now, and if an uninterrupted unity binds the present majesty to the mortal career, we are led to believe that the veil must gradually have worn thinner and more translucent, until, at least in high moments of visitation, He knew Himself the Son conditioned in and by humanity. In whatever ways the significance of His relationship to God betrayed itself, His unshared unity with the Father must at length have come to stand before His mind definitely as constitutive of His personality. Otherwise we should have to think of some moment of mysterious apocalypse—at the resurrection presumably—when in conditions to which we can attach no ethical significance the Risen Lord awoke to His own divinity. This has no relation to the data of the New Testament. The subject, however, of the gradual expansion of the Divine-human experience will come before us in the next chapter. I only note here in passing what will there be dwelt on.

It would seem that the self-imposition of limits by Divine love must be conceived of as a great supra-temporal act by which, in the almightiness of grace, the Son chose to pass into human life. An infinitely pregnant act; for in truth it involved all the conflict, renunciation, and achievement of the life to which it was the prelude. But it is not possible to conceive of this act as having been continuously repeated throughout the earthly life. We cannot think of the Incarnate One as confining Himself from moment to moment, by explicit volition, within the frontiers of manhood. That would simply lead back to the old untenable conception of a *krypsis* by which the Divine Self in Christ veils His loftier attributes, now less now more, and is actuated in each case by didactic motives. To return thus to a theoretic duality of mental life in our Lord against which all modern Christology has been a protest, is surely to sin against light. The acceptance of human relationships—to nature, to man, to God—belongs to the eternal or transcendent sphere, as a definitive settled act; it is not something consciously and continuously renewed in time. What *is* continuous with the decisive act of self-reduction is the moral quality of the life on earth, the permanent self-consecration of Jesus' will. But the self-limitation, transcendently achieved as a single, final deed, inaugurates a permanent condition or state of life, amid circumstances of change and suffering once for all accepted.

Two lines of argument often supposed to be vital to a complete Kenotic statement are noticeably absent from the foregoing exposition. First, no psychological theory is attempted as to the relations of the Divine and the human in Christ. All efforts to divide the ground here go astray. To construct a theory of how two streams of consciousness or will co-existed, or mingled, in the same personality, we must first ascertain that there *are* two streams; and this has never yet been proved. What seems evidence of the dualism is that mysterious clairvoyance on Christ's part, in hours of exalted self-consciousness, which recurs at intervals in the Gospel story. This, however, in no way represents a mental or spiritual duality; it is rather a profound and luminous intuition on Jesus' part of His own infinite significance both for God and man. Besides, the ethical interpretation of motive and meaning is of more importance than any psychological theory of method. Exactly how the Divine qualities in Christ, brought from the eternal sphere, were adjusted to the human lot we do not know and cannot tell; but the redemption He accomplished by life and death and victory is proof that the truth of Godhead was His inmost being, while yet He was our brother in humanity.

In the second place, our exposition is silent as to the "Word" or "Son" apart from His incarnation. In the older theology much is said as to the Logos *extra carnem*—in traditional phrase—as constituting the permanent and essential background of the Logos in flesh. It is held that we can make affirmations as to the unbroken maintenance of cosmic functions by the infinite Logos, "filling all things and uncircumscribed of any," even during the earthly life of Jesus; the Logos unlimited, that is, not only furnishes the power of the Incarnate life, but simultaneously lives in a universal creative relationship to the cosmos as a whole, to which the human and developing relations of the Incarnate sphere are simply additional, though with an independence of their own. The Word or Son is thus described as living at two centres, united indeed by what we may call continuity of personal being—as the bay is still one with the vast ocean—yet distinct in scope and dispensation: on the one hand, the Word omnipotent and omniscient, who dwells in all creatures by virtue of inalienable ubiquity, on the other the Word voluntarily restrained in manhood. And of these two co-existing states, the eternal and changeless state is the abiding dynamic ground of the temporal.

My reason for passing over this in silence is not that various analogies—more or less relevant and instructive—could not be adduced to illustrate the idea of a personality functioning in a dual relationship to its environment.[1] Yet even so, a closer scrutiny reveals the fact that all such analogies are defective at one or more vital points. Thus, to take one detail, the Logos incarnate has *ex hypothesi* no direct knowledge of the cosmic activities predicated of the Logos *extra carnem.* But there are two considerations of more importance. First, the New Testament data are insufficient. Bishop Weston has said that "the general tendency of the New Testament is towards the doctrine of the permanence of the universal life and cosmic functions of the eternal Word"[2]—their permanence, *i.e.*, during Christ's life on earth. But the phrases he has cited from St. Paul and the Epistle to the Hebrews can be made to carry his interpretation only by a *petitio principii*; for in both writers the term Son, as scholars are virtually agreed, has reference primarily to the historic and exalted Christ. Nothing else can be assumed to be in view. At most, then, apostolic statements on the subject—even if we suppose them to have had the problem before their minds—leave it undecided. St. John does not even know what is meant by the "Word incarnate" without looking at the story of Jesus; and we may therefore regard it as improbable that he would have cared to enter on speculations as to the non-incarnate Word.

Secondly, it is scarcely possible at this point to acquit certain traditional arguments of a tendency to ditheism. Thus it is urged that the cessation of the incarnate Word from His universal activities must produce a cosmic chaos. But a plea so dubious would seem to involve the far greater

[1] See for example Weston, *op. cit.* 151. [2] *Ibid.* 115.

religious peril of so separating the Father from the Son in a cosmic reference as to endanger the monotheistic view of the Trinity and negative the *inseparabilis trinitatis operatio* so memorably emphasised by Augustine. If the term "person" in Trinitarian doctrine is more than "aspect," it is certainly less than "individual." After all, it is a fundamental truth that the world is upheld by God, not by a constituent or part of God. There are spheres in which division of labour is unmeaning. We must simply confess that we know nothing of an existence of the Logos apart from but synchronous with His reality in Jesus, and that statements of a dogmatic character on the subject have no apprehensible reality for our minds.

It will be seen that these considerations bear with equal force on theories of an opposite kind. They bear, for instance, on Godet's view that during the period of the earthly life, when the existence of the Son within the Godhead was interrupted for a time, the Father Himself effected what is normally effected by the mediation of the Word.[1] But this is to be wise above what is written. Over all such problems there hangs a curtain, alike for discursive knowledge and for faith. And no employment can be less rewarding than the construction of hypotheses for which we possess no data.

Perhaps the strongest blow aimed at the Kenotic principle came from Ritschl, when he said that by very definition it deprives us of the right to say that we find God in Jesus. For the Kenotist, as he puts it, "Christ, at least in His earthly existence, has no Godhead at all."[2] Were the charge made out, it would mean that the incriminated class had repeated the mistake of the earlier Logos Christology, which, as we have seen, taught men to find in Jesus, not God Himself, but an inferior Divine essence. A full reply to the accusation would have to inquire whether the Ritschlian conception of what is meant by predicating

[1] *Commentary on St. John's Gospel.*

[2] *Justification and Reconciliation* (E.T.), 410.

Godhead of the historic Christ is itself satisfactory. It may be pointed out, however, that what Ritschl regards as an insuperable difficulty—the absence of certain Divine qualities—is simply essential to the personal advent of God in time. Surely there is truth in the argument of a suggestive writer, that wherever God reveals Himself, the veiling is as real as the revelation. "Chemistry does not show any more of Him than there is in chemistry; the revelation will be all shut up within its laws and limitations. May we not expect that in history, on the plane of human affairs, the same law will obtain? If God does not put more of Himself into chemistry than chemistry will hold, we may expect that He will not put more of Himself into humanity than humanity will hold. And thus the self-limitation, the self-emptying of Deity which we are told is an impossible conception, becomes the first condition of any revelation at all."[1] The position defended here is that only so—only by contracting His Divine fulness within earthly limits—could the redeeming God draw nigh to man. Further, the life of Jesus exhibits to us precisely that rendering of true deity in human terms, that absolute perfectness of life "in short measures," which answers to the Kenotic principle as rightly understood. We read the Gospels, and we find that in Jesus there was faith and hope and love in perfect fulness; that He lived in unbroken intimacy with the Father; that He manifested God to men as absolute holiness, love, and freedom; that He acted a Divine part in the experience of the sinful, forgiving their iniquities and imparting a new and blessed life. In Him there is realised on earth the human life of God, and it is a life whose chiefest glory consists in a voluntary descent from depth to depth of our experience. It is the personal presence of God in One who is neither omniscient nor ubiquitous nor almighty—as God absolute must be—but is perfect Love and Holiness and Freedom in terms of perfect humanity.

[1] Brierley, *Aspects of the Spiritual*, 35.

NOTE ON DR. SANDAY'S PSYCHOLOGICAL THEORY

In his *Christologies Ancient and Modern* (1910), Dr. Sanday has outlined a new and hitherto unexplored view of our Lord's person which we notice here both for its extremely stimulating quality and for the vivacious debate evoked by it. He is convinced that we understand the incarnation better by using the analogy of the meeting of Divine and human in ourselves. Now "the proper seat or *locus* of all divine indwelling, or divine action upon the human soul, is the subliminal consciousness" (p. 159). The influence of the Spirit plays upon the roots of our being. In comparison with conscious states the subconscious are "subtler, intenser, further-reaching, more penetrating. It is something more than a mere metaphor when we describe the sub- and unconscious states as more 'profound'" (p. 145). This is illustrated from another sphere. "The deepest truth of mysticism, and of the states of which we have been speaking as mystical, belongs not so much to the upper region of consciousness—the region of symptoms, manifestations, effects—as to the lower region of the unconscious" (p. 155). And the novel feature of Dr. Sanday's theory is the definite position that "the same, or the corresponding subliminal consciousness is the proper seat or *locus* of the Deity of the incarnate Christ" (p. 159). Thus we are to conceive the union of the human and Divine in Christ. We may draw a horizontal line, he writes, "between the upper human medium, which is the proper and natural field of all active expression, and those lower deeps which are no less the proper and natural home of whatever is divine. This line is inevitably drawn in the region of the subconscious. . . . Whatever there was of divine in Him, on its way to expression whether in speech or act, passed through, and could not but pass through, the restricting and restraining medium of human consciousness. This consciousness was, as it were, the narrow neck through which alone the divine could come to expression" (pp. 165–67). Dr. Sanday lays stress on this figure of the "narrow neck" as applied to our Lord's human consciousness. The expression is human, completely human; but that which is expressed is neither human alone nor Divine alone; but Divine and human fused or blended. While the Divine and the unconscious are not equated, it is held that the unconscious is the sphere within which Divine and human coalesce. Their mutual influence takes effect below the dividing-line at which the resultant consciousness emerges.

I can only summarise the objections to which this striking argument seems to be exposed. With Dr. Sanday's unreserved declarations as to the unity and consistency of Jesus' life, and his acceptance of the position that "there is no possible or desirable division between what is human in Him and what is Divine," there will, I imagine, be general sympathy. But we must ask whether his special solution of the problem can be permanently maintained.

(*a*) Is the superiority of the unconscious really tenable? Subliminal process is no doubt an indispensable concomitant of all mental life; psychology would, however, class it not as the higher form, but as a subordinate and ancillary condition of the fully conscious. Its content and quality are alike derived from consciousness; in Professor Stout's words, "it is an organised system of conditions which have been formed in and through bygone conscious experience." From the ethical point of view the difficulty is still graver, and I do not find it mitigated by what has been urged as to the "live" and active character of the contents of subliminal mind, or its independently receptive contact with the universe. Does the subconscious have moral qualities of *any* kind? It yields not merely the inspirations of genius or heroism, but the disordered and incoherent absurdities of dreams; is a vague and dubious magnitude of this sort calculated to help us to interpret Jesus? Why should we take this half-lit region of psychic life, regarding which we can only speak hypothetically or at second-hand—since it cannot of course be *known* directly—and say that it offers a truer and more worthy dwelling-place or medium of Godhead than is provided by the full intensity of consciousness? I question whether Christian mysticism is really on Dr. Sanday's side. The mystics appear to refer the soul's participation in God to His presence in their consciousness, their knowledge, will, and feeling—at least predominantly. Lastly, the subconscious has affinities rather with sleep, infant life, and animal instinct; which suggests that it is of a character too humble and inarticulate for Dr. Sanday's greater purpose.

(*b*) Inferentially the new theory involves a conception of

deity as unknowable. God is not conscious mind known to or in conscience and reason, but touches us rather beneath the line of clear thought and moral volition. Yet Christians define Him as love and holiness existing in the form of Absolute Personality; love conscious, ethical, rational. But this is something we simply cannot put in terms of the unconscious. We know what is meant by saying that the love which looked out of Christ's eyes, touching men's lives and making all things new for them, was literally the love of God Himself. But how shall we speak of a Holy Love whose fit home is in the subliminal? The only epithets rightly applied to deity have hitherto been drawn from the sphere of conscious will and reason; if they are vetoed, as the new theory appears to veto them, God becomes indescribable and unknown. Further, the facts which have been appealed to all through the ages in proof that in Christ deity and humanity were combined, are those of His spiritual authority, His sinlessness, His redeeming power, His filial consciousness, and the like. Certainly there is mystery in the manifestation, but the mystery *is in these forms of consciousness*, and is, I feel, in no way relieved by being referred to an inscrutable non-conscious background.

(*c*) Does the new hypothesis really evade the haunting dualism of tradition? It is proposed that instead of a vertical line between the two natures, as in older doctrine, we should draw a horizontal line between the upper human medium and the lower deeps where deity has a home. Dr. Sanday, it is true, insists that the interfusion of Divine and human is effected in the region of the subconscious, so that it is in a subliminal whole where the union has already been realised that the resulting full consciousness arises. But this in no way alters the fact that the full consciousness in question is merely human, so that to reach the Divine in Jesus we must still quit the human sphere. We still argue *from* one *to* the other, passing in either direction by a distinct movement of transition; we do not see them identified or merged in living oneness, as both faith and the ideal Christology are clear we must.

In a later pamphlet (*Personality in Christ and in Ourselves* 1911) Dr. Sanday concedes that he may have made the boundary-line between conscious and subconscious rather too sharp. The action and reaction between the two spheres is mutual and incessant. Nor does he wish, as he explains, to treat the subliminal as *per se* superior to the supraliminal. But if this be so, the question is whether one of the main arguments for his theory as a whole has not vanished. We must be able to predicate of the subconscious a deeper affinity with the Divine if it is to rank as *par excellence* the receptacle for indwelling or incarnated Godhead, an affinity which I have argued cannot be made out.[1]

[1] Cf. with the above two full and suggestive articles by Professor Henri Bois in the Montauban *Revue de Théologie* for July and September 1911, which deal at considerable length with Dr. Sanday's theory and its critics. Professor Bois agrees with Dr. Sanday in holding that the subconscious is the psychological *locus* of the indwelling of God in Jesus, but rejects the orthodox Trinitarian background of the new hypothesis.

CHAPTER XI.

THE SELF-REALISATION OF CHRIST.

ONE defect in traditional Christology, of which the best modern thought is sensible, is a tendency to construe our Lord's person in rigid and quiescent terms which are hostile to the idea of development. The Cyrilline theory, whatever its discretion in statement, left no place for growth in the Incarnate. He is represented as being complete *mit einem Schlage*, at a single stroke. The whole significance of His personality is given by fiat from the very outset. It is forgotten that a static theory of a dynamic reality must prove false, and that ethically qualified life unfolding within time is subject by definition to change and progress through which it attains to be explicitly and in act what it is by fundamental constitution. It was a symptom or consequence of this initial error that the fact of the historic Jesus' growth in power and knowledge came to be totally ignored, or, if not ignored, referred exclusively to His manhood. Humanity, even the humanity of God, it was conceded, must exhibit real modification and increase; hence the humanity of Jesus doubtless possessed these vital characteristics of a dilating and self-augmenting life. But to speak of Godhead as patient of change is self-contradictory. Deity is insusceptible of growth or diminution.

To-day, however, there is a natural reluctance to

LITERATURE—Dorner, *System of Christian Doctrine*, 1890; Forsyth, *Person and Place of Jesus Christ*, 1909; Weston, *The One Christ*, 1907; Orr, *Christian View of God and the World*, 1893; Edwards, *The God-Man*, 1895; Garvie, *Studies in the Inner Life of Jesus*, 1907; Bensow, *Die Lehre von der Kenose*, 1903.

break up Christ's single person into the two unrelated halves which any such view must postulate. His life, we are sure, is a unity both in being and doing; and all our efforts to show how it is one, and what sort of one it is, presuppose this unity as apprehended from the first by the Christian consciousness. If growth is predicable of one aspect of the whole, it is predicable of the whole to which that aspect belongs. It is inconceivable that what went on in Christ's manhood made no difference in His total person. Furthermore, change is a necessary condition of life in history, in which finite reality comes to itself through the issues of free and motived action. In particular, every reality of the kind called "ethical" not only realises but wins its life through interaction with a changing environment which serves to educe and reveal its latently moral character. Life for every moral agent lies open in the direction of the future; he is becoming that which he has not been and is not yet. He lives by moving; to make the same choice for ever would be to make no choice at all and *ipso facto* lapse from the moral plane. If, then, our Lord belongs to concrete history, His person cannot be a scene of stagnation; and the activity and movement constitutive of it is no mere evanescent accident, but vital to His individuality. There must be a sense in which His being is ever approaching completion. Finally, the maxim that development in Christ is excluded by the absolute immutability of Godhead is one, as we have seen, to be accepted only with great reserve. Inferences derived from the abstract conception of deity must be confronted, in this field, with the essential distinction between God *per se*, in His transcendent being, and God as He comes forth in self-impartation to spirits immersed in space and time. If the incarnation be a fact, it is obviously a fact involving the self-subjection of the Divine life to ethical laws and conditions of existence which are so far irrelevant to Godhead as such and apart from the incarnate relationship. The conception is difficult, of course; but the difficulty is one inherent in the assumed facts. God in man is by supposition otherwise qualified than God as absolute, "Himself unmoved, all motion's source"; and one deep-reaching qualification, apart from which there could be no true human life, is liability to real activity, growth, evolution within the time-series. And if, to leave these generalities, we contemplate the Christ of history, first at the outset of His career, next at its termination, we are clearly aware that the comparison reveals a movement between these points; a process whereby the significance of His personality has been enhanced. At the end it includes more of those qualities in virtue of which He is definable as Redeemer. "As God in manhood," writes Bishop Weston, "as God self-conscious in manhood, He is not at birth perfect in the sense of complete attainment; but only in the popular sense of being free from sin and from the lack of anything necessary to Him at the stage of life in which He was."[1] There is a becoming, and it yields an access of being.

We have the less need to dwell on these abstract principles, because stages or crises in Jesus' life can be indicated where, as in veins below the surface, the pulse and flow of movement is discernible, and the coalescence of the Divine and human within Him can be viewed as a process. To take only three instances: His baptism, His death, and His resurrection cannot have passed and left no mark. The result must have been to deepen the involution and co-inherence of the two mobile factors of His life and to secure their more perfect mutual irradiation. His baptism was in itself a token of a faith matured through resistance to early temptations; it sealed Him as One who had sustained unimpaired His filial relation to the Father, and in the long effort had acquired full ability and independence of moral life. And by sealing it, it made this moral character still more irrevocably fixed. But

[1] *Op. cit.* 291. It is noticeable that the evangelists do not place Jesus vividly before us till He has reached the maturity of His strength; they do not dwell on His childhood, for our attitude towards a little child is not the fitting attitude to our Redeemer.

this decisive act of self-identification with the sinful must have been inspired more by perfect faith than by a full perception of its implications, which only the future could disclose. When it transpired later that nothing would avail but the uttermost sacrifice of death, Jesus' acceptance of this final obligation, in a series of experiences interpretable at their height by the transfiguration—when love to men filled His expanding soul and by inward act He avowed His willingness to share their lot to the uttermost—raised Him to a yet sublimer plane, a more completely redemptive fulness and glory of moral being. But above all He fulfilled His person through His death and resurrection. Who can fail to see that Christ was more *Himself*—more fully and completely all that is denoted by the name Christ—when death was past, than when as a child He lay in Simeon's arms?[1] By His resurrection, St. Paul declares, He was installed as Son of God with power. Thus the Risen Life came not *ex abrupto*, or from without, but at the point when the life-content of Godhead had taken completely realised form within Him and become the mighty principle of an exalted and redeeming life in the Spirit. Mediated by experiences now past, and supremely by the experience of the cross, the identification of self-imparting Godhead with finite human forms was at last perfected, and the Divine noumenon, if we may call it so, become wholly one with the human phenomenon. And this *plerosis*, or development and culmination of the Redeemer's person, is an event or fact which answers spiritually to the great *kenosis* from which it had begun. The two are moral correlates. On the privative act of renunciation, lasting on in moral quality throughout the earthly career, there follows the re-ascent of self-recovery. He who lost His life for our sake thereby regained it.

It may help to make this general conception more luminous if we recur to the Christological axiom that our Lord's person and work constitute a single reality. If the work is dependent on the person, and moves through it to

[1] Cf. Kähler, *Angewandte Dogmen*, 65.

achievement, the person is in some real sense dependent on the work, fulfilled by its mediation, integrating all its virtue. It is not in our minds merely that the two condition each other, but objectively and in themselves. Now the work is admittedly a process. As part of history it could not be given *en bloc*; it had its times, its order, its movement from less to more. Hence real growth is predicable also of Christ's person; the union of God and man in Him was more completely actualised at death than at birth, when He rose than when He died. As the discharge of His vocation proceeded, His personality—which as an ethical constitution could not be *un fait accompli* from the outset—expanded into its own fulness. What He did flowed from what He was, but also He was in a real measure all that He did. He was creating Himself continually. In each moment of His present there was a constitutive persistence of His past, as His redeeming soul dilated in Divine capacity, not only modifying its quality but also increasing its intensity. Thus the cross was not for Him eventually a defeat; it was the last consummation of His person.

The principle touches every side of life. There is the ever-increasing degree in which His body became ministrant to the spirit; there is the growing moral stability which comes from duty done, from new responsibilities accepted. There is advance in His reasoning thought, in His mental fitness to be the medium of truth, His adjustment of personal relationships, His holy aversion to sin mingled with the knowledge that He is identified with the sinful, His awareness of supremacy over man and of oneness with the Father. He could be tempted, as God cannot. The creaturely weakness which quivered in Gethsemane had still to be clothed with power. All this, however, it is impossible to abstract from His person. It has no reality our minds can apprehend to say that He matured in mind, in character, in self-consciousness, but that His personality or Ego remained throughout immutably behind a veil, as a substratum unaffected by the phenomena of change. The word "person" has no content when we remove moral character, religious consciousness, and the mediatorial function which both subserve. Wherever reality exists of the kind we call "personal," it cannot be described adequately either by reference to a quite changeless Ego which abides untouched beneath the shifting mass of our whole psychical existence, the flux of experience, or in terms exclusively of the shifting flux itself. The fact is a combination of both. The conceptions of static identity with which our study of personality usually begins have to be laid aside, and we learn to conceive spiritual being rather as that which by its nature moves from potency to achievement. The concrete fact, in other words, presents itself as a moving continuity, a continuity which is *lived*—the core of it persisting, yet the modification of change not less real; while neither aspect, abstract and hypostatise it as we may, exists save in and through the other. Indeed, it is no bad figure which symbolises personality by a melody, in which each note is continuous with the rest and exhibits a tone-colour and value dependent on the whole, the melody meanwhile perpetually building itself up in successive notes which in turn subtly reflect the entire musical conception. However faulty the illustration, it serves to bring out the fact that the anterior stages of personal life pass, by a dynamic progress, into the later and richer stages, and that if we are to state the full truth, we must speak not only of a continuity of being but of a continuous becoming. It is no defect in finite personality that it should have this character; it is simply its nature. And already we have seen reason to contend that it was into this developmental form of existence that Divine love and life passed, when Christ was born to traverse all the authentic stages of human life.

Objections to this view may be raised from two sides. It may first be urged that the notion of an unperfected Life which still is perfect cannot be maintained. If we predicate change and progress of the Incarnate, not as man only, but in His one Divine-human personality, is not this to assert defect and shortcoming? If it be so, the fault lies with our human speech. "Imperfect," as meaning "uncompleted" or "inadequately realised," has become encrusted with illegitimate moral associations suggestive of sin or evil. But any given stage of a development short of the highest is not of course deficient in this moral sense. We distinguish the seed from the tree as "imperfect" only if we have first taken the tree as our criterion of reality. So regarded, imperfection is but a name for finitude; on the other hand, the finite, and it only, is capable of being perfected through the eventual realisation of its idea. It is of course this gradual and ethically mediated attainment of perfection which we ascribe to Christ. His life is a process which runs its course in time, and moves from a basis of constitution to a climax. To exist humanly is to unfold capacities originally present *in nuce*; the differential feature of Christ is the unique degree of capacity posited in the fact that He is God's Son in flesh. Whereas in any other child or youth there exists the potency only of a completed *finite* self-consciousness, in Christ the potency is infinite.

Secondly, it may be said that this application of the category of growth to Christ is equivalent to the assertion that though originally merely human, He *became* Divine. How can we think the life-content of Godhead as being gradually conveyed in its fulness to Jesus, the individual man, in proportion to His receptivity, without transferring the realities of incarnation to His life on earth, so that incarnation finally appears as the resultant of His human career, rather than its antecedent ground? This criticism is probably due to the frequent use of the brief but inaccurate phrase "gradual incarnation." But what is meant by those who use the phrase is simply to call attention to the ethically mediated development or self-fulfilment of a life which is, by original constitution, Divine-human. Such development they hold to be a moral necessity of the case, since, as Dorner puts it from an earlier standpoint, "the two-sided *Unio* cannot at the outset exist in the sphere of knowledge and volition proper, which presuppose self-consciousness; for neither human will nor consciousness can be actually existent at the outset."[1] This effort to construe the whole in ethical terms, which can never be satisfied by the juxtaposition or even the interpenetration of two disparate substances, leads naturally to a theory of the kind now described. To the Divine movement of self-impartation, a human recipiency in Jesus must answer at each point, the content more and more adjusting itself to the capacity of the form.

Our case then is this: First, it is never to be forgotten that there is a Christ at all only in virtue of an unspeakable Divine sacrifice. That fixes His proper plane; also it makes possible a redeeming Life in human form. Secondly, everywhere in the moral world, and so for Christ, it is a law that we have and inherit only that which we also win for ourselves, appropriating the initial gift by action, will, liberty. Thus we can believe that when Jesus came to Himself absolutely, through life, death, and the last victory, it was as fulfilling, and triumphantly entering upon, His implicit being. The gain of life for Him was in a sense regained. It was progress *in* personal unity with Godhead, not progress to it from outside. The life grew and moved onward to its mighty climax; death and victory set the crown upon it all; and the whole vast movement retains its moral quality because it came to pass through an unceasing conflict with sin and death and tragedy, sustained by perfect dependence on God and perfect love to man. So there unfolded in Christ that which had been enfolded within Him by the Eternal Love, to be restrained wholly by the bounds of manhood. Notwithstanding the personal identity which unites the Child of Nazareth to the risen Lord, this newness of life-content, this dynamic advance in ripened and articulated nature, is a cardinal element of the whole fact.

Thus the whole personality of Christ, as it has been expressed, "is not something given at the start by the

[1] *System of Christian Doctrine*, iii. 335.

existence side by side of the Divine and human natures, but something achieved by His life's action."[1] And of this self-fulfilment the presence of God in Jesus is the permanent underlying ground. It is not simply that God's care specially fostered a certain child, youth, man. Rather it is that the indwelling God, who is Love and Power, so formed and irradiated this expanding life that from within it became the perfected personality it was by potency. As instrumental factors of this growth many things may be specified—*e.g.* inborn disposition and the influences of ancestral piety—but the distinctive force is given by the personal inhabitation of God. There came—the order we cannot fix—the knowledge of His unshared connection with the Father. There came a sense of personal Redeemership, of a place and function answering to ancient promises of a Servant of the Lord who should save by vicarious pain. There came the discovery, through action, of His own inherent power to rescue lost men from all their sorest troubles, from the load of sin and the destroying powers of nature. Everything which can be truly said regarding the growth of His Messianic consciousness is in place here. Living in that age and land, He could only awake through certain thought-forms, coloured by ancient human experience, to His singular position in time and history. But the power resting on Him as Messiah He enjoys as His own possession. It could rest only on the Son. More and more He takes possession of it, till at last, on the immortal side of death, it fills Him in absolute and final measure.

But this general interpretation, as I believe, may be surveyed from a yet wider point of view, even if in candour we have to admit that a problem is far from completely soluble which contains, and is created by, two imperfectly known factors.[2]

[1] J. K. Mozley, *ut supra.*

[2] On what follows cf. Kähler, *Wissenschaft der christlichen Lehre*[3], 325–56.

The unification of Divine and human life in Christ may be regarded as the focus and meeting-point of two great spiritual movements of an essentially personal character. From above comes the creative initiating movement of God towards man, directed by the saving purposes of Holy Love. From beneath comes the yearning movement of man toward God, in faith and love and hope. These two personal currents—of salvation held forth and communion longed for—join and interpenetrate in the one person, Jesus Christ, in a fashion completely concrete, historical, apprehensible. In this confluent unification, which does not cease to be progressive because its *locus* has now come to be once for all within His single personality, is given the specific and final expression of an active relationship of God to the world posited with its very existence as His creation—rooted, therefore, in His eternal being. For Him redemption is re-creation; in it creation comes to its final goal. The writer who first named Christ "the Word" saw Him as the supreme expression of this Divine purpose for the world, so that all He utters by life and passion rests on and discloses some aspect of the Eternal Life as its ever-present background.

In all His relations to the finite, then, God appears in this specific light, this attitude of redemptive will. His presence in Jesus consummates the plan. It is He who calls the Divine-human person into history; it is He who sustains and perfects Him by a real indwelling which acts and re-acts upon a true human experience. In Christ, that is, the personal redeeming distinction or aspect in God through which He goes forth into the world, to save by truth and grace, takes historical form in the conditions of finite life. The Highest becomes a means to man's chief end. Recent attempts to conceive of God as Purpose, rather than as Infinite Thing or Quantity, are again raising our minds to the thought of Him as ever engaged with and on finite souls, moving toward them, energising within them, essentially directive, actual, and active.[1] But long before the Gospel had set this forth as the "far-off, Divine event to which the whole creation moves." And its whole centralised meaning and power is gathered up in Jesus. He is "the Incarnation, the Fulfilment, the expression in conditions of time and space, of that Intending Will which is coming to itself in the universe of human souls."[2] There is no longer any question of a quiescent Divine substance planted in bare mechanical juxtaposition with impersonal manhood; in Jesus' soul, rather, is given the spiritual life-content of God, the outgoing of His infinite redeeming Self into the experience of a growing finite spirit.

Further, on the human side the progressive and irreversible unification in Christ of life Divine and human was from the first conditioned by a unique basis of human personality, the ground of the future complete unity. The unity, as a fact lived out in time, was mediated by the gradual voluntary appropriation, on Jesus' side, of the Divine fulness of love, truth, holiness, power. In virtue of this appropriation, through the instrumentality of an obedience which never faltered, the human life of Jesus became the absolute organ of the Father's self-bestowal. The impartation of God is focalised in a decisive spiritual personality.

Thus on both sides, the originative equally with the receptive, real conditions can be found for that personal life-unity which was to be accomplished through the experiences of Jesus. In God all things begin from His eternal purpose to make Himself, in His Son, the means to the chief end of man; in Jesus is posited a uniquely qualified life, in special relations to the Father, and free like no other in history from the taint or disability of sin. These two, meeting and permeating in ways which the *kenosis* had made possible, issue finally in Godhead perfectly mediated into oneness with manhood. The basis and guarantee of that result are given *ab initio*; what

[1] Cf. W. Temple, *The Nature of Personality* (1911).

[2] Hutton, *Authority and Person of our Lord*, 9.

cannot be given, so long as the process remains moral, is the last consummate form. The life of Jesus, far from being episodic or accidental in the highest point of view, was constitutive of the person who emerged from it. In the words of Dr. Forsyth, whose exposition of this general view I have found deeply suggestive: "In Christ we have two things, the two grand actions of spiritual being, in final peace and eternal power. We have the whole perfect action of Godhead concentrated through one factor or hypostasis within it and directed manward both to create and redeem; and we have also the growing moral appropriation by man's soul moving Godward of that action as its own, as its initial Divine nature and content. . . . As His personal history enlarged and ripened by every experience, and as He was always found equal to each moral crisis, the latent Godhead became more and more mighty as His life's interior, and asserted itself with the more power as the personality grew in depth and scope. Every step He victoriously took into the dark and hostile land was an ascending movement also of the Godhead which was His base."[1]

Hence we may regard the union alternately and equally from two points of view, each of which is defined by the other. As the Father's gift, in a purpose infallibly sure of execution, it is Divinely real from the outset and *sub specie aeternitatis.* But also it is humanly actualised in time; it comes to fruition in One who "passes from a destiny to a perfection through a career." What we see during the earthly life is the aspect of creaturely unperfectedness, becoming perfect "in short measures"; at the resurrection it is made clear how much had always been latent in this Life by very origin, and how eventually, and, to the insight of faith, quite fully and irrevocably, the active and redeeming life of God is now become the vital content of humanity. If this be scouted as implying an antinomy, I should not be careful to deny it, nor do I think that the work of theology can be done without

[1] *Op. cit.* 338, 349.

encountering antinomies at every point where we touch the relations of eternity and time. At all events, this very difficulty meets us squarely as soon as we try to think out the meaning of Christian redemption. Redemption, as a concrete fact, insists on being contemplated in just these two ways. It is the outcome of eternal love, in whose designs there can be no breakdown; but also, as we know it, it is a temporal experience, successive, continuous, expectant. It *is*, yet is to be. Moreover, from the standpoint of theory it will always be impossible to interpret the receptivity in time of the believing soul as anything but the rival of the eternal grace which saves; in experience, on the other hand, grace fulfils itself in volition, and we find it liberty to yield to God. Thus religion itself is unintelligible if once we define eternity and time as sheerly disparate or mutually exclusive, or assume that our nature is impervious to God. And this Christian experience of being saved is positive evidence, given in immediate consciousness, that the union of God and man is a reality, achieved in regenerate men, however faintly, and that as a reality it is subject to conditions of growth in time.

If then we see clearly that God and man are not definable as opposites, and that time is susceptible of eternity, it will not seem incredible that there should have existed in Christ, under conditions never again repeated, a gradual coalescence of life Divine and human. It may be this is one reason why the New Testament does not hesitate to summon the Christian to share the very experience of Jesus—to be baptized with His baptism, to die His death, to live with Him the resurrection life. Divine though He be, it is not impossible that we should be one with Him. Such oneness is indeed the final end of His mission, and the nature of the real, always, is homogeneous with its end. Christ, in other words, was God incarnate in such modes that—in spite of the difference between Saviour and saved—we may follow Him on an ascending journey, and lay hold on a redeeming life which He has made real, near, and sure to us by translating it into the progressively appropriated content of His own soul. It is fact humanly given in Him, His by personal assimilation and ownership, that it may be saving fact received by man. First He lived the grace He was, finally He installed it in our world by death, and entered on universally redemptive sway. But the fount and origin of the whole was the vast pre-temporal transcendent act of self-abnegation on the part of God.

It will be agreed that if the self-limitation and the self-fulfilment of God in Christ, with which this chapter and the last have been concerned, are real and credible, they are also morally correlative. The juxtaposition is not accidental, or due to a mere craving for logical symmetry. Each answers to the other by an ethical necessity. The manifested Divine fulness which faith beholds in the exalted Lord, inconceivable though it be in one who grows on the soil of human nature, as merely human, is intelligibly continuous with the life prior to resurrection, and fitly crowns it. "*Worthy* is the Lamb that was slain to receive power and glory and blessing." Thus what He rose to requires that what He rose from—the frailty and the cross—should in turn have been the self-limiting of an absolute Life and Love, of a glory which could be resigned because it could also be resumed. This on one side. On the other, the moral glory of the *kenosis* points to the almighty consummation of the *plerosis* or re-ascent. God in His transcendence is not definable as moral character simply; there is a mode of being answering to the Holy Love which He is; and this Godhead of manifestation, unrestrained by phenomenal conditions, is visible in Christ as risen. Here, at the core of reality, the world of fact and the world of value interpenetrate. Once the Divine mode of self-revelation in historic life had ceased, the limitations of earth and nature dropped away; and Christ entered, by a transition of which we can see the moral fitness, into possession of all power in heaven and in earth. It is this conception which the New Testament sets forth under the guise of a reward bestowed on Christ for His obedience—"the Name which is above every name." We are led to think of Him as somehow greater for having lived. Finally, it is perhaps not impossible to mark the traces of these two corresponding moments or movements in our Lord's person. His being is as it were the theatre or *locus* in which the manward movement of God, characterised by redemptive self-limitation, blends with the Godward movements of man in obedient faith and hope and love. The sustained approach of the *Deus humilis* finds its essential counterpart in that rising perfection, that τελείωσις, as it is described in Hebrews, which He acquired as He successively seized the occasions which His vocation as Saviour placed before Him. What we behold is a personality creating its own form by a series of acts, of surmounted moral crises, of renunciations conceived and accomplished duly; the enlarging life thus offering an ever more adequate organ and medium of self-revealing Godhead. As He stooped to save, He grew in the stature of Divine humanity.

Apart from this strain or element of Divine-human self-realisation in Christ, our thought of Him must be always incomplete. Exclusive emphasis on the Divine self-reduction leaves a picture lacking in the glorious majesty of the Risen Lord. Along with the self-renunciation goes ever an ascending line of self-fulfilment and re-conquest, mediated in moral ways, and the two movements are distinguishable in the total experience of which Christ was Subject. Each shares the other's moral rhythm, and is fused or merged with it in spiritual unity.

Such thoughts, it may be said, are extravagant and metaphysical. Even if we believe them, can we actually think them; can we place them before our mind in articulate and lucid form? This notion of a Divine *kenosis*, restraining God by His own act to human measures, still more perhaps this companion idea of a *plerosis* or self-acquisition, whereby the synthesis of God and man in Christ, though given in potency, is also progressively actualised—can they be handled or even held by reason? They seem rich and imposing, as conceptions; may they not on examination prove bankrupt, their fancied wealth turned in a moment, like the fairies' gifts, to withered leaves? I am far from seeking to minimise the objections which may be raised on behalf both of tradition and of liberal theology. It is noticeable, indeed, that in certain classical treatises on Christology the two main principles set forth in this chapter and the last are viewed as essentially incongruous and antagonistic, not, as I have argued, mutually correlative. Nevertheless, I cannot avoid the conviction that it is in this direction, and no other, that we are led by the facts alike of the New Testament record and of experience; and that these facts are such as make it a natural task for the Christologian to discover, apprehend, and make patent, first to himself and then to the Christian mind, the harmonious structure of some general theory of this kind; to do this at least in its main outlines and dominating principles.

As for the charge of inconceivability, it is of course peculiarly hard to meet. Yet even here, the main ideas of which these chapters have been so faltering and imperfect an exposition may perhaps challenge comparison, as regards mere capability of being thought, with the constructions of recent speculative philosophy, be it Hegelian, Bergsonian, or materialistic. The conception of Godhead self-renounced and self-fulfilled in Christ is surely child's play in contrast to the marvels of the absolute dialectic, of the intuitive method, or of naturalistic evolution as interpreted in terms of matter. Whereas the Christologian has at least this advantage, that the mystery he reports is a mystery of grace. Holy love is his last criterion of reality. The greatness, the mercy, the glorious power of Jesus Christ, who ransomed us with His blood, and who, after all creatures have received of Him, is still as endless as in the beginning—these are facts which have conveyed to the human mind a totally new impression of what God is, and of the lengths His love will go to redeem the world. He who has stood by this ocean of Divine mercy, as it stretches from his feet to incomprehensible distances, will not too much complain that our estimate of Christ should thus bring us, ere we are aware, to the verge of silence. Still, if we are to think of Him at all, and to think consistently, there are certain ideas in which we are obliged to throw out our minds at the tremendous fact. One such idea is surely this, that if personal Godhead enters history, it must be in virtue of its own omnipotent self-reduction; another, that in the historic Christ—living, dying, risen—there is found a deepening and culminating synthesis, within a single integrate life, of the Divine and human factors to which faith bears equal witness.

CHAPTER XII.

CHRIST AND THE DIVINE TRIUNITY.

CHRISTIANITY, as heir of the Old Testament, is a form of ethical monotheism which yet has learned to conceive God in a new way. Naturally the experience of redemption through Christ was felt from the first as reacting on the idea of God who alone can redeem. It was felt as necessitating new distinctions in a Divine nature which had once been regarded as bare and unfigured simplicity. Those who look up to an omnipotent Christ, and who see in Him the very life of God incorporate, subsisting from before all time, are obliged, unless they resolve not to think, to adjust this conviction to the basal and commanding fact of the Divine unity.

But the operation of the Spirit is as characteristic an element of Christianity as the incarnation. If, in virtue of Jesus, faith is rooted in the actualities of the past, in virtue of the Spirit it finds its perpetual dynamic in the present. The principle of life and power known as "Holy Spirit" is no one casual factor in perfect religion by the side of others; it is that to which everything else converges, and apart from which nothing else—not even the revelation of Jesus—could take effect. So the Father disclosed in the Son is imparted in the Spirit. The

LITERATURE—Kirn, article "Trinität" *RE.* xx.; D'Arcy, article "Trinity" in *DCG.* 1908; Schleiermacher, *Sämmtliche Werke*, i. 2, 1836; Illingworth, *Doctrine of the Trinity*, 1909; Shedd, *Dogmatic Theology*, 1889; Fairbairn, *Christ in Modern Theology*, 1893; Orr, *Christian View of God and the World*, 1893; Rothe, *Dogmatik*, 1870; Hutton, *Theological Essays*[3], 1888; Drummond, *Studies in Christian Doctrine*, 1908; Armstrong, *The Trinity and the Incarnation*, 1904; Martineau, *Essays, Reviews, and Addresses*, II.; Adams Brown, *The Trinity and Modern Thought*, 1906.

presence of the Spirit comes but as a higher mode of Christ's transcendent influence, the climax of His work. "Through Him we have access by one Spirit unto the Father"[1] is a great comprehensive Pauline word; and in such a verse the experience out of which flowed the New Testament faith in a Triune God grows transparent. It is the experience of a differentiated yet single Divine causality in redemption. If then the Spirit belongs to the sphere of the Divine, not of the human even as redeemed, room must be made for it also within the believing thought of God. Its omission leaves that thought incomplete. We speak in the sense of the New Testament, therefore, when we say that "the Father, the Son, and the Spirit in their unity constitute the God whom we know as the God of our salvation."[2]

The doctrine of the Triunity found in Scripture, however, is naive and experimental. There is nothing of reflection or design about it, nothing *à priori*, nothing that consists in or comes out of the manipulation of abstract ideas. It is due to an irresistible induction as objective in its own way as that which established spectrum analysis. If God is in Christ, not figuratively but in reality, and if the Spirit gives a renewing Divine life, these central facts must somehow be gathered into a unitary conception of Godhead. The intuition, then, that God is triune is born of experience; this is the direction in which the Christian mind is spontaneously led: but there is no need to infer that a concept thus experimentally generated may not also have immense philosophic value. On the contrary, it may well prove, as Bagehot held, "the best account which human reason could render of the mystery of the self-existent mind." What does follow from the unspeculative thought of the New Testament is that we must not force upon it the distinctions of later times. These distinctions soon became rigid; apostolic language was alive and fluid. Thus 2 Corinthians, which opens with a double salutation in the name of "God our Father and the Lord Jesus

[1] Eph 2^{18}. [2] Denney, *DCG.* i. 744.

Christ," ends with a triple benediction invoking "the grace of the Lord Jesus Christ, and the love of God, and the communion of the Holy Spirit." Yet the God of whom in each case St. Paul was thinking is the same, and his variant phrases cover exactly the same ground. When the bipartite is replaced by the tripartite formula, no change in denotation is intended; except for the fellowship of the Spirit, the grace of Christ and the love of God would not be ours. No fourth name is ever added to the sacred triad, and Harnack is much less convincing than usual when he argues that at one point it was something like an even chance that "the Church" might have been given the place in the formula now occupied by the Spirit.[1] The fact is that the Spirit was unquestioned from the first, the epithet "holy" marking it off from spirit in general as exclusively and specifically Divine.

Spirit means life and power, the saving energy of God within human life; and it is the uniform teaching of the New Testament that Christ, who possessed this Spirit in its fulness, has mediated it to all believers. Hence to call the Spirit impersonal must ultimately be meaningless for a religion to which the gracious power of God can never be a mere "thing." Could the love of God be shed abroad in our hearts by the non-personal? Could a natural force enable men to confess Jesus as Lord? True, a monotheistic New Testament has nowhere described the Spirit as a "separate personality"; it is indeed more than questionable whether such a general abstract idea as "personality" had then attained general currency. Yet in the last resort the Spirit of God must be as personal as God Himself. So true is this, that it is only by interior union with the personal Spirit that our proper personality is consummated. To have within us, as the soul's life, the very Spirit that made the inmost being of Jesus, is bestowed by Jesus, and commends Jesus to the heart—this is to be perfected in personal being. By unity with such Spirit man first is fully man.

[1] *Constitution and Law of the Church*, 265–66.

We cannot too much ponder the fact that in Christianity the Spirit is identical with the Spirit of Jesus. This alone gives the idea precision and reality. For St. Paul, a path-breaker in this field, the phenomena of the Spirit, as an ethical power, drew their value and permanent significance from their connection with the personality of Jesus; and it is clear that so long as the Spirit mediates the historic Lord to men, distilling the Gospel (as it were) through His life and death, Christianity can never sink into impotent sentimentalism, but is secured by the native strength of fact against the pessimism and defective moral inspiration which so often accompany impersonal views of grace. It follows that in the sphere of practical religion it is impossible to distinguish between the Spirit and Christ in the heart. Each blends vitally with the other. The Spirit is but the form or mode of the Lord's presence. What is given in the Spirit is Christ transcendent and unlimited; otherwise, His Godhead would be a phrase and nothing more.[1]

The attempt to force a literal harmony on the untheorised Trinitarian utterances of, say, Romans 8 or St. John 14–16 is certain to be disastrous. Thus for St. John it is the Father who, in response to the Son, imparts the Spirit to abide with the disciples for ever. St. Paul, simply recording and enforcing what were to him facts of the spiritual life, can teach that the Father is Lord, and the Son is Lord, and the Spirit is Lord; while yet for his real mind there are evidently not three Lords, but one only. It would not be difficult, using barely arithmetical methods, to elicit from such passages an average view which reduced the Godhead to a species consisting of three individuals, with distinct departmental offices, and constituting one God only as collective humanity is man. This might be done, obviously, by a cold insistence on the antinomies of the letter. Nevertheless, the Trinitarian thought of the Church, be its shortcomings what they may, has been one

[1] Cf. Schaeder, *Theozentrische Theologie*, Erster Teil, 27, 144–45, 165–67.

sustained effort to show that this, as an interpretation, is wholly false and mechanical, and that minds whose sympathy and insight are quickened by religious faith can attach a profoundly real sense to what might seem only verbal dexterities in the sphere of the ineffable. All for whom the doctrine of the Trinity has any positive kind of meaning are at one in this conviction. They are clear that a view of God must be attained which will embrace vitally the Divine person of Christ and the not less Divine work of the Spirit.

Nor is this all. Up to a certain point, all Christians are unanimous as to the content of the required doctrine. They are unanimous in holding that God has been revealed in a threefold way. Redemption is a historical fact, or series of facts; and in that history there has been a manifestation of Father, Son, and Spirit. The Eternal has been disclosed in Jesus Christ, by whom He reconciled the world; He speaks in our heart still by a spiritual presence that guides to the truth contained in Jesus. This is a redeeming Gospel—it proclaims that God is not far off, approachable only at long last by hard thinking or ascetic sacrifice, but that He came amongst us in His Son, and still dwells in our souls as Giver of life. Now in essence the doctrine of the Trinity is but a brief confession of these facts; and thus far, let it be repeated, all believers are agreed. They are agreed as to the essential religious data which doctrine must assert, even though the Christian intelligence which asks questions may decline to stop short with this simple assertion.

At this point, then, there occurs a divergence between the advocates of what are called the economic and the immanent views of the Divine Triunity. According to the economic or modal view, we see the triune God in the revelation He has given, and in that vision we rest. Creation, redemption, renewal are the stages or phases of His self-disclosure. Why go further? Why pretend to step outside experience, or use language, which of course cannot be verified, as to the Divine nature in itself? The fact of Christ is ultimate; it is vain to get behind it and try to see its conditions. It is vain to hypostatise an element in Christ which never had discernibly a separate existence, but is simply *our* mental articulation of an individual reality, an aspect artificially detached by our thought. Enough for us to behold God in history and Christian life, and to confess Him as known within that field.

With the positive half of this theory no other view can have any quarrel. It is true that Father, Son, and Spirit are relative, properly, to the historic revelation. The term "Son," for instance, unquestionably points in the first place to the Jesus of the Gospels, not to the Second Person of the Trinity.[1] If theologians have given it an eternal or supramundane reference, the extension has been secondary and inferential. Not only so; its economic form was that in which the doctrine of the Trinity first came to be set out in theory. Tertullian's doctrine is of this kind. His consuming interest in monotheism led him to insist with all his powers that distinctions affirmed of Godhead are distinctions within a fundamental unity. So he teaches "a Trinity of dispensation or of function, like the assignment of parts or duties in a household: the work of the Father has special relation to the creation, conservation, and government of the universe; the work of the Son has special relation to the redemption of man; and the work of the Holy Spirit is the continuation of this."[2] With all his side-glances at speculation, Tertullian has not forgotten that the Trinitarian idea sprang out of history.

History alone, then, is our true point of departure; but when men call a halt at the outer boundary of historical experience on the ground that to transcend fact is to speculate, and that speculation is injurious to faith, it must be answered that all such proscription is unavailing.

[1] Moberly, *Atonement and Personality*, 181–99; cf. the important Note B to chap. viii. of the same work.

[2] Sanday, *Christologies Ancient and Modern*, 26.

In the first place, men will *persist* in thinking, whatever notice-boards may be set up by the well-meaning theological positivist to warn the trespasser of impending dangers. It is, moreover, illegitimate to insist on restricting the Christian mind to the supremely practical language of the first disciples, whether on the Trinity or any other aspect of the creed. There is no topic on which the theologian finds his material in the New Testament ready and merely waiting to be lifted. It is not thus we can deal with such topics as the Personality of God, of which no theoretical exposition is given in Scripture; or the Atonement, of which passionate apostolic utterances are not fitted, and were not designed, to anticipate the intellectual rationale demanded by each new age. So is it with the Trinity. Here too we search the New Testament in vain for theories; but assuredly we encounter great vital data which it is our duty to cross-examine and explicate and synthesise without being too much concerned by the recurrent charge of having strayed into the domain of metaphysic.

In addition to this, it is plain that some forms of the economic view, by the stress they lay upon its negations, go far towards cancelling the facts with which all theories must start. This occurs, for example, when it is contended that the threefoldness of Divine revelation is merely phenomenal. God appears to be triune; He is not really so. Our minds, according to this interpretation of the relativity of knowledge—which is here introduced, with all its ambiguous paralogisms, into the arcanum of faith—hide from us the real nature of things; we know objects not as they are, but as they seem to us. We can neither tell precisely what is the amount of distortion of truth indissociable from our processes of cognition, nor can we rectify the error. Now this theory of knowledge, which is ultimately agnostic, leaves phenomena in no positive or definable relation to reality. Applied to the Christian thought of God, it means that *for us* God is Father, Son, and Spirit; but these appellations in no way answer to real facts which qualify His essential being. But if in general we reject this singular view of the self-defeating nature of cognition, and insist, on the contrary, that our minds in very deed know real things, and that phenomena are a true index, though of course an incomplete one, of concrete being, there is no seriously tenable argument for ignoring this principle in the doctrinal construction of the personal life of God. Our believing apprehension of Father, Son, and Spirit is in contact not with appearance only, but with reality. If God shines through Christ to our believing apprehension, then by way of this historic medium we see into the Divine nature.

For the rest, it may be convenient to proceed by way of comment upon, or reply to, the best-known objections to the conception of a Trinity immanent in the Divine life.

(*a*) It may be urged that the notion of an immanent or ontological Trinity is an attempt, and a reprehensible one, to think the Godhead as God is in Himself, with abstraction from His relation to the world. Now, since God is *actually* related to the world, we are the subjects of hallucination (it is held) if we imagine that by leaving that relation out of sight we attain to a more profound and inward knowledge of His being. For out of that relation God is seen precisely as He is not, either in Himself or otherwise. Nor is this all. Religion surely has no concern with a Divine existence which by definition is conceived apart from the world and humanity. In the New Testament everything said about God has a direct bearing on man's redemption, on God's final purpose with His children; and there is no possible stage of thought at which we are justified in ignoring this vital reference.

This may be otherwise put by saying that the idea of an essential Trinity is condemned by its indifference to history. The concept of the Logos, applied early in the second century to denote the second Person in the Godhead, is bound up incurably with this grave fault. For what it primarily indicates is not the revealing significance of Jesus—in which sense it is quite legitimate—but cosmic reason, either as a principle of philosophic thought or as a rational Power permeating the universe. Now in this sense it is not a religious notion at all. The interest it satisfies is logical or cosmological. Hence the problems to which it relates have nothing to do with Jesus the Son of God; they pertain to the purely metaphysical problem of Infinite and finite, of the One and the many.

The burden of this first objection is then that the idea of an immanent Trinity has no religious meaning or importance. Now this is a point of view which it is not quite easy to appreciate. It is indeed self-evident if the Godhead of Christ be first denied, but otherwise it is as obviously erratic and short-sighted. For if Christ be Son of God essentially, religion has surely a real and keen interest in viewing the relation of Son to Father as unbeginning. By an irresistible impulse it will "eternalise" that relation, just as it does the electing love of God manifested to men in time. For the Christian mind it means everything, as was proved by the early controversies, that the Sonship of Christ is no mere temporal creation, but the expression within time of an eternal fact. Now to see that Christ is Son from before the ages is to see also that God is Father by inherent nature, that this is His essence. It is to plant the Fatherhood firmly inside the Divine, as the current Unitarian form can never do. Concede as we may that to lift the relationship of Father and Son to the eternal plane lends no *new* content to our knowledge of God's interior life; that the Trinitarian concept is empty if sundered from the roots of history and experience; that we become irresponsible and fantastic so soon as in our thought of God we cast loose from revelation within the world. Yet religion has assuredly an interest in noting that the meaning of Son *is* eternal or intrinsic, not adventitious, so that the Divine Fatherhood had not to wait for perfect self-expression till Jesus was born and grew to manhood. In such a view there is a final vindication of the Fatherhood which faith has always valued, and the absence of which is always felt keenly. It is not an idea divorced from history; it is an attempt, on the contrary, to set forth the absolute background of reality from which history derives its significance, and to exhibit the gift of Christ as flowing from the life of God. To contend, moreover, that it is a conception of no religious worth is flying in the face of experience. M. Reville, certainly no advocate of Church tradition, is noticeably emphatic on the point. "The Trinitarian God," he writes, "is a living God. He is not the unknown principle seated at the centre of all things, blind and deaf, producing worlds like a fermenting substance without knowing either what He is or what He does. Nor, again, is He the purely ideal term of the 'Universal Becoming,' *that* God in process of continual evolution who does not create the world, but is created by the world; a *future* God who will be, but at present is not, or who at least only murmurs as yet in the cradle of the human consciousness. Finally, He is not the dreary God of Deism, that supreme mechanician retired within the icy depths of His own eternity, and without permanent or active connection with the works of His capricious genius. None of these Gods is a being we can worship. To present them to the human spirit hungering after religion, is like giving stones to the poor instead of bread."[1] He proceeds, it is true, to recommend the notion of Divine immanence in the cosmos as a fit modern substitute for the Trinity; but it is plain that this notion, so far from mitigating the problems of sin and sorrow, leaves them precisely as they were before.

Certain suggestive writers have sought to present the Trinitarian idea to the modern mind by construing it in more general terms. It points merely to the richness of the Divine existence. It tells in broken human words that the life of God is various and deep and manifold. It

[1] *History of the Dogma of the Deity of Jesus Christ*, 153–54.

rejects the audacious yet contemptible illusion that we have fathomed or surrounded God by our eager cogitations. Along with this, it is sometimes asked why the Divine elements or factors should be only three; may there not be many others, as yet unknown to us, or revealed in other worlds?

Much in this contention, we may grant, is an index of great and imposing truths. The history of thought has proved the worthlessness of a conception of God which pictures Him as a bare, single, isolated unit of deity. Without active distinctions essential to His being, His own spiritual nature and His relation to the world are alike unintelligible to our minds. Life as such is ever complex, with a complexity that deepens and intensifies as it mounts in the scale of being. The inner structure of animate things reveals a constantly increasing differentiation, combined with and constituted by an always finer and more perfect unity. Variety and organic oneness exist in and through each other. Human life, moreover, unveiled to us on its inner side, is the very type and criterion of a manifold held together in vital unity, a multiplex fulness or diversity which yet is articulated and harmonised in one focal identity. It is an impressive argument, therefore, which holds that if Godhead also is seen as involving a real variety in unison—distinct functions irradiated vitally from a single centre—this ultimate intuition falls into line with, and completes, the lower forms of cognition. We have a right to ask whether deity can be an eternal *life*, or can be thought as such, except on terms implying a varied wealth of inner content. But while this is so, it is surely a departure from Christian ground to break off abruptly at this point. What the revelation mediated in history denotes is no mere vague wealth of Divine existence; but eternal Fatherhood, eternal Sonship, moving within the eternal life of Spirit. If we have real data for *any* transcendent induction, it is this induction we must make. The Christian mind has no interest, so far as I can see, in affirming that in God there is an *undefined* fulness or complexity, or that still other intra-divine factors, like those we call Son and Spirit, may one day be disclosed. Our thought is bound by the historic sources of Christian truth—the spiritual content present in Jesus and sealed to men in the Spirit.[1]

(*b*) Trinitarian doctrine of the type now in question implies at least a duality in the Divine life, in virtue of which God's love and knowledge are superior to time; but it may be held that this essential other-than-self is given in the universe as a whole. If we do not believe that the universe began to be, we have no need to speculate further as to the absolute existence of the Eternal. Moreover, the argument for a vital duality can never yield a trinity; it gives no help in conceiving the third Person of the Godhead, thus failing at a crucial point.

One feels that the last part of this objection is unanswerable, and must be accepted frankly. No speculative argument known to the present writer has the slightest value as proving a third Divine distinction which is either "Holy" or "Spirit." And the fact is a strong reminder that the origin of the idea of Spirit, in its Trinitarian meaning, lies not in philosophic thought, but in history and life.[2]

But the former part of the objection cannot be

[1] Cf. the striking words of Professor G. W. Knox: "The Johannine writings, which presupposed the Pauline movement, are a protest against the hyper-spiritualising tendency. They insist that the Son of God has been incarnate in Jesus of Nazareth, and that our hands have handled and our eyes have seen the word of life. This same purpose, namely, to hold fast to the historic Jesus, triumphed in the doctrine of the Trinity; Jesus was not to be resolved into an æon or into some mysterious *tertium quid*, neither God nor man, but to be recognised as very God who redeemed the soul. Through him men were to understand the Father and to understand themselves as God's children. Thus the doctrine of the Trinity satisfied at once the philosophic intelligence of scholars and the religious needs of Christians. Only thus can its adoption and ultimate acceptance be explained. Its doctrinal form is the philosophic statement of beliefs held by the common people, who had little interest in theology, but whose faith centred in Jesus" (from article "Christianity," *Encycl. Brit.* 11th ed. vol. vi. 284–85).

[2] Cf. Thieme, in *ZTK.* (1911), 84 ff.

sustained. Nothing is easier than to write vaguely of the world as adequate either to the knowledge or the love of God, yet on closer scrutiny nothing could be more unconvincing. After all, the only rational creatures known to us who are capable of appreciating God's love, and returning it, are human beings. That other spiritual beings may exist is of course very credible, but we cannot seriously be held to have direct cognition of them. Therefore it is to argue purely from our ignorance when the world, or the universe, is held to be a sufficient eternal object. If the world means the physical cosmos, it cannot properly be loved at all, not to speak of its loving the lover; if it means or includes finite spirits, we have no certainty that these have existed from the first, for men began to be quite recently. So that if we are in quest of an adequate object of the Divine love and knowledge, and if by adequate we intend, as we should, an object which not only receives the forthcoming of the eternal Self-consciousness but responds to it, with equal infinitude, then this object exists nowhere within the universe; it is to be found only in God Himself. Subject and object are correlative, be it in finite or in transcendent Mind. In perfect knowledge or love or action, object and subject are necessarily conceived as personal in quality; and when thought reaches the ideal limit of those relationships, it rests in a distinction which yet is mediated unity.

The value of such considerations may be illustrated by the well-known attempt of the late Dr. Martineau to resolve the problem. As against pantheism, which admits of nothing objective to God, since He is but the inner side of nature, Dr. Martineau (so far at one with Hegel and Spencer) argues powerfully that the Divine Spirit must distinguish itself from what is *other*. "The moment we conceive of mind at all," he writes, "or any operation of mind, we must concurrently conceive of something other than it as engaging its activity. . . . God, therefore, cannot stand for us as the sole and exhaustive term in the realm of uncreated being; as early and as long as he is, must also be something objective to him."[1] This other-than-self for God he discovers first in matter-filled space; later and more adequately, he believes, in finite centres of individuality, furnishing a province of real being objective to God in the complete degree. But if we refuse "to stake God's existence on the eternity of matter and finite creatures,"[2] while yet we agree with Martineau in regarding a personal self-expression or object as necessary for the Divine Spirit, it will be natural to resort to the great New Testament conception of the unbeginning Word, in whom is given the resonance of life vital to either love or knowledge in perfect form, yet not separate from God as we from other selves.

Thus reason may find its own in the Christian certitude that love Divine is from everlasting to everlasting. When we think of God in Himself, possessed of that subjectivity, that centralised thought, activity, and feeling without which self-consciousness is but a name, it is not as a formless Void that we conceive Him, or as a silent vast Omnipresence; it is as the home of the loftiest and most spiritual relations manifested in human life. Fatherhood is no acquired attribute; we cannot image that love as sleeping before it woke to shed its beneficence on an object other than itself. It is not creation which enables us to interpret the absolute Personality. Rather it is our view of that Personality which enables us to interpret creation; for no God complete in loneliness could feel the impulse to create, least of all to create potential sons. In other words, the relations of God and man become luminous in view of the interior Divine life. That life is neither loveless thought, nor abstract thought, nor mere boundless energy; we are nearest to the infinite truth when in Fatherhood and Sonship we symbolise vital distinctions apart from which Godhead cannot be.

It is easy, of course, to call this metaphysics, and so

[1] *Seat of Authority in Religion*, 32.

[2] T. Vincent Tymns, in *The Ancient Faith in Modern Light*, 32.

dismiss the topic with a word. But the accusation is a harmless one unless it can be proved that metaphysics, in this connection, is anything more than a name for persistent thinking. Faith in Christ will always constrain thoughtful men to construe in reason His ultimate relation to God and man, so far as this is possible; and the limits of possibility can be ascertained in no other way than by actual experiment. There is no mode of knowing whether we are on the way to truth save the process of knowledge itself. Religion, certainly, has no interest in suppressing the instinctive effort of the mind to follow out this supreme inquiry to the farthest point. As it has been expressed: "The reasons which prevent us from acquiescing in the proposal to banish the metaphysical element from our theology . . . are to be found in the nature of the metaphysical interest itself. That motive is not merely speculative; it is intensely practical. It is the desire for a unified world-view which voices itself in the demand for a philosophical theology."[1] No one to-day will dream of constructing a Trinitarian doctrine *à priori*; the sufficiency of the syllogism in such a realm has ceased to be obvious: but the clear duty of the Christian thinker—as will be acknowledged once more when the present disparagement of reason has passed by—is to relate Jesus Christ intelligibly to the inmost and eternal life of God. He has no option but to do this; his instinctive impulse is to do it; and the impulse is restrained only in obedience to a particular theory of knowledge. Why the effort to translate the initial certitude of faith—which no subsequent speculative procedure can impair—into a luminous conviction of the mind should be flouted as superfluous, or even as an attempt upon the Christian religion, it is not easy to see; and reason is sure to avenge itself by the gibe that faith, in submission to the unintelligible, is simply indifferent to the truth. There is room in theology for a knowledge that is not so much disinterested as interested purely in its

[1] Adams Brown, *Christian Theology in Outline*, 159. The whole of his finely-toned chapter on the Trinity should be read.

object, and cares enough about God to know Him in His own nature.

(*c*) It may be objected, finally, that the duality within the Godhead is the equivalent of ditheism. To say that love is not love if there be no beloved; to maintain that Divine love is "social," with an unbeginning relation of Father and Son—if at least by Son is meant a conscious being, distinct alike from God, the world, and the human Jesus; this, it is urged, is to drift into a polytheistic view of deity. Moreover, the "social" conception of God has not the slenderest title to pose as orthodoxy proper. It is notorious that Augustine rested upon a trinity in the individual human mind—memory, understanding, and will in one place; the mind, self-knowledge, and self-love in another—and that he used this psychological analogy without misgiving to interpret the supreme Godhead, arguing on this basis that each of the Persons singly is equal to all the Persons together: each, that is, is simply God in a certain aspect. In like manner, Aquinas views the three Persons as respectively the principles of Origination, Wisdom, and Will. There is obviously no tritheism in a construction based on the analogy of a single human self-consciousness.

It is of course undeniable that Church theology has often preferred a psychological line of this sort. One disadvantage, however, is that Trinitarian doctrine in this form has no perceptible relation to the historic Christ, whose true Godhead it was meant originally to record and synthesise with older conceptions of the Divine. Why "understanding" in Augustine's first theory should be the eternal equivalent of the Divine Son who lived on earth, it is difficult to comprehend. What he offers is but a distinction of ideas, or of psychical constituents, quite unrelated, so far as can be seen, to the historic antecedents by which the doctrine must be judged and sanctioned.

But when we turn to the form of doctrine inspired by the analogy of love as implying a real duality, a subject and an object in complete reciprocation, the difficulties of a genuine and unflinching monotheism become more grave.

True, the word "Person" is not in itself decisive. A high authority has said that "Person, in Trinitarian usage, is a mode of being which serves as a ground or basis (a *real* ground or basis) of special function, but just stops short of separate individuality. It implies distinction without division."[1] Words in such a realm are more or less arbitrary, and must be taken in a sense appropriate to their objects of denotation; and it is certain that *ὑπόστασις* in Greek theology, and *persona*, its Latin equivalent, do not mean now, and never have meant, what we usually intend by Personality. In strictness, then, as was argued previously, we use the word "Person" from simple poverty of language: to indicate our belief, that is, in the reality of Divine distinctions, not to affirm separate conscious beings, possessed of separate "essences." If it be said that this description of such interior distinctions is negative merely, the comment, however just, is by no means fatal to its validity. Most Christian thinkers are agreed that God is *causa sui*, and that He is omnipresent; yet when we look into our own minds, are not these phrases, however necessary, laden with a sense predominantly negative? When we use them, we are affirming that God owes reality to Himself alone, and that He is nowise limited by space. The conceptions, in other words, can never be positively defined, yet we are obliged to grant their truth.

At this extreme point we obtain most real help, perhaps, from the thought that in God conditions essential to love, which *in us* imply mutually exclusive personalities, may exist without such exclusion, in a unity that is more and deeper than the distinction. One feels that too often the criticism of Trinitarian doctrine has rested on a narrow, individualist conception of personal life; a conception animated and controlled by a static view of human experience. For it is clear that even in human love the inter-

[1] Sanday, *Personality in Christ and in Ourselves*, 19.

personal exclusion just referred to is largely overcome.[1] This is simple matter of fact, and the best philosophy has not been slow to recognise it. Take these words of Nettleship on the ideal of life as universal love. "So far as we can conceive such a state," he writes, "it would be one in which there would be no 'individuals' at all, in the sense in which individuality means mutual exclusion: there would be a universal being in and for another: 'consciousness' would be the consciousness of 'another' which was also 'oneself'—a *common* consciousness."[2] What if this transcendent ideal is for ever real in the life of God? May not we, looking still towards the innermost recesses, believe that in Him a merged and blended unity of love with its equal object is eternally attained; attained none the less because our divisive and spatialised logic is incompetent to set it forth without tritheistic error? Bergson has taught us that it is impossible to think even the vital unity of movement or of life, save intuitively; so the Godhead, which does not any more than life itself form a picture we can see, may signify Father, Son, and Spirit as members or manifestations of a single Divine life beyond the limits of time, forming together the supreme instance of individuality. This interfusion of personalities in a common life, never realised save imperfectly by us, may have been fully actualised and unimpeded in the love hid in God from all eternity.

Thus, faintly, under the form of idealised human relationships, we envisage that which perpetually evades our grasp. How can we, whose being is finitely individual and (so far) apart from other selves, apprehend God truly or with perfect clarity? We cannot place our minds inside that transcendence or perceive it inwardly by feeling; for only that which we have lived can ever become luminous to us. But at least we may refrain from imposing upon it our own particularity. If there be

[1] Cf. *supra*, p. 338 f.

[2] *Philosophical Remains*, vol. i. 42 (quoted by Temple, *The Nature of Personality*, 76). See also Moberly, *Atonement and Personality*, 156 ff.

mystery in the Trinitarian conception, a deeper mystery, and one aggravated by ethical enigmas, must always lie in the notion of a solitary God, without love, void of thought, incapable of movement, divorced from all reality. We read the great words: "Father, glorify Thou Me with Thine own self with the glory which I had with Thee before the world was"; and as their solemn and elusive wonder lingers on the soul we feel again how noble and subduing is that vision of the One God which beholds Him as never alone, but always the Father towards whom the Son has ever been looking in the Spirit of eternal love.

Yet it is in the unity of God as known in Christ that our minds come finally to rest. The triune life is apprehended by us for the sake of its redemptive expression, not for the internal analysis of its content. The problem can never be one of ontology mixed with arithmetic. Throughout, our aim is bent on history and its meaning, as we strive to apprehend the one God in His saving manifestation. To this point of view faith is constant. From this point the doctrine must set out only to circle round at last to its fruitful origin. God as Holy Love we name the Father; this same eternal God, as making the sacrifice of love and appearing in one finite spirit for our redemption, we name the Son; God filling as new life the hearts to which His Son has become a revelation, we name the Spirit. In this confession we resume the best it has been given us to know of the eternal God our Saviour.

APPENDIX.

JESUS' BIRTH OF A VIRGIN.

DURING the nineteenth century the words of the Apostles' Creed, "conceived of the Holy Ghost, born of the Virgin Mary," were more than once the subject of vehement dispute. Controversy prevailed among German scholars in 1877, and again in 1893; and on each occasion the after-swell of the storm beat upon British shores. The theme is one to be discussed quietly and without prejudice. For my own part, I should not think of regarding explicit belief in the virgin-birth of our Lord as *essential* to Christian faith—otherwise, St. Paul was no Christian; while, on the other hand, the story has an exquisite natural fitness, and its vogue is nearly impossible to explain save by the hypothesis of its truth.

The main aspects of the problem are two—the critical and the doctrinal; distinct, indeed, yet in no sense separate. Thus it is of the first importance to recollect that the birth in question is that of Jesus Christ. Virgin-birth is exceptional in character, as resurrection also is; and on any showing Jesus was, as a person, utterly exceptional. Apart from *Him*, the idea of supernatural conception is not even plausible. Hence, whether we are to call the birth-narratives only a childish attempt to utter Jesus' greatness, or valid testimony to a historic fact, will much depend on the spiritual impression He has made upon us. On the other hand, it is not less true that if virgin-birth cannot be put in any significant relation to Christ, and is merely irrelevant to the believing interpretation of His self-consciousness, its credibility is gravely lessened.

For a discussion of the critical problem, the reader is referred to the commentaries and special studies. We can touch only a few cardinal points.

In the First and Third Gospels, the higher Sonship of

Jesus is depicted as having been mediated in part by the reception of the Spirit at His baptism, in part by abnormal birth. Of the early variants in Mt 1^{16} it has been said recently that "such modifications as may be due to doctrinal prepossessions are designed to re-set or to sharpen the reference in the original text to the virgin-birth, not to insert the dogma in a passage which was originally free from it."[1] Nor has the case been made out for removing Lk 1^{34-35} as an interpolation, although this would give us a Lucan version of which virgin-birth at first formed no part. But Mark knows nothing of the story, nor does it seem to have found a place in Q. The genealogies which, if not contradictory, are certainly independent, connect Jesus with David through Joseph, not Mary; but this may mean that the evangelists have only imperfectly adapted these documents, which they found already in existence, to the purpose of expressing legal kinship but not physical parentage. In any case, Jesus must have ranked as Joseph's son before the law. Various writers have dwelt on the fact that Luke writes from Mary's point of view, Matthew from Joseph's. As might be expected, therefore, the narratives diverge; but they agree in the parents' names, the places of birth and boyhood, descent from David, and the special action of the Holy Spirit. It is not a grave objection that the evangelists repeatedly mention Joseph as Jesus' father. Quite consistently they may reflect or report popular opinion in certain places while giving elsewhere information drawn from a private source.

Outside these narratives, the New Testament is completely silent. Virgin-birth is not present in Gal 4^4, nor even hinted at; for the phrase "born of a woman" is a familiar phrase, used by Jesus Himself of men as such (Mt 10^{11}). Few would say, with Westcott, that virgin-birth is implied though not explicitly asserted in John 1^{14}: "the Word became flesh." Still it is difficult to believe that if John had regarded the story as inaccurate, he would have uttered no word of protest. The Synoptics were before him; silence, presumably, means not disapproval but tacit acquiescence, coupled with a statement in his Prologue of what he conceived to be a deeper truth. There is no contradiction, such as has often been alleged, between birth of a virgin and pre-existence, though in

[1] Moffatt, *Introduction to the Literature of the NT*, 251.

point of fact no New Testament writer happens to mention both. Luke, the Paulinist, can scarcely have been unfamiliar with the idea of pre-existence; and virgin-birth may have stood in his mind less as the ultimate ground of Jesus' Sonship than as the mediating occasion of His presence, as Son, in the world. It is not easy to see why a particular mode of birth should be thought incongruous with the idea of pre-temporal life. Resch and Blass have argued that with some ancient versions we should read the singular pronoun in Jn 1^{13}—not "who were born," but "who *was* born, not of blood, nor of the will of the flesh, nor of the will of man, but of God"; the subject thus being the Incarnate One. But this is hardly serious. In the case of St. Paul, again, silence can only mean ignorance of a story even then jealously guarded within a narrow circle. There is indeed much to be thankful for in the providential circumstance that the method of our Lord's entering the world was not at first made the subject of doctrinal reflection.

One thing, however, the silence of St. Paul does prove. It proves that an apostle could hold and teach the eternal Sonship of Christ without reference to virgin-birth; which in turn is good evidence that in the case of Matthew and Luke the belief need not have been an irresistible religious postulate. It was not a psychologically inevitable idea which had to be introduced at any cost. The evangelists felt that the testimony was good.

For history the really strong argument in favour of the virgin-birth is the difficulty of accounting for the story otherwise than on the assumption of its truth. Harnack, who traces everything to Is 7^{14}, enumerates thirteen other theories of origin;[1] and the curious list might be added to. If the Old Testament, however, shows any leaning, it is not to glorify virginity as opposed to marriage, but rather the other way. There seems to have been no expectation that the Messiah's birth would be abnormal; not a trace is discoverable of a Messianic exegesis of Is 7^{14};[2] while the far-fetched way in which the verse is adduced by Matthew shows that he is only clenching his statement with a proof-text, not inferentially deriving a new fact. He simply quotes Isaiah to repel innuendoes against Mary's honour.

[1] *Dogmengeschichte*[4], i. 113.

[2] See Professor Buchanan Gray's masterly argument in the *Expositor* for April 1911.

And the supposed influence of heathen mythology would require a longer time than New Testament criticism will allow. Further, in the Gospel story there is a pure and beautiful reticence which has nothing in common with Greek or Hindu narrations of birth from a Divine and a human parent; narrations which anyhow do not tell of virgin-birth at all, but of gods possessed with human passions. It is indeed strictly veracious, as Dr. Orr has proved,[1] to say that no ethnic parallel to birth from a pure virgin has been found. The contrary is often stated, but at the crucial point the alleged parallel invariably breaks down; and even radical critics are obliged to grant that pagan ideas, if adopted by the evangelists, were transformed out of all recognition.[2] Not only so; but the early chapters of Matthew and Luke are in tone intensely Hebraic. They must have arisen in Palestinian circles. The attitude of first-century Christians to pagan tales regarding the celestial descent of Alexander the Great, Plato, or Augustus, can only have been one of indignant horror. We are therefore entitled to believe that in reading these early traditions we have before us matter with a high claim to credibility. Nor does it come to us divorced from the rest of the evangelic story by a long, precarious interval of years. On the contrary, even so radical a critic as Johannes Weiss has expressed the view that the contents of Luke 1 and 2 may have circulated in the Jewish Christian communities of Judæa "in the 'sixties."[3]

At the same time, considerations of history are not decisive by themselves. The evidence might conceivably be much stronger than it is, though, as it has been put, it is "strong enough for rational acceptance." When we turn then to more theological considerations, it is necessary to have before us clearly what the negative argument exactly is.

While the origin of Jesus' person must be traced to God's creative power, and thus to miracle in the true sense, and while this is the proper religious significance of the words, "conceived by the Holy Ghost," no conviction (it may be held) is attainable as to the form or medium of this Divine creation. We know that the Saviour is from above; we do not know how He came to be here in that character.

[1] *The Virgin Birth of Christ*, chap. vi.
[2] Cf. J. Weiss in *Religion in Geschichte u. Gegenwart*, i. 1736–37.
[3] *Die Schriften d. NT*, i. 412.

Unless marriage is sinful, neither His sinlessness nor His unique Sonship requires the guarantee of virgin-birth. If we insist on such a guarantee, it is certainly not supplied by the absence of human paternity. There is also the motherhood of Mary, through whose natural relation to Him sinful dispositions might be as really transmitted as through normal birth.

With the inference drawn from these premises I do not myself agree; but it is undeniable that the term "miraculous" might justly be applied to the genesis of our Lord's manhood even on this theory. We can say out of our experience that He belongs to a higher sphere; that the resident forces of humanity were insufficient to produce Him. In this sense at any rate He was no child of earth; He was the Son of God. But we dare not call virgin-birth a *sine qua non* of Sonship. The immediate object of faith is Christ living, dying, and exalted; and we cannot imagine Christ Himself insisting on acceptance of the birth-narratives as a condition or preliminary of personal salvation. At the same time, strong grounds can be adduced for accepting the belief as in complete harmony with the Christian thought of Jesus, as dove-tailing into the rest of our conviction naturally and simply. But first it is well to say emphatically that arguments drawn from biology as to the possibility of what is called parthenogenesis are wholly beside the mark. If the virgin-birth is real, its meaning is indissociably bound up with its supernatural character; and this should be avowed frankly.

(1) There is the companion fact of the resurrection. Supernatural conception is a most credible and befitting preface to a life consummated by rising from the dead. This is an argument the force of which grows upon one the more it is considered. "It is in harmony," says Professor Denney, "with that unique relation to God and man which is of the essence of His consciousness, that there should be something unique in the mode of His entrance into the world as well as in that of His leaving it."[1] The alleged singularity, in other words, is appropriate to the character and the occasion. Leaving aside all efforts to prove virgin-birth a necessity (*e.g.* to break the sinful entail), we have a right to dwell on the fitness of such an exordium in a life which, if we grant the transcendent victory over death at its close, was in any case supernaturally qualified. The case is one

[1] *Standard Dictionary of the Bible*, 423.

more for the application of the category of τὸ πρέπον than of τὸ ἀναγκαῖον. It was through the resurrection that Christ entered on full activity as Lord; what more intrinsically congruous than that His initial work on earth should begin, as well as end, with that which marked Him off from all other children of men? If Christ is Son of God in a lonely and unshared sense, free from all taint of sin, and Head of a redeemed race, He is clearly so unexampled a person that we cannot assume Him to have been subject either in birth or death to all normal sequences. This is not indeed to prove the virgin-birth. As it has been put: "It does not follow that a thing actually happened, because it appears to us likely and becoming that it should happen." Nor is it to make the supernatural birth of Jesus the *ground* of, say, His sinlessness. A moral fact is not explicable ultimately by one which is physical. But we may reasonably insist on the vital unity or parallelism of spirit and body, finding it wholly natural that a unique human spirit should also have a body uniquely conditioned in its origin.

(2) One minor point may be glanced at. Some of those who reject the virgin-birth of Jesus, while maintaining His perfect sinlessness, explain this unique absence of moral taint by summoning to their aid other supernatural factors; and it then becomes a question whether such intercalated factors are not more miraculous, as well as more unintelligible, than the evangelic story. Schleiermacher, *e.g.*, has argued that birth took place in normal ways, whereas the creative power of God intervened to bar the transmission of inborn sin. Of this it can only be remarked that it too affirms a special act of interference on the part of God, and one for which there exists in the record not the faintest trace of evidence. *Mystère pour mystère*, the account of Luke and Matthew is to be preferred.

(3) The point of real importance is positive rather than negative; not the absence of a human father, but the overshadowing presence of the Divine Spirit. The evangelists do not lead us to regard the birth as derived from the Spirit acting as bare power; the event has an essentially ethical aspect. This is furnished, we may consider, by the faith and holy obedience of Mary, reacting upon the higher influences from above. There is no magic in the miracle; no absence of mediating forces in the spiritual and moral realm. Jesus is born a man, in a relation of true heredity to His

mother, and, through her faith, to the grace and piety of the past. His is a new humanity, unique in perfectness of initial constitution, but grafted by God's creative act into the older stem.

When we look at these two forms of evidence simultaneously—the excellence of the tradition together with the spiritual fitness of virgin-birth—they seem to involve each other, much like the arms of a great arch rising up to meet and join.

I have already expressed my complete incredulity as to the existence of precise heathen parallels to the Gospel story. But even if we grant the point, what then? Then we shall have once more to recognise that the ethnic world had been dreaming of great things yet to be. As with ideas like those of Incarnation, Atonement, Resurrection, and many more, some dim prevision of and craving for transcendent Divine realities had already visited the souls of men. It was into no unspiritual world that the Christian religion came, but a world rather of seething hopes and dreams and premonitory glimpses. These hopes the Gospel was to realise. But it realised them, we may believe, not by borrowing ideas, or decking itself out in ancient symbols, but by the exhibition of a fact within the field of history in which were more than fulfilled the inextinguishable yearnings of the world's desire.

In conclusion, I cannot deny myself the pleasure of the following quotation from the Bampton Lectures of 1911, *Creed and the Creeds*, by J. H. Skrine: "To some of us who the most earnestly contend for the divinity of Jesus, may we not say that this Underivedness is the truth for which they are really contending, when they champion certain articles of our creed which are of value only as the historical correlatives of that truth, or as symbols of it. Thus, they assert the Virgin Birth of Jesus, as if the Divinity of Christ stood or fell with that physical event. It is not so —the manner of the Birth can have efficacy for human fate only as a fleshly accompaniment of the spiritual event, the entry into the human current of a force not derived from humanity. This entry is what we have to prove. This ought we to do, and not indeed to leave the other undone, but still to assure our hearts that, proven or found incapable of proof or disproof, it cannot shake our faith that God sent forth His Son; sent Him forth made of a woman; but His Son. Sometimes now we fight for a symbol when we should fight for the substance; as ere now in campaigns of our countrymen, a regiment has lost a victory by a useless strife to save the colours. Are we not liable to do the same—to remember the banner, forget the battle?" (p. 176).

INDEX

I. SUBJECTS

II. AUTHORS

III. REFERENCES

Printed by Morrison & Gibb Limited, *Edinburgh.*